Wingate Pasha

Dedication
In Memory of Dennis Moore
and
for Kate

Wingate Pasha

The Life of
General Sir Francis Reginald Wingate
1861–1953

First Baronet of Dunbar and Port Sudan
and
Maker of the Anglo-Egyptian Sudan

ROY PUGH

Pen & Sword
MILITARY

First published in Great Britain in 2011 by
PEN & SWORD MILITARY
An imprint of
Pen & Sword Books Ltd
47 Church Street
Barnsley
South Yorkshire
S70 2AS

ISBN 978-1-84884-531-2

A CIP catalogue record for this book is
available from the British Library

Typeset by Concept, Huddersfield, West Yorkshire
Printed and bound in England by CPI, UK.

Pen & Sword Books Ltd incorporates the Imprints of Pen & Sword Aviation,
Pen & Sword Family History, Pen & Sword Maritime, Pen & Sword Military,
Pen & Sword Discovery, Wharncliffe Local History, Wharncliffe True Crime,
Wharncliffe Transport, Pen & Sword Select, Pen & Sword Military Classics,
Leo Cooper, The Praetorian Press, Remember When, Seaforth Publishing and
Frontline Publishing.

For a complete list of Pen & Sword titles please contact
PEN & SWORD BOOKS LIMITED
47 Church Street, Barnsley, South Yorkshire, S70 2AS, England
E-mail: enquiries@pen-and-sword.co.uk
Website: www.pen-and-sword.co.uk

Contents

List of Plates

Acknowledgements

Inevitably, as so many people associated with various organizations and institutions have assisted in the writing of this book, I am at a loss to know where to start in expressing my gratitude to them. Hopefully, any whose names are omitted will excuse my flagging memory and accept my sincere apologies.

In no particular order, I wish to thank Lorraine Holmes, Research Secretary, School of Government and International Affairs, University of Durham and Alistair Tebbit at Durham University Library. I am particularly indebted to Jane Hogan, Assistant Keeper, Archives and Special Collections, Durham University Library for her invaluable assistance in advising me on the Wingate Papers and also to her staff who kindly and unstintingly provided the many box files comprising the impressive Wingate archive in the Sudan Archive Department.

Thanks are also due to the staff of the National Archives of Scotland, Edinburgh, the National Library of Scotland and Edinburgh Public Library.

I would also like to acknowledge the invaluable co-operation and assistance of Sheila Millar, Ray Halliday and Craig Statham of the East Lothian Local History Centre and Gordon Mitchell of the Dunbar Castle Freemasons' Lodge. I am also grateful to Peter Gray, former Museums Officer, East Lothian Council Museums Service, for permission to photograph the oil painting of Sir Henry Macleod Leslie Rundle. Thanks are also due to Brian Robertson who took great trouble in producing the aforementioned photograph. I am also indebted to Joy Dodd, Scottish Genealogical Society, for her investigation and preparation of the Wingate family tree.

I am particularly grateful to Mark Beattie, Charles Carruthers, Alexander Knox and Verna Tennant, all of Dunbar, who kindly provided some of the illustrations and allowed the use of books and documents in their possession. I also wish to thank Grahame Smith, Dunbar photographer, whose professionalism is obvious from the quality of his photographs of Reginald Wingate and Captain George Miller Wingate and the Wingate grave. Special thanks are due to John Harris, not only for his invaluable information on Reginald Wingate's association with Dunbar Golf Club but also for proof-reading the first version of the manuscript and explaining the mysteries of computer technology to the 'technosaurus' that I am. I am also indebted to Kate Covey, whose support, encouragement and sympathy sustained me during the final months of preparing this book. Finally, I wish to thank Jamie Wilson, Publisher/Commissioning Editor, Richard Doherty, Editor, both of Pen & Sword Books Limited and of course, the publishers themselves who completed the process.

A: Wingate Family Tree showing Scottish links to Francis Reginald Wingate

William Wingate m. Isobel (Sarah) Carrick
c. 1762

- Janet
  b. 1763
  m. 1790

- Margaret
  b. 1765
  m. 1801
  George Sharp

- John
  b. 1766
  m. 1795
  Margaret Jamieson

- Louisa
  b. 1769
  m. 1801
  James Patterson

- Sarah
  b. 1773
  John Buchanan

- William
  b. 1775
  m. (1) Christine Miller 1802 m. (2) Margaret Miller 1807

- **Andrew**
  (1778–1860)

- Elizabeth
  b. 1782

Children of William:

- (Rev) William
  (1808–1899)
  [see **B** for issue]

- Christine
  b. 1810
  m. Joseph Oldham
  1834

- Sir George
  (1813–1874)
  [see **C** for issue]

- **Andrew**
  (1813–1862)
  m. 1845
  Elizabeth (Bessie) Turner

- John Edward
  b. 1819

- Jessie Carrick
  b. 1819
  m. 1836
  William Beers Huggins

- Louisa Jane
  b. 1822

Children of Andrew and Elizabeth (Bessie) Turner:

- Jane (Min)
  (1846–1919)

- Andrew
  (1847–1868)

- Richard Turner
  (1849–1898)

- William
  (1850–1917)

- Margaret Miller
  (1852–1937)

- George Edward
  (1854–1862)

- Henry
  (1855–1872)

- Agnes Norah
  (1851–1945)
  m. Brigadier Gen. Philip Greaney
  - John (Jack)

- **Francis Reginald**
  (1861–1953)
  m. 1888
  Catherine Leslie Rundle
  (1858–1946)

- Bessie Turner
  (1858–1910)

- Frederick Austin
  (1857–1910)

Children of Francis Reginald and Catherine Leslie Rundle:

- Ronald Evelyn Leslie
  (1890–1978)
  m 1916
  Mary Vinogradoff (nee Harpoth)

- George Andrew
  b & d 1892

- Malcolm Roy
  (1893–1918)

- Victoria Alexandrina Catherine
  (1899–?) m. 1922
  Capt. Henry Dane

- Paul Malcolm Henry (1925–?)

- Josephine Marion Catherine (1928–?)
  m. Wilfred Guy Street

- Louis Martin (1938–?)
  m. Jane Mary Patterson Smith

B: Family of the Revd William Wingate

Revd William Wingate   (1) m. 1834, Jessie Buchanan d. 1838
(1808 – 1899)   (2) m. 1843, Margaret Wallace Torrance

Janet Douglas
b. 1844

Sir Andrew 'Dan' F.
(1846–1936)
m. 1887 Henriette Catharine Pemberton

William John Douglas
b. 1848

Louisa Theresa
b. 1851

George
(1852–1936)
m. Ethel Orde-Browne

Alfred Douglas
k. 1915

Dan
d. before 1915

2 daughters

Orde Charles
(1903–1944)
m. 1935 Lorna Paterson

Orde Jonathan
(1944–2000)
(Wife's name Holly
issue 2 daughters)

Rachel

Sybil

Monica

Nigel

Granville

Constance
d. 1931

C: Family of Sir George Wingate

Sir George Wingate m. 1843 Agnes Muir
(1813–1874)   b. 1818

Elizabeth	Margaret Miller	Alice	Augusta	Mary J M	Edith J M	George Miller	Grace
b. 1844	b. 1846	b. 1847	b. 1851	b. 1851	b. 1855	(1858–1918)	b. 1860
						m. Emily Livingstone Wood	

George Frederick Richardson	Agnese Eudora	Reginald 'Rex' C.	Muriel Grace	Dolly	Rachel
m. 1905	m. 1907	k. 1915	m. 1912		
Amy Elizabeth Donaldson	Archibald Primrose		John Congreve Murray		
	Liston-Foulis		(1882–1917)		

Reginald Wingate's Military and Civil Honours

Nile Expedition 1883	Mentioned in Despatches, awarded medal with clasp, bronze star, 4th Class Osmanieh.*
1887	4th Class Medjidieh*
Toski, 1889	Mentioned in Despatches, clasp, Distinguished Service Order.
Tokar, Afafit, 1891	Mentioned in Despatches, clasp to bronze star, 3rd Class Medjidieh.*
CB (Civil), 1895	Companion of the Order of the Bath.
1895	Iron Crown, 2nd Class, Austria.
Firket, Hafir, 1896	Mentioned in Despatches, medal, two clasps.
1897	Star of Ethiopia, 2nd Class.
Atbara, Khartoum, 1898	Mentioned in Despatches twice, three clasps, medal.
KCMG, 1898	Knight Commander of St Michael and St George.
Um Dibkayat, 1899	2nd Class Osmanieh* with two clasps.
KCB, 1900	Knight Commander of the Order of the Bath.
1901	1st Class Medjidieh.*
1902	Coronation Medal.
1905	1st Class Osmanieh.*
DCL Oxford, 1905	Doctor of Civil Law
1911	Coronation Medal
GCVO, 1912	Knight Grand Cross of the (Royal) Victorian Order
GCB, 1914	Knight Grand Cross of the Order of the Bath

1915	Order of the Nile*
1917	Order of Mohammed Ali*
GBE, 1918	Knight Grand Cross of the Order of the British Empire
LLD, Hon., Edinburgh, 1919	Doctor of Law
KVO, 1919	Knight of the Venerable Order of St John
1920	1st Baronet Dunbar and Port Sudan
1927	Gold Medal, Royal African Society
TD, 1935	Territorial Decoration
1937	Silver Jubilee Medal

* Full title = Grand Cordon, Order of the Ottoman Osmanieh, Medjidieh, Nile and Mohammed Ali Medals.

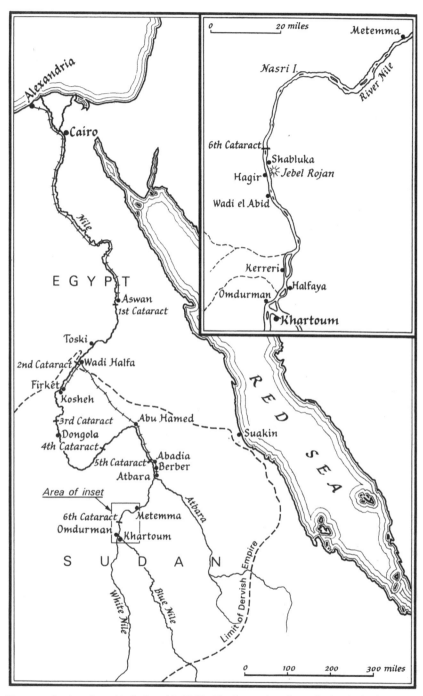

Egypt to the frontier with Sudan. (© Philip Ziegler – taken from the book *Omdurman*, Pen & Sword, 2006)

Sudan, showing provinces and frontiers.

WADI HALFA
No.1 Station
2nd Cataract
SARRAS
AMBIGOL WELLS
No. 2
No. 3
AKASHA
No. 4 (wells)
KOSHEH (105)
No. 5
No. 6 (wells)
KUROR
No. 7
DELGO
No. 8 desert
Nubian
3rd Cataract
No.9
KERMA (200)
ABU HAMED (230)
DAGASH
ABU DIS
River Nile
SHEREIK
4th Cataract
ABU SILLEM
5thCataract
KORTI
ABABIYA
BERBER
ATBARA (385)
Bayuda desert
River Atbara
METEMMA
6th Cataract
To Korosko
MURRAT OASIS

Distances (in brackets)
are from WADI HALFA

OMDURMAN (575)

Railways of the Sudan, 1898.

xvii

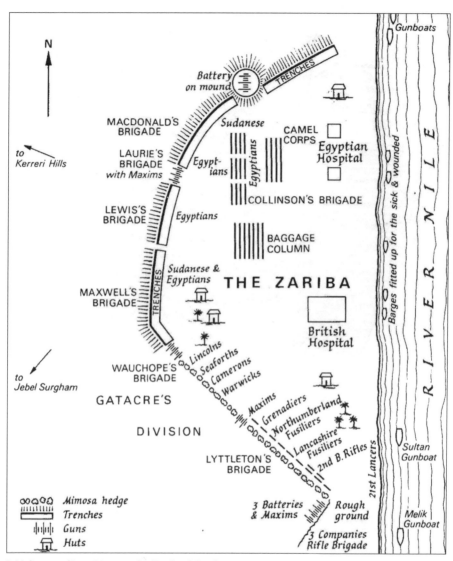

Initial troop dispositions at the Battle of Omdurman.

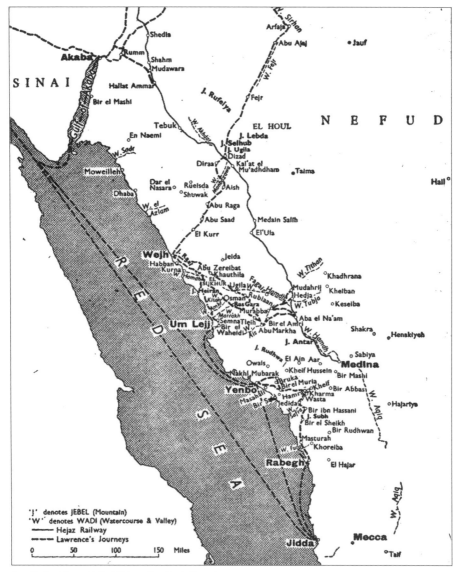

Saudi Arabia and the Hejaz: the Arab Revolt.

Foreword

History has a fascinating and occasionally infuriating habit of trespassing upon our lives whether we like it or not, often when we least expect it. The most common interference in the life of human society has been war. The two world wars of the twentieth century touched the lives of millions of ordinary people, arguably more so than in any other previous century. One hopes that wars on that scale will never occur again.

I consider myself fortunate never to have had to wear a military uniform, nor has my life been touched directly by war, although it was altered by it. It seems that war is part of the human condition, an insane, irresponsible and degrading fact of life in an animal species supposed to be supreme in the order of living creatures upon this earth. No century has been free from war and it seems that after the devastation and loss of life in America on 11 September 2001 and London on 7 July 2005, war, or a form of it in the shape of cowardly terrorism, will continue in the third Millennium.

Among the rapidly dwindling generations of the two world wars, there are still many in Dunbar who remember Francis Reginald Wingate – the *Sirdar*, as he was known locally – who began his military career at the height of the Victorian Age, when Britain was held in awe throughout the world. Wingate was a product of the British Empire, although he was often uneasy about his role in it. In the course of his life he encountered many famous people, some of whom remained lifelong friends. Among his earliest associates were Lord Cromer, Sir Evelyn Wood, Sir Francis Grenfell and, most importantly, General Charles Gordon who perished at Khartoum in 1885. Wingate was a serving officer and confidant of Lord Kitchener; his dear friend Baron Rudolph von Slatin accompanied him on visits to Balmoral as the frequent guests of Queen Victoria; Wingate knew and assisted Thomas Edward Lawrence in his quixotic quest to establish an independent kingdom of Arabia and he was a confidant of General Sir Edmund Allenby. He moved in circles that included Prime Minister and later Foreign Secretary A. J. Balfour, Lord Curzon, Viceroy of India, Edward VII and George V. In the closing years of his life, he sponsored his great-cousin* Orde Wingate of Chindit fame, an unorthodox soldier who led the special forces trained in jungle warfare against the Imperial Japanese Army in Burma in 1943 and

---

*This is a Scottish genealogical term for first cousin, once removed.

1

1944. Reginald Wingate regularly found himself in the company of the statesmen of his day and he was a personal friend of Winston Churchill. Wingate was known widely and approvingly in Foreign and War Office circles until his fall from grace in 1919. He first came to East Lothian in 1899, drawn to it by his love of golf, making Dunbar his permanent home from 1909 in his prestigious Edwardian mansion of Knockenhair. By 1919 his best days in public service were behind him; he retired from the public arena that year to devote the rest of his life to a successful business career which ended shortly before his death in 1953. In Dunbar, he was treated with reverence, a Grand Old Man of the Victorian Age.

Reginald Wingate experienced what were later to become known as the 'Little Wars' of the Victorian Age and served on the fringes of the Great War. If the wars of the eighteenth century may be described as familial and dynastic, those of the following century resulted from rising nationalism in countries incorporated into the British Empire, when the interests of the superpower were at variance with the aspirations of those governed. Thus the 'little' wars came about. Any serious student of the military conflicts throughout the nineteenth century will appreciate that war is always a political act which is justified – by the victors at any rate – in the hope that a better situation will emerge when peace is restored. We have the recent example of the war with Iraq as proof. The wars of the twentieth century are generally accepted as capitalist in origin, although the Great War was a mixture of patriotism – and thus a product of nineteenth century values – and the dismantling of an aristocratic class system, which occurred in the twentieth century. The First World War was the result of dynastic quarrels between the ruling classes; the Second World War is generally considered the peoples' war. While Wingate did not participate directly in the latter, there is reason to suppose that he was covertly involved in it, although this is difficult to prove.

To some historians Wingate is something of an oddity, a man who does not quite fit the military pattern of any age. He was primarily an academic, one of many who often stray into military life, upsetting the apple cart by beating soldiers at their own game. He entered the Army at a time when colonial government was at its height, first in Egypt, then in the Sudan and finally in the Middle East. In the art of colonial administration he demonstrated con-siderable ability, astutely assessing the character and ambitions of those around him, both British and Anglo-Egyptian. His was never the unqualified arrogance of a dedicated imperialist, for he genuinely cared about the welfare and development of the two countries with which he was most associated, Egypt and the Sudan. He cared about justice, tempering his administrative responsibilities with an understanding of the religion and culture of the peoples over whom he was placed. Perhaps that is a Scottish rather than an English trait. He supported – albeit in a necessarily muted approach – the Egyptian nationalists who began to challenge the Imperial British govern-ment, particularly a powerful Foreign Office, which considered nationalists as little more than troublemakers. Wingate sensed the sea change in world politics at the turn of the nineteenth century, a man of vision who foresaw that the demise of the Empire over which the sun never set was a historic inevitability. In the end, he could not conceal his beliefs behind a façade of pious platitudes or consensus politics and was sacked for showing his hand. Perhaps never as appealing to the Egyptians and Sudanese as the charismatic Charles Gordon of Khartoum – even today, Gordon enjoys an almost saintly reputation – Wingate left his mark on the Sudan and his name was long remembered and praised by the native population for many years after his departure from the Middle East in 1919. One has to ask the question: had Britain and Wingate or someone like him continued to rule the Sudan, would we be witnessing the present-day troubles in that country?

During his long life, Reginald Wingate – known as Rex to his friends and family – attracted intense affection, loyalty and respect in the Sudan and, in the latter stage of his life, people from all walks of life in his adopted home of Dunbar, East Lothian. He was a man who had a great capacity for making friends and keeping them. Although his military career effectively came to an end in 1899, he continued to serve his country as Governor General of the Sudan and as Sirdar (Commander in Chief) of the Egyptian Army until appointed High Commissioner of Egypt in 1917. During the Great War he was given military control of the Hejaz region of Saudi Arabia, supporting the leaders of the Arab Revolt and T. E. Lawrence, its charismatic and inspired champion; Lawrence was one of several quasi-mystical soldier-academics thrown up by the British military system, a man who excelled in guerrilla warfare and today is remembered as Lawrence of Arabia. Such men appealed to Wingate, possibly because, from his comfortable armchair, he harboured dreams of emulating their achievements. His great-cousin Orde Charles Wingate was of the same stamp as Lawrence, even if he considered Lawrence a flawed genius.

A seasoned military campaigner turned statesman and administrator, Wingate was at ease in both roles. The object of this biography is to re-appraise the character of the man, with passing reference to his visits to and activities in Dunbar. It has to be borne in mind that when Ronald Wingate wrote *Wingate of the Sudan*, his account of his father's time in the Sudan rather than a biography of his entire life, the political scene in the Middle East was vastly different from that of today. The British Empire was in its dying stages, Egyptian and other nationalist movements were demanding independence and change was in the air. While in no way wishing to detract from Ronald Wingate's excellent account, perhaps a fresh and unbiased look at the man and his life is now due.

A quiet, self-effacing man of small height – he was only 5 feet 6 inches – Wingate nonetheless had presence; apart from being the most decorated soldier-statesman of his day, his contribution to the world in which he lived was considerable. By 1919 his career in public life had come to an end and less is known of him in the remaining thirty-four years of his life. The

Haddingtonshire Advertiser and the *Haddingtonshire Courier* (now the *East Lothian Courier*) faithfully reported his Dunbar comings and goings and his part in the social life of his adopted town. Freemason and keen golfer, he was chairman of the local lifeboat institution and many other organizations, a popular guest at important official and social functions in and around Dunbar.

I have two personal memories of Reginald Wingate. The first occasion that his name came to my ears was in the late 1940s, when my cousin Dennis Moore was employed as an apprentice gardener at Knockenhair; he probably began his apprenticeship after leaving school at age fourteen. In those days gardening was regarded as a trade with a five-year apprenticeship. So when Dennis reached age eighteen in September 1947 he had one year of his apprenticeship to serve. He was called up for National Service that year but could have deferred this service until he had completed his indenture. Wingate advised him to do otherwise.

Dennis was a regular visitor to our house on Sunday mornings when he played cards with my uncle and elder brother. On one such Sunday he informed my family that he had decided to take Sir Reginald Wingate's advice and not defer his national service, Wingate having promised to keep a position open for him on his return. A tall, erect young man, he was drafted into the Scots Guards and a few days before joining the colours, he came to say his farewells to the family. We never saw him again.

Dennis Moore was posted to Malaya, where the British government was pursuing what was euphemistically called 'a police action' against Communist-inspired Malayan nationalists seeking independence. This 'policing' was largely undertaken by young conscripts. On 25 September 1949, three days before his twentieth birthday, Dennis was part of a three-man patrol tracking a group of 'bandits', or insurgents. They caught up with three terrorists in the jungle and killed them. Unknown to them, a fourth terrorist hid near the scene of the ambush; while the British patrol was inspecting the bodies, the survivor threw a hand grenade among them, killing all three. The incident was widely reported in the national press, particularly the *Daily Express*, from which my mother sadly read us the account. From that day, the name Wingate was rarely if ever mentioned in our household without a sense of bitterness. It is easy to speculate that had Dennis deferred his national service, he might be alive today. Dennis Moore was one of about 600 casualties – largely national servicemen – who gave their lives in the 'emergency' until Malaya was granted full independence in 1960.

The second occasion I came into direct contact with Wingate was in 1950 (or 1951) when, at the annual Armistice Sunday parade, he shook my hand. I was nine or ten years old, a member of the local Life Boy Troop, the junior arm of the Boys' Brigade. That day, it was my good fortune to carry the troop pennant and as such was afforded the distinction of shaking the Grand Old Man's hand. It was, as I recall, typical Armistice Sunday weather – cold, wet and miserable. All the local youth organizations and representatives from the British Legion were present, parading in front of Belhaven Church. The Boys' Brigade was arguably the smartest of the youth organizations, wearing pillbox hats with chinstraps, blancoed belts and dark suits; the officers wore brown leather gloves and forage-style caps with black ribbons. The Life Boys stood beside them. Among the other organizations were Scouts in kilts and wide-brimmed hats, attendant Cub Scouts, Girl Guides and Brownies. The British Legion men and women were smart, the standard-bearers wearing heavy white gauntlet gloves and carrying various flags, including the Union Flag. On the pavement beside Wingate were the local dignitaries – my mother's cousin Provost Alexander J. Manderson, Burgh councillors, the Town Clerk and other officials. I recall that Wingate stood beside the Reverend J. S. McMartin, minister of Belhaven Church, who was dressed in the uniform of an officer in the Boys' Brigade. Wingate was resplendent in top hat and a velvet-collared greatcoat with the obligatory poppy in his lapel. The Reverend McMartin, a former army chaplain in the Second World War, intoned a prayer, after which the Grand Old Man walked up and down the serried ranks, shaking hands here and there. Finally, the bands struck up and the whole parade moved off to attend the ceremony at the local war memorial.

For me it was – and remains – a sombre, moving event which deeply impressed a young boy. Our school at Woodbush always trooped out into the quadrangle every 11 November to observe the two minutes' silence as poppy wreaths were laid at a trough in the quad in memory of fallen former pupils. I knew we were honouring the dead of our parish in two world wars and I was proud to, unlike the children of today who seem to have lost that sense of occasion. But on that Armistice Sunday of so many years ago, I was also paying tribute to my cousin whom I had admired so much and whose name is inscribed on the local war memorial.

Personal grief freezes such emotional moments for all time – well, the time we are allotted. That Armistice Day parade is as fresh in my memory over half a century later, mainly because a beloved member of my family was being honoured. It was many years later that I learnt that the diminutive, Churchillian figure who had shaken my hand was an eminent Victorian, Wingate of the Sudan, a man who was a personal friend of Lord Kitchener, Gordon of Khartoum, Lawrence of Arabia and countless others of his time, men I was later to read about in historical biographies. I had shaken hands with history. Of course, even in my tender years, I was aware of the esteem in which Wingate was held. He had touched my life twice and would touch it for a third time, in January 1953 when he died.

As 2011 is the 150th anniversary of Sir Reginald Wingate's birth, perhaps it is appropriate that a book devoted to his memory should appear. It is now over half a century since the late Sir Ronald Wingate, CB, CMG, CIE, OBE, 2nd and last Baronet of Dunbar and Port Sudan (Honour *defunctus* in 1978) published a highly entertaining and informative account of his father's time in the Sudan and Egypt. Wingate senior *made* the Sudan, although it is a backward, impoverished country today, suffering drought, famine and war as it had before his stewardship.

Francis Reginald Wingate enjoyed a long life, a great deal of it spent in public service. Unlike his contemporaries – Gordon, Kitchener, Cromer, Lawrence and Allenby – little has been written about him. Having read extensively about the Middle East over the past centuries, from the Crusades to the Iraq war, I was struck by the fact that there are only a few passing references to Wingate's career in accounts of the Middle East between 1885 and 1919; often, his name appears only as a footnote. Having studied his extensive archive housed in Durham University, I was impressed by his sympathy – empathy – for the Egyptian, Sudanese and Arab peoples over whom he was set. He was a man before his time, sacked for his views about that region by an atrophied Foreign Office. What is ironic is that his blueprint for the future of Egypt and the Sudan, rejected by the British government in 1919, was implemented during his own lifetime. That must have lain heavily on his heart. Within three years of his death, Egypt's Colonel Gamal Abd-el Nasser declared that the Suez Canal would be nationalized; a brief but ignominious war followed in which British prestige was severely damaged, with only Israel emerging from the conflict with any honour. In 1956 Britain's eighty-year control of the canal came to an end. I wonder if Wingate would have been surprised by the fact. The British Empire continued to flicker until its demise in the 1960s, almost a decade after Wingate's death. To many Wingate remains a mere footnote in history, often confused with his great-cousin Orde (1903–1944). Sir Reginald Wingate's name has already faded in a small town which has few heroes. There are still some from his time in Dunbar who remember the man, but they are a dwindling band. Perhaps this book will go some way to ensure his name is not forgotten. Nor should it be.

Until fairly recently a book of this kind could not have been written. It has only been made possible by the assiduous industry of archivists in the Sudan Archive Department at Durham University Library who have painstakingly catalogued the archival material which comprise the Wingate Papers. The writing of this book has been made easier through judicious study of the many documents written to and by Wingate. These documents enlighten us to the thoughts, actions and to a certain extent the character of the man. Wingate wrote prolifically about his life in the service of his country, yet so far, there has been only one biography, *The Sirdar*, written by an American, Professor M. W. Daly; Professor Daly's book has never been retailed in the UK, which is a great pity, as it is a well-researched study of a Victorian administrator of imperial Britain. Professor Daly's book unfortunately fails to explore fully the background to Wingate's uneasy relationship with those controlling the Foreign Office. For example, he overlooks the nuances of tradition and nepotism rife in the Foreign Office in 1919, a government department largely staffed by Old Etonians and aristocrats who undoubtedly coloured the views of the Cabinet – themselves products of the Etonian system – who sat in judgement of Wingate. These individuals considered his reports and accurate assessment of the political situation in Egypt in 1919 but ignored his warnings. Consequently he was ignominiously sacked from his post of High Commissioner of Egypt for daring to tell the truth. I hope this book will add to our knowledge of a man loyal to the British government who devoted a large part of his long life in the service of king and country.

R. J. M. Pugh
Dunbar, 2007–2010

Chapter 1

Early Years
(1861–1885)

Situated in the east-facing aspect of Dunbar Parish Church cemetery, in a quiet, secluded corner overlooking what was once the main road to Spott Village, a couple of miles south of Dunbar, stands a plain, unprepossessing granite Celtic cross. It is inscribed with the following, fading words:

FRANCIS REGINALD WINGATE
BORN 25 JUNE 1861 – DIED 28 JANUARY 1953
FIRST BARONET OF DUNBAR AND PORT SUDAN
GCB. GCVO. GBE. KCMG. DSO.
THE MAKER OF THE ANGLO-EGYPTIAN SUDAN
R.I.P.

Pausing to read this inscription – if you are of an imaginative mind – you sense that you are standing before a testament to history enshrined in stone. It is an unobtrusive monument, one of many in a crowded part of the cemetery. Several nearby monuments inform the casual visitor that in that quiet corner repose the remains of several residents of Dunbar who spent most of their working lives in the service of the British Empire. The Celtic cross which marks Wingate's grave is opposite an impressive triptych monument erected by the Keith family who resided at St Margaret's, Winterfield, the latter once a thriving farm and now a golf course. The inscription on the Keith monument informs us that the family provided the Anglo-Indian administration with a senior civil servant, a lawyer and an educationalist. Thus Wingate lies among men of similar stamp to himself. There are many other gravestones scattered about the cemetery bearing testimony to the military and civil administrators who were born in Dunbar or lived there, men who served the British Empire upon which it was once said that the sun never set. Reginald Wingate was not born in Dunbar but he was a confirmed part of the community, spending the last thirty-four years of his life in the town.

Francis Reginald Wingate – always known as Rex to his family and friends – was the youngest of eleven children and the seventh son to Andrew Wingate and Elizabeth (known as Bessie) Turner, daughter of Richard Turner of Hammersmith, County Dublin. Reginald was born on 25 June 1861 in Broadfield, his parents' house at Port Glasgow, Renfrewshire (now

Inverclyde). The Scottish branch of his family originated in Stirlingshire, probably in the twelfth century. Two centuries before Wingate's birth, the family had been minor landowners in the vicinity of Craigengelt and Gargunnock in St Ninian's Parish, Stirlingshire. Wingate's grandfather William was an affluent merchant in the family business at Port Glasgow, to where the Wingates had moved early in the nineteenth century. Wingate's uncle, the Reverend William Wingate (1808–1899), furthered the family fortunes during the Industrial Revolution until he got religion and disassociated himself from commerce to devote his life to that of an evangelical preacher. In 1829, William had yet to discover Christianity; he was a partner in the family firm dealing in cotton textiles; by all accounts, he was a popular young man who had good connections in Scottish social circles. His biographer describes him as follows:

> He entered into commercial life with zeal and diligence, a leader at the same time in all sorts of sports, balls, dinners etc, and devoted to horsemanship, keeping generally one or two hunters, a member of the Harriers' Club, and joining often in the foxhunt.[1]

William Wingate was therefore what the eminent lexicographer Dr Samuel Johnson would have termed 'a clubbable man'. With a promising future ahead of him, William's life changed dramatically when his wife of only three years, Jessie, died in childbirth in 1838. Thereafter, he gave his life to Christianity, becoming an evangelical lay missionary in Glasgow until deciding to devote himself to the conversion of Jews – God's chosen people – to Christianity. He completely abandoned his business career, relinquishing the partnership with brother Andrew and was appointed to the Church of Scotland's mission to the Jews of Hungary. Ordained in Budapest in 1842, he worked there until the 1850s, converting many hundreds until the mission was disbanded. He returned to England to continue evangelical preaching until his death in 1899.

The Reverend William Wingate appears to have been the first in the family to research the family tree. As he wrote:

> They [the Wingates] are said to have come over with William the Conqueror in the eleventh century from Normandy, their French name being Winguet. They were effectively divided into two branches, one which settled in Scotland, the other in England. To the latter, I hope, Euston Wingate belonged, [the magistrate] who imprisoned John Bunyan. I had once a Latin book sent me written by a Wingate in Edinburgh at the Reformation period in the days of Knox.[2]
>
> Ours are the Stirlingshire Wingates. My grandfather was William Wingate of Craiginhelt [sic] Stirlingshire, and my grandmother was Sarah Carrick, sister of the celebrated physician, Dr Carrick of Bristol. Both were earnest Christians and he was an ordained elder in St Ninian's Parish for over fifty years.[3]

Without doubt, the Wingates came from Norman stock. It is also more than likely that the Scottish branch descended from a younger son of the English Wingates invited to settle in Scotland by King David I (1123–1154). David owned extensive lands in England and visited them regularly. Impressed by the Norman achievements in administrative – both civil and ecclesiastical – and military matters, he offered lands in Scotland to the younger sons of Norman families, men who were unlikely to inherit their fathers' estates in England, as right of inheritance was the prerogative of eldest sons. Thus, through David's generosity, a steady flow of Norman knights came to Scotland, intermarrying with indigenous Scottish noble families. A gentle Norman Conquest of Scotland followed. David's motives were not altogether altruistic; he hoped to civilize his semi-barbaric kingdom with the help of his Norman *parvenus*.

The Scottish Wingates took great pride in an ancestry they believed traced back to Robert the Bruce (1274–1329); in claiming this they were in error, although it is recorded that a Sir Richard de Wongatte fought for Bruce at Bannockburn. Yet another spelling of the family name was Windgeat, signifying a place where the wind forces its way through a narrow space and which survives in many place-names in Derbyshire, Durham, Northumberland and Scotland. Sir Ronald Wingate, Reginald's eldest son, would later claim that the English branch lived in Northumberland as the family provided some twenty recruits of that name in the armies of Edward III (1312–1377) during his Scottish campaigns.[3] (It is interesting to note that Earl Gospatric II of Dunbar owned a vill, or manor, called Windygates in the Serjeanty of Beanley in Northumberland, near Morpeth and Wooler. Was there a Dunbar connection even then with the Wingate family?)

After the Reformation in Scotland, the Wingates became staunch Presbyterians and Episcopalians; in the eighteenth century, they favoured the Episcopalian form of worship, supporting the cause of the Jacobite Pretenders to the British throne, respectively James VIII and Charles Edward Stewart. Reginald Wingate's forebears possibly fought at Sherrifmuir in 1715, Prestonpans in 1745 and Culloden in 1746. During his time in Dunbar, Reginald Wingate upheld family tradition by worshipping at St Anne's Episcopalian Church.

In later life, Reginald Wingate also attempted – unsuccessfully as it turned out – to trace his Scottish roots with the assistance of an eminent Edinburgh genealogist and antiquarian, James Mackenzie. Wingate was obliged to concede defeat in this venture as he admitted in a letter to a Mrs Dalrymple of Gargunnock, Stirlingshire:

> I have the full details of the English branch of the family dating back from [sic] the eleventh century, but even then it is difficult to establish the actual point when the Scottish and English branches separated, and then again we have an American branch, which appears to me to be of

undoubtedly Scotch [sic] origin, though of course the English family was apparently the English stock.[4]

Wingate's grandfather had established a flourishing shipping business in Glasgow, dealing in raw cotton at the end of the eighteenth century. Wingate's uncle William then became a partner in the family firm in 1829, at the age of twenty-one, until he became an evangelical preacher. Subsequently, Wingate's father and Wingate's brother William ran the business, the former becoming senior partner in 1838 until his untimely death in 1862.

The family business had gone from strength to strength from the late eighteenth to middle nineteenth centuries. At the height of the cotton boom, there were sixty factories in Glasgow employing 20,000 men and women. When Reginald was born on 25 June 1861, the American Civil War had broken out two months earlier. The Southern Confederate States of America had enjoyed unprecedented wealth from the sale of cotton to Glasgow and Lancashire in the 1850s, exporting about 70 per cent of their crop to Britain. If in Britain coal was king, then cotton reigned supreme in America; it would become the principal weapon in the Confederates' armoury and a major influence on the foreign policy of the day. When the Civil War erupted, the Southern States deliberately ceased sending cotton to Britain; it was made clear that the embargo would continue until Britain formally recognized the Confederacy. By 1862, the supply of raw cotton to Britain had been reduced to one-third of the pre-bellum South's exports, putting 75 per cent of British cotton-mill workers out of work and consigning the rest to short-time working.

It has been claimed that the export of Confederate cotton to Britain was restricted by the effective blockade of the Union Navy on Southern seaports. This is only partly true, although the Confederate government were content that the British believed this. It was a good ploy. In fact, Southern cotton went north to unscrupulous traders and profiteers who provided the South with money, salt, bacon, flour, shoes, clothing, gunpowder and bullets, helping the Southern armies to continue the struggle against the Northern States. War has often produced such anomalies.

The American Civil War put an end to the Wingate family business; as early as 1862 it was already failing. Probably due to stress, Wingate's father Andrew who was managing the textile business in Glasgow, suffered a fatal heart attack in 1862, although the cause of death was officially recorded as pneumonia. Reginald Wingate's distraught mother Bessie took her impoverished and fatherless family to Jersey in the Channel Islands during May 1864, at that time a cheap place to live. Thus the youngest Wingate and his nine siblings (his eight year-old brother George had died in May 1862, six weeks before his father's death) were brought up in relative poverty in Jersey.[5]

Bessie Wingate was so poor that she was unable to meet the high fees charged by the prestigious public schools of the day, so her youngest son

11

was sent to St James Collegiate School in Jersey. In those days public schools like Eton and Harrow followed an education system which was geared to churning out servants of the British Empire – statesmen, administrators, military men – whose sole purpose was to serve its vast territories.

Reginald Wingate entered St James School, Jersey in 1866 and graduated in 1878, aged seventeen. By all accounts he was a diligent scholar, showing promise through a power of concentration combined with a natural gift for taking the initiative. He was nothing if not resourceful; at the age of eleven, he and a fellow pupil decided to cross to France during the summer of 1872, a year after the Franco-Prussian War (1870–71) had ended. The two boys failed to inform their parents of their whereabouts. Apparently, with little or no money, the youngsters embarked on a walking tour of the recent battlefields. Thus at an early age, Wingate demonstrated his ability to be resourceful and independent – if not a little foolhardy – in his desire to explore unfamiliar territory. The boys returned home three weeks later, much to the relief of their worried families.

Further sadness was visited on the family; eldest son Andrew died in 1868, then another son, Henry, died at sea in 1872. After completing his secondary education, Wingate – orphaned in 1877, the year his fifty-five-year-old mother died – passed into the Royal Military Academy at Woolwich, known affectionately as 'The Shop', on 18 December 1878. Founded in 1721 the Academy was designed by Sir John Vanbrugh; its domes were heavily influenced by Indian architecture, which Vanbrugh had studied as a young man. Many of the recruits passing through the Academy's portals would later see service in the Indian continent.

Wingate was gazetted as Gentleman Cadet on 14 January 1879. Applying himself to his studies, he came tenth in his class (as would his son Malcolm in 1912). After passing out as a Lieutenant, or subaltern, in the Royal Artillery on 27 July 1880, Wingate underwent a short assimilation course at Shoeburyness, Essex. Subsequently, he was posted to Kandahar in Afghanistan at the end of the Second Afghan War. In going to the Indian sub-continent, he was following not only a Scottish but a family tradition; his first cousin Andrew was British Resident at the Royal Court in Rajputana, at Chittore; another cousin George (father of Orde Wingate, with whom Reginald Wingate is often confused) was an officer on the Indian Staff Corps, while another cousin Alfred, George's brother, served with the Indian Cavalry. Wingate's brother Richard held a good position in the Bombay Residency and yet another brother William was a chaplain on the Indian Establishment.

Reginald Wingate joined the British Army when the British Empire was at its height, unchallenged save by minor dissidents in places like the North-West Frontier of India and Egypt. Service in far-off countries was considered ideal training and character-building for young officers. Wingate arrived in Bombay in March 1881 from where he proceeded to Kandahar, when the last stage of the Second Afghan War was coming to an end. The frontier skirmishing had been encouraged by Imperial Russia which had for long cast a jealous eye on British possessions in the East, particularly India, the jewel in the crown of the Empire.

Wingate spent almost a year in Afghanistan. Undoubtedly, he began to hone his career as a young soldier who did not find service in a hostile environment and climate in any way irksome. It was good basic training for a man who would spend almost the next forty years in the Sudan and Egypt.

A staunch Christian – he attended church twice every Sunday – Wingate soon displayed a remarkable gift for languages. He could write French and German well but was also a fluent speaker in Arabic – a difficult language – Hindustani and Turkish. He was popular with his brother officers, possessing another great gift – that of comradeship. Like his future Commander in Chief, Lord Kitchener, he was a freemason, in time becoming Grand Master of Egypt and the Sudan and Grand Warden of England. In retirement, he became a member of the local lodge in Dunbar.

On 25 February 1882, the heavy Royal Artillery battery to which he was attached was transferred to Aden, a British protectorate and Crown colony with its important seaport town and fuelling station for ships passing through the Suez Canal. It was an unpleasant posting: Aden is a dry and barren place, where heat and disease took their toll in Wingate's day. His battery was positioned in the Crater District, a particularly unsavoury part of the town where sunstroke, dysentery, prickly heat and fever were rife. No matter, Wingate plunged himself into work, continuing to study Arabic and visiting his brother William, or Bill, who had also been posted to Aden as regimental chaplain.

At this time, reports of unrest in Egypt were the main topics of conversation and rumour among the garrison troops at Aden. Like others in his battery, Wingate speculated on his chances of a posting to Egypt that August; sadly, his hopes were dashed when other units were transferred. The revolt by disaffected officers in the Egyptian Army had led to decisive British intervention; an expeditionary force commanded by Sir Garnet Wolseley and Sir Evelyn Wood was despatched to quell the uprising. In Aden, Wingate's commanding officer, General Blair, had engaged him as a supernumerary ADC as he was impressed by the young officer's knowledge of Arabic. All Wingate's hopes of active service in Egypt ended with Wolseley's defeat of the disaffected Arabi Pasha at the Battle of Tel-el-Kebir. Blair had recommended Wingate to Wolseley without success; he did the next best thing however. He wrote to Sir Evelyn Wood who had recently been appointed *Sirdar* (Commander in Chief) of the Egyptian Army and was re-organizing it. Wingate was hopeful that Blair's recommendation to Wood might bear fruit; he was desperate to escape the barren rocks of Aden. Blair's approach on Wingate's behalf was refused on the grounds of Wingate's short service. Career postings required service with a line regiment for a minimum of five years; Wingate had only two years. (History would repeat itself in 1927, when

Wingate's cousin Orde was initially turned down for a posting to the Sudan under the same War Office ruling.)

By way of consolation, Wingate was posted to a mountain battery at Khandala, near Bombay. Although he was no doubt relieved to be away from the hostile environs of Aden, one of his first and unpalatable duties was to arrange the public execution of a Pathan soldier found guilty of murdering a British battery sergeant major.

However, events next took a sudden and unexpected turn. On 17 April, barely six weeks after his departure from Aden, Sir Evelyn Wood wrote to Wingate, offering him an appointment in the 4th Battalion of the Egyptian Army. The five-year rule was conveniently forgotten, undoubtedly on account of Wingate's fluency in Arabic. The young officer could not believe his good luck. He confided to his diary for May 1883 that:

> my orders to go to Egypt had come ... to proceed forthwith provided my transit did not cost the government of India anything ... [I] sent a line to Genl. Wood saying 'orders received, start twentieth [May] in Canton.[6]

He left India for Egypt in late May. When he stepped ashore at Suez on 3 June 1883, Wingate was three weeks short of his twenty-second birthday. Slim, dapper, with fair hair, he cut a handsome figure in his uniform, although he was only 5 feet 6 inches in height. A photograph taken a few years later in service dress shows him in formal pose, with penetrating eyes and a firm chin. His strong mouth was set off by a luxuriant moustache twisted at the ends, a mouth that more than hints of a sense of purpose. In later photographs as Governor General of the Sudan and High Commissioner of Egypt, Wingate looks every inch the Victorian statesman even if his hair had begun to recede. The determined set of his mouth never changed; it gives the impression of an aloof, even snobbish man who knows he enjoys considerable power and status. On the contrary, the opposite is true; away from the camera lens, Wingate was sincere, friendly, clubbable and kind.

Two days after his arrival in Suez, the young officer booked into the prestigious Shepheard's Hotel in Cairo. In those days, Shepheard's was a popular watering-hole frequented by unattached, pretty, young women – debutantes from Britain, collectively known as the Imperial Fishing Fleet – drinking morning coffee and seeking future husbands among the young officers stationed in the city. It was also the meeting-place of rich Europeans coming to Cairo and finishing the winter season in Egypt.

It was in this salubrious setting that Wingate met Major Andrew Haggard, King's Own Scottish Borderers, brother of the Victorian romantic novelist Sir Henry Rider Haggard.[7] The following day, Wingate met Leslie Rundle, a young officer in the Egyptian Army who would become his brother-in-law in 1888, when he married Rundle's sister Catherine, known as Kitty.

After paying the customary respects to the Sirdar, Sir Evelyn Wood, Wingate was introduced to the Khedive, or Prince, of Egypt, Tewfik Pasha. Wingate spent the next few weeks acclimatizing himself, although with typical honesty, he admitted that his knowledge of infantry drill was woefully inadequate, ruefully confiding to his diary:

> I do not know the bayonet exercise and have no idea of the Turkish words of command and little or nothing of Egyptian Arabic – I fear I was not much use.[8]

No matter, in time he would remedy those shortcomings. In July, a cholera epidemic reached Cairo, reputedly carried in cargoes of wood landed at the nearby seaport of Damietta. The disease quickly spread and caused panic among the native population and the occupying army as well as the resident and newly-formed units of the Egyptian army. On 14 July Wingate was ordered to set up a special isolation camp for all British soldiers returning from leave. The tented camp was supplemented by a ruined house which Wingate whitewashed and converted into a makeshift hospital. On 22 July the first cholera case arrived. In his diary of that time Wingate recorded the toll taken by the disease. He spent many hours at the bedsides of the victims and, though he never contracted the disease himself, he was afflicted with typhoid. By mid-September, he was fit enough to be sent home on leave, which he spent in Scotland. During that visit he fell in love with a Norah MacFarlane, whom he followed to Cannes, France but Norah's parents ended the affair by letter. In that year of 1883, Wingate was presented with the 4th Class of the Order of Osmanieh by the Sirdar, on behalf of the Khedive of Egypt. It was the first of many decorations Wingate would receive in the service of Egypt and the Sudan.

At this time rebellion erupted in the Sudan. To understand the cause, it is necessary to explore Egypt's recent history and relationship with the Sudan. When Wingate came to Egypt in 1883, he entered a country whose finances had been rescued from bankruptcy by the intervention of Britain and France. Egypt had been under Turkish rule since the sixteenth century, when it became a province of the Ottoman Empire in 1517. By the time of the Napoleonic Wars, Egypt had managed to secure semi-independence from the Sultan of Turkey until it was invaded by Napoleon in 1798. The French Emperor had long cast acquisitive eyes over Britain's interests in India which would have been threatened if the Middle East were occupied by France. Britain reacted by sending Admiral Horatio Nelson whose brilliant naval action had sunk almost the entire French fleet at Aboukir Bay but not in time to prevent a French army landing in Egypt. It took until 1801 for the British to finally dislodge the French when they were decisively defeated at the Battle of Alexandria. After the expulsion of the French, the British Government restored Turkish suzerainty over Egypt.

In the next half-century, Egypt prospered, mainly due to its cotton exports. However, the impressive income from cotton was squandered by the first Khedive Isma'il (or Ismail) Pasha, who had succeeded his uncle in 1863. A speculator on the stock market of the day, Ismail was known to the world as a spendthrift whose profligacy would ultimately consign Egypt to seventy-three years of European domination. He fancied himself as a sophisticated businessman, indulging in grandiose and ambitious aims for Egypt's agricultural and industrial development. Encouraged in these aims by the cotton boom in Egypt as a result of the American Civil War, he was determined to modernize the country and enrich himself at the same time. He borrowed money from foreign merchants and negotiated long-term loans from European banking houses. The money was borrowed at crippling interest rates; Ismail's development schemes came to nothing or failed to generate the anticipated income. The British government sat passively on the sidelines, curious to see how the fiasco would end. In 1875 Prime Minister Benjamin Disraeli took advantage of Ismail's financial predicament and purchased Egypt's shares in the Suez Canal. From this time on, Egypt was in Britain's pocket. In time, Sir Evelyn Baring, later Lord Cromer, was appointed to oversee Egypt's finances and bring them out of the red.

Ismail had been keen to modernize Egypt and her satellite state, the Sudan. His main ambitions were to utilize western expertise and technology and abolish the notorious Sudanese slave trade. In 1877 he accepted the British-appointed General Gordon as Governor of the Sudan. Knowing that the charismatic general was an evangelical Christian, Ismail was confident that Gordon would conduct a vigorous campaign against the evil of slavery, thus proving to the western world that he, Ismail, was an enlightened, modern leader to his people. In the same year, Ismail signed the Anglo-Egyptian slave trade convention, prohibiting the sale and purchase of slaves by the year 1880. This was in keeping with the campaign in Britain which led to the abolition of slavery throughout the British Empire in 1833, a full three decades before slavery was outlawed in the United States during the American Civil War.

Gordon set to work with the zeal of an evangelist; his crusade completely disregarded the effect that the campaign would have on the culture and economy of the Sudan, a largely Muslim country. Apart from the ensuing economic crisis he brought to an impoverished nation, the Sudanese leaders believed that Gordon had violated the tenets and practices of Islam. By 1879 a strong current of disaffection had arisen against Gordon and his policies; after all, he was perceived as a Christian infidel. Gordon's chief critics were the leaders of the rich and influential Baqqara (or Baggara) tribe whose wealth derived principally from the slave trade.

An increasingly financially straitened Egypt forced Khedive Ismail to reduce Egypt's public expenditure. Ismail was naïve in his attempts, his first target being the Egyptian army. He had backed the wrong horse, antagonizing his officer class by putting them on half-pay and thereby caused a minor revolt which he personally had to subdue. A second uprising for the same reason occurred in 1881, a revolt led by Arabi Pasha, a serving officer and committed Egyptian nationalist. Under pressure, Ismail admitted Arabi Pasha to his Council of Ministers which caused consternation among his

British and French 'advisers.' Arabi's slogan was 'Egypt for the Egyptians'; he strove to throw off the financial yoke of the Christian infidels – Britain and France – which imposed financial constraints over his country and were running it in all but name. On his dismissal from the Council of Ministers, Arabi declared war on Britain; during his rebellion, several Europeans were slaughtered. A fearful British government sent an expeditionary force to Egypt under Sir Garnet Wolseley who defeated Arabi's 25,000 strong army at the Battle of Tel-el-Kebir on 13 September 1882 with the loss of only 400 British troops.

During the period 1869–79, the British and French had attempted to re-float the Egyptian economy. Britain established the Bank of Egypt, while France provided funds to build the Suez Canal. The vital waterway, brainchild of a former French diplomat and engineer, Viscomte Ferdinand de Lesseps, had greatly enhanced European and Egyptian trade when it was opened in 1869. However, despite these initiatives, Ismail plunged Egypt deeper into debt; in 1879, he was forced to abdicate in favour of his son Tewfik Pasha, the second Khedive. As we saw earlier, an astute Disraeli brokered a secret deal with Tewfik in exchange for Egypt's shares in the Suez Canal. In return, Britain underwrote Egypt's vast debts and, along with France, took control of the economy. Thus by 1880 Britain's involvement with Egypt had assumed an entirely different character.

After the defeat of Arabi Pasha at Tel-el-Kebir, Britain found herself in absolute control in Egypt and – technically at least – the Sudan. From 1882 Egypt was effectively ruled by a British Consul-General, the first being Sir Evelyn Baring, with Sir Evelyn Wood as Sirdar of the newly reorganized Egyptian Army charged with ensuring the security of the Suez Canal. Baring instituted reforms in government, Wood in the military structure. Wood arranged for the secondment of several British officers from the British Army to the army of Egypt and created a Gendarmerie of para-military police commanded by General Valentine Baker whose remit was to police Egyptian towns. The combined force totalled 8,500 of which 6,500 were soldiers in the Egyptian Army.

Change for the better had come to Egypt but the same could not be said for the Sudan, its satellite. In Arabic, Sudan means 'the country of the black people'. The country was inhabited by Arabic-speaking Muslim tribes in the north and savage pagans in the south. The Sudanese economy had long been based on slave-trading; Egyptian rule was considered oppressive in the Muslim-dominated north, non-existent in the pagan south. Opposition to General Gordon's anti-slavery policy reached a climax in May 1881, when on Aba Island on the White Nile, 200 miles south of Khartoum, Ahmad ibn Abdallah, a religious fanatic and self-styled Mahdi (Messenger) proclaimed that he had been chosen by Allah to free the Sudan from the infidels. The faithful called him the Guided One or Expected One. Sudan was soon in the grip of a pan-Islamic revolt. It would take men like Charles Gordon, Herbert

Kitchener and Reginald Wingate to defeat this fanatical idealist and his successor in a campaign which would last for the next sixteen years.

It is appropriate here to note that in strictly theological terms and fundamental doctrine, Mahdism had no place in the orthodox beliefs of Sunni Islam. It derived from the Messianic doctrines of the heretical Shiahs or Shi'ite followers who believed that divine attributes descended from the prophet Mohammed by a form of apostolic succession through a line of *Imams*, or holy men, and that one would appear as the Mahdi to guide the people. There had been a succession of Mahdis, Ahmad ibn Abdallah being the latest of these. In 1881, he raised his standard in Kordofan Province, west of the White Nile and 250 miles south-west of Khartoum. It was here that Abdallah ambushed and destroyed an Egyptian force, capturing quantities of arms and ammunition. A long campaign against several Egyptian garrisons raised his status; it was no coincidence that the Mahdi flew his flag there as it was smack in the centre of territory occupied by the rich and warlike Baggara tribe who were increasingly disaffected by Egyptian rule and Gordon's vigorous anti-slavery measures.

The Sudan is a harsh, unforgiving region of Africa where extremes of temperature are awesome and forbidding even to its own inhabitants. The Arabs said of the area, 'When Allah made the Sudan, he laughed.' It would prove extremely difficult to set the Sudan free from the Mahdi and his fanatical followers.

In September 1883 Sir Evelyn Baring arrived in Cairo to take up his appointment as British Agent a few days before Reginald Wingate was sent home on leave to England. A large force commanded by General William Hicks, a retired Indian Army officer, left Khartoum for El Obeid, the capital of Kordofan Province, now in the Mahdi's possession. The British government confidently expected Hicks Pasha to defeat the Mahdi and restore Egyptian authority in Kordofan. Baring, who did not arrive in Cairo in time to cancel the expedition, considered it extremely foolhardy.

The expedition against the Mahdists which left Dueim on the White Nile on 27 September 1883 was doomed from the start. Hicks Pasha fell out with his Egyptian colleagues and the quarrel was widely spread among the troops; it sapped morale and undermined the army's chance of a quick victory. As Hicks advanced into Kordofan, his column was harassed by a strong contingent of Dervish warriors. Proclamations issued by the Mahdi were scattered along the line of march, propaganda that further weakened the morale of Hicks' men. The pamphlets warned the Egyptian troops that it was hopeless to fight against the soldiers of God. On 5 November 1883 Hicks and his army of 10,000 officers and men were annihilated by the Mahdist forces at Shaykan, south of El Obeid. All the officers including Hicks and the Governor of Kordofan, Ala al-Din, were killed. The action lasted only fifteen minutes, resulting in terrible loss of life, with many guns and ammunition stocks captured. The defeat of Hicks Pasha brought unprecedented prestige to the Mahdi; henceforth, he would be known as the Great One.

It is often a mistaken view of historians of the time that the Dervishes or, as the Mahdi preferred to call them, his *ansars* (helpers) were little more than savages, warriors rather than soldiers. They were possessed of incredible fighting qualities. It was often said that their bravery was fuelled by religious fanaticism, which of course is true, but such devotion does not explain how these tribesmen fearlessly attacked well-prepared positions defended by modern weapons – howitzers, Maxim guns and rapid-firing rifles in the hands of well-trained and disciplined soldiers. The Dervishes were personally brave and fearless, so much so that they were able on at least one occasion to break a British infantry square, something that Napoleon's troops at Waterloo had failed to do.

The news of the defeat of a modern army led by British officers by a force of half-naked warriors armed only with swords, spears and a few obsolete single-shot muskets ran like wildfire through the disbelieving and distressed corridors of Whitehall. El Obeid was seen as another Isandhlwana where, in 1879, the Zulu *impis* of King Cetewayo had massacred 1,500 British and native troops during the Zulu War. A shocked British government was frozen with inaction, its anti-imperialist Prime Minister William Gladstone reluctant to become embroiled in yet another 'Little War'. However, public outcry and the jingoistic press demanded a response. Gladstone had opposed the Afghan Wars; now he was refusing to respond to the problem in the Sudan. The British people called for an expeditionary force to avenge Hicks; Gladstone resisted as long as he dared before finally giving in to public opinion. The people wanted their hero General Charles 'Chinese' Gordon to lead the expeditionary force, a man who in their eyes came from the same mould as Lord Nelson, the victor of Trafalgar in 1805.

Born in 1833, Charles George Gordon was one of several quirky, unorthodox soldiers which Britain produced during the long period of its Empire. Idealistic, energetic, blessed with foresight, devoted to religious evangelism, Gordon was also naïve and over-trusting. He spoke or wrote no Arabic, a skill which would have given him a certain advantage over his adversaries. He put his trust in interpreters, men who were not always reliable or trustworthy. Normally patient, he was not above violent displays of temper, especially when his aims were frustrated by those in higher authority. His sense of humour tended towards the sardonic. He had served in the Crimean War (1854–56) and the Chinese Opium War of 1860 – hence his epithet of 'Chinese' Gordon – where he had gained fame and a reputation as a guerrilla leader *par excellence*, anticipating T. E. Lawrence and equalling him in eccentricity and anti-establishment posturing. He had also governed the Sudan between 1874 and 1879; during his time as Governor General, he had set himself the almost impossible task of ending the slave trade in a country where nearly 90 per cent of the population were virtual, if not actual, slaves. The Sudanese economy was largely based on this degrading and inhuman trade and, as we saw earlier, Gordon made himself highly unpopular among those who benefited from the vast profits made from dealing in human flesh. He resigned from his post after the abdication of Ismail Pasha, the first Khedive, believing that he had been unfairly treated by the Great Powers. Perhaps now he saw himself as the obvious choice to lead an expeditionary force – or was he?

The disaster of the Hicks expedition was only a prelude to what would come. In Cairo, Baring urged the British government to reach a decision about the Sudan, a satellite of Egypt and therefore Britain's responsibility. Following Hicks' defeat came less dramatic but worrying defeats at Sinkat, Trinkitat and Tokar; at Trinkitat, the British Consul at Jedda had been murdered and the Egyptian garrisons of the three towns had been slaughtered.

Drastic action was needed. Baring, with the support of the Egyptian government, recommended to the British government that the proposed withdrawal of British troops from Cairo should be postponed. He also recommended that the Sudan be evacuated except for the towns of Suakin and Wadi Halfa. The Egyptian government was unhappy about the second proposal, taking the view that the Sudan was an integral part of Egypt and essential to her security and prosperity. On 13 December, Lord Granville, the British Foreign Secretary, accepted both recommendations and advised the Egyptian government accordingly. Baring subsequently recommended that a British officer of high authority be sent to the Sudan to organize the evacuation of all Egyptian garrisons and make the best arrangements possible for the country's future government. Enter General Charles Gordon ...

On 20 December 1883, Reginald Wingate returned from leave but was not declared medically fit for active service as he was still suffering from the after-effects of a bout of typhoid fever. By the end of the month, Wingate, now holding the brevet rank of major, was appointed aide-de-camp (ADC) to Sir Evelyn Wood and also acted as his Military Secretary. Thus Wingate began a long and loyal friendship with Wood and Sir Evelyn Baring (later Lord Cromer). Less than three weeks after Wingate's return to Cairo, the British government took action; the Cabinet insisted that all Egyptian troops be withdrawn from Khartoum and the Sudanese interior. Public opinion in Britain was incensed; the people saw this as a weak climb-down. Baring equally insisted that Britain was simply preparing Egypt for self-government and he was lukewarm in his enthusiasm for a British expeditionary force entering the Sudan. A reluctant British government was persuaded by pressure in the press to alter its decision slightly. General Gordon would be sent to the Sudan to advise on the most effective way of withdrawing Egyptian troops and then personally supervise the evacuation of the city. This was no more than political expediency. Gordon was briefed on his role; the British Cabinet emphasized that he would go to Khartoum, his sole purpose being to evacuate its population. It is difficult to accept that Gladstone was naïve enough to believe that a man of such character and honour would comply with this ignominious order. Gladstone had been extremely reluctant to send Gordon to the Sudan; he distrusted the man and knew in his heart that Gordon would be unlikely to give up the Sudan without a fight. Gladstone was even more reluctant to send a relief force to rescue Gordon from Khartoum in 1884 when he got into difficulties, eventually being forced to give way under pressure just before the parliamentary summer recess that year. The relief expedition was late in starting, poorly supplied and missed the seasonal Nile high waters. It would eventually arrive in Khartoum two days too late to save Gordon.

On 18 January 1884 Gordon left England with express orders: all Egyptian personnel were to be brought out. The Sudan was to be abandoned to its fate. On 23 January Wingate recorded in his diary that 'The Sirdar [Sir Evelyn Wood] went to Port Said to meet General Gordon and try to induce him to come to Cairo'. Gordon had intended to go directly to Khartoum via Suakin. Although he disliked Wood he agreed to accompany him to Cairo; this change of direction gave Wingate an opportunity to meet Gordon. Wingate found the man quiet and pleasant although prior to a dinner held in his honour, Gordon succumbed to a fit of the sulks and demanded to be served soup in his hotel bedroom. In Cairo, Gordon was formally re-appointed Governor General of the Sudan – a somewhat hollow accolade, given the nature of his mission – and, on 25 January, Wingate was among the small group of officials who saw him off on the night train to Khartoum. It was a propitious date; Khartoum and Gordon Pasha would fall exactly a year later.

It is difficult to see how Gordon could have carried out his orders to the letter, since Khartoum was virtually surrounded by the Mahdi's Dervishes. He had been expressly forbidden to stand against the Mahdi and involve Britain in yet another 'Little War' which Gladstone wished to avoid at all costs. Evacuation of the Sudan would be seen by the Mahdi's supporters as the infidel Christians cocking a snook at pan-Islamic prestige and the Mahdi's reputation, despite this also being a loss of face on the part of Britain. The Dervish army would do all in its power to prevent the evacuation; at the same time, the Dervishes would prove to the European powers that the Mahdi could not be ignored.

After Gordon's departure from Cairo, activity in the Sudan shifted to the east, where a British-led force of Egyptians was en route to relieve the Egyptian garrison at Sinkat commanded by Tewfik Bey, a resourceful officer who had effectively disrupted the plans of Osman Digna, one of the Mahdi's guerrilla cavalry leaders. Now under siege, Tewfik Bey requested reinforcements; the first contingent of 150 men was virtually wiped out, the second from Suakin consisting of 500 men was beaten at El Teb, a third of its strength being killed and the rest scattered. Four days later, Tewfik Bey evacuated Sinkat and was overwhelmed a mile and a half from the town. News of these defeats was met by further clamour in the British press for direct action, so a force commanded by General Sir Gerald Graham set out from Suakin to confront Osman Digna. Graham attacked the rebels at El Teb, decisively defeating them; the second Battle of El Teb resulted in more than 2,000 killed among the Dervish army of 6,000 with the loss of only thirty-four killed and 155 wounded on the British side. This proved something of a hollow victory however; when Graham marched back to Tokar, he allowed Osman Digna to re-occupy the territory.

The Egyptian Army not only had to contend with a resourceful and formidable opponent but also the severity of the terrain over which they fought, one of the worst in the world. The climate is appalling, with extremes of heat and cold; there is little greenery and its deserts are unremittingly harsh. Any re-conquest of the Sudan would be entirely dependent on the use of the Nile and the desert railways.

Meanwhile, the situation at Khartoum was far from clear. Gordon had not evacuated the town, determined to defend it at all costs. In September 1884, he sent a party downriver to report on the situation but the steamer carrying his aide, Colonel Herbert Stewart, was wrecked with all on board lured to the shore by a supposedly friendly Sheik in the Mahdi's pay and murdered. This left Gordon a virtual prisoner in Khartoum. Nothing so absorbed the attention of the Victorian British public as a threat to men they considered heroes. Now public opinion and press pressure forced Gladstone to mount a relief expedition led by Lord Wolseley who arrived in Cairo on 16 September with strict orders to bring Gordon safely out. Before that, Wingate and his commanding officer Sir Evelyn Wood were sent to Wadi Halfa, the advance base for collecting stores, camels and organizing the necessary river transport. They left Cairo on 13 August to prepare the way for Wolseley's expedition. On 8 October Wolseley arrived in Wadi Halfa, from where he organized his campaign. Wingate had arrived in Wadi Halfa on 29 August and remained there until 23 December. At the end of December, Wolseley had moved forward to Kurti (or Korti), where he divided his force in two; one wing designated a Desert Column travelling overland was delayed in its advance, the troops having to be trained to ride camels. The second wing, a River Column, proceeded by steamer up the Nile. By 11 January, Wood and Wingate arrived in Korti. By now, the end was near for Gordon ...

To illustrate the problems facing Gordon, a brief comment is necessary here on the general state of the Sudan in 1884. At the outbreak of the Mahdi's rebellion in 1881, between 30,000 and 40,000 Egyptian troops were stationed in various garrison towns. Only a few thousand of these would return alive to Cairo, the rest being killed on active service. On arriving at Khartoum in January 1884, Gordon had made an inventory of the stores, weapons and ammunition. He decided he would make a stand; in his opinion, a sense of duty to the loyal Sudanese and British prestige left him no other choice. He set about creating a defensive ring around the town, mining the approaches and setting up strongpoints on the defensive perimeter. He rationed the food and distributed grain which unscrupulous merchants had stockpiled to inflate its price. Despite these measures, unless Khartoum was relieved, it would fall to the Dervishes.

The relief expedition reluctantly authorized by Gladstone finally lurched into action on 5 October 1884. Had it left two days earlier it might have saved

Gordon. However, British involvement in the Sudan had always been ineffective and haphazard; that came to an abrupt end when Khartoum fell on 24 January 1885, two days before the leading elements of the relief expedition arrived.

Wolseley, leading the expedition, was an old acquaintance of Gordon from the Chinese Opium War. He was familiar with Gordon's eccentricities and knew that he would never surrender Khartoum without a fight. Almost from the outset, the relief expedition ran into difficulties when the Desert Column was badly mauled by the Dervishes. The River Column made slow progress – some historians consider its tardy rate of advance was deliberate, although it has to be remembered that the steamers and gunboats had to negotiate several Nile cataracts which required the boats to unload before proceeding to the next stretch of clear water, and then re-load. In the advance of the River Column up the Nile, a humorous – if grotesque – incident occurred on board one of the steamers. Wingate must have known of it, as he sailed on one of the boats provided by Thomas Cook, founder of the future tourist agency. Due to a scarcity of wood, some of the steamers had taken on board a gruesome reserve fuel –mummified bodies from the Valley of Kings at Luxor. One can only marvel at the ingenuity of the British captains who acquired the dry cadavers. A story is told of Colonel Bagnold of the Royal Engineers who distinctly remembered hearing the captain of the steamer on which he was travelling call for more steam. The engine room officer informed him that, as fuel was low, he could not comply with the order. The captain then ordered the chief stoker to use what was available. His words were pure *Grand Guignol*, 'All right. Just throw on another Pharaoh!' Bagnold no doubt recounted the tale to his sister Enid, later author of the children's book *National Velvet*. His son Ralph, a major in the Royal Engineers, would join Count Ladislaus de Almasy's Libyan Desert expedition in 1932 to find the lost oasis of Zerzura (see Chapter 10).

Khartoum fell on 24 January, exactly a year after Gordon's departure from Cairo. In his book written several years after the fall of Khartoum,[9] Wingate records a supposedly near eye-witness account of Gordon's last hour as related to him by Fiki Medawi, one of the Mahdi's Emirs and an officer in the force besieging Khartoum. According to Medawi, when the Dervishes reached the walls of the palace, they

> dashed up the steps leading to Gordon Pasha's room; they found him standing by the door of the office at the top of the staircase, and he asked them who was their leader [presumably he wished to surrender his sword to that leader]; but they took no notice of what he said, and one of them rushing up, stabbed him with a spear, the others then followed, and soon he was killed. His death took place just before sunrise ... his head was cut off, wrapped in a handkerchief, and taken to the Mahdi. Gordon's body lay in the garden all that day, and many Arabs came and stabbed it with their spears; the next day, I heard it was thrown into one

of the wells ... as far as I know, Gordon was killed by spear and sword wounds only, and I have never heard that he made any resistance.

This report must be suspect. How can it be a true eye-witness account if it contains the words 'as far as I know, Gordon was killed by spear and sword wounds'? It is only one account of several detailing the last moments and circumstances of Gordon's death, one of 4,000 casualties at Khartoum. As it purports to be an eye-witness account given to Wingate, one has to give it certain credence but it is hard to accept that Gordon meekly accepted his fate. This was the view of Karl (or Charles) Neufeld, a German who combined trade in gum-arabic – the Sudan supplied 75 per cent of the world's needs – with acting as an Arabic interpreter to the Egyptian Army. Neufeld was captured by the Khalifa in 1887 and held prisoner until the fall of Omdurman in 1898. After his release, Neufeld questioned the account given of Gordon's death by the native who presumably was the same man who had spoken to Wingate. The native, a deserter from Khartoum, was a known liar; Gordon had threatened to cut out his tongue for his inveterate lying. Clearly, escaping from Khartoum and reaching Cairo, the man wanted to make a name for himself. Neufeld also questioned the accounts given by Rudolf Slatin and Father Joseph Ohrwalder, both prisoners of the Mahdist forces at Omdurman; these accounts were virtually the same as that of the mendacious Sudanese refugee. In Neufeld's view, it would have been out of character for Gordon to go like a lamb to the slaughter. Neufeld was not present at the death-scene but either wishful thinking or hero-worship convinced him that Gordon would have met his end defending himself. Neufeld has Gordon emptying his revolver three times into the horde, then killing sixteen or seventeen Dervish with his sword. An implied thirty or so casualties seems unlikely, even for a man of Gordon's stature and bravery, but we will never know the truth. Heroes are made, not born; we create their image in order that they live in memory.

When his victorious tribesmen brought him Gordon's head wrapped in a handkerchief, the Mahdi was enraged; as a religious man, he knew the power and appeal of martyrdom, which is why he had ordered that Gordon be brought before him alive. Today, it is Gordon, not the Mahdi, who is remembered whenever talk turns to Khartoum. The fall of the town was perhaps symptomatic of what was wrong with Imperial Britain's attitude – not only towards the Sudan but to many similar countries which Britain believed were better served by courting her friendship. As for Gordon, his death was felt personally by the public in Britain; he became the people's hero. The establishment took a different view of the unorthodox, eccentric soldier-statesman. Lord Cromer later commented that despite express orders to evacuate the Sudan, Gordon 'threw his instructions to the wind' and described him as 'half-cracked', while Thomas George Baring (Lord Northwood, Viceroy of India) thought him a 'mad man'.

The fall of Khartoum precipitated a complete withdrawal of Anglo-Egyptian troops and administrators, leaving the Sudan to face years of terror, misery, tyranny, slavery, torture and famine. It would remain thus until 1898, with the defeat of the Dervishes at Omdurman. For the moment, Wolseley evacuated his men and Britain virtually abandoned the Sudan. Wingate had served in the relief force sent to Khartoum; he was with Sir Evelyn Wood during the closing stages of the withdrawal to Korti from Khartoum. For his part in the expedition, Wingate could at least console himself with being Mentioned in Despatches.

Wood, disillusioned by the failed campaign and in poor health, resigned as Sirdar and left Egypt for a posting to England. He was followed by Wingate who arrived in London in June 1885, taking up an appointment in Gosport, Hants. The year would prove momentous in the young man's emotional life. A few months later, now a captain, he remained in England for the longest period in his military career to date. Having passed a promotion exam in January 1886, on 1 April – did he find it ironic in any way that it was April Fools Day? – his supernumerary and temporary appointment as ADC to Sir Evelyn Wood was made official. He joined Wood, now General Officer Commanding the Eastern District of England at Colchester in Essex. It was about this time that Wingate met and fell in love with Catherine, sister of his brother-officer Leslie Rundle. By all accounts, Kitty (as she was known) Rundle was an extremely pretty young woman; both she and Leslie were adult orphans and although Kitty 'came out' during the debutante season in London, she was impoverished and relied on a guardian for her upkeep. Wingate's proposal of marriage was accepted but as his pay was a pittance and mess bills were prohibitive, marriage would have to be postponed until 1888. However, they were engaged on 1 May; he also resigned as Wood's ADC, having accepted an invitation from Sir Francis Grenfell, appointed Sirdar in Wood's place in 1885, to rejoin the Egyptian Army.

After the death of Gordon, the Mahdi died of typhoid in June 1885 and was replaced by the Khalifa, (in Arabic, *khalifa* means Successor) Abdullahi ibn el Sayyid Mohamed, himself the son of a holy man of Kordofan and Darfur. Abdullahi, who was of the Baggara tribe, turned his attention to the conquest of Abyssinia, a country on the southern border of the Sudan. The confrontation with Abyssinia was essentially religious, the Khalifa believing the Abyssinians to be a more worthy foe than the 'Turks', as the British and Egyptians were known to the Dervishes. Furthermore, King John or Johannes, a Christian, had occupied some Islamic territory near Harat and had been offering assistance to the retreating Egyptians during the withdrawal from the Sudan. A succession of bloody contests followed, mainly at frontier towns. The Abyssinian war would continue until 1889, by which time it was confined to border skirmishing.

Wingate, now increasingly becoming engaged in intelligence gathering in the Sudan, candidly reported the political situation leading up to Gordon's year in Khartoum. He wrote that until the Mahdi had united the several disparate tribes of his country, the Sudanese had been

smarting under the tyranny of their former governors [meaning Egypt and Britain]. They welcomed the expected Mahdi, who was to set them free and enable them to become once more the rightful owners of their lands. But as time went on they saw their spiritual leader steeped in the wildest debauchery, and blindly led by his chief [sic], Khalifa, Abdullah Taaski who ... ruled the land with an iron hand. In place of a religious kingdom, where the inhabitants would live in peace, where there should be a communism of property and poverty should be unknown, they found the country drifting into a state of anarchy. Rapine [robbery], bloodshed and horrors filled the land. [10]

Of course he would be likely to write in such vein. Wingate was but thirty years old when he penned these words, still young enough to be inspired by the idealism of youth. While not wishing to accuse him of economy with the truth, the author finds these words somewhat hollow and, to a certain extent, unworthy. In time, Wingate would support the cause of Arab nationalism, and later Egyptian nationalism during and after the First World War. He would ultimately be sacked for such anti-imperialist views in 1919. In 1891 he was still fired with a desire to see justice for the people of the Sudan, a people he rightly believed were sold short by their leaders. Many countries in the British Empire would have a long wait for full independence, particularly India which did not achieve it until 1947. In his written record of this period, Wingate espoused the benefits that the British Empire bestowed on the native populations an iron hand as he saw it, which, gloved with velvet, certainly improved the lot of those governed. But the question has to be asked: were the Mahdi and his successor the Khalifa so cynically dismissive of the people over whom they were set? It is hard to believe they were, although their regime was harsh. It is true that all societies which are controlled by religious rather than civil law can be repressive and brutal. Scotland's own history proves this time and again, especially during the witch-hunts conducted by the Church of Scotland during the sixteenth and seventeenth centuries, the Kirk of that time driven largely by hysteria and superstition. Fundamentalist Islam is not unique in being a repressive religion but Wingate never denounced it because he was a devout Christian seeking to understand other religions. He was in no doubt that Islam was the proper religion in the Sudan and the Middle East and was prepared to defend the rights of its followers to practise it. Wingate is to be applauded for this belief, even if, in his heart, he knew that it had a tendency to extremism.

In the Britain of 1885, Queen and country were united in their censure of what they saw as Gordon's unnecessary death at Khartoum. Both reviled Prime Minister Gladstone for failing to act quickly and decisively to save Gordon. One has a certain sympathy for Gladstone, the Midlothian MP who, as a Liberal Prime Minister had introduced a Home Rule Bill for Ireland; this tells us much about his desire to give power to the indigenous populations of countries ruled by Britain. But public opinion is fickle; the British people soon forgot Gordon and the Sudan until 1895, ten years after his death, when Gladstone had retired from political life. Gladstone's administration was replaced by that of Lord Salisbury, former Secretary of State for India and a robust supporter of the British Empire and all it stood for. Imperialism was back in fashion and respectable. The re-conquest of the Sudan would take a further thirteen years and it would be the making of Reginald Wingate who, in turn, would forge a more enlightened Anglo-Egyptian Sudan.

Notes

1. *Not in the Limelight*, RELW.
2. Thought to have been Nicholas Winzat, a fervent Catholic and opponent of the Reformation in Scotland.
3. *Life and Work of the Reverend William Wingate*, Carlyle.
4. Letter dated 31 August 1911, WP 235/2, SAD, DU.
5. It is interesting to note that another impoverished family by the name Lawrence also lived in Jersey for a time. Wingate would later meet T. E. Lawrence (of Arabia) in the Middle East, at the outbreak of the Arab Revolt in 1916.
6. WP 102/7, SAD, DU.
7. Rider Haggard's first novel *Cetewayo and His White Neighbours* had been published the year before. Cetewayo was the King of the Zulus against whom the British fought a 'Little War' in 1879.
8. *Wingate of the Sudan*, RELW.
9. *Mahdiism and the Egyptian Sudan*, FRW.
10. *Ibid.*

Chapter 2

Intelligence Officer
(1886–1898)

In 1886 Wingate was back in England, languishing under the routine life in army barracks. Obliged to dine in the officers' mess, he found the bills exorbitantly high and British Army pay abysmally low. As for marriage, that would remain out of the question for another two years. Unless he could somehow engineer another overseas posting offering better pay, subsistence allowances and promotion prospects, he was stuck in a career and financial rut. He ran into debt which increased every month he remained in England. He took Sir Evelyn Wood into his confidence and explained his predicament; Wood generously agreed to release him only a month after appointment as his ADC. Through Wood's good offices, Wingate received welcome news from Egypt; the Sirdar, Sir Francis Grenfell, offered him a posting to the Egyptian Army.

Grenfell had been as good as his word, appreciative of Wingate's fluency in Arabic. (It was his impressive linguistic ability which would, in time, provide Wingate's escape route from everyday military routine.) Posted to Cairo, Wingate arrived on 31 May 1886, where he was appointed Assistant Military Secretary to Grenfell. Wingate immediately felt at home in Egypt, working and playing hard; his off-duty time was divided between squash, tennis and riding. In his new post he attended many official functions hosted by the Sirdar, mixing freely and confidently with leading Egyptians, thanks to his by now impressive knowledge of Arabic.

Wingate visited England on leave in 1887 and in 1888; in the latter year, on 18 June, he married Kitty Rundle at St Mary Abbot's Church, West Kensington, London.[1] Kitty and her brother Leslie were the children of the late Captain Joseph Sparkinhall Rundle RN who, as mate of HMS *Volage* in 1839, had led a landing party in an action against the Arabs in Aden, planting the Union Flag in the desert and claiming the territory for Britain.

Perhaps it is appropriate here to describe Kitty Rundle's life in more detail. Born on 26 October 1858 in England, she and Leslie were brought up by a guardian who acted *in loco parentis*. Although little is known of these years, we know that brother Leslie entered the army. After marriage to Wingate, her first real home was a flat near the War Office in Cairo. Like most women married to men in the service of imperial Britain, Kitty was obliged to take refuge behind a shield of formality, a requirement of the time, even though junior British officers and officials formed the backbone of the ruling class in countries of the Empire. By all accounts, she was a model wife; in these days, wives of British officials were never considered the 'other sex'; in the words of the French novelist Simone de Beauvoir, women were the 'second sex'. Kitty Wingate embodied the Victorian qualities expected of her – propriety, dignity, strictness, kindness, sentimentality – and a burning ambition to further her husband's career. In private life she was a sensitive wife loyal to her husband and their three children. In Cairo she spent her days educating the children. In his book *Not in the Limelight*, her firstborn son Ronald describes her as a strict disciplinarian. As the years passed and her husband's income increased, she was able to hire a governess to look after sons Ronald and Malcolm. In their early married years she frequently spent long periods separated from her husband, taking holidays in England, France and Switzerland. Even when she and Wingate were together in Khartoum, when he was appointed Governor General of the Sudan, she was often alone while her husband toured the Sudanese provinces. There were compensations; Khartoum became a popular resort for European tourists and Kitty proved herself an excellent hostess by virtue of her grace, vivacity and humour.

Kitty Wingate spent the winter months of October to April with her husband in Egypt; when their children were born, she returned to England in April and took them on holiday to small hotels in Switzerland or France. The children also stayed with their great-aunt Ag[nes] Mackenzie, a widow who owned a vast Victorian mansion on Broadwater Down, Tunbridge Wells; another summer residence was that of friends in London, at 31 Great Cumberland Place.[2] As pre-school children, Ronald, then Malcolm and finally daughter Victoria lived with their parents in a large Cairo flat, Maison Rolo, in a square close to the old War Office.[3] In some respects the Wingate children were more fortunate than their counterparts with fathers serving in India in either military or administrative appointments; these youngsters often did not see their parents for months, even years, on end. (Most of Wingate's brothers and cousins served in India in various capacities, so he considered himself fortunate in being posted to Egypt, a place which allowed his children long visits.)

Meanwhile, in the Nile Valley, the immediate threat of a Dervish invasion of Egypt had been extinguished on 30 December 1885, when an advance force of Dervish warriors had been decisively defeated by General Stephenson's Anglo-Egyptian force at Qinis (or Ginnis). For the moment Egypt remained secure.

In August 1886 Wingate's appointment as Assistant Military Secretary to the Sirdar put him in charge of recruitment for the Egyptian Army which now numbered 10,000, or two divisions. Then, at the beginning of 1887, he was given the additional duties of Assistant Adjutant General for Intelligence. Wingate's skills were wasted on recruitment, a mundane and bureaucratic task; the second of these appointments suited his temperament and ambition. In that year, Wingate received his second honour, the 4th Class Medjidieh. In 1888 the Sirdar, Sir Francis Grenfell, impressed by his young and energetic aide, promoted Wingate to the post of Director of Military Intelligence when Britain began to assume a more aggressive role in the Sudan.

Wingate was delighted to be back among old friends such as Andrew Haggard, Leslie Rundle and even the reserved and remote Herbert Kitchener, the last two with whom he had served on the expedition to relieve Khartoum in 1884–85. By 1886 the Mahdists had driven the British and the Egyptians out of every Sudanese province except for the northern triangle of Suakin, Wadi Halfa and Aswan. The Frontier District, as it became known, was a desert area constantly under attack by the Khalifa's marauding forces. The Khalifa Abdullah who had succeeded the Mahdi on the latter's death in June 1885 made known his intention to invade and conquer Egypt, a not entirely hollow boast, as the defence of Egypt was now solely in the hands of the small, albeit efficient, Egyptian Army. The Frontier District became the base from which Wingate launched his intelligence operations and where he established his organization of spies and agents to infiltrate Dervish territory immediately to the south of the Wadi Halfa–Suakin line. He still continued to act as recruitment officer for the Egyptian Army but, as time went by, Wingate became increasingly involved in establishing what would become a highly efficient and impressive intelligence department, providing invaluable information in the years to come. He gathered about him a small coterie of skilful intelligence analysts and interrogators; his right-hand man was Milhem Bey Shakoor, a Syrian Christian who would play a vital role in rescuing men like Father Joseph Ohrwalder and Rudolph von Slatin from Dervish captivity. Another asset to the small organization was Naium Bey Shuqair, another Syrian professional intelligence officer who would remain in British service from 1886 until his death in 1922.

One of Wingate's first duties was to receive a delegation of four Baggara tribesmen sent by the Khalifa bearing letters addressed to several leading British officials and Queen Victoria. The letter to Victoria demanded nothing less than her conversion to Islam, which may have led her to comment that she was not amused. The Khalifa's absurd demands only strengthened the opinion of the British Establishment that he was an ignorant, upstart savage who needed to be put in his place.

Wingate's spy network began to take shape. To modern eyes the organization was naïve and amateur, with more than a whiff of the *Boy's Own* comic popular at the time. Wingate engagingly referred to his spies as Number One, Number Two, Number Three and so on, a far cry from the sophisticated twentieth century MI5 or the spy fiction of Ian Fleming, with his triple number operatives 'licensed to kill'. It must be admitted that, in the early days of his spy network, a fair portion of the information Wingate amassed was virtually useless from a military point of view. (For example, one of his operatives dutifully reported that the Khalifa owned a harem of

105 wives and concubines.) That apart, Wingate was able to build up a picture of conditions in the Khalifa's Sudan – the strength of his army at Omdurman, troop dispositions and the names of those commanding them in the various provinces. Another valuable intelligence asset was the report of shortages in food and the fluctuations in food prices – always an indication of plenty or want. Wingate's spies and agents were usually well paid. They had to be; if they were captured by the Khalifa's men, it would mean torture and even death. The Khalifa operated his own highly effective spy network; some of his operatives almost certainly acted as double agents, feeding Wingate with both true and false information. Several of Wingate's operatives were indeed taken prisoner and suffered a grisly death.

Occasionally Wingate strayed beyond his remit in the Sudan. For example, on one occasion he made use of the right-hand man of an old slave trader, Zubeir Pasha, a confidant of Charles Gordon and once considered for the position of Governor in a province of Sudan, as he opposed the Mahdi. Zubeir's man was called Rabeh. Little more than a brigand, Rabeh challenged French expansionism in Chad, around the huge Central African freshwater lake, a focal point on the French-African and British-Nigeria frontiers. Observing the old adage that my enemy's enemy is my friend, Wingate encouraged Rabeh to attack French settlements, offering him unspecified assistance – probably gold. The French in Chad believed that Rabeh was in the pay of the British, as Wingate would discover to his embarrassment many years later (see Chapter 11).

Usually Wingate remained in Cairo where he was metaphorically chained to a desk, overwhelmed with paperwork – the Egyptians named him *Abu Hibr* or Father of the Ink – although occasionally he was able to escape the tedium of bureaucracy and visit the Frontier District, mainly the towns of Suakin and Wadi Halfa, on some intelligence mission. These visits would gradually increase when significant Dervish activity was reported in the region.

Despite his virtual control of the Sudan, things were not going smoothly for the Khalifa. In 1887 he suffered a minor defeat at Sarras, about sixty miles south of Wadi Halfa but, apart from occasional unplanned and uncoordinated raids and border skirmishing, neither he nor the Egyptian Army made much progress against each other. He continued to boast of his intention to invade Egypt, in a more propagandist than militarily effective way. By 1889 his proposed campaign to invade Egypt had all but flickered out, although he continued to threaten *jihad*, or holy war, against the infidels, boasting that he would reform Islam in the whole of Africa, Arabia, Mesopotamia and Turkey. His military activities achieved little other than a shaky occupation of Darfur Province in western Sudan, although he had a firm grip on other regions.

By 1889 Wingate had been relieved of his irksome recruiting duties and was able to devote his entire energies to intelligence work as Director of Military Intelligence, a somewhat grandiose title. He was the sole European officer in the department until he was joined by Rudolf von Slatin in 1895. Wingate's remit was clear and unequivocal; he was given the task of gathering as much information as he could on the strength of the Mahdist Army, assessing the political and economic situation in the Sudan and the Khalifa's relations with Abyssinia on the eastern Sudanese border. Lastly, he was asked to ascertain the state of the European prisoners in Omdurman, regarded as a humanitarian rather than a military objective. His agents covered the territory from Kassala in the east to El Obeid in the west; he also maintained a fifth column in Omdurman, monitoring the comings and goings of the Khalifa's lieutenants.

A minor incident in 1888 had brought Wingate to Suakin on the Red Sea coast just north of Trinkitat which had been under intermittent siege since 1883 by Osman Digna, the elusive Dervish guerrilla leader. In December 1888 Osman launched the first of two attacks on the Suakin area but he was easily repulsed by the Sirdar, Sir Francis Grenfell, who lost only six Egyptian troops to Osman's 500. In 1889 the Khalifa was experiencing difficulties in maintaining his grip on several provinces, notably Dongola, where unrest was interfering with his planned invasion of Egypt. Nevertheless, he persisted with his plans, sending a force of 13,000 Dervishes led by Emir Abdel Rahman Wad el Nejumi, the brave and fanatical Muslim who had annihilated Hicks at Shaykan, near El Obeid in 1883, and breached Gordon's defences at Khartoum in 1885. Nejumi's strategy was to advance west of the Nile, avoiding the Wadi Halfa strongpoint, and strike at the Egyptian garrisons some sixty miles within the Egyptian border. Almost from the outset, Nejumi was plagued by difficulties with supplies and an acute shortage of water, losing both men and pack animals to desertion and sickness. His motley force consisted of 5,700 warriors and 8,000 camp followers; on his own, Nejumi presented little threat, although it was feared that his army might be strengthened by recruits from the indigenous population.

Just north of Wadi Halfa, an Egyptian force of 2,000 defending the village of Argin and commanded by General Sir Joseph Wodehouse successfully repulsed part of Nejumi's army which suffered heavy losses. Undaunted by this setback and even though short of drinking water, Nejumi pressed on, engaging in minor skirmishes with Egyptian cavalry patrols until his rapidly shrinking force was finally brought to Battle at Tushki (or Toski) on 2 August 1889. By then Grenfell had assembled the bulk of the Egyptian Army at Toski, although, surprisingly, he was reluctant to attack Nejumi's depleted force – he believed it to be 10,000 strong – without the addition of a British battalion to reinforce his already superior number of native troops. However, the British battalion failed to materialize (or else Grenfell's request was ignored) in time for the battle which took place on 3 August.

Wingate was present on the field and recorded his experience. It is not entirely clear how many Dervishes fought at Toski; estimates are contradictory. Some historians give 10,000 and claim it was a major action; other more realistic accounts consider the force to be half that number, perhaps as low as 3,000. We will never know the true figure, even were it possible to exhume the graves on the battlefield which is today submerged under Lake Nasser. The action at Toski was the culmination of the Khalifa's attempts to invade Egypt, so it was important from that perspective. Nejumi was beaten before he started the battle and was fatally wounded during its course. Wingate received the DSO and was Mentioned in Despatches, Grenfell compiling an official account of the action which was published in *The Times*.

For his part, Wingate sent a handwritten memorandum to Queen Victoria, depicting the less than competent Nejumi as a brilliant warrior in the same mould as Salah el Din, the scourge of the Crusader armies several centuries before. To be fair, Wingate genuinely admired Nejumi on account of his victories at El Obeid and Khartoum. However, his memo was a conscious and deliberate attempt to stir public opinion and imagination in Britain, aimed at convincing the establishment that it was now time to take decisive action in the Sudan and avenge Gordon. Wingate played the media for all it was worth. He even arranged for himself to be appointed as the official *Reuters* correspondent in Upper Egypt, a conflict of interest that would not be tolerated today. (He preceded a young Winston Churchill in this; Churchill had no scruples in combining his profession of soldier with that of journalist during his early years.) Wingate enriched himself by the sum of sixty guineas (£63) as retainer or fee from *Reuters* for his reportage. Sir Francis Grenfell turned a Nelsonian blind eye to this blatant conflict of interest, salving his conscience by insisting that Wingate's motive was for political rather than financial gain. Wingate was aware that his memo to Victoria was nothing short of propaganda; he blatantly exaggerated Nejumi's pathetic last stand, describing it as a great Egyptian victory simply because he and others like Herbert Kitchener wanted to stir up enthusiasm for a British commitment to re-conquer the Sudan. No matter, despite Wingate's memo, the British government remained unmoved.

Osman Digna's second major campaign occurred in February 1891. In Cairo, Sir Evelyn Baring persuaded Lord Rosebery's government to authorize an expedition to Tukar (or Tokar) which was said to be only lightly held by the Dervishes – or so War Office intelligence reports suggested. These reports turned out to be wide of the mark. (Baring later admitted that had he known of the true Dervish strength, he would never have recommended an advance on Tokar.)[4] The town proved a tough nut to crack but eventually, British-led Egyptian troops occupied it. It was a considerable prize; both sides recognized Tokar as the granary of the Sudan. The high command in Cairo saw that if Tokar was reclaimed this would not only relieve the pressure on Suakin, held by Egyptian troops, but also deny Osman Digna food supplies for his army. A brief, sharp fight at Afafit, near the town of Tokar, also weakened Osman Digna's capacity for further activity in that part of the Sudan, where Egyptian authority was firmly established. Wingate received further honours for his part in the actions at Tokar and Afafit.

The Egyptian victories at Toski, Afafit and Tokar in no way alleviated the sufferings of the Sudanese people who endured terrible privations between 1883 and 1891 and beyond. Years of famine and disease took their toll of human life, then as now. In his day the Khalifa blamed it all on the Christian infidels. He did precious little to alleviate the sufferings of the people he had 'liberated' from the autocratic rule of the 'Turk'. As for Wingate, he put his intelligence-gathering information to personal gain. Drawing on the documents he had acquired, he gave an account of the state of the Sudan in his book *Mahdiism and the Egyptian Sudan* which was published in 1891. Sir Francis Grenfell, the Sirdar, wrote the introduction and was fulsome in his praise of Major Wingate for his invaluable mastery of the Arab language which had enabled him to personally interrogate Dervish prisoners of war and refugees fleeing from the Khalifa. In the conclusion to his book, Wingate contended that the Khalifa would have to be defeated in battle before order was restored in the Sudan. While Wingate was writing from the perspective of contemporary European values, his words ring with more than a little truth; he described the Khalifa as a 'despotic and tyrannical leader, utterly ignorant and regardless of all recognized laws and forms of government'.[5]

It has to be said that Wingate's motives for writing his account of Mahdiism were primarily aimed at earning money and fame. The book received mixed reviews in the British press. *The Saturday Review* described the work as 'a godsend, especially just before a General Election.' *The Athenium* argued that Wingate's book had been 'written with the manifest object of bespeaking favour for an Egyptian reconquest of the Soudan [sic].' Several reviewers criticized its style, considering it dull reading. The book was hardly a commercial success – only 300 copies were sold in the year of its publication – possibly because it was large (600 pages) and consequently expensive. Besides, vivid accounts of recent events in the Sudan were already in print, dwelling on the (exaggerated) heroic exploits of British officers, written in the purple prose style of the cheap novelette so beloved of Victorian readers. These were largely fanciful, but history can be a dry subject, often failing to capture the imagination of those who prefer the blood-and-guts treatment. Wingate's book was heavily larded with details and facts which reduced its appeal to the general reader of the time.

Let us return to the conditions which Wingate describes in the Sudan of more than a century ago. The Khalifa was undoubtedly an autocratic despot, yet his administration served the Sudan more effectively than his modern European detractors may care to admit. The fact of the matter was that his methods appealed to the instincts – and more importantly – the religious prejudices and biases of his tribal subjects. They had survived under the authoritarian – and corrupt – Ottoman Empire for centuries, but at least their Turkish masters were Muslims like themselves. The Sudanese people lived in a country in which progress and modern development were alien, slow to come about. The sudden and dramatic intervention of a Western, civilized power brought confusion to a people who for centuries had accepted their lot as the will of Allah, content to live by ancient customs and habits. In the contemporary and more enlightened eyes of the British, the Khalifa was corrupt and savage, with his thirty-four wives and sixty concubines – not unusual in the culture and country of his time – but often these wives were acquired by the Khalifa discreetly ordering their lawful husbands to divorce or face execution. Holding his medieval court in the small town of Omdurman, the capital of the Mahdi's brief empire, the Khalifa treated the population as his personal property to do with as he pleased.

Omdurman, opposite Khartoum, was a reasonably secure base. The southern approach to it was protected by a fort which ironically had been built by General Gordon while Governor General of the Sudan between 1874 and 1879, a building later extended and strengthened by the Mahdists. Its western aspect was open desert, offering no cover to an attacking army. The town itself was dominated by the impressive tomb built in 1885 for the Mahdi's remains. It consisted of a large white dome 50 feet in height, surmounted by the Muslim crescent symbol, two enormous spearheads thrusting into the sky from the centre.

In the final pages of his book *Mahdiism and the Egyptian Sudan*, Wingate ends on an optimistic note, his wish being that

> a new and better Sudan will be raised up over the ashes of Gordon, and all those brave officers and men who have perished in the loyal performance of their duty is the fervent hope of every well-wisher for the prosperity of Egypt.[6]

He might have added the words 'and Britain' after 'Egypt' but perhaps that is being unfair to Wingate. His subsequent administration of the Sudan between 1899 and 1917 was not only effective and efficient, it was fair. He displayed a genuine concern for the welfare of the people over whom he was set. But that was still several years away. It would take much more than optimism to breathe life into his wish for a better future in the Sudan. In time he would prove his worth in the long campaign to bring the Sudan closer to something resembling a modern and civilized state. It has to be said, however, that, ultimately, Britain's campaign to reclaim the Sudan was aimed at preserving her interests in Egypt and preventing other European powers from gaining a foothold in the region. The late nineteenth century would see an undignified scramble to acquire possessions in Africa by the French, Belgian, Italian and German nations.

Wingate's book was published in the same year he was awarded the 3rd Class of the Order of Medjidieh. At the age of thirty, the young man was fast decorating his breast with awards.

In 1892 two major events occurred in Egypt which would have far-reaching consequences for the British administration. Returning to Egypt from leave in England in November 1892, Sir Evelyn Baring (now Lord Cromer) who, as a professional banker, had brought Egypt out of near bankruptcy, found a distinct change in the political atmosphere in Cairo, largely due to the attitude of the new Khedive, Abbas Hilmi. Hilmi had been appointed Khedive on the death of his father Tewfik Pasha. Hilmi inherited a kingdom enjoying economic stability and sound government; his rule was also more secure than that of his late father. However, he made no secret of his animosity towards the British in general and Consul-General Cromer in particular. The second event was the appointment of Herbert Kitchener as Sirdar on the resignation of Sir Francis Grenfell, British officials Abbas Hilmi also detested. Cromer was a capable and resolute administrator, not unduly concerned by the Khedive's opinion of him. As for Kitchener, he probably regarded his elevation to Sirdar as something of a mixed blessing. An entirely different man from Grenfell, who was not only wealthy but popular and trusted by the Egyptians, Kitchener was shy, distant, withdrawn, with no familial private means and few friends. Such was the extent of his reserve that he had little personal contact with the men who served him. His closest associates were Leslie Rundle and Reginald Wingate; he appointed Rundle as his Adjutant General and Wingate Director of Intelligence.

It is probably appropriate here to examine Kitchener's background and career prior to his appointment as Sirdar. Like Wingate, he had entered the British Army via the Royal Military Academy at Woolwich, passing out as a young subaltern in the Royal Engineers. From 1870 to 1882 his career was that of a typical Army officer, serving in places like Palestine, Egypt and Asia Minor, where he was largely engaged in mapping and surveying work. Not surprisingly, he was noted for his meticulous attention to matters of detail, probably on account of his cartographic skills. In 1883, the year Wingate arrived in Egypt, he was one of the first British officers to be seconded to the Egyptian Army and promoted to the rank of captain (Bimbashi) and appointed second-in-command of the Egyptian Army's cavalry division. In 1884 he played a key role in Wolseley's ill-fated relief column to rescue Gordon from beleaguered Khartoum. (It is interesting to note that Gordon had written to Cairo that year, recommending Kitchener as a possible Governor General of the Sudan. Gordon's advice would be implemented posthumously in 1886.)

Kitchener was a man with a mission – to avenge the death of Gordon, a man whom he considered a heroic figure. During the period 1886–92, Kitchener's career went from strength to strength. Despite the failure of the Wolseley expedition, Kitchener quickly ascended the promotion ladder; he was appointed Adjutant General of the Egyptian Army, Inspector General of the Egyptian Police, then he became Governor General of East Sudan (Suakin and the Red Sea Littoral, or shoreline). Finally, in 1892, he was appointed Sirdar of the Egyptian Army.

On 17 February 1888 Kitchener fought his first action against the elusive Osman Digna, arguably the best of the Khalifa's cavalry commanders. The battle took place near Suakin, where Kitchener's tactics were found seriously wanting; his direction of the fighting was little short of chaotic, although he managed to extricate his command intact. For this he was promoted to

Colonel, serving as Sir Francis Grenfell's Adjutant General. He was given full command of the Egyptian cavalry at the Battle of Toski in 1889, when the Khalifa's invasion of Egypt was repulsed with heavy loss. Three years later he was Sirdar; some historians consider he hardly merited an appointment which had been largely engineered by Lord Cromer. In time Cromer's judgement would be justified. In the year of 1892 Kitchener began his association with Reginald Wingate.

Wingate became one of the privileged few whom Kitchener allowed to get close to him; perhaps Wingate possessed some quality which touched a vital nerve in the aloof and lonely man's emotional make-up. Although Kitchener would have been embarrassed by it, the plain fact was that Wingate had an infinite capacity for friendship. They both shared an interest in freemasonry, although it is unlikely that Kitchener enjoyed the conviviality of that brotherhood, never having been a clubbable man. Kitchener became a freemason in 1893; by 1895, he was a member of five lodges in Cairo. He became Past Senior Grand Warden of Egypt and was a founder member of the Drury Lane Lodge in London, close to the renowned theatre. Wingate was appointed Grand Master in Egypt and the Sudan, then Grand Warden of England; later, in 1926, he would become a member of Dunbar Castle Lodge 75, his name heading the roll that year.

Following Kitchener's appointment as Sirdar, Wingate rose to prominence through his intelligence activities, developing his already impressive spy network in the Sudan. Despite his unceasing efforts, the Khalifa's lieutenant Osman Digna continued to lead the British and the Egyptians a merry dance up and down northern Sudan. His hit-and-run tactics seriously damaged Kitchener's plans for confrontation. Despite Kitchener's propagandist efforts – based on Wingate's information – to discredit the Dervish leader and create an anti-Dervish league of Sudanese tribes, Digna, an Arab equivalent of the Scarlet Pimpernel, continued to outfox his opponents, becoming a veritable thorn in Kitchener's flesh. To complicate matters, Kitchener's authority was also undermined by an even bigger irritation in the person of his supposed ally and nominal leader Abbas Hilmi, the eighteen-year-old Khedive of Egypt, who would rule Egypt from 1892 until he was deposed in 1914.

Hilmi was young, idealistic, wayward, frivolous and politically naïve; he resented British influence in Egypt and the financial control Britain exerted over it. He took every opportunity to denigrate the British and their political and military presence on which Egypt's security depended. Hilmi did not stop at mere verbal criticism behind closed doors; he actively encouraged his Council of Ministers and his subordinates to provoke anti-British feeling amongst his people and undermine the Egyptian Army's loyalty to the Sirdar, Kitchener. In 1893 the redoubtable Lord Cromer confessed to Lord Rosebery that he was exasperated by the young man and did not know how to deal with him.[7]

Kitchener, suffering the Khedive's personal attacks on his character and efficiency in diplomatic silence, finally brought things to a head on 19 January

1894, when Hilmi reviewed the Egyptian garrison at Wadi Halfa, the frontier between Egypt and the Sudan. Hilmi was accompanied by his Egyptian War Minister, Kitchener as Sirdar and, among others, Wingate. Hilmi repeatedly declared that Kitchener's troops – Egyptians – were slovenly, of different height and marched out of step. He publicly declared that this was the fault of the Sirdar personally, along with his British officers.[8] After a long harangue about the incompetence of British officers, Hilmi announced that the army was a total disgrace to Egypt. This was the last straw for Kitchener. Outwardly a patient man, he reacted sternly against any unfair criticism levelled at his officers and men as well as at himself. Tendering his resignation to Abbas Hilmi in person, he let it be known that all British officers serving in the Egyptian Army would leave with him and that none would replace them. His bluff worked: a shocked and shaken Hilmi begged him to withdraw his resignation. At first, Kitchener stalled, sending a cable to Lord Cromer, the Consul-General, informing him of the situation. Cromer, supported by Lord Rosebery, the Prime Minister and Foreign Secretary, advised Hilmi to apologize to the army. Kitchener now agreed to withdraw his resignation; his relationship with the young Khedive was restored in the interests of diplomacy but from that day onwards both men made no secret of their dislike of each other. In support Wingate threw in his tuppenceworth. In a letter to the War Office, he wrote of his 'absolute conviction that in dealing with Orientals, half measures are fatal … sooner or later [there will be] another explosion'.[9] After which 'explosion' he suggested it would be advisable if Kitchener left Egypt.

Kitchener was acutely aware of the difficulty of his position; he would have to tread very carefully, if not actually attempt to impress Hilmi or pander to his whims. Kitchener must have found this prospect difficult, being the kind of man he was. He did not want to jeopardize his great dream – the re-conquest of the Sudan and pay tribute to the memory of Charles Gordon, a man he believed had been poorly supported by Gladstone and the Foreign Office in 1884. Time and time again, he had lobbied the Foreign Office for authority to invade the Sudan, his stated aim being to recover it for Egypt and re-establish British prestige; privately, however, his real motive was to avenge Gordon's death. He saw that his first objective in any forthcoming campaign must be the recovery of Dongola Province, south of the official Frontier District line between Wadi Halfa and Suakin.

We saw earlier that, in 1889, the Khalifa had turned his attention to the lucrative prize of Egypt. However, his ambition to conquer Egypt was little more than a pipe dream; the defeat at Toski had extinguished it. By this year the Khalifa held in captivity several important people in Omdurman, the capital of Mahdist Sudan. Among these were Rudolf von Slatin, Father Joseph Ohrwalder and Father Paolo Rossignoli, the last two being Catholic missionaries to the Sudan.

Ohrwalder, an Austrian like Slatin, was among several Europeans to be taken by the Mahdists; in 1882, his mission station at Dilling in Kordofan

Province fell to the Mahdi. Slatin, acting Governor in Darfur, was taken prisoner in 1885. In 1891 Ohrwalder and Sisters Venturini and Chicarini were rescued by Wingate's operatives. This was a propaganda scoop for Wingate, who urged the priest to write an account of his years in Dervish captivity. Wingate edited Ohrwalder's account, wringing from it as much propaganda as he was able in order to stimulate British public interest in a re-conquest of the Sudan. Despite Wingate's massaging of the account, there is no doubt that Ohrwalder and the two nuns suffered severe hardship and privation during their ten years as captives in Omdurman. Several priests died in the squalor and filth of the internment camps there. By no means a professional writer, Ohrwalder nevertheless faithfully jotted down his personal memories; his drafts were translated from German into English by one of Wingate's aides in the Cairo Intelligence Department. Wingate then produced a narrative suitable for British consumption, filling in gaps and providing additional material from his intelligence files. Ohrwalder's book *Ten Years' Captivity in the Mahdi's Camp from the Original Manuscripts of Father J. Orhwalder* (translated and edited by Major F. R. Wingate) was duly published. Wingate's London publishers, Sampson, Marston and Low, brought the book out in October 1892. It was a harrowing account; under Wingate's directional hand, the book revived British and European interest in a seemingly forgotten part of Africa. It is a personal account, both colourful and lurid. The Egyptian Nationalist press characterized it as a vehicle for British propaganda; Ohrwalder's account had been manipulated to serve British interests. The Nationalist press was not far short of the mark; the account's tone of sustained hostility to the Mahdist regime was intended to persuade Europe of the rightness of Britain's policy regarding the Sudan.

When the Khalifa was informed of Ohrwalder's flight, he summoned Rudolph von Slatin to his court and accused him of complicity in the missionary's escape. Slatin truthfully and robustly denied the accusation. The Khalifa chose to believe him as he happened to like the little Austrian and Slatin was soon back in favour. Shortly after his capture, Slatin had converted to Islam to ensure his survival; however, he was becoming increasingly alarmed by the whims and eccentricities of his captor. He renewed plans for his own escape, contacting Wingate through the latter's intelligence operatives.

Ohrwalder brought Wingate invaluable information about the Khalifa and the situation in Omdurman. Wingate decided to publish the Austrian priest's account as a follow-up to his own book *Mahdiism and the Egyptian Sudan*. Ohrwalder's account nearly suffered the fate of many failed manuscripts, despite the fact that Wingate had recommended its publication to his London publishers who argued that the work would have little appeal for the general reader. Wingate persisted and the book became a best-seller, a seventh edition coming out in December 1892, less than three months after the first edition. Queen Victoria was pleased to receive a complimentary copy, as was Lord Rosebery, former Secretary of State for Foreign Affairs in

Gladstone's cabinet. The account was translated into German and published in Innsbruck. Not all the reviews were favourable, however, especially in Egypt, where the book was castigated by reviewers hostile to British influence. The Egyptian national press predictably reproached Father Ohrwalder for seeking to bolster British ambitions in Egypt and the Sudan, which to some extent was true. *The Journal Egyptien*, an anti-British newspaper, attacked Wingate, accusing him of embroidering Ohrwalder's tale for British political ends but Ohrwalder's book sold over 2,000 copies in just two months.

1892 was a mixed year for the Wingates' fortunes. Wingate went on leave in July to join his wife who was then pregnant with their second child. They met up on the Isle of Thanet in Kent, where, on 27 August, Kitty was safely delivered of a boy, whom they named George Andrew Leslie. The baby lived only two weeks, succumbing to an unspecified illness on 11 September. In the same year, Evelyn Baring was awarded a baronetcy which was good news for Wingate, given his growing friendship with Baring.

Through Ohrwalder's book and Wingate's intelligence reports, the latter's name became known in the corridors of power in Whitehall, particularly in the Foreign and War Offices. Wingate, already enjoying Queen Victoria's favour for his memorandum on the defeat of Emir Nejumi at Toski, was increasingly being talked about in London.

While Wingate immersed himself in intelligence gathering and preparing reports in 1893, Kitty returned to England in June; at Newton Abbot, South Devon, she gave birth to their son, Malcolm Roy, on 28 August, a year and a day after little George's death. Wingate joined Kitty, young Ronald and the new baby in September, spending some time in London where he sat and passed an examination which would bring him further promotion.

The next escapee from confinement in Omdurman came in 1894, while Wingate was Governor of Suakin province. At the year's end, Father Paolo Rossignoli managed to slip away in the night, bringing Wingate yet more valuable information. Wingate had hoped to free Slatin rather than Rossignoli; he knew that Slatin would bring more vital information about the weaponry and military capacity in Omdurman. A French newspaper noted for its anti-British stance went as far as to say that the Intelligence Department in Cairo had sent an agent to rescue Slatin but the agent – a native Egyptian – had been unable to distinguish one European from another and that he had brought out Father Rossignoli by mistake! There is a hint of truth in this; Wingate had hired an Abada tribesman to bring out other European prisoners, Karl Neufeld, a German merchant, or Father Rossignoli.

As with Ohrwalder, Wingate edited a book about Rossignoli's captivity. It eventually appeared in 1895 entitled *A Story of the Sudan: the Experiences of Father Rossignoli for Twelve Years a Captive of the Mahdi*. (The fact that the Mahdi had been dead for nearly ten years did not deter Wingate from using his name in the title, probably for propaganda reasons.) Wingate's new publisher, Edward Arnold, warned him there should be no padding, window-dressing or references to recent history as had occurred in the case of Ohrwalder's book in 1892. Arnold argued that any attempt to use the Rossignoli book as propaganda would affect its reception by the general British reader. (In point of fact, both books were best sellers in Britain.)

On his rescue, Ohrwalder informed Wingate of the plight of his fellow Austrian, Rudolf von Slatin, prisoner and former Governor of Darfur Province. Born in Vienna in 1857, Slatin was the son of a silk dyer. He first visited Egypt in 1874 as a young man, when employed as a clerk to a Cairo bookseller; finding this onerous, he went on an exploration of Darfur. He returned to Vienna in 1875, writing an account of his travels in the Nuba Mountains of the Sudan. Slatin liked the Sudan so much that he asked a colleague of General Charles Gordon to draw his name to Gordon's attention. By 1876 he was serving as a sub-lieutenant in the Austrian Army, undergoing compulsory national service. In 1878 Slatin's friend Dr Emin had recommended his name to Gordon; the young Austrian was delighted to receive an invitation to join Gordon's staff in the Sudan. Slatin jumped at the opportunity as he had found garrison duty in Bosnia oppressive and lacking adventure. He arrived in Khartoum in January 1879 and would spend the next thirty-five years there. His first duties were in Gordon's finance department, which he found not to his taste. He longed for military adventure and decided to resign from Gordon's staff. Gordon, however, encouraged his favourites and refused to accept Slatin's resignation; being a good judge of character and recognizing Slatin's potential, he appointed him Governor of Dara in Darfur Province in command of a division of Egyptian soldiers whose principal duty was to protect the local tax collectors.

When the Mahdists overran Kordofan Province in 1884, Darfur and Slatin were isolated, with little hope of reinforcement. At this point Slatin adopted the Islamic faith but not merely as a means of self-preservation during his subsequent captivity, an act which would later attract the opprobrium of his future Christian (British) colleagues. Even before he was taken prisoner by the Mahdi, Slatin had converted to Islam when he realized the Muslim forces he led regarded him as one who had brought bad luck with a succession of defeats in skirmishes with the Mahdist forces. His Muslim troops attributed this lack of success to Slatin being an infidel Christian. Slatin would later defend himself against criticism that he had converted through mere expediency. (This is a plausible argument but hardly holds water; the Egyptian Army of the day was officered by serving British Army officers who were of course Christians. Having said that, there is no trace in Slatin's writings of an intellectual interest in religion, be it Christian or Muslim.) Slatin was a survivor however; on the surface a romantic idealist, underneath he was level-headed and practical, as many romantics can be. He had converted to Islam for purely practical motives, although his account of conversion in *Fire and Sword in the Soudan* is larded with mawkish sentiment. The book is, by some accounts, a ponderous, shapeless, poignant tome running to more than 230,000 words; despite this, it became an overnight success. The book's appeal lay in the sincerity of its spontaneous style and Wingate's skilful editing which made it attractive to the general British reading public. Its tone is condescending towards the Egyptians and the Sudanese people are regarded as children.

Modern historians tend to allow a measure of sympathetic consideration for Slatin's conversion to Islam; in 1884, when he surrendered to the Mahdists, more than half of his 5,000 troops had been killed fighting the Dervishes, the remaining 2,000 being wounded or unfit for duty. He had little option but to surrender and thus began a captivity which would last for twelve years, as one of several European prisoners.

In many respects Rudolf von Slatin was an extraordinary little man. He could have stepped straight out of the pages of a John Buchan novel. Soldier, administrator and bon-viveur, he counted among his many friends several famous figures of the day. Like Wingate, he spoke excellent Sudanese Arabic, French and English. The Egyptian press put it about that Slatin was a captive of the Mahdists on account of his loyalty to Britain, which was of course true. The same press concluded that Slatin was a spy working for British intelligence to enrich himself and Britain's interests in the Sudan, and perhaps Egypt's along the way.

From the outset of his captivity Slatin ingratiated himself with the Mahdi. During the siege of Khartoum the Mahdi sent Slatin in chains to negotiate Gordon's surrender. Typically, Gordon refused. It is said that the Mahdi did so on the grounds that Slatin had renounced his Christian faith but that seems specious. Gordon was not the kind of man to give up his command without a fight. For his part, Slatin maintained that Gordon had acted uncharitably towards him, even if he understood perfectly the man's refusal to surrender (to modern eyes, this seems a contrivance by Slatin to divert attention from himself). Whatever the truth, Slatin reputedly even saw Gordon's severed head when the Dervishes brought it to the Mahdi.

After the Mahdi's death in June 1885, Slatin had won the confidence of the Khalifa Abdullahi, who had a soft spot for him. He adopted the Arab name of Abd el Quadir and was appointed in the role of minor court official, acting as runner or messenger and sometimes as advisor. In *Fire and Sword*, Slatin writes that he was required to sit outside the Khalifa's door, waiting to be summoned. His account also emphasizes the Khalifa's propensity for cruelty, which is not in dispute; but Slatin failed to comment on the fact that, cruel and capricious as the man was, he never put to death any of his European (Christian) captives. However, Slatin's animosity towards the Khalifa is understandable; throughout history, few captives are generous in praise of their jailers. The Khalifa's affection for the little Austrian did not prevent him from accusing Slatin of complicity in Ohrwalder's escape, which Slatin robustly and truthfully denied.

Following the successful escapes of Ohrwalder and Rossignoli, Wingate made plans to free Slatin, whom he considered the star prize. In June 1894 Wingate provided camels, guides, food and water to bring Slatin out. The venture came to grief, possibly because as stated above, the guides mistook Father Rossignoli for the little Austrian. Another version of the story, one which has an authentic ring to it, was that Wingate had not offered enough money in bribes to his operatives. The second attempt on 20 February 1895 was, however, successful; that night, Slatin rode a donkey to rendezvous with his Arab guides with camels, food and water. After three weeks in the desert, with Slatin and his guides suffering from hunger, thirst and heat exhaustion, the small party finally reached the frontier post at Aswan on 16 March. A few days later, Slatin arrived in Cairo, dressed in the shabby clothes of an Arab beggar. (One is tempted to make a comparison with the dramatic scene in the film *Lawrence of Arabia*, when Peter O'Toole as Lawrence arrives in Cairo dressed in native garb to inform General Allenby that his beloved Arabs had captured Akaba.)

News of Slatin's escape fired the imagination of the British press and the public in a way that neither Ohrwalder's nor Rossignoli's had achieved, despite the success of their published accounts. As before, Wingate gained valuable information about conditions in Omdurman; his dossier on the Khalifa's army was growing steadily.

To his discredit, Wingate published a lurid account of Slatin's escape on 17 March 1895. Moberley Bell, a journalist on the staff of *The Times* complained to David Rees of *Reuters* that the Khalifa had in fact allowed Slatin to escape on payment of a bribe and that Wingate's article, claiming the credit, was a 'humbug'. A week later Wingate penned a longer memorandum, a less emotive and more accurate account of Slatin's escape. It was truthful in all but one respect. Wingate claimed that General Gordon had appointed Slatin as Inspector General of the entire Sudan in 1875; Slatin's substantive position as Governor of Darfur Province fell far short of that. However, when Wingate was appointed Governor General of the Sudan and Sirdar of the Egyptian Army, Slatin became his Inspector General.

Wingate was correct in his conviction that Slatin's escape was more important than that of the priests. He said so in a long letter to his London literary agent Arnold P. Watt; Slatin's escape and account of his years of captivity were, in Wingate's view, a 'scoop'. However, it must be said that Slatin's account, *Fire and Sword in the Soudan* (1896), is understandably biased, despite the reasonable treatment he received from the Khalifa. That apart, Slatin was able to provide Wingate with vital information about the Khalifa's resources – the size of the Dervish army in Omdurman, which he put at 105,000, a suspect figure. Slatin also estimated that the Dervishes possessed 40,000 rifles and seventy-five field guns, although ammunition for both was in short supply. One wonders how Slatin managed to make such precise counts. Slatin's book credits Major F. R. Wingate as translator and it was dedicated to Queen Victoria.

In Egypt, the Nationalist press, ever increasingly hostile to Britain, saw the book as nothing more than propaganda intended to promote British expansion in the Sudan. Slatin was accused of being a plant in the Mahdists' camp, a spy who could report the state and size of the Mahdi-Khalifa forces to Cairo. There is no foundation to the story, even if Slatin had in fact provided Kitchener with an estimate of the Khalifa's manpower, firearms and ammunition.

Within days of his freedom Slatin became a celebrity. A photograph was taken on 19 March 1895 at Cairo's Bab el Habib railway station only a few days after his safe arrival from Omdurman. Slatin is in centre, dressed in white *mufti*, wearing a red fez and incongruous tennis shoes – these were the only footwear he could suffer after years of going barefoot – and carrying a cane. Facing him is Baron Heidler von Egeregg, the Austrian-Hungarian Consul-General and his staff. Behind Slatin are Father Joseph Ohrwalder and Wingate, also wearing a fez and carrying a stick under his arm. (A description of the moment appears in Richard Hill's *Slatin Pasha*.)

After publication of the three captives' books, Kitchener relied on Wingate even more, taking him into his confidence along with a few other select confidants – they could hardly be called friends, Kitchener being cold, aloof and lacking any degree of emotion. He informed Wingate that Sir Evelyn Baring, the British Agent in Cairo, did not share his enthusiasm for a punitive expedition into the Sudan. Neither did Lord Rosebery until succeeding Gladstone as Prime Minister in 1894. Wingate, the astute administrator and future statesman, while agreeing with Kitchener, was a realist, well versed in the fickleness of politicians. Perhaps he advised his Commander in Chief to exercise caution in any proposed campaign to re-conquer the Sudan. After a flurry of correspondence between Kitchener and his superiors in London, a disaffected and lonely Kitchener confessed to Wingate, 'Now I will have to be quiet for a while.'[10] The disappointment in that terse sentence speaks volumes about Kitchener's inner conflict. He had resigned himself to the waiting game. Despite Wingate's efforts in obtaining more detailed information about the state of the Sudan, the lack of real and reliable information about the country forced Kitchener to sit on his hands during a period of frustrating inactivity.

Wingate and 'Rowdy' Slatin took to each other immediately. They would work together in the Sudan, remaining friends even during the Great War, when Slatin would end up on the opposing side. Their friendship ended only with Slatin's death in 1931. After a brief stay in Cairo to regain his health, Slatin went to visit his family in Vienna, returning to Egypt via England, where he received a hero's welcome. Slatin's book *Fire and Sword in the Soudan* required editing by Wingate with an eye to its chief value – propaganda against the Mahdist regime. Its success was as much a benefit to Wingate as to Slatin; from it, he would ultimately reap fame, honours, promotion, money and support for the re-conquest of the Sudan and the ultimate avenging of Gordon's death. Slatin's book in fact boosted Wingate's flagging career at that time. *Fire and Sword* exceeded the sales of Father Ohrwalder's book and also ran to several editions. As a work of literature, however, it has little to commend it and contains nothing remotely approaching the brilliance of

Lawrence's *Seven Pillars of Wisdom*. However, it fired the imagination of the British press and people and was widely read in Europe.

We should pause here to examine the remarkable similarities of Wingate and Slatin. Both were dapper, well-made men, Wingate being the shorter of the two at 5 foot 6 inches; when off duty, Wingate wore fashionable plus-fours, while Slatin often affected to wear the Tyrolean leather shorts of his homeland. To modern eyes, the pair resemble Vaudeville comedians in off-duty dress. Despite their lack of taste in *haute couture* (Wingate was however a stickler for proper Victorian dress both on and off duty), they were practical men in a world dominated by practical considerations, neither being particularly interested in the abstract affairs of this world. Both were possessed of great patience, the virtue of those who are wise. Wingate was articulate on paper, Slatin was the entertaining conversationalist. As to their faults, Wingate was over-possessive of his command, reluctant to delegate; Slatin would lose his temper readily in the face of those who refused to listen and thus were considered stupid.

Perhaps theirs was a friendship which would have existed wherever they had met and in whatever era. Like Slatin, Wingate was a European; being a Scot, he was not of the breed he detested, that of the Little Englander who had held power in India and the Sudan for too many years. Wingate had not been privileged to enjoy a public school education; he did not play football or cricket like his contemporaries, although he enjoyed squash and tennis. It is probable that his Channel Island education, with its emphasis on French, gave him a love of languages. He spoke and wrote excellent French; he acquired an impressive knowledge of Arabic in Egypt and was a first-class interpreter of Turkish. He also understood men like Rudolf von Slatin.

Slatin returned to Egypt with a rock-solid reputation. Wingate appointed him as his assistant in the Intelligence Department; in time, under Wingate's patronage, he would become Inspector General in the Sudan. In 1895 Wingate prepared a detailed memorandum on the Sudan based on Slatin's account of his captivity. Further honours fell into Wingate's lap. The Emperor Franz Josef of Austria awarded him the Iron Crown (2nd Class) for his part in engineering Slatin's escape; then, in the Queen's birthday honours list of May 1895, he was made a Companion of the Order of the Bath, a civil order and rare distinction for a young army officer – he was only thirty-three.

Slatin's appointment as Assistant Director of Military Intelligence in the Egyptian Army in March 1895 raised more than a few eyebrows in Cairo clubs like The Turf and The Gezira as well as in the officers' mess. Some senior military commanders with an eye on protocol expressed concern that Wingate, a lieutenant colonel and a mere *Bey*, should appoint Slatin, a full colonel with the higher honorific of *Pasha*, as his assistant. Conservative Egyptians were confused by the decision.[11] The *Egyptian Gazette*[12] suggested a simple and practical solution – elevate Wingate to the dignity of Pasha. Certain French newspapers hostile to Britain more than hinted that such things could always be arranged to suit circumstances in British political circles. This apparently did not trouble Wingate Pasha in the least.

The world of intelligence suited the temperaments of both men, as can be testified by their almost obsessive attention to matters of detail, vital in the profession of intelligence gathering. Wingate and Slatin compiled innumerable lists – payments to secret agents, countless memoranda on movements in the desert, notes, endless accounts of interviews with people from all walks of life, notes on press correspondents, military strategy, weaknesses and troop dispositions.

Wingate was steadily perfecting entirely new military intelligence techniques which would prove invaluable to Kitchener in the coming campaign. Having already fired the British public's imagination with his publications, Wingate's organization was rapidly becoming the focus for those British military minds intent on the re-conquest of the Sudan. He had already proved he was a skilled manipulator of public opinion and was now influencing both Cabinet members and government in Britain. The Prime Minister, Lord Rosebery, would never have committed Britain and Egypt to war without strong support at home. Wingate subtly and adroitly engineered that support, ably abetted by Slatin. Slatin's book *Fire and Sword in the Soudan* was nothing short of intelligence propaganda and, like the best of its kind, identified weaknesses, particularly the British government's lacklustre strategy. The Mahdi was viewed as little more than a religious imposter, while the Khalifa was portrayed as a sadistic monster, descriptions reinforced by war correspondents in Cairo. Popular writers of the day took up this theme: novels were published by authors like A. E. W. Mason, George Henty and Arthur Conan Doyle; in particular, Mason's *The Four Feathers* paints a graphic portrait of the fighting qualities of the Dervishes.

Home on leave in the summer of 1895, Wingate and Slatin were summoned to Osborne on the Isle of Wight, one of the Queen's official residences. Wingate was awarded a CB, an honour bestowed on Slatin in October the same year. On 19 August, Wingate and Slatin were the dinner guests of the Queen's private secretary, Sir Arthur Bigge, who wrote to Wingate the following day intimating that Her Majesty wished to meet Slatin again. He also informed him that the Queen and Princesses Louise and Beatrice wished to have photographs of Slatin. In September, the Queen, through Wingate, arranged to have Slatin's portrait painted in his Dervish dress. The Queen may not have given Wingate and Slatin their nickname of 'The Sudanese Twins' but she certainly referred to the two men as such.

If the British Army gave Reginald Wingate, with his gifts as a linguist, an opportunity to put his talents to good use as spymaster and Imperial servant, Wingate repaid the debt in full. This was acknowledged by a contemporary writer:

He will learn [sic] you any language you like to name in three months. As for that mysterious child of lies, the Arab, Colonel Wingate can converse with him for hours, and at the end know not only how much truth he was told, but exactly what truth he [the Arab] had suppressed. He [Wingate] is the intellectual as the Sirdar [Kitchener] is the practical, compendium of British dealings in the Sudan. With that he is, himself, the most practical of men, and few realize how largely it is due to the system of native intelligence he has organized that operations in the Sudan are now certain and unsurprised instead of vague, as they once were. Nothing is hid from Colonel Wingate, whether in Cairo or at the court of Menelik [Emperor of Abyssinia] or Lake Tchad [Chad].[13]

Fulsome praise indeed.

During 1895 Kitchener fretted in Cairo, unable to apprehend an elusive Osman Digna who continued to mount minor hit-and-run raids in the Northern provinces. On the political front, he no doubt welcomed the fall of Gladstone's Liberal government to a Conservative administration under Lord Salisbury which augured well for a possible commitment to re-conquer the Sudan, with British troops supplementing the small Egyptian Army. Even so, despite Kitchener's and Wingate's recommendations to the British Agent in Cairo, Lord Cromer, to seek approval for an invasion of the Sudan, Cromer was not enthusiastic. With his banker's mind, Cromer argued against it on grounds of an expense which promised little reward. He was more persuaded by proposals to fund the building of a dam at Aswan which would bring direct returns and stimulate the Sudanese and Egyptian economies. Whitehall listened to Cromer, reluctant to expend blood and gold on what might prove a costly adventure. The year of 1895 might be termed Kitchener's wilderness year, one frustrated by political prevarication. Military men are not usually kindly disposed towards politicians; their proper concerns are logistics, manpower, strategies and tactics. To the military, politicians are necessary only to formulate policy, then provide them with the tools for the job. As for Kitchener's right-hand man, Wingate, his young but invaluable intelligence officer, his was the approach of a reflective academic rather than a man of action. It is not certain if, in the course of his studies of the Sudanese terrain, he ever read the Koran, the better to understand its people. Wingate was certainly familiar with the book, but whether he studied it closely seems unlikely. He was perhaps aware of the pronouncement of another Scot on the Koran, the writer-prophet Thomas Carlyle, who did take the trouble to read it and found it 'as toilsome reading as I ever undertook ... nothing but a sense of duty could carry any European through the Koran'. Carlyle considered the book tedious, its prose ranging between the purple and the turgid.

Wingate returned to Egypt in November 1895 when Cairo was buzzing with rumours about a possible campaign to liberate the Sudan, although the development of the proposed dam at Aswan in Upper Egypt was very much at the top of Cromer's agenda. As events turned out, the Aswan Dam was not begun until 1898 and took four years to construct. Cromer still had no desire to waste public money on an expensive military campaign which might prove unlikely to enrich either Egypt or Britain.

The catalyst for the start of operations in the Sudan came in 1895, when French ambitions in Africa took on a new dimension. Rumours abounded that France was preparing to mount an expedition to the Upper Nile Valley with a view to occupying the area. Such an initiative would give the French control over the waters of the Nile and be disastrous for continued British control in Egypt. Thus the need to re-conquer the Sudan now became imperative. Cromer made his displeasure known to the government, causing him to remark that 'This abominable Sudan business' and its expense would jeopardize his Aswan Dam project.[14] On 8 March Cromer approached the Earl of Kimberley, who had taken over as Foreign Secretary, intimating that he proposed to extend the Nile Valley railway to Aswan and advance the telegraph lines to Abu Hamed. As he wrote, 'I look upon both these measures as steps to facilitate the ultimate re-conquest of the Sudan.'[15] These words must have almost choked Cromer. His approach was hardly that of an imperialist or military strategist but he reluctantly accepted that should Egypt fail to occupy the Sudan the French or the Italians would. In April 1895 he consulted Wingate who informed him that the Khalifa's strength was much the same as it had been in 1891 but that the Khalifa would be unable to contain a large-scale French invasion in the Upper Nile. Was this yet another Wingate ploy to convince the British government that full-scale intervention in the Sudan was now imperative? For good measure, Wingate added that the Khalifa would not give up Khartoum without a fight.

In 1896 Kitchener's wilderness year came to an end. In that year occurred a momentous stroke of luck for British interests. The French threat apart, Italy, which had recently colonized parts of Abyssinia (modern Ethiopia) appealed for assistance from the British government when an Italian army suffered a crushing defeat at the hands of Abyssinian forces at Adowa in March. A desperate Italian ambassador in London pressed Lord Salisbury to create a diversion in the Nile area of Abyssinia. The Italians' aim was to distract the Khalifa from menacing the vulnerable Italian garrison at Kassala in western Abyssinia. In addition, the French and the Belgians were pursuing their own colonial ambitions in the sub-continent. Thus it was Italian, rather than French, ambitions which would act as the catalyst for British activity in the Sudan. However, the Quai d'Orsay in Paris made no secret of the fact that France intended to occupy the upper reaches of the Nile waters upon which the Egyptian economy depended. For the moment, a proposed occupation of Sudan was put on the back-burner by both France and Britain.

The British government responded to Italy's plea for help. The Italian government probably never learnt of one British officer's unfettered joy when he was ordered to lead a limited expedition into the Sudanese heartland. Herbert Kitchener, the officer in question, received the news with surprise and unconcealed delight – he is said to have danced in his pyjamas on the lawn of the *Sirdarieh*, the palatial residence of the Sirdar in Cairo – when he received a telegram from Whitehall ordering him to invade the Sudan. Thus in 1896 began what was known as the Dongola campaign, mounted ostensibly to relieve Abyssinian pressure on the Italian garrison at Kassala. International politics would now take precedence over the economics of Lord Cromer.

Let us briefly examine Italy's involvement in the Sudan at its periphery with the Sudanese-Abyssinian border. In 1887 the Italian government was intent on expanding its territory in Abyssinia, whose King Johannes or John had defeated an Italian expeditionary force at Dogali, near Massawa. In 1888 the Dervishes had invaded Abyssinia and compelled King John to withdraw his forces from Massawa, thus leaving the Italians a free hand in that area. In March 1888 John was defeated and killed by the Dervishes, his successor being Menelik, Prince of Shoa, whom the Italians now backed. In the following year the Italians helped Menelik to defeat a pretender to the Abyssinian throne. Due to Menelik's benevolence, Italy was able to advance closer to the valley of the Upper Nile, which lay beyond the foothills of Kassala. In 1894, Italy, from its colony of Eritrea, moved to secure its foothold by taking Kassala, a Sudanese border town. Under the terms of an Anglo-Italian agreement of 1891, the occupation of Kassala was permitted as a temporary defensive measure. In the same year the British were aware of France's intention to occupy the Upper Nile. The scramble for Africa by the European powers was gathering momentum. Wingate correctly assessed the political situation; in his view, it would not be the Mahdists under the Khalifa 'which will draw us into an expedition [into the Sudan], it is the pressure of France and other European nations towards the Nile Valley, which will force England to go to Khartoum'.[16]

Shortly, Menelik fell out with Italy and the Italians holding Kassala let it be known their presence was primarily to act as caretakers on Egypt's behalf. This suited Britain. Meanwhile, Menelik began making overtures to France as a more amenable European ally. With French assistance, Menelik defeated the Italians at Amba Alagi, thus opening the way for a Dervish attack on Kassala. The defeat of Italy at Adowa prompted the British government to authorize an expedition up the Nile to relieve pressure on the Italians. This was effected solely with the aim of bolstering the Triple Alliance between Britain, Italy and Germany.[17]

What is unusual – though not unique – about the re-conquest of the Sudan is that there was virtually no economic gain or incentive to Britain, no financial carrot to justify the invasion. It was a combination of European politics and British foreign policy. Kitchener, of course, saw it differently: for him, it was a personal crusade. Unromantic though he undoubtedly was, he viewed the recovery of the Sudan as a matter of chivalry, of regaining British honour and prestige lost when Gordon was murdered. Such sentiments were diminishing by the turn of the nineteenth century; they would finally expire on the killing fields of the Somme in 1916.

The Prime Minister, Lord Salisbury, was anxious to reinforce the Triple Alliance aligned against France and Russia. For their part, the French saw an opportunity to establish themselves in Upper Egypt encouraged by a new ally, Menelik. France supported Abyssinian claims in Sudanese territory to the east of the White Nile from Lake Victoria to Khartoum. The Italian appeal to Britain was aimed at safeguarding their interests in the colony of Eritrea, which Salisbury saw as countering French ambitions. France responded by mounting a small expeditionary force led by Commandant Jean-Baptiste Marchand with orders to raise the *tricolour* at Fashoda (modern day Kodok), in the Upper Nile basin. France had occupied Tunisia and Morocco and, in 1896, was casting ambitious eyes on the Upper Nile, where a dam could be constructed to regulate the free flow of the Nile waters. Without adequate water, Egypt would wither on the vine. In that year the French president, François Faure, authorized Marchand's expedition. (Faure's otherwise un-spectacular administration is remembered in history for three events – Franco-Russian alliance, the re-trial of the wrongly imprisoned Jewish Captain Alfred Dreyfus for alleged spying and what became known as the Fashoda Incident of 1898, which almost brought Britain and France to war.) Marchand set off on his expedition in June 1896; try as they might, the British attempted but failed to beat Marchand to Fashoda, as we shall see in the following chapter. Thus Britain, Italy and France were engaged in the eternal shadow-boxing of international politics, the occupation of the Sudan being central to the outcome.

Perhaps, with hindsight, the Anglo-Egyptian invasion of the Sudan was inevitable, brought about by a real threat from French ambitions in the Upper Nile. In its last months of office in 1895, the Liberal government remained reluctant to commit Britain to a re-conquest of the Sudan, a position which alarmed even Lord Cromer, who nonetheless shared Wingate's concern about France's aspirations. In the event, an urgent request from Italy, not Egypt, convinced the Conservative government which ousted the Liberals in June 1895 that France, rather than the Dervish regime, was the main threat to the Sudan. The Abyssinians then defeated the Italians at Amba Alagi on 7 December 1895, thus opening the way for the Mahdists to re-occupy Kassala or at least cut its communications to the coast. On 10 December the Italian ambassador in London sought British help, which was duly promised. On 1 March 1896 the Abyssinians again routed an Italian army at Adowa and Britain kept her promise. On 12 March the British Cabinet author-ized Kitchener's advance to Akasha, half way between Wadi Halfa and Dongola. British public opinion, already aroused by Slatin's book (by now a copy was in every British library) wholeheartedly supported the govern-ment's initiative. The British press positively slavered over Slatin's words: in true tabloid fashion, they dwelt on the blood, slavery, sadism and sexual excesses, the tyranny, savagery, lawlessness and corruption. They viewed the invasion of the Sudan in the manner of a crusade.

However, the Conservative Prime Minister and Foreign Secretary, Lord Salisbury, ordered a limited campaign – in the Khedive of Egypt's name – for the occupation of Dongola province, south of Wadi Halfa. Despite his awareness of the threat from an expansionist France, Lord Cromer in Cairo was disappointed by the turn of events: he had employed all his considerable political and economic skills to rescue the Egyptian economy from bankruptcy. Thanks to his reforms, Egypt was in a sounder economic position than before and Cromer was concerned that all his good works would be frittered away by international politics and military extravagance in the Sudan. However, he was obliged to bow to his superiors in Whitehall. At least he could draw some comfort from the fact that Kitchener, as Sirdar, would keep the cost of the campaign to the minimum; Kitchener was renowned for his cheese-paring approach in military matters. (There never was much personal accord between the two men, although they enjoyed a good working relationship, as they understood each other's minds.)

The campaign to re-occupy Dongola was a purely Egyptian affair, financed by Egypt. Kitchener's army consisted of 18,000 Egyptian and Sudanese troops, for which Egypt footed the bill. Only one British battalion – 1st North Staffordshire Regiment – was attached to the army and was hardly ever used. True to his reputation for keeping costs to the bare minimum, Kitchener made do with a small staff of fourteen officers including Wingate and Rudolf von Slatin; his chief of staff was Leslie Rundle, Wingate's brother-in-law.

The advance from Wadi Halfa was commanded by Lieutenant Colonel Hector MacDonald, known to his men as 'Fighting Mac'. MacDonald was a tough, no-nonsense soldier who had risen from the ranks. MacDonald advanced forty miles, taking Akasha with little difficulty. Akasha was some ten miles distant from Farka (or Firket) where MacDonald rested his Sudanese Brigade to await Kitchener's main force. On 7 June 1896 the entire army overwhelmed Firket, where Egyptian losses were a mere twenty dead and eighty wounded against Dervish losses of 800 dead and roughly the same number wounded – almost half of the Dervish force engaged. For his part in Firket, Wingate was Mentioned in Despatches. Two days later, Kitchener took Suarda, about twenty-five miles further on.

In September 1896 the *London Court Journal* recorded that

It is impossible to praise too highly Major Wingate's efforts on behalf of the [Dongola] expedition. No man knows as much about the Soudan [sic] as the Director of the Egyptian Intelligence Office, who had an eye or ear at every keyhole in the Khalifa's dominions ...

Before this praise, Wingate had informed Lord Cromer on 7 April that the Dervish strength in Dongola totalled 10,000, with an advance unit of 400 at Firket. The Battle of Firket hardly deserved the name but it was a psychological victory which stiffened the morale of the Egyptian Army.

After his success at Firket, Kitchener advanced to al-Kusha (or Koshesh). By 18 September the Dervishes had crossed the Nile to occupy Hafir on the west bank, near Dongola town. Kitchener ordered up his gunboats which came under accurate sniper fire until the boats were sent upriver to Dongola. Faced with the vastly superior numbers of the Egyptian Army, the Dervishes abandoned Hafir and retreated to Dongola, where Kitchener engaged the Dervish Army in strength near the town on 23 September. Dongola hardly deserved the name of town, being little more than a collection of mud huts; nor could it be described as a battlefield. There was in fact no battle for Dongola; the Dervishes restrained their leader, Emir Muhammad Bashara, who was carried bound from the field before he could mount what could have been a suicide attack on Kitchener's army. Thus Dongola was won cheaply, easily.

Kitchener recovered Dongola province with the loss of forty-seven killed and 122 wounded in actual combat; however, he had suffered fatal casualties of nearly 1,000 in a cholera epidemic in June 1896. Given Kitchener's fairly comfortable victories, it would not be long before the British government would order a complete recovery of the Sudan, especially with the French advance on Fashoda in prospect.

At the start of 1897 Kitchener took a definite step forward by constructing a railway line from Wadi Halfa to Berber (see Chapter 3). Despite his orders to mount a limited campaign in the Sudan, nothing less than complete conquest would satisfy him. He was less enthusiastic about confronting the French at Fashoda, which was entirely understandable. Sir Rennell Rodd of the Foreign Office and Wingate in the Sudan urged Kitchener to advance up the Nile to beat the French to Fashoda. Such a strategy was hardly feasible from Dongola; between it and Omdurman lay an unquantified number of Dervishes but, if the British government ordered a march south from Dongola, Kitchener was the man for the job. Lord Salisbury's comment on a possible French occupation of Fashoda was typically desperate in the face of the difficulties lying ahead of Kitchener, 'Well, let us hope that he [Marchand] won't get there!'[18] Immediately after the occupation of Dongola, a carbon copy of Kitchener's report on the outcome was sent on his behalf to Queen Victoria, celebrating her Diamond Jubilee:

> On this auspicious anniversary of Her Majesty's glorious reign … I beg to report I have just occupied Dongola. The Dervishes are in full retreat …

It was designed to impress the Queen; there had been no battle at Dongola, although it was occupied on the same day that Victoria celebrated the longest reign of any sovereign in England's history.

As for Wingate, during the Dongola campaign, he was affectionately known as the White Knight, arguably the most eccentric character in Lewis Carroll's *Through the Looking Glass* (1871). While Wingate was not noted for falling off his horse like his fictional counterpart, he was so nicknamed because of a habit of festooning his person with apparently useless items of equipment. Unlike the White Knight, whom Alice criticized for wearing his knapsack upside down with the lid unfastened 'to keep out the rain' and thus losing all its contents, Wingate certainly had uses for his supposedly 'useless' equipment.

Aided by Slatin, Wingate operated in advance of Kitchener's army; isolated in his tent every night, he would prepare detailed reports on Dervish activities, telegraphing these to his Commander in Chief.

There is no doubt that Wingate was possessed of outstanding qualities which Kitchener recognized and valued. A personable man, Wingate made more friends than enemies during his long and distinguished career. He had the uncanny knack of making solid and enduring personal relationships with men from all walks of life, men to whom he remained loyal and who for the most part reciprocated. As Kitchener's military eyes and ears, Wingate's services were inestimable throughout the Sudanese campaign. Military intelligence suggests an exciting occupation, with spies engaged in dangerous cloak-and-dagger activities; in reality, it is tedious and frustrating, requiring much patience and endurance, often for little reward. One supposes that Wingate would have been comfortable in the role of 'M' in Ian Fleming's James Bond books; equally, he would have appreciated 'M's' frustrations. Wingate had the necessary temperament to endure long hours at his desk or in his tent, sifting through reports from his operatives who did not always provide him with the information he sought. At least, with his impressive knowledge of Arabic, Wingate was able to question Dervish prisoners in their own tongue, learning to distinguish those lying and those telling the truth. He could never be sure when his own operatives were engaged in a double game, taking both his – and the Khalifa's – gold sovereigns. Wingate was also acutely aware that his loyal agents faced torture and certain death if captured. Wingate earned – and deserved – his reputation in the Sudan campaign. He had few resources at his disposal other than human flesh. His equipment was poor or non-existent; maps were unreliable and aerial photography did not exist at the time. Wingate was alone and yet he produced the goods for Kitchener, paving the way for his victory at Omdurman.

Notes

1. Catherine (or Kitty) Rundle, later Lady Wingate, received honours during her lifetime. The first of these was the DBE (Dame of the British Empire), Dame of Grace of St John of Jerusalem, Grand Order of Kemal of Egypt and the Coronation Medal of 1911.
2. *Not in the Limelight*, RELW.
3. *Ibid.*
4. *Cromer in Egypt*, Marlowe.
5. *Mahdiism and the Egyptian Sudan*, FRW.
6. Ibid.
7. *Cromer in Egypt.*
8. *Ibid.*
9. *Ibid.*
10. *A Good Dusting*, Keown-Boyd.
11. *Slatin Pasha*, Hill.

12. *The Egyptian Gazette* was a mouthpiece for Egyptian Nationalism. Founded in 1899 it advertised itself in 1941 as having 'enjoyed 42 years of unrivalled leadership in Egyptian affairs' and announced that as from 3 November 1941, it would become an evening newspaper.
13. *With Kitchener to Khartoum*, Steevens.
14. *Cromer in Egypt*.
15. *Ibid*.
16. Wingate to Major J. G. Maxwell (Cairo Intelligence), 29 June 1894, WP 257/1, SAD, DU.
17. FO 633/6 No 235, dated 8 March 1895.
18. *Cromer in Egypt*.

Chapter 3

Omdurman and Fashoda
(1898–1899)

As early as 1891 Wingate's spies and intelligence reports confirmed that the Khalifa considered the plains of Karari (or Kerreri), near Omdurman as his chosen ground where he swore to engage any invading infidel army in battle. Why he should choose terrain eminently suited to the deployment of modern weapons and cavalry remains a mystery to this day. It is tempting to speculate that either Kerreri had some religious significance for the Khalifa or that he was confident of success, despite the fact that he was painfully aware of the destructive power of well-officered, well-trained and disciplined troops possessed of modern weaponry. The Dervishes had come off badly against the Egyptian Army on several occasions, notably at Toski, Firket, Tokar and Afafit and had suffered significant losses. The Khalifa's strategy appears to have been to lure the invader deep into the Sudanese interior, where the natural weapons of thirst, disease, heat exhaustion and supply problems would do their work, sapping morale and weakening resolve. But Kerreri was close to the Nile and Kitchener would be able to supply his force by riverboat.

The Anglo-Egyptian Army, now numbering 20,000, had reclaimed Dongola province with almost contemptible ease, although it has to be said that the Dervish commander had not committed a body of troops comparable in size to the Egyptians thus far in the campaign. Kitchener knew this, so he exerted pressure on Wingate to step up his intelligence activities. Tireless as ever, Wingate strengthened his elaborate spy network throughout the Sudan, particularly in the district around Omdurman, where he knew battle would be drawn.

Perhaps it is appropriate to re-visit the circumstances which had brought Kitchener thus far. As indicated earlier, Kitchener had been lobbying the British government for permission to lead a full-scale invasion of the Sudan since 1896. In November that year he was on leave in London, reluctantly attending many official functions, including dinner and lunch respectively at the Queen's residences in Windsor and Osborne. His ambitions were met, not as a result of the force of his argument but because of the French expedition, now en route to the Upper Nile basin. Kitchener returned to Cairo with the welcome news that an all-out invasion had been authorized. He held a staff conference to discuss his proposals for the invasion. Outlining his strategy, Rundle, Wingate and others on his staff were astonished to learn that a pivotal element of Kitchener's tactics hinged on a new major railway which he would build, linking Wadi Halfa and Berber. This was a feat on a scale which not even Charles Gordon had contemplated; Gordon had envisaged a small-scale railway running parallel to the Nile. Kitchener planned to lay the tracks through the Nubian Desert, shortening the distance to Khartoum by several hundred miles in bypassing the wide curve of the Nile between Wadi Halfa and Korti. Perhaps, on reflection, it would have made more sense to extend the existing railway from Wadi Halfa beyond its terminal at Kerma, 200 miles from Wadi Halfa, and then follow the river to Abu Hamed (see Map 3 on p. xv).

The proposed railway was a daunting task which would stretch the resources of Kitchener's Royal Engineers, with their limited manpower. The cost of building the line would also consume half the budget of £2.5 million allocated for the campaign. Kitchener, himself a former Royal Engineer officer, never underestimated the logistical problems involved; lack of finance apart, his officers pointed out that scarcity of water in the desert would be a major obstacle. Kitchener's response was blunt – find it on the way. Surprisingly, in that inhospitable environment, water was indeed found. The first sleepers and rails were laid at Wadi Halfa in February 1897. Gradually, the line would inch forward to Abu Hamed, its first objective. Kitchener was ignoring the fact that Abu Hamed was occupied by the Dervishes; for the moment, that fly could stick to the wall.

With Dongola province firmly in Anglo-Egyptian hands, Kitchener's force began a cautious advance upriver. Progress on railway construction was painfully slow due to a combination of shortages of material and skilled manpower. Work did not start in earnest until midsummer and, by mid-July, the railway had reached a point about a hundred miles from Wadi Halfa. Kitchener called a halt there as it was imprudent to proceed further without taking Abu Hamed, from where the Dervishes could mount spoiling raids, disrupting the line by menacing the lives of the labourers hired to build it.

Meanwhile, all was far from well in the Dervish camp. The Khalifa seems to have discounted the Desert Railway in the planning of his counter-campaign. He believed that Kitchener, like his predecessor Wolseley, would advance on a route through the Bayuda Desert from Korti to Metemma. The latter town was occupied by Abdullah Wad Saad's Jaalin tribe which had long been disenchanted with the Mahdists and could not be trusted with the defence of Metemma. (Abdullah Wad Saad had sought Anglo-Egyptian aid against the Khalifa in 1894 and might do so again. The Khalifa was taking no chances on this recurring.) He ordered Saad to evacuate Metemma, replacing him with the pro-Mahdist Baggara tribe under its leader, Mahmud Ahmed, the Khalifa's arrogant young nephew. Saad was worried about the fate of his people at the hands of the ferocious Ahmed, so he sent word to the Anglo-Egyptian Army requesting rifles and ammunition to defend his tribe against the rapacious and unruly Baggara. Major General Leslie Rundle, Kitchener's Chief of Staff, saw this as an opportunity and responded by despatching weapons to Saad under escort through the Bayuda Desert. Incredulously, Saad foolishly sent a message to the Khalifa, challenging his authority. Showing as much haste as Rundle, the Khalifa ordered Mahmud Ahmed to attack Metemma and subdue the rebellious Jaalin. To his credit, Ahmed did attempt to negotiate Saad out of Metemma but without success. Rundle's rifles had not arrived, so the Baggara stormed Metemma, slaughtering most of the troops and inhabitants. The only survivors were young girls whose lives were spared for the use of Mahmud's tribesmen. Only a few troops escaped into the desert, among them Ibrahahim Muhamad Farah who would raise an irregular force of Jaalin and other anti-Mahdist tribesmen, later known as the 'Friendlies'. No doubt Wingate put them to good use in his spy network. The remnants of the Jaalin survivors who managed to escape from Mettema encountered Rundle's convoy with its consignment of rifles; on learning of the fall of the town, Rundle turned back disconsolately to Korti.

Mahmud's army at Metemma had numbered about 10,000–12,000. His advance on Metemma was the Khalifa's first major act of aggression since the Egyptian Army's invasion a year earlier. Acutely aware that Mahmud was capable of reinforcing Abu Hamed's and Berber's understrength Dervish garrisons, Kitchener had to move fast. Surprise was of the essence and the Intelligence Department – minus Wingate who, as we shall see, had only recently returned to the Sudan from the Rodd Mission to Emperor Menelik of Abyssinia – was working to full capacity, no doubt under the energetic supervision of Rudolf Slatin, Wingate's subordinate.

The Khalifa's several recent reverses had boosted the Egyptian Army's morale and the troops sniffed the scent of further blood. Kitchener was no Wellington however, although he shared some of the Iron Duke's prejudices and characteristics. Square-headed – often the mark of a stubborn man – Kitchener was tall and, it has to be said, cross-eyed. (If you look at the face of the man staring out from the famous First World War recruiting poster, an intimidating forefinger pointing straight at you, one is struck by the image of a man you should ignore at your peril. In that famous poster, Kitchener's rogue eye seems to be wandering, as if attempting to detect something behind him.)

Kitchener rarely smiled; like Charles Gordon, he was possessed of a sardonic sense of humour. He had a violent temper which he was rarely able to control; it frayed easily when his views were questioned by men he considered inferior. His eyes were blue and cold. This physical characteristic is often present in idealists, T. E. Lawrence being a classic example. Kitchener sat a horse well, cutting an impressively poker-backed figure on the parade ground, seemingly moulded to his mount. He was a confirmed bachelor with only one (unconsummated) romantic liaison with a woman. His hobbies were surprisingly effete: he enjoyed collecting delicate porcelain and loved flowers. Perhaps these pursuits were the only outlet for a well-hidden emotion. He would have made a good priest, being celibate by inclination. However, the cross-eyed crusader who would ultimately defeat the Dervishes could do no wrong in the eyes of the British public and press. And yet for all his later glorious triumph at Omdurman, as a commander he was no Alexander, no Robert E. Lee. Kitchener was unable or reluctant to delegate responsibility which is often characteristic of those with no faith in subordinates. Furthermore, he rarely took the trouble to explain himself to officers, with a few exceptions; he confided in Leslie Rundle and Reginald Wingate, although even these men suffered his displeasure and were sent to Coventry on occasion. Kitchener was not the kind of man to coax or wheedle, nor praise and encourage those who served him. He had no poetry in his heart. In an argument his practice was to repeat a point over and over again until he exhausted all opposition. When, in later years, he was appointed Secretary of State for War in Asquith's First World War cabinet, he acted as if still living in a feudal society.

As we have seen earlier, Kitchener had repeatedly lobbied London to authorize his advance into the Sudan. With some success already gained during 1897, it would have been a great gift to him if the Queen had made public her desire for the complete conquest of the Sudan, thus avenging the death of Gordon. The Queen wanted it, the British media wanted it and, most important of all, the British public demanded nothing less than outright victory.[1]

Thus there was immense pressure on the British government to provide the necessary funds for a further advance into the Sudan. However, all was not sweetness and light between himself and Wingate in the months leading up to the Battle of Abu Hamed in August 1897. Wingate was in temporary disgrace for challenging his chief on the matter of privileges granted to a journalist. Although Wingate was inordinately loyal to and fond of Kitchener, he rarely allowed himself the luxury of hero worship, knowing this might impair his judgement. He was subjected to a veritable tirade for disagreeing with Kitchener about the aforementioned journalist, more of which appears below. The ensuing coolness between the two men led Wingate to complain to his diary that Kitchener was keeping plans and tactics 'secret from me' which was the last thing he needed. Kitchener detested journalists, considering them no better than parasites; on one occasion, he strode through a group of them, denigrating them as 'scribblers and drunken swabs'. Perhaps Kitchener wanted to be rid of Wingate for a while, so it was agreed to second him to the fruitless Rodd Mission to Emperor Menelik of Abyssinia. Sir Rennell Rodd's mission was publicly announced as one aimed at defining the boundary between Abyssinia and the Sudan. There was another agenda however. Rodd's primary objective was to obtain Menelik's agreement not to assist the Dervishes. Unable to secure Menelik's co-operation to either, Rodd and Wingate returned to the Sudan, no doubt both men feeling their time had been wasted, although Wingate was awarded the Star of Ethiopia 2nd Class for his efforts. (Menelik refused to accede to British demands to remain neutral on the grounds that Britain continued to support the Italians who would not allow Abyssinia to import arms and ammunition via the Sudan.)[2]

Thus far Wingate and Slatin had been inseparable but, at this juncture, they parted company at Merowe in October. Wingate, now holding the brevet rank of Lieutenant Colonel, returned to Wadi Halfa, the HQ of the Intelligence Department, Slatin remaining at the branch office at Merowe. Was this a deliberate ploy on the part of Kitchener? It would seem so. The 'Sudanese Twins' were perhaps too powerful a team for his liking.

Kitchener's next major thrust against the Dervishes began on 29 July. A force of about 3,600, commanded by Sir Archibald Hunter and comprising mainly of Lieutenant Colonel Hector MacDonald's Sudanese Brigade, six field pieces, two Maxims and supported by a troop of cavalry, made good progress. As a consequence, Kitchener shifted his HQ to Merowe. On 4 August his advance column reached El Kab, well over halfway to their target at Abu Hamed. Hunter, now appraised that Dervish reinforcements were en route from Berber to stiffen the garrison at Abu Hamed, marched his men to the village which was lightly defended by a nonetheless determined garrison of 700 Dervishes. Hunter attacked on 7 August, taking the entrenched village with the loss of only fourteen killed and fifty wounded. Learning of the fall of Abu Hamed, the Berber reinforcements turned back. On 31 August the 'Friendly' Jaalin Sheik Farah occupied Berber, whose Dervish garrison simply melted away. Hunter entered the town on 5 September; now Kitchener could mount the last stage of his campaign against the Khalifa's forces at Omdurman.

All was going well for the campaign although Kitchener was plagued by a fear that the former Sirdar, Sir Francis Grenfell, who had recently been appointed to command the British army of occupation in Cairo, might replace him. Kitchener was also suffering from stress and exhaustion; on 18 October, such was his state of mind that he cabled his resignation to Lord Cromer, who ignored it. The two men met in Cairo in November, where Cromer assured Kitchener that he, Kitchener, would remain in command even if and when British troops were sent to reinforce his Egyptian and Sudanese battalions.

Kitchener's Desert Railway duly reached Abu Hamed on 31 October. During the closing weeks of 1897, Wingate – now restored to Kitchener's confidence – put it about that the Khalifa was preparing the reinforcement of his nephew Mahmud in Mettema. The boastful young Emir Mahmud, a man who normally did not take advice from subordinates, accepted Osman Digna's suggestion that he should march away from the Nile, thus drawing the Anglo-Egyptian Army from its water supply and outflanking it.

In November 1897 Cromer warned Whitehall that further advances into the Sudan would be prohibitively expensive to the British Treasury. He reported to Lord Salisbury that Egypt was at the end of its financial tether. However, events in late December cut the ground from under Cromer's firmly planted feet. Wingate reported to Kitchener that the Khalifa was about to march at the head of his entire host to occupy Berber in strength. Kitchener relayed

Wingate's report to Cromer who passed this alarming news to Lord Salisbury in London, adding that the Egyptian Army could not stem the advance alone. Two days before Christmas the British Cabinet gave Cromer a free hand, also promising British troops. Wingate's information was, however, incorrect on this occasion, perhaps deliberately so.[3] Modern historians consider that Wingate's report was either based on rumour or was deliberately fabricated to bring British troops to the Sudan. If it was a ruse, it worked. For his services in 1897, Wingate was promoted to the rank of Brevet Colonel, received a vote of thanks from Parliament and was made an extra ADC to Queen Victoria in December.

In January 1898 Slatin visited Wingate at Wadi Halfa and suggested to Kitchener that it would be preferable if he could be stationed there instead of at Merowe, where General Leslie Rundle was insisting he remain. Rundle was over-ruled; Slatin returned to Wadi Halfa, thus allowing Wingate to move forward with Kitchener and the army. Slatin had anticipated that he would accompany Wingate to the front and believed that he was being put on ice and that Kitchener was trying to get rid of him, as he confessed in a letter to Wingate. Kitchener held no such motive; he was unaware of Slatin's unease until Wingate drew the matter to his attention. He made it known that Slatin would be welcome to join the final advance on Omdurman but only after all the necessary intelligence work had been completed. Wingate, ever the diplomat, wrote thus to his friend, 'If you were shot, our enemies would rejoice and there would be political consequences at home.'[4]

In February 1898 a British infantry brigade commanded by Major General William Gatacre arrived in the Sudan. Gatacre's command consisted of the 1st Battalions of the Warwickshire, Lincolnshire and Cameron Highlander regiments, later joined by the 1st Battalion Seaforth Highlanders.

In mid-March Kitchener moved his by now 14,000-strong army to Ras el Hudi to the dry riverbed at Atbara, only a few miles from Mahmud's *zariba*, or circular thornbush enclosure. Mahmud made elaborate but flexible preparations at Atbara; his strategy would give him a choice between a frontal confrontation and a speedy withdrawal if necessary. His defensive fortifications were impressive; built on a strategic point above the riverbed, they consisted of a stout zariba, with wooden firing platforms, backed by a stockade, trenches and a dried mud blockhouse. Mahmud was ideally placed to observe Kitchener's movements and make a stand if necessary, or he could withdraw and menace Kitchener's flanks on the approach to Omdurman.

Kitchener sensed that victory was in his grasp; if he could destroy Mahmud, the road to Omdurman would be open and the campaign would be over before the end of the year. At Atbara it was clear to Wingate that a confrontation was inevitable. Kitchener, Gatacre and Hunter seriously over-estimated Mahmud's strength, which they believed numbered at least 25,000; some modern historians contend it was nearer 19,000. The usually dependable Wingate seems not to have known the precise figure. Kitchener's plans were flexible; reluctant to commit his entire force until ready to make a frontal attack or a flanking movement, he bided his time. He was encouraged by the steady stream of deserters from Mahmud's army, as many as 3,000 in a few days. Kitchener held a war council which included Sir Archibald Hunter – a man of whom Wingate said Kitchener was afraid – Wingate himself and the brigade officers. Kitchener, unlike other military commanders, only resorted to councils of war when he was uncertain whether to engage the enemy. The consensus of opinion was that Kitchener should not mount a frontal attack, advice which he overruled. He was implacable, although he felt it necessary to wire a belt-and-braces telegram to Cairo and London reporting his situation and intentions. The responses from Cromer in Cairo and Salisbury in London advised him to do what he thought best, which in Victorian spin meant 'you are in command, do not blame me if it all goes wrong'. Kitchener's request was a clear indication that he had, in fact, lost his nerve; he needed reassurance.

Despite wavering, Kitchener knew that if he could destroy the formidable corps of the Khalifa's army he would shorten the war. He was proved right but prevaricated, fearing for his reputation. (Kitchener was rarely resolute and confident in the manner of men like the Duke of Wellington, possibly because he was from humble stock; he certainly lacked confidence in his own ability.) Rudolf von Slatin provided him with accurate intelligence reports on the state of the Khalifa's army which pointed to victory if only Kitchener would take the initiative. Kitchener had two options – to attack the Emir Mahmud at Atbara or allow the enemy forces to disperse. Slatin recommended that Kitchener should attack but the man prevaricated to such an extent that it was said he went into a 'blue funk'. Kitchener's staff finally persuaded him to attack the Dervishes. Atbara presented an opportunity to reduce the Khalifa's awesome superiority in manpower. Wingate remained ever resourceful; he urged his agents to spread it about that British (Christian) troops would not fight on Good Friday, 8 April. Friday is also a day sacred to Muslims.[5] Wingate's ruse worked. An unsuspecting Mahmud found himself under heavy attack at 6.15 that morning; the artillery launched a devastating barrage which lasted for an hour and a half. The zariba occupied by Mahmud and his lieutenant, Osman Digna, was repeatedly pounded. When the barrage was lifted, the British, Egyptian and Sudanese troops moved forward in parade-ground precision, with drums beating and bagpipes skirling. The Anglo-Egyptian Army crashed through the zariba shouting 'Remember Gordon!' A frontal assault with the bayonet, then fierce hand-to-hand fighting carried the day. By 8.00am, all resistance was over; it was a massacre. A wounded Mahmud was brought before Kitchener, Major Lord Edward Cecil (son of Prime Minister Lord Salisbury and one of Kitchener's ADCs), Brevet Colonel Wingate and Major General Hunter. Osman Digna, true to his nature, once more escaped capture. Anglo-Egyptian casualties amounted to eighty-one dead and 487 wounded, the bulk of the casualties suffered by the Scottish regiments.[6] Dervish casualties were estimated at 3,000 dead and 4,000 wounded.

Despite his modest casualties, Kitchener wept when he heard the losses had included two of his British officers – one each from the Cameron and Seaforth Highlanders and twenty-two British Other Ranks. For the rest of his life, Kitchener considered Atbara rather than Omdurman his 'crowning glory'. For his part in the battle, Wingate was Mentioned in Despatches[7] and received three clasps to his growing collection of medals. After the battle he interrogated Mahmud Ahmad; a contemporary photograph unfortunately masks both Ahmad's and Wingate's features. A decidedly portly Wingate is depicted in what today would be described as a laid-back pose. Smoking a cigar, he looks like he is giving an order to a subordinate. It is hardly the portrait of a conquering hero. However, his awards were tinged with sadness; the day after Atbara, Wingate learnt that his brother Richard, aged forty-nine, had died from malaria contracted in India.

Emir Mahmud was led away from the bloody field of Atbara; despite being wounded and bound, he had lost none of his courage or arrogance. As he was led into captivity he confronted Kitchener with defiant words, 'You will pay for this at Omdurman. Compared with the Khalifa, I am but a leaf.' Four days later Kitchener entered Berber, welcomed by cheering crowds of anti-Mahdist Sudanese waving flags; women spat at Mahmud, the butcher of Mettema, as he was led through the streets, hands tied behind his back yet nevertheless strutting haughtily through the jeering crowds. He died in prison in 1906, aged forty.

After the Battle of Atbara, the Egyptian Army went into summer camp while plans were drawn up for the final assault on the Khalifa at Omdurman. The question on everyone's mind was whether the Khalifa would sit behind the protecting walls of Omdurman and snipe at Kitchener's forces or fight in the open. Wingate assured Kitchener he would do the latter, having learnt in 1891 that the Khalifa had chosen his killing ground on the plain of Kerreri, north of the town. The Anglo-Egyptian Army, now strengthened by the Seaforth Highlanders, was joined in August by the 1st Battalion Grenadier Guards (Lord Edward Cecil's regiment) and the 21st Lancers, the latter's ranks including an ambitious young subaltern whose influential mother had repeatedly lobbied the government in London for her son's transfer to the army of liberation in the Sudan.

When he learnt that Lady Randolph Churchill's son Winston had joined his army, Kitchener was extremely angry. Not only had he previously rejected the young man, he disliked serving officers doubling as war correspondents and journalists. In his view, such men clogged up vital telegraph lines, getting drunk at every opportunity. He had already treated Wingate to the sharp edge of his tongue in an incident relating to drunken journalists. The tirade had been sparked off by the arrival of Colonel Frank Rhodes, brother of the empire-builder and businessman Cecil Rhodes, as official war correspondent with Kitchener's army. Kitchener did not want Rhodes: Wingate did. Kitchener refused to tell Rhodes to his face that he was unwelcome, so Wingate, who supported Rhodes' application, refused to do Kitchener's dirty work, simply informing the man that Kitchener did not want him. Fortunately, the problem was solved when Rhodes went elsewhere. Kitchener made known his displeasure about the incident to Wingate. The shy and reserved Sirdar was perhaps no fool; he possibly foresaw that his personal rejection of Rhodes might not only alienate him but also harm his reputation. With powerful and influential connections, Rhodes could indeed have discredited Kitchener, especially in the event of a possible setback at Omdurman. Directing his displeasure at Wingate was unfair, even if it was Kitchener's privilege as Commander in Chief. As events turned out, his successful handling of Omdurman would be reported not from the pen of a professional journalist but one of his own men – Winston Churchill.

Kitchener was enraged that Churchill had been foisted on him largely because of Lady Randolph Churchill's political influence. Churchill had recently taken part in actions on the North-West Frontier of India against the notoriously aggressive Pathan tribesmen. He had served with distinction there and was Mentioned in Despatches, singing his own praises afterwards. Returning to England in May 1898, manipulative as he undoubtedly was, Churchill sent a copy of his account of the Pathan rebellion to the Prime Minister, Lord Salisbury, who subsequently interviewed him. A few days later, Churchill was informed that he was to be posted to the 21st Lancers, serving in the Sudan campaign.

Kitchener made it abundantly clear that he did not want Churchill. In addition to Kitchener's prejudice, it seems that Churchill was unpopular with his brother officers, never missing an opportunity to inform them of his destined greatness. We do not know if Wingate attempted to smooth Kitchener's ruffled feathers in the matter; perhaps he remained wisely in the background, leaving Kitchener to resolve the problem by pretending that Churchill did not exist.

By August, Kitchener had moved his HQ to El Hajir, a few miles north of Omdurman. Being in close proximity to Omdurman, Wingate recalled his spies and agents to El Hajir, as they had completed their work. One of his operatives, Taib el Hussain, a former official in the Khalifa's governing council, brought Wingate invaluable information about Dervish strength in and around Omdurman and a fairly accurate version of the Khalifa's proposed strategy.

All was not well in the Anglo-Egyptian Army among the British officers. There were constant disputes with Kitchener, personal slights and disagreements about strategy and tactics. Wingate possessed the ability to moderate Kitchener's arguments and soften his harsher orders but Kitchener's paranoid secrecy undoubtedly hampered Wingate's effectiveness. Slatin was also routinely and ruthlessly insulted. Leslie Rundle and the majority of the Egyptian Army staff were kept to the rear, with little to do. Wingate, on the spot, suffered his chief's ungracious behaviour, being often snubbed and taken for granted. To console himself, Wingate confided to his diary that Kitchener was a 'time server ... the quintessence of a coward'.[8] (Another critic was Margot, wife of Herbert Asquith, the Liberal Prime Minister; she once described Kitchener as 'that great cad'.)

Yet another bone of contention proved to be the arrival of Wingate's wife Kitty at Aswan. The celibate Kitchener made no secret of his impatience with officers who made concessions for married life. Wingate would later write to his wife that even mentioning her name would bring 'a sneer in which he [Kitchener] airs his views on the mistake of officers marrying'.[9]

The Battle at Atbara was the prelude to Omdurman, the *entrée* to the main course, although the Anglo-Egyptian Army would suffer a long, hot summer of inactivity in that final year of the Sudan campaign. On 24 August Kitchener reviewed his troops at Wadi Hamed for the last time; these now numbered about 30,000, of which 8,000 were British. Then, in the last week of August, Kitchener ordered the bulk of his troops to march along the west bank of the Nile, while others travelled by river steamers and barges. Those who travelled in the river transports were the unlucky ones, being packed on board like sardines. By 31 August the army had reached the small village of El Egeiga, where Kitchener bivouacked for the night, ordering his men to construct a stout thorn zariba on the west bank of the Nile. The Anglo-Egyptian Army camped near the hill of Jabel Surkab, known to British historians as Jebel Surgham, a small eminence about six miles from Omdurman. When the advance elements of Kitchener's army reached the Kerreri Hills, they saw 50,000 Sudanese warriors below, drawn up in orderly formations. The two armies would confront each other on the plains of Kerreri, as the Khalifa had promised.

On the afternoon of 1 September 1898, Kitchener was enjoying lunch when a heliograph flashing from a small hill caught his eye. Mounting his white Arab horse, he cantered leisurely towards the position, which he knew was occupied by the 21st Lancers. Ahead, he saw a lone rider galloping towards him from the hill. When they met, Kitchener's was confronted by the man he detested – Winston Churchill. That day, the two men met face to face for the first time. The young Churchill reined in beside his Commander in Chief, breathlessly delivering the message that 60,000 Dervishes from Omdurman were advancing upon the Anglo-British position.

Kitchener was cool, confident of victory. Like Bernard Montgomery in 1942, preparing for the Battle of El Alamein against Rommel, Kitchener had trained his infantry to the peak of perfection. The men were lean, fit and eager to engage the enemy. One of the brigades was commanded by Lieutenant Colonel Hector MacDonald who had risen from the rank of private in the Gordon Highlanders; the following day, MacDonald would give Kitchener the victory he had craved for so long. MacDonald's brigade of Sudanese troops was stationed on the right flank of the Anglo-Egyptian Army at El Egeiga which was deployed in a wide arc before the village and protected by a thorn zariba on the west bank of the Nile. Trenches had been dug, artillery batteries, howitzers and Maxim machine guns placed in strategic positions to support the infantry. Morale was high simply because the ordinary soldiers were eager to get the job done.

Nonetheless, the sheer volume of the advancing force must have been awesome, momentarily unnerving all who witnessed it. Then, quite suddenly and unaccountably, the lumbering Dervish army came to a halt about three miles distant. Just what was the Khalifa's plan? All that hot afternoon the Dervishes remained motionless, the heat waves shimmering and distorting the massed lines of men, horses and camels. That night Kitchener ordered his men to spend the night at their battle stations; he suspected that the Khalifa intended to attack under cover of darkness which might have been tactically successful, possibly inflicting serious casualties on the Anglo-Egyptian Army and forcing it to retreat or dig in to await reinforcements. Certainly the superior firepower of Kitchener's forces would have been less effective in the darkness. The army spent a nervous night on constant alert, apprehensive at the sound of the least inexplicable noise. The following morning Kitchener confessed to one of his senior officers that he believed the enemy would have penetrated his defensive zariba had they attacked at night.

General Sir Archibald Hunter probably captured the mood of many, echoing Kitchener's own thoughts: 'When the sun rose on 2/9/98, I never was so glad in all my days.'[10]

Dawn came at 5.00am. The men in Kitchener's army were no doubt relieved to see the sun. There was a definite movement in the Dervish camp at dawn, signalled by the reflection of sunlight from thousands of spears, swords and rifles. Then the mass of Dervishes began to advance to the north of Kitchener's position. Where was the Khalifa going and for what reason? The nervous, excited troops formed up outside the El Egeiga zariba on the west bank of the Nile. On the east bank, Major General Stewart-Wortley, the Hon E. J. Montagu and his 'Friendlies' – native tribes hostile to the Mahdist forces – secured the area to prevent any attack from the rear. The Dervish front line, still hardly discernible, stretched for four or five miles with its extreme left resting on the Kerreri Hills. British, Egyptian and Sudanese battalions shuffled in parade-ground order, dressing from right to left. It was a move designed to steady the troops, a fact appreciated by Wellington at Waterloo who famously said that anything that wasted time before a battle was an important factor in boosting morale.

Part of the Dervish Army was hidden behind the Kerreri Hills; numbering 5,500 the corps was commanded by Ali Wad Helu. Some way to Helu's right and forward of his position was the main body of Dervish, comprising 28,000 warriors and commanded by the Khalifa's son, Shayk al-Din. To his right, facing Kitchener's zariba was Osman Azrak's 8,000-strong contingent; then behind the knoll known as Jebel Surgham, facing Kitchener's left, were the Khalifa and his brother Ya'Qub (or Yakub) with a force numbering 21,000 grouped beneath the Mahdi's sacred Black Flag.

Facing these four formations totalling 62,500 men were Kitchener's battalions – 8,000 British regulars, comprised of the Grenadier Guards,

Northumberland Fusiliers, Lancashire Fusiliers, Rifle Brigade (Green Jackets) of 2 Brigade, commanded by Brigadier N. G. Lyttleton on the extreme left (*see map*); to Lyttelton's right was 1 Brigade under Brigadier General A. G. Wauchope, consisting of the 1st Warwicks, Lincolns, Seaforth Highlanders and Cameron Highlanders. These two brigades were commanded by Sir William Gatacre (known to his officers as 'Fatacre' because he constantly interfered with their duties; the Other Ranks called him 'Backacre' on account of his habit of pushing them to the limits of their endurance). To Wauchope's right were positioned twenty-six of the forty-four guns of 32 Field Battery, Royal Artillery. Next to the guns stood the first section of the Egyptian Division commanded by Lieutenant Colonel J. G. Maxwell, three battalions of Sudanese and one battalion of Egyptian troops. To Maxwell's right was Lieutenant Colonel MacDonald ('Fighting Mac') whose brigade consisted of four battalions, three Sudanese and one Egyptian. Fighting Mac was destined to become the real hero of the battle; some historians rightly claim that he, not Kitchener, won the day. On the extreme right with his back to the Nile was Lieutenant Colonel D. F. ('Taffy') Lewis with four Egyptian battalions, reputedly the weakest formation in the entire army. In reserve was Lieutenant Colonel J. Collinson's brigade comprised of three and a half battalions of Egyptian infantry. Thus the stage was set for the final battle of the Sudan.

With his usual attention to observation and tactical analysis, Wingate remained close to Kitchener, trying to assess the situation as they watched the Khalifa turn away from the Nile. What passed between the two men is not recorded; in truth, it is more than likely that neither knew what the Khalifa intended.

Studying the Dervish Army's advance – if advance it was – the British cavalry moved in the direction ordered. It is not known whether Wingate's spies had spread misinformation in the Dervish camp that Kitchener's main position was concentrated in the Kerreri Hills but the Khalifa believed that it was and that the force at El Egeiga was a lure. Kitchener had despatched Lieutenant General Broadwood's small command to the Kerreri Hills, hoping that the Dervish Army would follow him to Kitchener's prepared position. This less than elaborate chess game did not last long; Kitchener opened fire at 6.25am with 32 Field Battery firing its first salvoes at a range of 2,700 yards, followed by the Egyptian Field Artillery and the rapid-firing Neufeldt guns from the Nile gunboats. The large force pursuing Broadwood broke off, wheeled round and advanced on the El Egeiga zariba. The defenders stood calm, reassured by their rapid-fire rifles, Maxim guns and field artillery firing canister shrapnel that would wreak havoc on the advancing Dervish hordes.

It was an unequal fight from the outset although, as eyewitnesses would later recall, they were awestruck by the bravery of the thousands of Dervish warriors hurtling towards them, their black and green banners flying, spears and swords held aloft, glittering in the early morning sun. Kitchener in his white uniform and seated on a white Arab charger sat stock-still, seemingly indifferent to what confronted him. He had taken up position behind the Cameron Highlanders, stationed at the left centre of his line. Perhaps, as he sat in isolation and silence, his mind strayed to the comment made by the French Marshal St Arnaud on the pointless Charge of the Light Brigade during the Crimean War, 'C'est magnifique, mais ce n'est pas la guerre.' (It is magnificent, but it is not war).

Through field glasses, Kitchener studied the mass of men charging towards him; the enemy seemed to be keeping good order despite the shells thinning their ranks. (One cannot resist comparison with the Confederate General Pickett's charge at Gettysburg during the American Civil War, when on 3 July 1863, the flower of Old Virginia was destroyed in a single afternoon.) Kitchener was unmoved, seemingly detached from it all, possibly in an effort to encourage his troops. Then, as the Dervishes closed in for the last 400 yards, he ordered the artillery to shorten range and give their all. Deadly canister fire tore great gaps in the ranks of the howling warriors. Kitchener watched the clouds of dust settle over empty spaces which seconds before had been densely packed with men. Recent historians have estimated that in the first phase of the Battle of Omdurman, some 200,000 rounds of small arms' ammunition were used and 1,000 rounds of shells. Only the Dervish standard-bearers got close to the zariba, the nearest falling 300 yards from it, having been shot at by half of Wauchope's Brigade.

As the Dervishes drew closer, the Maxim guns did their devastating work, a prelude of what would become a daily occurrence in the trenches of the Great War. At 800 yards, the infantry began delivering volley after volley into the heaving, swirling mass of men. Surely the sight of hundreds of trembling white-smocked bodies lying on the sand moved even the unemotional Kitchener, an appalling sight that must have remained with him until his death in 1916.

Despite the awesome firepower ranged against them, the Dervishes came on, leaving dead and wounded in ordered lines behind them. Undoubtedly, there were young men in Kitchener's lines that September day who would live to see the carnage on the Western Front eighteen years later. Perhaps in the Flanders mud they remembered their first experience of the devastation that Maxim guns could inflict on advancing infantry. (One wonders if their feelings were moved by memories of Omdurman when 20,000 of their comrades would fall similarly on the first day of the terrible Battle of the Somme on 1 July 1916.)

While the first attack was in progress, beyond the main camp and forward of Kitchener's right flank, Broadwood with the horse artillery, a small contingent of Egyptian cavalry and the Camel Corps cavalry were observing the battle from the Kerreri Hills. Broadwood had been given a minor role although he was in essence Kitchener's eyes, on the blind side of his position. The only other 'eyes' were the 21st Lancers, the light cavalry regiment posted on Kitchener's left flank. The Lancers resented the fact that Broadwood had been given a more important role than theirs – well, that is how it seemed to their commander, Lieutenant Colonel Rowland Hill Martin. The regiment was ordered to prowl around the vicinity of Jebel Surgham, scouting for concentrations of Dervish. For the moment they felt they had been cast in a subsidiary role, which annoyed Martin. His regiment lacked battle honours, unlike its sister regiment, the 17th Lancers which had taken part in the disastrous Charge of the Light Brigade.

The Mahdist advance, perhaps unnerved by the devastating firepower from the zariba, began to drift from left to right; it was a suicidal move, for the line was exposed to the entire fire of the Anglo-Egyptian army and was within range. The British observers could only stare in astonishment, although at the time it was thought that the reason for this move was ordered by the Khalifa because he assumed the zariba at El Egeiga was weak and that Kitchener had concentrated his main force, hidden from view, in the Kerreri Hills.

The Dervish force advancing on the zariba was still a long way off, a smudge of smoke and dust in the distance. Despite the appalling and accurate firepower from the allied army, eyewitness accounts confirmed that the shrapnel shells had little effect on the moving mass of men on horses, camels and foot. Still they came on. Their screams seemed like the plaintive calls of distant seagulls until the warriors drew closer and their voices became loud and human. Until then they appeared to have been untouched, an irresistible force that simply shivered each time a canister or shrapnel shell exploded in their midst. It was as if the moving mass of men were liquid, absorbing the impact of the projectiles as a pond absorbs stones thrown into it.

Suddenly, a large body of Dervish split away like water diverted by an obstruction in its path, flowing away from the main course. The human river ran down the hill of Jebel Surgham, threatening to engulf the allied army at El Egeiga. Only moments before this move, Kitchener's troops stationed on the right flank had begun to think they would be on the periphery of the battle. Now they saw that had changed.

The relatively small contingent of Dervish attacking the zariba – 8,000 at most – was a deliberate tactic of the Khalifa as he still believed that Kitchener's main army was concentrated in the Kerreri Hills. It was a fatal mistake, even if his contingent were reinforced by elements of the Dervish force at Jebel Surgham, which added a further 10,000 to the force commanded by Osman Azrak, the Emir who had been charged with the assault on El Egeiga.

Modern firepower had arrived with a vengeance. The age of innocence – if innocence is a word that may be applied to warfare – was over. The British Army had become a killing machine. It was a case of 'We have got the Maxim gun, which they have not'. On the plains of Kerreri, thousands of Muslim Dervish met – in the eyes of the faithful – honourable death. The fallen were the elect of Allah, going straight to Paradise as promised by the Prophet Mohammed, each man to be cosseted by seventy-two virgins in Paradise.

Omdurman was a killing field with thousands of casualties. Even their opponents on the day of the battle and for many years to come grudgingly admired the Dervishes' courage at Omdurman until the generation which had cheered Kitchener had passed, giving way to a generation which would suffer even worse carnage on the Western Front. Some modern historians have deprecated Kitchener's callous slaughter of a people. What else could he have done? It was the cultural and religious beliefs of the Dervishes which drew them inexorably on to the guns.

In the first phase of the battle, the closest any warrior got to Kitchener's lines was a mere 300 yards. Successive standard-bearers who bore the Army of the Green Flag's emblem fell, only for the flag to be carried forward by another. It was during this phase of the battle that most of the few British casualties were sustained – five killed and ninety wounded. By 8.30am the Dervish attempt to smash through the Allied zariba had all but disintegrated. The desert was littered with thousands of corpses, their white robes fluttering on the breeze. Several hundred wounded began to crawl away from the battlefield, dying later in obscure hollows and among the rocks. One modern account graphically describes Kitchener advancing towards Omdurman across a wasteland 'on which the white-clad corpses lay strewn like crumpled newspapers'.[11] Eyewitnesses later said that the Emirs, men who were personally brave, were the first casualties; many were found dead wearing chain mail and carrying swords looted from Christian Crusader soldiers over six centuries earlier.

Meanwhile, as Osman Azrak's battalions were being slaughtered before El Egeiga, Broadwood and his small force held their positions in the Kerreri Hills, acting as forward protection for the vulnerable right flank of the zariba held by Lewis's all-Egyptian brigade, which contained at least one battalion of doubtful quality. Broadwood's force consisted of nine squadrons of cavalry, eight companies of Camel Corps and a horse artillery battery. The small force was about to find itself in deep trouble. Soon Broadwood found himself facing 20,000 Dervishes racing towards his position. Every inch the professional soldier, Broadwood despatched a galloper to Kitchener, informing him of this unexpected development. Kitchener immediately ordered Broadwood to fall back on the zariba but it seemed too late to do so. In his hasty retreat, Broadwood lost two field pieces that had come to grief, much to the delight of the advancing Dervishes; the rest of the artillery escaped under the protective screen of cavalry squadrons commanded by Captain Douglas Haig, who would later become a field marshal in the Great War. The Camel Corps was in danger of being overtaken and annihilated, being almost a mile from the protection of the zariba and the Nile. The Dervish hordes were literally snapping at its heels when help came from the gunboats *Melik* and *Abu Klea* whose commanders trained their fast-firing guns on the pursuers, killing and wounding hundreds until the chase came to a standstill.

Now it was the turn of the 21st Lancers, stationed near the zariba, fretting at their hitherto inactive role. At 8.00am the cavalry regiment was ordered forward to scout the left flank of Kitchener's forces; they were sent to Jebel Surgham ostensibly to harass the remnants of the Khalifa's army and prevent a retreat to Omdurman. It was an unrealistic order for a regiment of light cavalry numbering less than 400. Kitchener was unaware that he was sending the regiment to confront 12,000 of the Khalifa's best and bravest warriors, hidden behind the knoll of Jebel Surgham. Lieutenant Colonel Martin, commanding the regiment, no doubt welcomed the order. The Lancers were spoiling for a fight and needed a battle honour for their flag. The regiment, with Winston Churchill in the forefront, trotted forward. Unknown to Lieutenant Colonel Martin, he was heading towards a superior force commanded by the resourceful Osman Digna who had set a trap for the Lancers. Digna concealed his men in a dry watercourse south-east of Jebel Surgham; in his many guerrilla raids, Digna had lèarnt to respect Anglo-Egyptian infantry squares which he knew were rarely broken. However, he also knew that the cavalry were vulnerable if they could be induced to charge over broken ground defended by concealed infantrymen. The Lancers thought they were mopping up a mere few hundred Dervish to their front.

As the forward troop negotiated the ridge, they were surprised to find a considerable body of the enemy around them. 'Bloody Hell!' was supposedly Winston Churchill's only comment as he galloped over the ridge into Osman Digna's massed foot soldiers, shouting 'La Llaha illa Llah wa Muhammad rasul Allah!' (There is one God and Muhammad is the Messenger of God).

In the few moments of that charge, 40 per cent of the British casualties in the Battle of Omdurman were sustained; Lieutenant Grenfell, a nephew of the former Sirdar, and twenty men were killed and fifty officers and men wounded. The charge of the 21st Lancers achieved nothing of military value; it did, however, provide young Winston Churchill with good copy for the newspapers and, no doubt, it also gave a lift to the recruiting sergeants in the regiment. Omdurman was one of the last occasions when a British cavalry regiment would charge an enemy, the last occurring in Chanak, Turkey in 1920. Churchill set down his brief part in the Battle of Omdurman the following year.[12]

Phase two of the battle began at 9.00am. A large number of Dervishes remained unbloodied and uncommitted; the Army of the Black Flag numbering 17,000 was under the command of the Khalifa's brother, Yakub. Also, a large force under Ali Wad Helu, which had swept across the van of the zariba at El Egeiga was still in the field, reasonably intact. No matter, Kitchener sensed victory and ordered a general advance on the Khalifa and his brother, leaving his right flank protected by Lieutenant Colonel MacDonald. It was at this point that the allied effort almost came to grief.

Hector MacDonald had made his way through the ranks on merit rather than through patronage, the usual way of gaining promotion for the time. He showed a total contempt for danger, placing little value on his own life, possibly because he knew that soldiers of his generation rarely expected to survive to middle age. MacDonald was of humble birth, the son of a Dingwall tailor; he joined the Gordon Highlanders as a private in 1870 and saw action in the First Afghan War, then in the First Boer War in 1880. He was commissioned in the field and decorated three times. In 1880, fighting the Boers, he had distinguished himself by defending his post at Laing's Nek in South Africa with only twenty men against a greatly superior force. He fought for seven hours at Majuba Hill, being one of only two survivors in that action. A year later he was posted to Egypt and took part in the relief expedition to Khartoum. Transferred to the Egyptian army with the rank of captain, he trained the native troops in the Highland way of fighting, substituting the bayonet for the claymore. He learnt Arabic, was loved by his men and known to them as 'MacDonald Pasha'.

Kitchener had given MacDonald the doubtful honour of defending the right flank of the zariba and ordered him to hold the line if attacked by Sheik al-Din and Ali Wad Helu. Attempting to remain in line when Kitchener ordered a general advance, MacDonald found himself confronted by a large body of Dervishes who charged his Sudanese Brigade which numbered only 3,000 men. MacDonald informed Kitchener of his precarious position and that he was being attacked by superior forces. Kitchener's blood was up and he sent a galloper to MacDonald with an Olympian response, 'Can't Colonel MacDonald see that we are marching on Omdurman? Tell him to follow on.' Kitchener's decision could have cost him the victory he so sorely sought. MacDonald's force was isolated, alone. The cool-headed Scot acted quickly, re-positioning his brigade on an alignment of ninety degrees, an L-shaped formation which withstood the assault from the Kerreri Hills. His Sudanese troops were undaunted by the mass of warriors advancing on them, pouring irregular rifle-fire into the front lines. MacDonald had to force them to stand fast and cease their uncoordinated volleys. He knew a substantial force was in front of and on his right flank; 20,000 Dervishes commanded by Sheik al-Din and Ali Wad Helu. MacDonald was ordered to withdraw, but he refused to obey the order: 'I'll no' do it. I'll see them damned first.'

MacDonald met the attack with a barrage from his three batteries of field artillery supported by a battery of Maxim guns, stopping the onslaught 300 yards before his line. He noted that the Khalifa's Black Flag lay only 250 yards from his position. Despite his robust defence, Mac's part in the battle was not over; elements of the Green Flag were menacing his right flank and he had only just enough time to bring forward a fresh battery of guns to meet the new threat. His infantry broke the columns of charging cavalry with rifle fire. Had Sheik al-Din and Ali Wad Helu managed to overcome MacDonald, they could have turned the battle in the Dervish favour.

MacDonald's Sudanese were down to their last few rounds but they stood firm, ready to use the bayonet when their ammunition ran out. Then at the crucial moment, the 1st Lincolns were ordered to assist MacDonald, supported by a further three batteries of field artillery. The rest of 1 British Brigade came over the ridge, comprising the 1st Seaforth, 1st Camerons and 1st Warwicks, turning what had almost been a disaster into a crushing victory. The Dervishes were now completely outflanked; the last of Ali Wad Helu's force destroyed themselves in suicidal charges against MacDonald's line. MacDonald then ordered a general advance with the bayonet, driving the remnants of Helu's shattered force back into the Kerreri Hills, ensuring that they could not return to join up with the Khalifa. MacDonald's fortitude and courage had won the day, although at the time he was never given the credit he deserved for his part in the battle. His efforts went unrecognized, Kitchener receiving all the glory.

It is appropriate here to record the last few years of Hector MacDonald's life. He went on from the Sudan to take command of the Highland Division in the Second Boer War in 1900, restoring its morale after a serious defeat at the Battle of Magersfontein. His was a tragic and controversial death, not in battle but by his own hand. In 1903 he was posted to Ceylon where there was an undisclosed complaint against his character. It was rumoured that, while travelling on a train, MacDonald had interfered with some schoolboy of noble birth. MacDonald had not been popular in Ceylon. Sir John J. West Ridgeway, the Governor General of Ceylon, had made no secret of his dislike of Mac-Donald to the British government and wanted him out of Ceylon. MacDonald was despised by others in Ceylonese Establishment circles who resented having to answer to someone of 'low breeding'. One day MacDonald yelled at some wealthy political figure wandering about the army camp during military exercises. It was later said that this person was responsible for the subsequent rumours about MacDonald's sexual preferences. An anonymous letter appeared in *The Times* of Ceylon suggesting he did not 'like ladies' and he was 'pleasantly surprised to find he has dropped on [sic] a spicy little Isle where ladies were few and far between'. Further letters appeared in the press; Ridgeway read MacDonald the accusations made against him; the latter's response was that the Governor General 'was in no position to judge him'. Ridgeway ordered MacDonald to return to the UK to answer the charges or face a court-martial. MacDonald complied, hoping to petition Edward VII at court; the King ordered him back to Ceylon to answer the accusations against him. En route, while staying in the Hotel Regina, Paris, he read an article in the *New York Herald* featuring an account of his alleged misdemeanour, its headline bearing the words 'Grave Charge Lies against Sir H. MacDonald'. MacDonald returned to his room and shot himself with his service revolver. He was survived by a wife and son. The British government offered Lady MacDonald a state funeral but she declined. It was said that MacDonald was in poor health, suffering from dysentery and depression but he was the victim of spite, jealousy and slander. Today Hector MacDonald is remembered with pride in his hometown of Dingwall, whose people have seen fit to erect a statue to his memory.

The final phase of the Battle of Omdurman was something of an anticlimax. Kitchener had steeled himself for street fighting in Omdurman, expecting significant casualties; many had predicted there would be a final, bloody stand. The Dervishes had no stomach for further bloodshed however;

the entire force was scattered, the Khalifa being among those who escaped from the blood-soaked desert sands between the Kerreri Hills and Jebel Surgham. It was still only 11.30 in the morning. The flower of the Dervish army had been utterly destroyed. Surveying the battlefield through his glasses on the knoll of Jebel Surgham, Kitchener remarked that the enemy had been given a 'good dusting'. No doubt Wingate, at his side, agreed. On hearing heavy firing to his right, Kitchener blandly remarked, 'That'll be Mac[Donald].'

Wingate, ever vigilant, surveyed the battlefield from a knoll some 2,000 yards from the Khalifa's last position. He watched him withdraw with the remnants of his 60,000 warriors, leaving thousands of his tribesmen dead, dying and wounded on the desert floor. The allied cavalry chased after him, hoping to make contact and end the battle there but the Khalifa was determined to live on and fight another day.

As the infantry columns passed through the battlefield they must have been sickened at the carnage. Inert bodies lay in profusion and, as for the wounded survivors, it seemed as if an army of snails had crawled over the sand, leaving not trails of silver slime in their wake but blood. The Allied casualties were minimal, most being incurred during the charge of the 21st Lancers. Three British and two native officers were killed, with twenty-five British and eighteen native Other Ranks; the wounded amounted to 153 British and 281 Egyptian and Sudanese. The Khalifa's losses were appalling by any standard, not out of place in the later Great War; the butcher's bill was estimated as at least 11,000 dead and 16,000 wounded; there were 5,000 prisoners. The figure for the dead is an approximation, as many wounded Dervish crawled away to die undiscovered in rocky outcrops and dried-up watercourses.

An anonymous verse lamenting the Khalifa's defeat was circulated afterwards:

The woe which befell us has now befallen the ansar [helper]
English gunfire, and slaughter, and wretchedness.
The Sirdar [Kitchener] takes up his quarters in the Khalifa's courtyard.
Shayk al-Din is a prisoner, and Ya'Qub carries firewood.[13]

(This cannot have been written until after the Battle of Um Dibaykarat in November 1899, where Wingate defeated and killed the Khalifa and took Sheik al-Din prisoner.)

Later that day the Anglo-Egyptians entered Omdurman itself. The scene which greeted the soldiers was straight out of Dante's *Inferno* or the lurid paintings of Hieronymous Bosch. Battle-hardened troops vomited unashamedly as they searched the streets for the expected last-ditch defenders. Dead men, women and donkeys lay every few yards, victims of the previous day's bombardment. The last shots were fired on the Mahdi's massive tomb by 37 Battery, still operating from the east bank of the Nile. As the allied army entered the town, they were faced not with bullets, swords or spears but an unbearable stench of the unburied dead on that hot September afternoon. Captain D. W. Churcher, in command of a Maxim-gun battery, confessed he was nearly sick on several occasions that afternoon. Some minor street fighting did occur as the last few Dervishes still in the town sold their lives as dearly as they could, but by nightfall all resistance had ceased. The few European captives found in Omdurman included Karl Neufeld, the German trader who had been in captivity for several years. (In 1895, Wingate had attempted to rescue Neufeld on more than one occasion, but Neufeld never found it convenient to escape, possibly because he had taken one or two Dervish women as wives. Wingate recorded in his papers that the German 'was a bit of a humbug'. Neufeld did not like Rudolph von Slatin, his fellow captive and, of course, Slatin became Wingate's staunchest supporter in the Sudan. Perhaps this throws some light on Neufeld's subsequent behaviour towards Wingate who regarded him as a troublemaker right up to the outbreak of the Great War, when Neufeld was ordered to leave the Sudan as an undesirable alien.)

It is perhaps interesting that Neufeld wrote an account of his captivity with the Mahdists, *A Prisoner of the Khalifa* published in 1899. Neufeld's book was openly hostile to Slatin and challenged the latter's account *Fire and Sword in the Soudan*, casting doubts on the book's veracity. Neufeld suffered from a lack of prestige; Slatin was in the limelight, he was ignored.

We have a rare, endearing description of Kitchener, resting on his laurels – or, more prosaically, lying on his back in a makeshift army cot under the stars that night, dictating letters to Wingate for despatch to Lord Cromer and the Queen. Wingate, the faithful dog, lay at his feet on his stomach, writing down his Commander in Chief's words. It is said that, like Oliver Cromwell after the Battle of Dunbar in 1650, Kitchener thanked 'The Lord of Hosts for giving us victory'. Lieutenant Churchill of the 21st Lancers recalls this image when he visited Kitchener's HQ that night; he described the Sirdar as 'lying on his bed in well-deserved repose' while noting that Wingate was 'stretched out on the ground, busily writing by an uncertain light the telegrams announcing the victory'.[14] Wingate wrote to his wife Kitty a few days later, giving her an account of his part in the battle:

> I am thankful to say that I am quite fit and more thankful than I can say that all is over and that our victory has been so complete ... H. M. L. [his wife's brother Leslie Rundle] and I were practically together and we were well up in the front [of El Egiega] at the capture of the [Khalifa's] Black Flag. We afterwards celebrated it with a drink from your father's little flask which I had in my holster. On two occasions the Sirdar and Staff were nearly shot by our own men ... old Rowdy [Rudolf von Slatin] was most useful and behaved well throughout; he pursued with the cavalry in the hope of catching his old friend [the Khalifa] but failed ... I never saw the Dervishes fight better.[15]

On 4 September Kitchener himself entered Khartoum; in the midst of the ruins a memorial service was held for General Charles Gordon. Gordon's death had at last been avenged; it had taken fourteen years to accomplish but Kitchener could now sleep at night. It was tastefully done, with due Victorian pomp and circumstance, regimental bands playing music befitting the occasion. The pipes and drums of the Scottish regiments – 1st Seaforth and 1st Camerons – played appropriate laments. Salutes of guns were fired, cheers were ordered among the British, Egyptian and Sudanese troops. It was all very emotional and quintessentially Victorian. No one present that day would have dared question Gordon's earlier determination to remain in Khartoum, even though he could have evacuated and saved the lives of many of countrymen.

When the news of the victory at Omdurman reached Britain – well, England at least – the Queen was beside herself with joy. Overnight, Kitchener's name became a household word; he was toasted in every community up and down England. Not surprisingly, he was accorded every accolade, elevated by Victoria to Baron Kitchener of Khartoum. Thus the legend that was Kitchener was born; his reputation would last until his death by drowning in June 1916.

Like so many men of distinction, Kitchener had his detractors, even enemies, but after Omdurman he was the nation's darling. However, at least one voice of bitter acrimony was raised against him in England. Wilfred Scawen Blunt, poet, revolutionary, idealist, romantic and – perhaps most important of all – anti-imperialist and friend of nationalists throughout the British Empire in general and Ireland in particular, where he supported Home Rule, took issue with Kitchener's 'victory' at Omdurman. When Blunt read of the slaughter he was so shocked and sickened that he mounted a campaign against Kitchener, drawing attention to the brutal suppression of the Dervish people. Apart form the terrible loss of life, it was said that Kitchener had also desecrated the Mahdi's tomb; he was accused of ordering the tomb to be broken and the skeleton tossed into the Nile less its skull, which Kitchener intended to send to the Royal College of Surgeons in England. Victoria herself protested at this and the Mahdi's skull was subsequently buried at Wadi Halfa.

There are various versions of Kitchener's treatment of the Mahdi's remains. Some reported that Kitchener ordered young Major William 'Monkey' Gordon – nephew of his hero at Khartoum – to dig up the corpse. It was also said that Kitchener intended to use the Mahdi's skull as an inkwell or drinking-cup. These stories may be considered apocryphal, although there is never smoke without fire. Several of the Mahdi's fingernails were said to have been destined for White's Club in London. Kitchener put the blame for the controversy on 'Monkey' Gordon, probably justifying himself by reminding the British public that young Gordon was the nephew of the great man. A friend of the younger Gordon wrote a letter to the *Daily News* which printed Kitchener's version of the facts alongside Gordon's account, the article being

entitled *The True Story*. Whatever the truth of the matter, Kitchener's reputation remained intact; in the eyes of the British public he had become little
short of a god.

It is perhaps otiose to dwell on the final facts of the desecration of the
Mahdi's tomb by Kitchener. However, Kitchener allegedly wrote to the
Queen, admitting that the Mahdi's remains had indeed been exhumed and
dumped into the Nile and that some 'waggish' officers under his command
had suggested he make an inkpot out of the holy man's skull. There was
some justification for Kitchener's actions, insensitive though they may have
been. He did not want the tomb to become another Mecca for pilgrimages
by fanatical Muslims. The tomb at Omdurman has since been restored to
its former glory. Modern Sudanese consider Kitchener a butcher, although
Charles Gordon enjoys something approaching a reputation of sainthood.
Such are the vagaries of history.

The campaign over, Kitchener set himself the task of tending for the
Dervish wounded. Hospitals were hastily erected but tended only a small
percentage of the enemy. Many were left to die on the battlefield or at the
hands of looters. Kitchener did not personally supervise the scant humanitarian effort as he was more interested in restoring Khartoum to its former
glory – if indeed Khartoum had ever been a glorious Sudanese town. He
wasted little time mourning. He began to make elaborate plans to rebuild
Khartoum which would include the creation of the Gordon Memorial
College. He set in motion a scheme for public subscription for the College,
money which would be readily made available by an adoring British public.
Just as the century had begun with tributes to Lord Nelson for his victory at
Trafalgar in 1805, it would go out on a high note with Kitchener's victory –
even if the two events bear little comparison. In making his preparations for
the reconstruction of Khartoum, Kitchener would put Wingate's considerable
talents to another use. In January 1899 he ordered Wingate to 'loot like blazes.
I want any quantity of marble stairs, marble paving, iron railings, looking
glasses and fittings of all sorts'.[16] This may have seemed strange to Wingate
at the time, for he knew how his Commander in Chief spurned ostentation
in his own personal life. However, nothing was too good where Gordon's
memory was concerned.

Immediately after Omdurman, Kitchener was faced with another poten-
tially more serious problem. On 5 September Wingate was busily engaged in
writing intelligence and situation reports when a steamer flying Dervish flags
arrived from the south. The captain had not learnt of the Khalifa's defeat at
Omdurman and immediately surrendered. Under questioning he informed
Wingate that he had been ordered south on a raiding mission; arriving at
Fashoda, he had been attacked by black troops commanded by white officers.
The captain described them simply as 'Turks'; Wingate was anxious to deter-
mine the type of flag flying over the fort at Fashoda. According to his account
written forty years later, he claimed to have handed the Dervish his riding

crop and asked him to draw the flag in the sand. The man supposedly drew the French *tricolour* although later historians have disputed this.

Wingate, with his intelligence network and in the knowledge that the French were in the vicinity, was able to work it out for himself. He immediately informed Kitchener who already knew the unidentified force must be that of the French expedition led by Commandant Jean-Baptiste Marchand with a contingent of Senegalese troops.

Kitchener was carrying sealed orders from Lord Salisbury with instructions on how to treat the French in the event of their occupying the Upper Nile Valley. He had sewn the orders in the lining of his jacket for safekeeping. Verbal instructions from Lord Cromer had been both clear and obscure. His and Salisbury's were clear insofar as Kitchener's orders were that he should inform the French they were trespassing on territory which belonged to the Khedive of Egypt. However, both statesmen were vague as to how each should act if the French refused to leave. Kitchener at once ordered a flotilla of five gunboats to steam up and proceed upriver to Fashoda, taking two Sudanese battalions and a company of Cameron Highlanders with Maxims and artillery. On 10 September the flotilla disembarked, Kitchener and Wingate travelling aboard the steamship *Dal*.

Marchand's mission had begun in French Equatorial Africa in March 1897; it took him over a year to reach Fashoda. He had arrived on 10 June and taken possession of its ruined fort. It seemed Kitchener might have another fight on his hands, one which could have international consequences. Military action could even have led to all-out war between Britain and France. He would have to employ what diplomatic skills he possessed to defuse the situation.

On 18 September Wingate drafted a letter for Kitchener to send to Commandant Marchand, informing him of the Anglo-Egyptian victory at Omdurman and Kitchener's imminent arrival in Fashoda. Resting at Kaka, a village about fifty miles north of Fashoda, Kitchener was preoccupied with his next move, acutely aware of the delicate situation. He also knew that at the time, French prestige was low, the nation still suffering from the ignominious defeat inflicted by the Prussians in the Franco-Prussian war of 1870–71. France needed to regain confidence in Europe and in Africa; occupation of the Upper Nile Valley would be a *coup* as well as countering British expansionism in North Africa. For his part, Marchand, an over-exuberant nationalist, behaved as if he were acting in a comic opera; the Fashoda incident contained more than a whiff of farce, although, at the time, there was a real danger of war breaking out between two great European nations.

Kitchener was decidedly weak in the field of diplomacy, given his temperament and character. At Fashoda he must have felt extremely uncomfortable. Yet he rose to the challenge; his subsequent handling of the affair bore testament to his discretion and caution. Perhaps his recent victory had taught him a few lessons and he had Wingate, a skilled negotiator, at his side to advise him. Aware that he could have easily defeated Marchand and his small force, Kitchener could afford to be magnanimous. In his first official contact with Marchand, he congratulated him on having brought his expedition safely through a hostile part of the continent. Appealing to an opponent's vanity rarely fails to bring results. Then he announced his decisive victory at Omdurman, that he had reclaimed the Sudan and that he had come to Fashoda to re-establish the Khedive of Egypt's authority there as elsewhere in the Sudan. Marchand could hardly take offence at these announcements.

On the morning of 19 September Kitchener and Wingate stood on the upper deck of the *Dal*, supported by the gunboats *Sultan*, *Fateh* and *Nasr*. Kitchener wore the uniform of the Egyptian Army, a diplomatic touch possibly suggested by Wingate. He and Wingate saw the French flag fluttering over the fort at Fashoda. Kitchener invited Marchand and his second-in-command to join him and Wingate on the *Dal*. Awaiting a response, they saw a small craft flying the *tricolour* making for them. As it hove to, they saw it bore a Senegalese non-commissioned officer – a deliberate insult to Kitchener – who handed the Sirdar a reply from Marchand, styling himself High Commissioner, but of where? Kitchener's response was to order the gunboats to train their guns on the French fort. It was stalemate ...

After a few anxious hours, Kitchener received Marchand and his aide on board his steamer; the ensuing conversation was friendly, if strained. Fortunately, both men took to each other immediately. The Englishman said he was bearing orders to the effect that French presence in Fashoda was a violation of the rights of Egypt and her protecting power, Britain. The Upper Nile was not undisputed territory as the French appeared to have assumed. For his part, the Frenchman informed Kitchener of his orders, which were to occupy Fashoda; he informed Kitchener that he would have to await further orders from his government before he could give answer. At no time did the two men lose their tempers, probably because both were aware of the extremely delicate nature of the situation. Then Marchand stated bluntly that he was prepared to die where he stood, as French military honour demanded. Even at the height of the tension, the two men toasted each other's health, while the Diplomatic Corps in Whitehall and Paris exchanged a flurry of telegrams and attended hastily arranged meetings. The Fashoda incident was assuming alarming proportions, with possible war looming.

In the British camp there was only one difference of opinion between Kitchener and Wingate in the proceedings. Kitchener wanted to fly the British flag beside that of Egypt when he arrived in Fashoda. Wingate rightly argued that it might ease the tension and encourage more relaxed negotiations if the flag of Egypt alone was flown. After a brief argument, Kitchener conceded to Wingate's better judgement: 'Damn it, have it your own way.'

As we have seen, French prestige was at an all-time low, not simply because of their defeat in the recent Franco-Prussian war. The French government and the establishment had been rocked by the famous – or infamous – scandal of the Dreyfus Affair. Alfred Dreyfus, a Captain of artillery and staff officer in the French High Command, was a Jew who had been arrested in 1894 for allegedly passing military secrets to a foreign power, thought to be Germany. After a secret court-martial, Dreyfus was convicted of treason and sent in 1895 to Devil's Island, Cayenne, to serve a life imprisonment. His case became a *cause celebre*, defended by the influential writer Emile Zola who, in his open letter *J'Accuse* to the French newspaper *Aurore*, made serious charges against the French General Staff and the government itself. It was subsequently discovered that Dreyfus had been framed and the court-martial illegal; the real traitor was another officer by the name of Ferdinand Esterhazy. Dreyfus was acquitted and re-instated in the French Army in 1899. One is tempted to the view that Fashoda was little more than a publicity stunt to rescue the besmirched reputation of the most powerful institution in France – the Army.

Kitchener knew of these events and of the low esteem the French army was held in at home. He assured Marchand that the French government could not in all conscience support him under any existing international law. Matters dragged on until 4 December 1898, when Marchand finally accepted the inevitable. France declared publicly and internationally that she had no ambitions in the Upper Nile Valley and that Marchand would be recalled. The Fashoda Incident became but one of many diplomatic episodes in the 'Scramble for Africa' during the late nineteenth century.

Kitchener and Wingate returned to Omdurman on 24 September 1898. Awaiting Wingate was a telegram from General Sir Francis Grenfell, the former Sirdar, conveying the Queen's hope that Colonel Wingate and Rudolf von Slatin were both safe. Wingate met up with Slatin; leaving Leslie Rundle in charge of intelligence at Omdurman, the two friends travelled to Cairo, where they and Kitchener were feted on 6 October. Wingate was made a Pasha of Egypt and Adjutant General of the Egyptian Army. Kitchener left for England on 17 October, arriving to a tumultuous reception in London from jingoistic crowds, delighted that, at last, Charles Gordon had been avenged. In Cairo Wingate was left to prepare a new budget for the Sudan, no doubt at the request of Lord Cromer. In London the shy Kitchener had to attend a dinner in the Mansion House at which he launched an appeal for funds for the Gordon Memorial College in Khartoum. His personal reward for Omdurman was to be elevated to the peerage; Wingate was made a Knight Commander of St Michael and St George.

The position in Egypt was that Britain was now virtually in control. Both countries had made significant financial contributions to the re-conquest of the Sudan, although two-thirds of the money came from the Egyptian Treasury. Who would reign supreme there? Lord Cromer, the inveterate economist, came up with a solution; a Condominium agreement which would oversee the finances of Egypt (and, by extension, the Sudan) and would be controlled by Britain and Egypt. The Khedive and the Queen would jointly rule the Sudan, with British and Egyptian flags flying side by side. The supreme military and administrative command would be vested in a

Governor General appointed by the Khedive but nominated by the British government. Cromer's agreement was signed on 19 January 1899.

Perhaps due to a combination of stress, hard work and exhaustion, Wingate fell ill at this stage, suffering from influenza or pneumonia – or perhaps both – and was sent home to England at the end of April to recuperate. In that year he spent his first summer in Dunbar, East Lothian, rejoining Kitchener in Khartoum in August. The Khalifa was still at large with a force of about 10,000; as long as he lived Anglo-Egyptian rule in the Sudan would be threatened. Kitchener had unsuccessfully attempted to capture him about seventy miles from Fashoda. In November Wingate was ordered to lead a flying column of 2,000 men and some artillery pieces. His small force inflicted a minor defeat on the Dervishes on 23 November, although the Khalifa was still free somewhere in Kordofan Province, west of the Nile. Wingate was determined to track him down and capture if not kill him.

On 23 November, Slatin wrote to Wingate from Vienna:

> My Dear Old Francis,
> It is an age that I had not a line from you, but you are so busy defeating the Dervishes and you have undoubtedly still your large correspondence well-known to me. My heartfelt congratulations to [sic] your splendid success against Ahmad Fasil [Fedil] ... I am fit and fat and still a bachelor.
> Yours affec.
> Old Rowdy.[17]

Slatin must have been studying *Reuters News*. Cromer in Cairo received a telegram on the same day. Slatin had written:

> Wingate found Nefissa [Drefissa] evacuated and pushed on to Abu Aadil ... when Ahmed Fedil's [?force] was found encamped. They were at once engaged by mounted troops under [Lieutenant Colonel] Mahon with four Maxims, two guns and Jehadia [native troops] under [Major] Gorringe. The Dervishes charged with all their own dash to within 80 yards of the guns. Wingate arrived with infantry in time to support Mahon and cleared the whole Dem. [?] The Dervishes bolted through the bush followed by mounted troops. Wingate estimates Fedil's force to have been 2,500, of whom 400 have been killed. He has also taken a considerable number of prisoners, quantity of grain, rifles, spears etc.[18]

Wingate's casualties were one dead and two wounded.

A few days later, Wingate achieved even greater success at Um Dibaykarat. This was the sole occasion when he held an independent command during his Army service. Wingate later admitted that it was luck rather than design which brought him to the Khalifa's zariba. It was yet another massacre. In the brief and unequal fight, a thousand Dervishes were killed and 9,400 men, women and children surrendered. The ever-elusive Osman Digna managed to escape yet again. Wingate's losses were negligible; four killed and twenty-nine wounded. Only native troops were engaged in the action – the 9th and 13th Sudanese Battalions – with the Camel Corps, cavalry and 'Friendly' cavalry. There was no gloating in Wingate's report of the defeat. As he afterwards wrote:

> The way the whole of the Dervishes fell into our hands makes one feel, as the Arabs say, that their day had come and that it was arranged by Higher Powers than us poor mortals.[19]

From contemporary newspaper clippings held in the Sudan Archive Department of Durham University, it is reported that Wingate attacked at dawn.

In the closing stages of the action, the Khalifa led from the front. Here is Wingate again:

> Seeing his followers retiring, he made an ineffectual attempt to rally them, but recognizing that the day was lost he had called on his Emirs to dismount from their horses and seating himself on his *firwa* or sheepskin – as is the custom of Arab chiefs who disdain surrender – he had placed Ali Wad Helu on his right and Ahmed Fadel on his left, whilst the remaining Emirs seated themselves round him ... and in this position they had unflinchingly met their death [sic].[20]

The Khalifa had met his end at the hands of the advancing 9th Sudanese, facing Mecca, as every Muslim should. Among the dead lying beside him were Khalifa Ali Wad Helu who had fought at Omdurman, Emirs Ahmad Fedil and the Khalifa's two brothers. The Khalifa's son, Osman Shayk al-Din was taken prisoner. In England, Wingate's son Ronald, attending Hillbrow School, near Rugby, recounted that, in the November of his first year there, the headmaster interrupted a school concert to announce that Wingate Senior had defeated and killed the Khalifa. No doubt the young lad was ecstatic and cheered by his schoolmates.[21]

As for Wingate himself, flushed with success, he allowed exhilaration to go to his head. In response to Cromer's congratulatory telegram from Cairo, he replied that 'Mahdism received its *coup de grace* ... I hope a new era will now open for the unfortunate Sudanese people.'[22] To his wife he wrote more ecstatically, 'Hurrah Mahdism finished am returning at once, best love.'[23] These were understandably emotive responses written not by a conquering hero but a man who was relieved that a long ordeal was finally at an end. A year later, when Cromer visited the Sudan in December 1900, Wingate, as proleptic Governor General and Sirdar spoke of his ambition to introduce a form of administration which would 'show the inhabitants that a new and brighter future dawned for them when Mahdism received its deathblow'. These fine words were in accord with personal ambition but they were not enough in themselves to extinguish Wingate's haunting fear of future political instability in the Sudan.

There is a bizarre postscript to Wingate's victory which is contained in his archive. The newspaper *Union Conservadoro* in the Canary Isles reported the following:

Colonel Wingate with a body of native troops utterly defeated a strong British [sic] Column commanded by Abaed Fidil, killing 400 British soldiers and taking 300 prisoners. The news of this defeat has been badly received, and has much aggravated the situation in England ...

The sender of the clipping which is dated 6 December 1899 has written in the margin 'Good gracious! How awful of you!'. Perhaps the reporter had had a more than usually convivial (liquid) lunch when he wrote the piece and was conforming to Kitchener's low regard for journalists!

There is another equally bizarre postscript to Wingate's final encounter with the Dervishes. The story appeared on television during the 1990s. During the course of a travelogue on the Sudan describing how Thomas Cook had pioneered the tourist trade after arranging the transport for the doomed Khartoum expedition in 1884, a retired Army officer holidaying in Egypt was interviewed. He had the following story to tell. In describing the origins of Thomas Cook, he mentioned Wingate of Dunbar. It transpired that the officer had begun his army career in the 165th Officer Cadet Training Unit (OCTU) at Castlepark Barracks, Dunbar during the Second World War. The officer said that his Commanding Officer had been asked to select a number of young cadets to meet Wingate at Knockenhair on the latter's invitation for sherry. The cadets were duly briefed about the Grand Old Man's military and colonial career and were suitably impressed when they met Wingate that evening. During sherry, Wingate noticed one cadet studying what was clearly a trepanned skull in the drinks cabinet; he commented on it and the odd silver cup that had been inserted in the hollow. Wingate asked him if he would like to study it closer and removed it from the cabinet, casually informing the young man that the skull was that of a Dervish chief whom he had pursued through the Nile marshes after the Battle of Omdurman. Whether or not there is any truth in this story is difficult to prove; however, Wingate assured the young man that he was in the habit of drinking his claret from the grisly receptacle on the annual anniversary of the Khalifa's death! Perhaps he was indulging in a bit of leg-pulling or a put-down of young idealistic warriors about to go off to fight their own war.[24]

Another example of *Grand Guignol* which emerged in Wingate's later years was a photograph he had taken of the dead Khalifa and his Emirs in November 1899; he kept it until 1927, when he gave it to his cousin Orde on the latter's visit to Dunbar before embarking for the Sudan. The story goes that Orde Wingate showed it to one of the native soldiers under his command in the Sudan Defence Force in 1928. Apparently, he did this in an attempt to befriend the young soldier who seemed somewhat aloof from the rest of his battalion. Orde described him as tall, erect and almost regal. Trying to thaw him out, he showed him Rex Wingate's photograph of the dead Khalifa. The ruse tragically misfired; the young man was shocked, saying 'I am the Caliph's [Khalifa's] youngest son'.[25]

At last, the might of the Dervishes had been finally vanquished. Wingate, the conquering hero, returned to Cairo on 1 December to learn of his baby daughter's birth on the very day of the Khalifa's death. He was pleased that the Queen indicated a wish to sponsor the little girl; she was christened Victoria Alexandrina Catherine, although during her lifetime she was known as Catherine.

Now events were changing fast; the hierarchy in Egypt was altered by the outbreak of the Second Boer War. Kitchener was transferred to South Africa to take up appointment as Lord Roberts' ('Bobs') Chief of Staff on 21 December 1899. Wingate was knighted and, on 22 December, was appointed as Kitchener's successor as Sirdar of the Egyptian Army and Governor General of the Sudan – who else was qualified to assume these responsibilities? One of his proudest moments in these roles was to accompany Kitchener to Khartoum to attend the inauguration of the Gordon Memorial College in 1902.

What was the butcher's bill in money and human life for the re-conquest of the Sudan? Some 1,500 Egyptian and British lives had been lost. The campaign had cost £2.5 million, half of which had been expended on Kitchener's railway from Wadi Halfa to Berber. A good deal of the remainder was spent on the rebuilding of Khartoum, whose streets were laid out in the pattern of the Union Flag. It is pure speculation on the author's part that Wingate would have preferred to take the Khalifa alive so that he could question him. No matter. Wingate was spared the need to attend a formal trial, which would have undoubtedly resulted in the Khalifa's probable subsequent imprisonment or even execution. Nor would Britain be faced with yet another martyr to spark off future rebellions in the Sudan. Wingate must surely have breathed a sigh of relief.

A postscript to the campaign story is that the elusive Osman Digna – Sheik al-Din – was finally captured in 1900 by the Anglo-Egyptian army; he spent the next eight years in captivity until released and allowed to live at Wadi Halfa. He died in 1926, aged about eighty-six.

The last surviving soldier of the campaign, Regimental Sergeant Major James Richard ('Paddy') Miles who had fought at Omdurman, serving as a rifleman in the 2nd Battalion Rifle Brigade, died at Weymouth on 20 January 1977. His last recorded comment on the epic battle was simple, delivered to an officer of his old regiment, 'If you will pardon the expression sir [it was] bloody hot.'[26] Thus the re-conquest of the Sudan was finally achieved. For Wingate, at the end of 1899, it proved to be the beginning of a new and fulfilling career, as we shall presently see.

Notes

1. *Slatin Pasha*, Hill.
2. *Cromer in Egypt*, Marlowe.

3. *Ibid.*
4. *Slatin Pasha.*
5. *A Good Dusting*, Keown-Boyd.
6. *Sirdar and Khalifa*, Burleigh.
7. Kitchener's despatch dated 10 April 1898 to Sir Francis Grenfell, Major General commanding in Egypt: 'My thanks are due to Brevet Colonel Wingate, and the intelligence staff under him, who kept me fully informed' (Quoted in *Sirdar and Khalifa*, Burleigh).
8. Diary entry, 23 January 1898, WP 102/1, SAD, DU.
9. Wingate to his wife, 15 May 1898, WP 233/5, SAD, DU.
10. *A Soldier's Hero: The Life of General Sir Archibald Hunter*, Doolittle.
11. *Between Two Flags*, Brooke-Shephard.
12. *The River War*, Churchill.
13. *A History of the Sudan*, Holt and Daly; translated by S. Hillelson.
14. *The River War.*
15. Wingate to his wife, 6 September 1898, WP 233/5, SAD, DU.
16. *Wingate of the Sudan*, RELW.
17. Slatin to Wingate, 23 November 1899, WP 269/11, SAD, DU.
18. FO to Cromer, 23 November 1899, WP 269/11, SAD, DU.
19. Sudan Government Archives, National Records Office, Khartoum; letter from Wingate to Kitchener, 25 November 1899 quoted in *The Sirdar*, Daly.
20. WP 269/11, SAD, DU.
21. *Not in the Limelight*, RELW.
22. Wingate to Cromer, 24 November 1899, WP 269/11, SAD, DU.
23. Wingate to Lady Wingate, 24 November 1899, WP 269/11, SAD, DU.
24. Henry Keown-Boyd's recent book *A Good Dusting*, discounts this story, arguing that it would not have been in character for Wingate to sully the memory of a worthy adversary. He maintains the story is false or that it was confused with the desecration of the Mahdi's tomb in Omdurman, a grisly deed for which Kitchener was blamed. Be that as it may, the author personally witnessed a television documentary containing a story recounted by a former British Army officer who served in the 165th Officer Cadet Training Unit at Castlepark Barracks at Dunbar in the 1940s. The man confirmed that the skull was on display in Wingate's drinks cabinet at Knockenhair.
25. *Orde Wingate, the Official Biography*, Sykes.
26. *A Good Dusting.*

Chapter 4

Governor General and Sirdar (1899–1917)

Thus the Sudan was again brought under Anglo-Egyptian control. Its recovery would have one unforeseen consequence – a boost to the aspirations of Egyptian nationalists seeking independence from Britain over the subsequent two decades. In 1899 the astute Lord Cromer brokered the Condominium, an agreement purportedly described in Whitehall as 'the only constitution this hybrid government [of Egypt] would ever have'. Under the Condominium Act, Egypt and Britain were nominally given joint responsibility for the administration of the Sudan but, in effect, it became a British possession in all but name.

In the eyes of Queen Victoria and the British public, Baron Kitchener of Khartoum and Aspall was perceived as a hero – much to his acute embarrassment. In 1899 he simply wanted to knuckle down to the business of rebuilding Khartoum, a town in ruins, then to establish stable, effective government in the Sudan. He and Wingate had often discussed plans for the future; both men saw that the first priorities were to restore the confidence and well-being of the indigenous population and lay the foundations for a sound economy. The advent of the Boer War abruptly ended Kitchener's appointment as Governor General of the Sudan, a position which Wingate would fill with distinction. In December 1899 Kitchener was transferred to South Africa where he became Lord Roberts' Chief of Staff, and Commander in Chief of the British forces in November 1900, when Roberts resigned. In October 1899 Wingate was officially appointed Governor General of the Sudan and Sirdar of the Egyptian Army. Wingate's brother-in-law, Major General Leslie Rundle, was also posted to South Africa, no doubt on account of his having served as Kitchener's Chief of Staff during the Sudan campaign.

Before proceeding to examine Wingate's stewardship of the Sudan over the ensuing eighteen years, we should examine the state of the country at the close of 1899. The terrain amounted to roughly 1,000,000 square miles of mainly desert, scrub and yellow grass, with swamps and uncharted areas to the south and west. In the north-west was the province of Darfur, an area which today has problems of political unrest, famine and disease. The south-west was inhabited by black Africans as yet uncontacted by Europeans. The economy was in ruins, exhausted by the depredations of the Mahdi and the Khalifa. Prior to the Mahdi's rebellion, the population had numbered about 8,000,000; by 1899 it had shrunk to just under 2,000,000 inhabitants. The people were predominantly nomadic, although certain areas close to the Nile and the Egyptian border were permanently settled, agriculture being the main source of subsistence. The population was almost exclusively Muslim, a mixture of Arabs and black Africans. The recent rebellion had resulted in the destruction of many settled towns and villages, particularly those inhabited by tribes hostile to the Mahdi and his followers. Cultivated areas were sparse and distant from each other; the main exports were gum-arabic – used in the finishing and dressing of fabrics and thickening the colours of calico, in pharmacy, in ink production and making crayons – maize, millet and cotton. The capital, Khartoum, was a deserted ruin and nearby Omdurman was a town of stinking, fetid hovels where disease was rife.

When Wingate first arrived in the Sudan, the country was a backwater ripe for economic development. During his stewardship as Governor General, the relationship between ruler and ruled, capital and labour would be reworked. Wingate saw that the Sudan was a melting-pot, ready for improvement; with his fluency in Arabic, his understanding of and respect for its people, he believed he could better the lot of the Sudanese people, seeing further into the future than many of his contemporaries.

The Sudan posed what must have seemed an insurmountable task for the newly-appointed Governor General but Wingate did not shrink from the task. A devout Episcopalian, imbued with the Protestant, Presbyterian belief in the work ethic, Wingate was more than equal to the job. In theory, he was responsible to Abbas Hilmi, the Khedive of Egypt and his Council of Ministers; in practice, his masters were the British Cabinet and the Foreign Office through Lord Cromer, the Controller General in Cairo. As Sirdar, Wingate was answerable to the Egyptian Minister of War and the Khedive, again in theory. Even in this role the War Office in London still exerted influence over him. The cost of administering the Sudan was entirely borne by the Egyptian government; this included defence and capital investment in public works. The sole financial contribution made by the British Treasury was the upkeep of a single battalion of British troops stationed at Khartoum.

Wingate's staff in Khartoum were predominantly British, with a sprinkling of Egyptians, Syrians and, later, Sudanese. One of his most notable and invaluable British assistants was Edgar Bonham Carter (1870–1956) – later Sir Edgar Bonham Carter – who served Wingate well for fifteen years. At the age of twenty-nine, Bonham Carter was appointed by Cromer with express instructions to devise, implement and administer a system of civil and criminal law in the Sudan where, before 1899, no formal legal system had existed. Related to Florence Nightingale, the 'Lady of the Lamp' in the Crimean conflict of almost a half century earlier, Bonham Carter became judicial adviser and legal secretary to Wingate.

Wingate's superior, Evelyn Baring, now Viscount Cromer (1841–1917) had entered the British Army as a young officer in the Royal Artillery in 1858, a beginning he shared with Wingate. Appointed Commissioner of Public Debt in Egypt in 1877, two years later he became Consul General in Egypt. Noted for his financial acumen (he was nicknamed 'Over-bearing' and 'Evelyn the First'), Cromer rescued Egypt's parlous financial state from a succession of profligate Khedives. When he retired from public service in 1907 he left Egypt in a prosperous condition. A powerful figure, he would drive in an open carriage through the Cairo streets to the Khedival Palace, preceded by a mounted escort which cleared a path through the crowds. He was king in all but name; his name was on the lips of every British and Egyptian politician and official. European and British visitors wintering in Egypt returned home with glowing accounts of his efficient administration. It is interesting to note that despite the close association between Kitchener and Wingate, the former recommended General Sir Archibald Hunter as his replacement as Governor General in the Sudan in 1899 but Cromer overruled him, preferring Wingate as the man for the job. Lord Edward Cecil described Hunter, a Scot of whom it was said Kitchener was afraid, as 'a real live Cromwellian, brutal, cruel, licentious, religious, brave, able, blunt and cunning'. Cromer shared Cecil's view. Despite his blinkered banker's outlook, Cromer was a good judge of character; he knew that Hunter, as Governor General of the Sudan, would have been an aggressive dictator, ruthlessly suppressing the population. Hunter, some soldiers' hero at Omdurman, completely lacked Wingate's velvet touch which Cromer rightly believed would win the confidence of the Sudanese people.

Almost immediately after appointment Wingate was faced with a crisis. Word was put about in Egypt that following a series of humiliating defeats inflicted on the British Army by the Boers – Black Week in December 1899 – Sudanese troops would be sent to reinforce the British in South Africa. Unrest in the 14th Sudanese Battalion, officered by Egyptians and stationed in Omdurman, was triggered in January 1900. Wingate's tactful handling of the situation prevented a widespread mutiny in the Sudanese and Egyptian Army. The Egyptian officer class in the Sudan contained nationalists intent on turning the Sudanese against the British with a view to expelling them from the country. In the course of the mutiny, the 14th Sudanese and its associated battalion were ordered to surrender their ammunition to Colonel Maxwell, then serving as Governor of Omdurman. Maxwell had received an anonymous letter threatening his life, so he acted quickly to defuse a volatile situation. Wingate reassured the soldiers that the rumour of their impending transfer to South Africa was false. One of the two battalions handed in their ammunition; the second refused to do so. Wingate came up with a clever – if not entirely honest – ploy to defuse the situation; he invited any officer with a grievance to appear before him and state it. Those who did so were arrested; in the ensuing courts-martial, several officers were dismissed from the army.

Wingate's achievements in the Sudan are well documented but, at this juncture, we should attempt to understand the nature of the man, something which has never been satisfactorily explored. We know from his son Ronald that he was a happily married man possessed by a high moral sense who attended church twice every Sunday.[1] At Knockenhair, his mansion in Dunbar, prayers were said every day before breakfast. Ronald Wingate, who wrote *Wingate of the Sudan*, admits in his second book, *Not in the Limelight*, that he knew little of his father than what he saw during his childhood years. His first book was more a history of the Sudan during his father's time than a biography. In the later book he candidly admits that he rarely saw his father until visiting him in Dunbar in 1919 and 1938, then not again until 1946, on his demobilization from military service.

Little is known of the young Reginald; we know more about the man after his marriage to Kitty Rundle, a marriage made in heaven. Their love was spontaneous and, to a great extent, their marriage escaped the colonial constraints endured by many wives of officials in the service of the Empire who were virtually subservient to queen and country. When she married, Kitty Rundle was aware that she would live the life of a woman separated from her husband for long periods.

In Cairo the Wingates were fortunate to be blessed with the presence of their children,[2] the first of whom was Ronald Evelyn Leslie, then Malcolm Roy and finally Victoria Alexandrina Catherine. Another son, George Andrew Leslie, had been born in 1892, between Malcolm and Catherine, but died at two weeks of age. Ronald Wingate describes two early memories of his father in Cairo.[3] Wingate Senior pomaded his stiff, bristly moustache and wore a dark blue uniform and red *tarboosh* or fez which he detested, conscious of the fact that such headwear could (and did) look ridiculous on a squat, stout little man. Ronald also recounts how he and brother Malcolm watched their father playing tennis and golf at the Gezira Sporting Club in Cairo. Wingate was instrumental in creating the nine-hole golf course at Gezira, inviting James Hastie, a young assistant at Dunbar Golf Club, to become the Cairo Golf Club professional, instructing Wingate's friends in the ancient and honourable game.

An early photograph of the Wingates taken in Dunbar in 1899 shows baby Victoria sitting on her mother's lap; Wingate is seated to her left, Malcolm Roy is seated to her right, wearing the awful boots so beloved of middle and upper class Victorian families for their male offspring. Standing behind Malcolm is his brother Ronald; behind Ronald is Rudolph Slatin, with a Sudanese servant and an unknown man, possibly a local dignitary.

Dunbar had been recommended to Wingate by Sir Arthur Bigge, Queen Victoria's Private Secretary, not only as a healthy seaside resort but for its excellent golf course. Bigge had spent holidays in Dunbar, enjoying his favourite pastime on the East Links. In 1899 Wingate and his family spent their first summer in Kerridge's (now the New Bayswell) Hotel in the up-market West End of Dunbar. The Wingates spent the following four summers in one or two of the many local boarding houses. Then, between 1904 and 1908, Wingate rented the prestigious Stafford House overlooking Bayswell Shore, about 100 yards away from Kerridge's. Although he spent most of the year in the Middle East, he rented Stafford House at Christmas and Easter when his children were on holiday from boarding school.

During their school years the Wingate boys toured the Sudan in the company of Lord Kitchener and Rudolf von Slatin. They shot sand grouse[4] in the desert and were taken by their father to view the Sphinx and pyramids outside Cairo at Gezira. In *Not in the Limelight*, Ronald Wingate writes that he and brother Malcolm were fortunate to live with their parents in Cairo, where they were educated by their mother, then by a succession of governesses, until they were sent to preparatory and boarding schools in England. By modern standards, Lady Wingate was very strict in their upbringing but the Wingate children had a happy childhood, despite the discipline. The boys enjoyed themselves in Cairo and loved their two pet donkeys, Firket and Toski, named after battles in which their father had played a part during the re-conquest of the Sudan.[5]

Again, in *Not in the Limelight*, Ronald Wingate vividly describes his early memories of Lord and Lady Cromer's sumptuous balls and children's parties at the Cairo Residency. In his opinion, the Cromers' New Year fancy dress party was the major event of the year. British and other European diplomats and anyone who was anyone in Cairo society attended the Cromers' New Year ball. On one occasion, Cromer arranged for the officers of a Scottish regiment stationed in Cairo to give a demonstration of Highland reel dancing before the guests went in to supper. The event was not an unqualified success. One of the guests, Monsieur Maskens, the Belgian Consul, accompanied by his young daughter, took exception to the display. The young officers wore the kilt in the true tradition of Scotsmen, whirling about like the Dervishes the Anglo-Egyptian army had recently conquered. Monsieur Maskens was so affronted by the spectacle of half-naked – from the waist down – Scottish manhood that he removed himself and his daughter during the proceedings. The sight of Scottish nether region flesh was too much for the puritanical Belgian, though it was said that Mademoiselle Maskens was taken home very much against her wishes![6]

During Wingate's years as Governor General in the Sudan, when he was joined permanently by his wife, he arranged for a summer residence to be built near Khartoum, a hill station where he and his family could spend the hottest months of the Sudanese year. Wingate, or rather his wife, located an ideal spot at Erkowit in the Red Sea Hills, a convenient vantage point for observing the important sea port of Suakin. The Wingates' house at Erkowit was known as 'Kitty's Leap' in honour of Lady Wingate.[7] (Kitty Wingate did not actually 'leap'; she simply walked to the promontory, declaring the view splendid.)

With its mild climate, Erkowit was ideal, even if in November and December it was shrouded in a mist the natives called a *shabura*. The station was suitable for growing pomegranates, grapes and most European vegetables, although the date palms had been cut down by Osman Digna during the Mahdist rebellion.

Vacations at Erkowit were a pleasant escape from the almost unbearable heat of Khartoum, but it is equally certain that the Wingates always looked forward to their Dunbar holidays. In 1899 a local newspaper reported the Wingate family holiday at Kerridge's Hotel.[8] The article was to be the first of many recording Wingate's visits to the town. Ronald Wingate recalls that his family spent the summer of 1900 in a 'seafront hotel'[9] which was almost certainly the same establishment. Reginald Wingate's cousin Captain George Miller Wingate may have been the first of the family to visit Dunbar as he took the tenancy of Number Eleven, Marine Road in 1900.[10,11] George Wingate would not own a permanent residence there until 1905 which is confirmed by a local newspaper account of his purchase of land adjacent to Number Eleven, a vacant lot then owned by the Forest Land Committee. (In 1905, Captain Wingate asked the local Dean of Guild[12] to alter the road fronting his new property, which he had decided to call 'Craigengelt' for the Stirlingshire village where the Scottish branch of the Wingates had lived for at least two centuries, owning land there.) Captain Wingate was still in possession of the property in 1910–11.[13,14] The house must have been built by 1905 as, in that year, the same local newspaper announced the forthcoming marriage of Captain Wingate's eldest daughter Agnese, living at Craigengelt, to Captain A. P. Liston-Foulis of the South-East Scottish Royal Field Artillery.[15] The couple were married in St Anne's Episcopalian Church, Dunbar, on 31 October 1907 and were presented with a gift of a silver rose bowl by the local Traders' Association. (In 1920 Craigengelt House passed to the Craig family[16] who subsequently converted it into a fine hotel; many local people erroneously believed the hotel was named for Tom and Emily Craig. Today, the building is still a hotel, known as The Rocks for the fine view it has of the approach to Dunbar Harbour.)

The family spent at least two summers at Kerridge's and, according to Ronald Wingate, others at modest Dunbar boarding houses until 1904, when Wingate first rented Stafford House; the family resided there in the summers of 1904 to 1906. However, in 1907, Wingate was unable to rent Stafford House. Disappointed, he resolved to build his own permanent residence in the town. During the years he managed to rent Stafford House, Wingate arranged for his eldest sister Jane – Ronald Wingate refers to her as Aunt Min – to open up the house to accommodate his sons Ronald and Malcolm during their Christmas and Easter holidays from preparatory school in England. Ronald recalls spending holidays with his 'great-aunt Ag' Mackenzie, a widow who owned a sumptuous Victorian pile at Broadwater Down, Tunbridge Wells. Ronald also remembers staying at Number Thirty-One, Great Cumberland Place, London, home of a family friend, Mrs Elkin Mocatta, who regularly accommodated Lady Wingate and her children when they visited England.[17]

The Wingates' holiday in Dunbar in 1900 was eventful; they arrived in June and stayed until September. Almost immediately, Wingate was honoured by the local burgh council and the townspeople who that June were celebrating the fall of Pretoria during the Boer War. Apparently the local people stood outside Kerridge's, giving the Sirdar three rousing cheers. The same day Provost John Gibb sent Wingate a letter welcoming him back to the town; as noted in the local newspaper,[18] Wingate dutifully responded as follows:

> your hearty words of welcome this evening caused my family and myself very deep gratification, and I felt most highly honoured by the kind manner in which you referred to my return to Dunbar ... and I heartily congratulate you ... on the excellence of the arrangements to celebrate Pretoria Day.* I need hardly tell you that an honour, such as you and the town of Dunbar have paid me today, goes far to help us [sic] soldiers ... to carry out our duties to our beloved Queen ... I only hope that our comrades in South Africa could have witnessed today of their countrymen's appreciation of their gallant deeds ... which have been achieved under the able leadership of Lord Roberts.'[19,20]

In that summer of 1900 Wingate was pleased to meet his old friend Rudolf 'Rowdy' Slatin in Dunbar, where the latter spent a holiday at the Hotel Belle Vue (now a complex of luxury flats for senior citizens). In August Wingate held a dinner at the Belle Vue to honour his friend, an occasion no doubt attended by Provost Gibb and other local and county dignitaries such as the Lord Lieutenant of Haddingtonshire.[21] In July that year the Wingates were also dinner guests of the Prince and Princess of Wales at Marlborough House, the royal residence in London.[22] They were then summoned to Balmoral as guests of Queen Victoria. That same month, Wingate escorted the Khedive of Egypt, Abbas Hilmi, to London and Windsor on an official visit to the Queen.

It seems that in 1900 Wingate had not enjoyed good health which was put down to strain. However, his stay in Dunbar, with its bracing sea air and golf course soon restored him. The local newspaper reported that he had not only played on the Dunbar East Links course but also at Muirfield and Luffness near Gullane, partnered by his friend and colleague James Currie, Director of Education in the Sudan.[23]

That same summer, Arthur Bigge, Queen Victoria's Private Secretary, wrote to Wingate from the royal residence at Osborne on 12 August informing him that he and his family would be staying at the Hotel Belle Vue on 4 September. Bigge said that Lord Cromer in Cairo had asked him to 'impress upon Wingate not to think of returning to Egypt until he is perfectly well'. Bigge also commented ruefully on the Boer War which he said 'drags on'. Bigge followed up this letter with another dated 24 August, asking Wingate if he could have a game of golf with him on the morning or afternoon of 6 September; in passing, he asked how Slatin was 'getting on' with his golf.[24,25]

The third major event of that summer brought a further accolade to Wingate, a pleasant end to a memorable holiday. Provost Gibb proposed to

---

*Free beer had been laid on by the local brewery at the instigation of the burgh council.

the burgh council that Wingate be made a burgess of Dunbar and given the freedom of the burgh. At 3.00pm on 5 September, Gibb held a ceremony in the Corn Exchange to honour Wingate in recognition of his service as a soldier in Egypt and the Sudan. Wingate was ushered in, dressed in resplendent uniform, decorated with his many medals and accompanied by his aide who wore a Turkish military uniform. The ceremony was reported by local newspapers.[26] Before entering the hall, Wingate passed through the Town's Corn Exchange Close, lined by a guard of honour comprised of local men who had served in the Army. After Wingate received his burgess ticket and the freedom of Dunbar, he presented Provost Gibb with two proclamations he had 'liberated' from Omdurman in 1898, both signed by the Dervish leader, the Khalifa. A few days later, he sent Provost Gibb £5 to be distributed among the veterans and local policemen who had acted as his guard of honour, a touching gesture reminiscent of the Middle Ages custom of paying 'drinksilver' to commoners loyal to the kings and nobles of Scotland.

In the summer of 1900 Ronald Wingate recalled playing with children he called his 'Wingate cousins' – they were in fact great-cousins – at a large house beside the sea. That house surely must have been Number Eleven, Marine Road, where his father's cousin and golfing partner, Captain George Miller Wingate resided. The George Wingate children numbered six – two boys and four girls. Ronald Wingate only names two of the children – Agnese Eudora and George Frederick Richard (see family tree for others).[27]

We know that as a young Lieutenant in the British Army George Wingate was present at the Battle of Tel-el-Kebir in 1882, when Sir Garnet Wolseley defeated a force of Egyptian nationalists. (In that action Lieutenant Wingate was awarded the Bronze Star with clasp.) Captain Wingate, Royal Artillery (retired) was a keen golfer who captained Dunbar Golf Club in 1909. He lived at Craigengelt until his death at the age of sixty on 9 April 1918 at Southsea. His widow was still residing in Craigengelt that year.[28]

Other summer friends of the Wingate children were Major Peter Marrow and his wife Mary who owned the impressive Belhaven Hill mansion opposite what later became Winterfield Golf Course; the house was set in extensive grounds with north and south lodges guarding its entrances. The Marrow children numbered six – one boy and five girls. We know the names of four of the girls – Alison, Eileen, Molly and Petrina. Molly lived on after the Second World War in the nearby village of West Barns;[29] Alison was one of five bridesmaids at Victoria Wingate's wedding in 1922. Major Marrow died before 1923, in which year his wife Mary was obliged to sell the estate. Belhaven House and its extensive grounds became a prestigious prep school for the sons of the wealthy and, today, it caters for both boys and girls, as exclusive as ever.

Reginald Wingate's chief interest in Dunbar in these years was also golf and Dunbar was, and still is, fortunate to have an excellent course at the East

Links. In 1904 he won the Merchants' Cup. He would remain associated with the club, playing there until age and ill health prevented him from doing so.

Ronald Wingate relates an incident at Dunbar Golf Club, when his father and Major Marrow were partnered in a golf tournament sometime between 1905 and 1907. The author's view is that the incident occurred in 1905 when Reginald Wingate was serving a second consecutive term as club captain. Ronald remembers Major Marrow handing his father two golf balls wrapped in tissue paper at the first tee. Marrow informed Wingate that he had just received a box of twelve balls from America; these were known as Haskells after the maker, a ball which revolutionized the game of golf. Constituted of wound elastic, they bounced on the fairway, adding many yards to a golfer's drive, something which Reginald Wingate viewed with unconcealed delight. (Unfortunately, Ronald Wingate does not tell us the precise date of the Marrow-Wingate match.)

Despite Wingate's popular but firm rule in the Sudan, danger was never far from the surface, particularly in Egypt, where nationalist enclaves were active. Was it pure coincidence that, when travelling to Alexandria on 8 July 1901 to take ship for his summer leave in Dunbar, Wingate's train was derailed at Damanhur? Six heavy railway sleepers had been laid on the line; fortunately, no one was injured but an inquiry was launched into the derailment.[30] Another attempt would be made on Wingate's life in 1912, as we shall presently see.

In the summer of 1902, when Wingate was holidaying at Dunbar, Lord Kitchener visited Prime Minister Arthur J. Balfour at nearby Whittinge-hame.[31] The purpose of his visit is not clear, although it may have been combined with a desire to meet his old friend Wingate. There are various theories behind Kitchener's brief stay in East Lothian. One is that he had been ordered to Whittingehame to be informed that he was to be appointed Commander in Chief of the Indian Army. In addition, Kitchener may have been asked to arrange the security for Edward VII's forthcoming visit to East Lothian. Whatever the real reason behind Kitchener's visit, he was non-plussed by an incident at Dunbar Railway Station when about to depart for London. To his dismay, he was besieged on the platform by a crowd of local people. One man approached him and asked, 'Are ye Lord Kitchener, for if ye are, I'd like to shake yir [your] hand.' Like his contemporary, T. E. Lawrence, Kitchener hated being touched. He managed to avoid the Dunbar man's proffered paw, nervously smiling at his admirers as he closed the window of the carriage, thereby escaping the unwelcome attentions of the unwashed patriots of Dunbar.

In the autumn of 1903, the *Haddingtonshire Advertiser and East Lothian Journal* contained a short article on Wingate, summarizing his career to that year. The reporter was fulsome, though qualified, in his praise:

> like so many famous military men, he is by no means Herculean in his structure, but his figure is well-knit, and he is exceptionally active ... The

youngest major [general] in the British Army, he was also considered the best looking [among the] officers. The King [Edward VII] is said to have a very high opinion of the present Sirdar.

The article ends by describing Lady Wingate as 'gracious and charming'.[32]

Wingate's temporary summer sojourns in Dunbar came to an end when he was able to live in his new, permanent residence at Knockenhair.[33] His first choice of site for the house was somewhat unrealistic, a precarious, windswept promontory on the clifftop walk known as The West Promenade; it is not known whether he was advised that the cliff was subject to erosion but sense prevailed. Wingate next chose Knockenhair, a bleak, windswept hill. Ronald Wingate later wrote that everyone in East Lothian advised his father against the second site.[34] (There is a local legend that the hill was named for the widows of fishermen who went to sea on a Sunday in the sixteenth century to fish Belhaven Bay where a sudden storm overwhelmed them. The womenfolk stood on the hill and watched the fishermen drown. The incident is recorded in the *Diurnal of Occurrents in Scotland* and drama-tized by local historian James Miller, 1791–1865, in his poem *The Luckless Drave*. Knockenhair, the place where the widows reputedly tore out their hair, was not, however, named for them at all; the name derives from the Gaelic *cnoc-an-aire*, or lookout hill.)

Knockenhair was surmounted by a small windmill which was converted to a lookout station during the Napoleonic Wars, a feature which probably appealed to Wingate's role as spymaster in the Sudan campaign. He incorporated the watchtower into the house; it is occupied to this day.

Knockenhair Hill had for long been one of the town's rabbit warrens and provided pasture for cattle, both supplying meat for local butchers. It was also the meeting place each year for the gypsies who came to Dunbar, some of whom were allowed to sell horses at Lochend, the home of the Warrender family, until they had been ejected in 1825. It was said that, in 1897, when Queen Victoria celebrated her Jubilee and visited Dunbar she met another monarch, Esther Blyth, Queen of the Gypsies.

Ronald Wingate never understood why his father chose Knockenhair as his family home. He said that apart from its exposed situation, it could only be approached by a steep road which exhausted family and visitors alike. Bleak and remote, the house could be mistaken for some medical institution. However, its redeeming feature is an unrestricted view of the North Sea, the May Island and the Bass Rock. The foundation stone for Knockenhair was laid on 22 November 1907 by Wingate's eight-year-old daughter Victoria who was presented with a silver trowel to mark the occasion. The stone, at the base of the north-east-facing wall, still bears her initials 'VACW' and the date.[35] The foundations had to be blasted out of unstable rock to give the house a firm base before the architect, Robert Weir Schultz, could begin work on the building; he crowned the natural contour of the ridge with his impressive edifice which incorporated a square, ogee-style tower and the windmill.

The interior walls were decorated with Dervish weapons – spears, cowhide shields, swords and ancient muskets; one staircase was carpeted with leopard skins. The house was draughty, lit by gas and heated by coal fires providing a constant supply of hot water; Ronald Wingate said that his father ordered coal by the railway wagonload from a local coal merchant.

In July 1908 workmen were laying out the landscaped gardens; the house was not yet ready, so the Wingates were obliged to spend another summer at Stafford House. Knockenhair was completed in December 1908[36] but it would be the summer of 1909 before the Wingates could finally enjoy their new home.[37]

Knockenhair still has an uninterrupted view of the North Sea, overlooking what is now Winterfield Golf Course, formerly Winterfield Farm owned by the Anderson family. One of the family's ancestors, Major General William Cochran Anderson, Royal Artillery, was present on the field of Waterloo. (On the centenary of the battle, 18 June 1915, the Royal Artillery marked the occasion by laying a wreath of roses on 'Waterloo Willy's' grave in Dunbar Churchyard.) In 1935 Winterfield became Dunbar's second golf course, Wingate being largely instrumental in its foundation. In recognition, the Club immediately appointed him Honorary President. At some point, certainly by 1928, as confirmed by the *Dunbar Valuation Roll* (1928–29), Wingate owned a sizeable piece of land to the immediate west of Knockenhair. Known as Kirk Park, due to its proximity to Belhaven Church, the land was rented out to a local farmer (today, it is the site of a private housing estate). In Wingate's day, there were fields to the south-facing front of Knockenhair and on either side of it, with an unrestricted view of Doon Hill.

It goes without saying that Wingate chose Dunbar as his family seat, not only for its bracing sea air but also for its excellent golf course at the East Links. He, his sons Ronald and Malcolm, his cousin Captain George Miller Wingate and George's son George Frederick, were members; at one time, there no fewer than eight Wingate members.

Ronald Wingate remembers various distinguished visitors to Knockenhair. Lord Kitchener visited on several occasions; he managed part of a day there in August 1912, breaking a journey from Balmoral to London.[38] Rudolf von Slatin was another frequent visitor, usually en route to Balmoral during the summer; his last visit to Knockenhair occurred after the Great War when Lady Wingate was 'cool' towards him – perhaps because her son Malcolm Roy had been killed during the war. Other prestigious visitors were Louis Bernstein Namier (later Sir Louis Namier), an eminent historian, Captains Charlton and Vaughan, who would later become generals in the British Army, Sir James Currie, the first principal of the Charles Gordon Memorial College in Khartoum, and the Bishop of Khartoum, Henry Gwynne. Ronald Wingate also recalled his father playing golf with A. J. Balfour and Balfour's brother Gerald at the course in North Berwick, although it is not certain if they ever visited Knockenhair.

Unfortunately for the historian, Ronald Wingate's two books about his father offer little by way of insight into his father's character. He limits his comments to his father's role in the history of the Sudan, although he enlivens both accounts with the occasional anecdote about Wingate's hobbies – golf, reading detective novels and collecting Dervish weapons. (Wingate's love of detective novels may explain the close friendship with his golfing partner, Sir Arthur Conan Doyle, the creator of Sherlock Holmes.)[39]

Ronald Wingate candidly admits that *Wingate of the Sudan* was largely about the history of the Sudan; in *Not in the Limelight* he writes that he and his siblings knew little about their father during their school years in England apart from their few weeks' holiday in Dunbar every summer. Ronald attended preparatory school at Hillbrow, then Bradfield, the latter which he describes as a lesser establishment than Eton or Winchester. After his secondary school education, he entered Balliol College, Oxford from where he graduated. He had hoped to make a career in the Sudanese Civil Service which his father had formed, or serve in some other capacity. Wingate advised his son to seek a career in the Indian Civil Service, saying he would be obliged to give him the poorest jobs in the Sudan lest he be accused of nepotism. That tells us much about Reginald Wingate and his ideas of fair play which surely stem from his Scottish, Presbyterian, upbringing. It was probably wise advice.

Ronald never saw his father again at Knockenhair until 1919, when Wingate had been effectively sacked as High Commissioner of Egypt. He said he was inconsolable, spending many hours isolated in his study at Knockenhair, brooding upon his fall from grace. Ronald tells us that Wingate had a terrible temper which he was at great pains to control. He paid tribute to his father's two great qualities – his single-minded dedication to work and his effortless gift for making and retaining friendships. Throughout his lifetime, Wingate was obsessed by only one bitter prejudice – his unqualified hatred of the Foreign Office; Ronald Wingate admits that his father's hatred and criticism of the FO were expressed in words which were 'unprintable'. No wonder, for when he was sacked – and that was never officially intimated to him – Wingate wrote a memorandum suggesting the best way forward for Egypt which was first ignored by the FO, then implemented three years later, in 1922. Wingate's subsequent city and business life in London were poor compensation for the loss of a brilliant and dedicated career in imperial administration. Wingate was also denied the ultimate accolade for those who had distinguished themselves in imperial service – a peerage. He had to content himself with a baronetage which became defunct on the death of his son Ronald. Had Wingate been awarded a peerage, he would have had a seat in the House of Lords, where he could have 'named names' in diatribes against those in the Foreign Office who had brought him down in 1919. It is virtually certain that, for this reason, he was denied the honour that was rightfully his.

The Wingates turned Dunbar from seasonal to permanent residence in 1919; in their young years when they visited Dunbar, the children played on the broad sandy expanse at Belhaven which may have reminded them of their times in the deserts of the Sudan. Ronald and his brother Malcolm were avid collectors of lead soldiers, building forts out of children's bricks and firing toy cannon at the French cavalry in their re-enactments of the Battle of Waterloo.

The Wingates' annual visits to Dunbar were dutifully and respectfully recorded by the *Haddingtonshire Courier*. In 1907 the paper reported that Wingate was conducting trials on Belhaven Sands with what he described as his 'desert motor car'.[40] During that summer Wingate had bought an Arnold Johnston, something of a rarity in Dunbar – the first car seen on the town's streets had only occurred in 1904. The local populace flocked to the beach to watch the machine being put through its paces. The *Courier* reporter covering the incident described the machine as having 'solid tyres of exceptional dimensions'. Wingate was on hand to enlighten the spectators that he proposed to use the car in the Egyptian desert – hence his reason for testing it on Belhaven's drifting sand dunes. The car's rear wheels had been adapted to give more purchase; Wingate had it fitted with iron strips to the axles with staples which gave the vehicle the appearance of a paddle steamer. He was ahead of his time in owning a car; not only were they a novelty outside London but motorized transport in the Middle Eastern deserts was then virtually unknown.

Wingate's love of the motorcar, like his golf, remained with him for most of the rest of his life. (One is tempted to compare him with Toad in *Wind in the Willows* who fell in love with an early version of the car.) It is interesting to note that, in 1932, when his great-cousin Orde Wingate mounted an expedition into the Libyan Desert, the younger man professed his preference for the camel, the ship of the desert. At first Reginald Wingate agreed with him, then pointed out the benefits of motorized transport which he had first tried out in Dunbar twenty-five years earlier. Orde Wingate should have listened to his older relative, as a rival expedition by car in the Libyan Desert beat him to his goal in 1932 (see Chapter 10).

In April 1909 the local newspaper reported the forthcoming marriage of Captain George Wingate's eldest son George Frederick Richard to Amy Elizabeth Donaldson.[41] In August that year, Rudolf von Slatin spent a few days at Knockenhair as he and Wingate had been invited to Balmoral as guests of Edward VII; Slatin went alone that summer as Wingate was suffering from a chill. Around this time, the *Courier* carried several reports that Wingate was about to retire from the Sudan – he was then in his early fifties – but these proved idle gossip.

In 1912, George Wingate gave his second daughter Muriel Grace (known to the family as Betty) in marriage to John Congreve Murray. Her bridesmaids were sisters Dolly and Rachael. The wedding took place in St Anne's Episcopal Church, Dunbar. Afterwards, 100 guests were invited to a reception at Craigengelt, the family residence.[42] Reginald Wingate was unable to be present though he wrote to his cousin from Aswan. Two months later, Wingate and his wife in Khartoum attended the consecration service at the Anglican Cathedral in Khartoum by the Bishop of London on 26 March. In the afternoon the Wingates hosted a garden party in the grounds of Khartoum Palace. During the tea and cucumber sandwiches, Wingate, the Bishop of London and Bishop Henry Gwynne of Khartoum delivered speeches.[43]

Wingate enjoyed a special relationship with the Town Council of Dunbar, even if he never stood for election. He received many accolades congratulating him on his achievements from successive Provosts and he was often the honoured guest at dinners arranged by the Council. However, this special and cordial relationship did not prevent him from lobbying the Council about their duty to maintain the public thoroughfare which ran past Knockenhair. For example, in 1910, he asked the Town Council to install street lighting in the side road fronting his property, reminding them that he paid exorbitant taxes and rates for the privilege of living in the sole house in the vicinity at that time. (Given that, at his death, he bequeathed Knockenhair to the people of Dunbar, it was a modest request.)

Wingate's generosity to the community of Dunbar should not go unrecorded. In his early years he made a gift of a billiard table to the local Social Institute; other gifts included a Wingate Swimming Medal, a Wingate golf trophy (the Sirdar Medal), a gift of ten guineas (£10.50) to the local Comrades of the Great War for their social institute scheme which provided recreational amenities – billiards and a reading room – for local war veterans. He also made a gift of £50 towards the Dunbar Burgh and Parish War Memorial in special recognition of his son Major Malcolm Roy Wingate DSO, MC and *Croix de Guerre*, Royal Engineers, who gave his life in the Great War. Wingate entered the social round, involving himself in the local Royal National Lifeboat Institution, Dunbar Rugby Club and other local organizations; he was an enthusiastic member of Dunbar Golf Club and, on at least one occasion, he played host to some of the town's fishermen (mainly the volunteer crews of the local lifeboat) and their families at Knockenhair.

However, we now return to the Sudan where Wingate would become what might be termed a benign dictator. In the first months of 1900 he remained in Khartoum, coping with the changes in personnel resulting from Kitchener's transfer to South Africa during the Boer War. While different in temperament, the two men shared common visions for the future of the Sudan in general and Khartoum in particular. Both came from impoverished backgrounds, both served in specialist branches of the British Army – Kitchener the engineer and Wingate the artilleryman – and both were staunch Christians. They also shared a healthy and often justified distrust of the Foreign Office mandarins of the day. (As the Sudan was not a British Crown Colony, Wingate was obliged to report to the Foreign Office, an arrangement he at best found irksome, at worst distasteful.)

From the outset, Wingate embarked on a personal crusade to understand the Sudanese people and work for their well-being, respecting their culture and religious beliefs. The Egyptian newspaper *Al-Ahram* was full of obsequious praise quaintly expressed in its appreciation of Wingate's promotion:

> Egyptians, in general, were never pleased in appointing an English [sic] official in an Egyptian post as they were pleased this time in the appointment of His Excellency Wingate Pasha to be Sirdar and Governor General of Soudan [sic]. He is well known for his manners and his good treatment to [sic] the natives. He is a good soldier and rewards well those who serve him. All Egyptians know that he was the principal organ in the expedition which destroyed the Madieh [sic]. He is a good administrator and knows the country and its manners. It is very much hoped that he will open a new way to improve the connection between England and Egypt, because we know he is inclined to listen to the demands of the Egyptian officers and to treat them justly, and also he is the man to treat Egypt with kindness. If what we hope in him becomes a fact, we are sure that the result will be good and everyone will be happy.[44]

During his time as Governor General Kitchener had taken the same course, albeit to a lesser extent; his appointment was brief but he shared Wingate's enthusiasm for the people over whom he was set. In this they differed from some arrogant empire-builders of their time – usually but not exclusively Englishmen who displayed ill-concealed contempt for the indigenous population. Most were woefully ignorant of and totally uninterested in the lives of those they controlled. Having said that, Kitchener and Wingate were products of imperial Britain and so were also content to go with the flow. With Kitchener as his friend and Lord Cromer as his mentor, Wingate was able to introduce policies in the Sudan which would serve the country well and facilitate the development of sound and enlightened government which not only paid dividends for the Sudanese and Egyptian economies but assured him his place in history. He richly deserved the epithet which adorns his grave monument in Dunbar's Churchyard – 'Maker of the Anglo-Egyptian Sudan'.

During the Wingate years in the Sudan, several 'false prophets' in the mould of the Mahdi had to be suppressed; all were harshly dealt with by the still insecure government of Egypt. Wingate combined the duties of Governor General and Sirdar of the Egyptian Army until 1919; these offices were separated in 1924. The Sudan was divided into provinces, each controlled by a governor responsible directly to Wingate during his time as Governor General. Religious policy was determined by considerations of national security – hence the constant need to defuse possible rebellions stirred up by 'false prophets'. To combat the influence of popular Islam, Wingate created a Board of religious representatives (*ulemas*) in 1901. All government proposals concerning Islam were referred to this board but it was largely ineffective, mere window-dressing on Wingate's part. Religious policy in southern Sudan differed greatly from that in the Muslim north. Ever vigilant as to the potential dangers posed to internal security by fanatical radicals, Wingate and his subordinates strove to control Muslim influence in the southern provinces of Darfur, Kordofan and the Upper Nile.

Kitchener and Wingate shared a joint dream of rebuilding Khartoum as a lasting tribute to Charles Gordon's memory. Wingate transformed the town from ruin to fashionable winter resort for British and European royals, wealthy aristocrats and tired businessmen. With his love of good food, whisky and cigars, Wingate enjoyed a sybaritic lifestyle to the full. He travelled through the Sudan with a large retinue in the manner of medieval kings, confident that such displays of pomp and glitter would impress a largely peasant population. His was a proprietary appointment, the gift of the British monarch in whose name he served; despite the lavish lifestyle he enjoyed, it never distracted him from what he considered his prime duty – the efficient and effective government of the Sudan and its people.

Wingate welcomed Lord Cromer's ambition to modernize and improve the Sudanese economy. Under Wingate's administration, the railway system was upgraded, telegraphic communications were extended and steamers sailed up and down the Nile more frequently, bringing food and, more importantly, tourists to the region in general and Khartoum in particular. Wingate must take credit for the creation of a new deep sea harbour on the Red Sea, replacing the by now outdated Suakin. He suggested it should be named Port Cromer in deference to his master in Cairo; Cromer returned the compliment by proposing it should be called Port Wingate. Ultimately, it became Port Sudan, officially opened by the Khedive in 1909.

In October 1900 Wingate returned from his Dunbar holiday and was joined by his wife Kitty and baby daughter Victoria at Christmas. Lady Wingate set herself the task of cultivating the Residency gardens; she would be particularly remembered for her cultivation of roses. She was also active in the hospital and nursing services as well as with several welfare organizations.

In 1901 Wingate received yet another accolade; he was awarded the 1st Class Mejidieh medal by the Khedive of Egypt. For the next thirteen years Wingate travelled extensively throughout the Sudan, inspecting public works, making speeches and listening to carefully worded petitions from local sheiks, administrators and holy men. His year was usually spent as follows: three weeks in the early summer in Cairo, then the hill station at Erkowit for the hot season, followed by three months' leave in Dunbar and a further three weeks in Cairo before his return to Khartoum. Even after Queen Victoria's death in January 1901, Wingate and Slatin continued to be regular summer visitors at Balmoral, guests of Edward VII and Queen Alexandra who delighted in their company, enjoying their conversations about mutual acquaintances in the upper echelons of British and European society. In 1901 Wingate accompanied Slatin to his native Austria, spending some time in Vienna, then returned to Dunbar via Karlsbad, where he undertook the 'cure' at that famous spa town. The following year, reports that the Khedive of Egypt, Abbas Hilmi, was demanding Wingate's resignation as Governor General were widely disclaimed in the British newspapers.

Soon after the end of the Boer War, the Sudan Plantation Syndicate was formed; under its auspices, several thousands of inhospitable desert acres between the Blue and White Niles were transformed by irrigation into fertile cropping land. The main crops were sorghum, a species of millet for feeding cattle and poultry, millet for human consumption and, most important of all, cotton. (By 1933, the value of the Sudanese cotton crop alone brought in revenues of £2.5 million. Management of this highly lucrative venture had, since 1909, been in the capable hands of Donald P. MacGillivray, yet another enterprising Scot and Cairo banker.)

In 1902 the Gordon Memorial College was inaugurated by Lord Kitchener who had personally raised £135,000 – a colossal sum for the time – to create it. James Currie, a Scot, was appointed to the dual role of Principal and Director of Sudanese Education. Wingate was instrumental in enlisting the support of his friend Sir William Mather who provided two educational workshops for the College. With his family background in the cotton trade, Wingate readily saw that cotton could become king in the Sudan, so he personally provided facilities for young Sudanese men to study its cultivation and harvesting. In time the Gordon Memorial College would contain several departments of excellence, including those devoted to the study of bacteriology, entomology and geology; it also provided facilities for artisans, trainee teachers, the Kitchener School of Medicine, a military school and schools in agriculture, veterinary services, engineering and law. In 1908 the College admitted female students, a revolutionary breakthrough for the time in a stringently male-dominated Muslim society where women were seen as little more than hewers of wood, drawers of water and for breeding children.

In 1903 Wingate, ever the diplomat and peacemaker, abolished the annual commemoration of the Battle of Omdurman on 2 September, a holiday introduced during Kitchener's time as Governor General. Wingate astutely saw no reason to rub salt into the wounds of a large proportion of Sudanese people, many of whom were former supporters of the Mahdi and the Khalifa, as well as people bitter at the defeat and death of several thousand of their countrymen. In this respect, Wingate was ahead of his time, recognizing that conciliation rather than confrontation was the way forward. One wonders how different Europe might have been if Wingate's philosophy had been applied after the Great War, when the conquering powers squeezed Germany until the 'pips squeaked' at Versailles.

After an exhausting tour of the Sudan between March and June 1903, Wingate arrived in Dunbar on 18 June on summer leave. Even then, his official duties did not cease. He attended the King's dinner in London for the Khedive on 29 June, a royal ball held in honour of French President Loubet on 6 July and the Prince of Wales' ball a week later. Only after these events could he return to Dunbar to enjoy his beloved golf. On the East Links course

Wingate, with a handicap of eighteen, won the Roxburghe Gold Cross among other prizes and was appointed captain of Dunbar Golf Club for two consecutive years, 1904 and 1905.[45]

The following summer Wingate dined with the Prince of Wales and the Khedive in London on 14 July. Two days later, he was granted an audience with Edward VII. In Dunbar, he won a prestigious local golf tournament known as the Merchants' Cup before returning to Cairo in October with his wife and baby daughter Victoria.

Despite his prestigious position as representative of Edward VII – which of course he was – and left no one in any doubt of – in the Sudan – Wingate made do with a small secretarial staff; most of his senior administrators were officers seconded from the British Army. Being a practical man, he accepted the fact of, and even showed a preference for, military assistants since, unlike professional public administrators, they were hardly likely to pose a threat to his authority. Having said that, he privately harboured doubts about an administration drawn from the military, which to modern eyes appears alarmingly close to being that of a junta. His long-term aim was to govern the Sudan not with soldiers but civil servants who were then thin on the ground. Even so, Wingate appointed his friend Rudolf von Slatin to the post of Inspector General, a military appointment. Like Wingate, Slatin was constantly on the move, inspecting regions of the Sudan but, unlike Wingate, wearing military uniform. Wingate administered the Sudan with a small coterie of British Army officers and non-military technical experts in charge of river transport, forests and game preserves. He welcomed and appreciated the contributions made by two of his non-military officials, James Currie the educationalist and Edgar Bonham Carter, his legal secretary. Bonham Carter was young but well versed in law; civil and criminal law were practically non-existent in the Sudan in 1900, so Lord Cromer had suggested Bonham Carter to Wingate. Both Bonham Carter and Currie were indispensable to Wingate in his role as Governor General over the next fifteen years.

The lives of Ambassadors, Consul Generals, diplomats and other Foreign and Colonial officials in the service of the British Empire have always contained an element of danger, particularly during periods of political unrest in the countries to which they were posted. Perhaps this danger was slight in the outposts of the Middle East, particularly the Sudan, despite its unhealthy environment and climate.

In the Wingates' day, one of the most serious incidents in the history of the Diplomatic Corps occurred in China in 1900, when the dowager Empress, last of the ancient Manchu dynasty, openly supported an insurrection by a faction known as the Boxers. The Boxers were a Chinese secret society of fervent nationalists with an intense hatred of foreigners in their country. They began by murdering native Christian and European missionaries, then began to demand removal of 'the foreign devils' from 'the Forbidden City', as Beijing (formerly Peking) was then known. The European Legations – British, French, German, Austrian, Italian, Russian and Japanese, each with military units of about 150 personnel – were in danger of being massacred. With their small combined force of 1,000 soldiers, the Legations managed to survive a long siege (this siege was later the subject of a dramatization in the 1963 film *55 Days at Peking*). Wingate would have read about the siege in the newspapers and would have also been heartened to learn that the first naval relief force sent to Peking was commanded by Sir George Warrender of Dunbar. The Boxer rebellion failed; during a decade of clamour for reform in China, the Manchu dynasty fell and China became a republic in 1911. However, the Boxer uprising rang alarm bells in a Foreign Office intent on suppressing any bids for independence from Britain by India and Egypt.

All this was distant from the Sudan, where conditions would vastly improve and be welcomed by the Sudanese people during Wingate's benign dictatorship. But let us consider his wife Kitty, who, at the end of 1899, was thrust into a role for which she had never been prepared. Nevertheless, she rose to the challenge admirably, proving capable of embracing her duties as wife of the Governor General. It was a difficult role but she mastered it with grace and dignity. In 1900 she was living in a country where plague was rife and swept through like a forest fire. Ever present were the threats of smallpox, cholera and the deadly sand-fly fever that would carry off many Europeans. Kitty Wingate took it all in her stride. Apart from the hostile environment, she was beset by the strictures of protocol in which, as part of his daily functions, her husband was obliged to entertain an endless procession of government officials, royal guests, dignitaries, rich tourists escaping the smog-ridden streets of London and native Sudanese leaders and holy men who needed placating.

The Sudan was considered a backwater but had its compensations. Wingate and his wife lived in a palace with many rooms, the most spectacular being the dining room illuminated by its crystal chandeliers and resplendent with decorative native furniture. Even if Khartoum never reached the height of luxury comparable to the Viceroy of India's palace, it was still impressive. The rooms rang with the sound of pipes and drums when formal occasions demanded. The palace hosted frequent receptions, dinners, balls and coffee mornings. Kitty Wingate was blessed with a strong character and quickly adapted to a hectic life in the back of beyond.

No doubt she learnt a few tips from the helpful, if starchy, handbook written by a Major S. Leigh-Hunt in 1883 for the advice of women living in the Tropics, namely *Tropical Trials: A Handbook for Women in the Tropics*. Leigh-Hunt meant well and some of the book's advice was sensible, even if prosaic and ponderous. His foremost recommendation – a must – was that women going to hot countries should purchase several gossamer veils to be worn over a topee. Leigh-Hunt also recommended that ladies provide themselves with 'a Most Liberal [sic] supply of tulle, net, lace, ruffles, frillings, white and coloured collars and cuffs, artificial flowers and ribbons'. Another writer, Flora Annie Steel, published a celebrated guide entitled *The Complete Indian Housewife and Cook* in 1888, offering more practical advice than

Leigh-Hunt's. Some of Mrs Steel's suggestions seem eccentric to modern eyes. (For example, her remedy for dealing with any hysterical European woman was to administer whisky and water with 'a little wholesome neglect'!) Mrs Steel made an almost exhaustive – not to say exhausting for the porters who had to bear the weight of luggage – list of items essential to the wardrobe of women whose husbands were in the service of Empire. She recommended an abundance of nightgowns for cold nights, silk or thin woollen ones for hot nights, dresses for morning, afternoon and evening, summer and winter tea-gowns (tea-gowns were the equivalent of modern dressing gowns, though worn in public without attracting the least moral censure). Other 'musts' in the wardrobe were an Ulster, or stout waterproof cloak, the Mackintosh raincoat, a riding habit with light jacket, suitable footwear for indoors and outdoors – tennis shoes, walking shoes and boots, house shoes and evening shoes. The underwear recommended for the wives of diplomats was combinations (a single undergarment covering body and legs) made of calico, silk or wool. In addition, bodices, petticoats in layers, stays (corsets) and cami-knickers were considered essential. In these days women wore a minimum of five petticoats, long lace-trimmed drawers, a bodice and a camisole (under-bodice). How on earth could the poor creatures breathe in such a hot climate?

One wonders how Kitty Wingate felt when she arrived in Khartoum at the end of 1899 to join her husband. She had taken the long sea journey from Tilbury Docks, London to Suez, then an uncomfortable train journey from Cairo to Khartoum. When she stepped off the train, she would have been engulfed by a throng of humanity – men wearing red fezes, suits and the more ubiquitous peasants in their tattered clothes displaying their sores and beggars demanding money or food. Of course, she would have been spared the indignity of rubbing shoulders with the crowd when met by her husband, whose entourage would have cloven a path through the unwashed poor. She would have been accompanied by an abundance of Sudanese servants – mainly women – bearing trays of beautiful flowers, fruits and cold drinks. Transport to the palace at Khartoum would have been an open-topped, pale gilded carriage lined with crimson velvet and fringed with silver and gold. Her mounted escort – men from the Sudanese cavalry units at Khartoum wearing their fine, dress uniforms – would have ridden in front and behind, perhaps numbering twenty troopers. Kitty could not have failed to be impressed by the pomp and circumstance, coming as she did from an impoverished family; she and brother Leslie had no doubt suffered under the rigid discipline of their austere guardian. Kitty must have felt she had really arrived.

Kitty's life would now change dramatically and suddenly. Her responsibilities remained principally domestic but on a much grander scale, entertaining people from all walks of life and nationalities. At first, the prospect must have been daunting but Kitty soon settled into the role, creating a harmonious household in the palace, where she was sheltered from a hostile landscape and where the effects of an equally hostile climate were mitigated by its cool walls. She certainly fell in love with the palace gardens and immediately took charge of their supervision, improving the flowerbeds and formal layout. Kitty was delighted with the wisteria-sheltered balconies, the masses of blooms, the scented herbs, vegetables and fruit, and was also beginning to propagate roses. One of her achievements was to cultivate the Charles Gordon rose, a yellow bloom, to commemorate the fallen general, even successfully transplanting a specimen to the Knockenhair garden.

Kitty quickly learnt the finer points of diplomatic life – protocol, etiquette and of course the placement, or seating arrangements, at formal banquets and dinners. She would discover that at such functions her husband, as host, was served last. In the hot summers, showing her guests round the gardens, she learnt that a white umbrella occasionally dipped in water proved efficacious in making a garden walk more pleasant. When the Wingates occupied their hill station at Erkowit on the Red Sea coast, she would dress in the thinnest of white outer and undergarments. She also learnt to turn a blind eye to the almost naked (and sometimes completely naked) female servants who laboured in the kitchen.

The Wingates enjoyed a domestic harmony because, in addition to being middle rather than upper class, they took the trouble to understand servants. Wingate spoke Arabic, which endeared him to the native Sudanese, a white man who had actually learnt to speak their own language.

The word 'duty' is unfashionable today but, a century ago, the Wingates, like their contemporaries, set great store by it. Kitty Wingate may be rightly described as a daughter of Britannia during her twenty or so years in the Sudan and Egypt. Diplomatic wives then depended more on servants, often their only contact with the native population. The servants in Khartoum Palace shopped for their mistress, knew how to keep the palace cool or warm depending on the season and understood how things were done in the town. Kitty faced the same problem as other colonial wives living in Muslim countries at the time, that of male servants considering it demeaning to take orders from a woman. She was advised not to give orders but to make 'requests' of her male servants, a ruse which soon had the desired effect.

The wives of Foreign Office officials took in their stride the setting up of new homes abroad, although they sometimes succumbed to feelings of isolation and loneliness. However, on the whole, official residences became their home and the staff their extended family. The Governor Generalship of the Sudan differed from other Foreign Office posts in that it was less formal in its day-to-day administration, although Wingate was a stickler for protocol and proper dress. He was industrious and worked long hours, often well into the night; his happiest leisure times were spent on leave in Dunbar and at the hill-station at Erkowit. In the latter case, moving an entire household would have been a feat of immense proportions; the Wingates would pack their belongings – appropriate clothing, linen, pots and pans and crockery as well as books and other items to pass the time – into large wooden trunks requiring a dozen or more camels to transport them.

At Erkowit there was a prolific garden providing fruit, vegetables and flowers; the mornings were pleasant, with cool breezes from the sea until midday, when it became oppressively hot until late afternoon when the breezes resumed, bringing the temperature down and allowing walks in the vicinity of the bungalow. At evening, after dinner, the Wingates could relax on the verandahs; during the day, these were sheltered from the sun by stout rush-woven blinds which were dowsed with water to keep the air cool. One can picture Kitty propagating the oleanders, lavender and zinnias in the garden in the early hours of the morning and late afternoon. In the evenings nightingales sang, adding to the restorative pleasure of Erkowit. Years later, Wingate would look back on this time in the Sudan as his happiest.

Kitty also enjoyed her time in the Middle East. In the Residency at Khartoum she ritually observed the red letter days – Queen Victoria's birthday, then Edward VII's and George V's, the St Andrew's Day dinner, the children's Christmas party. No doubt other occasions were celebrated – the victories at Waterloo and Omdurman, the relief of Mafeking and Ladysmith – all significant events in the Imperial Calendar. At Khartoum, there were Sunday tennis matches, afternoon teas and evening bridge parties attended by the officers and wives of Wingate's small and predominantly military staff, living *en famille* in the Residency. The palace displayed the icons of Empire – the Union Flag, ubiquitous statues of lions and unicorns, photographs of monarchs and Prime Ministers, the Tower of London with beefeaters, Buckingham Palace with guardsmen dressed like toy soldiers in uniforms of scarlet. All this was accompanied by the resident band playing the National Anthem and other patriotic pieces. The British (English) have always striven to impress native populations of those countries they occupied but it was a world that would begin to crumble after the First World War and which virtually disappeared after the Second.

A Sudanese civil service was some four years away, even if the top posts would be held by British and Egyptian officials. The development of the country was still in the hands of British military personnel; among them were Sir Edward Midwinter who built extensions to the railway, Sir M. R. Kennedy who reconstructed Khartoum and Port Sudan, Colonel the Hon. Milo Talbot of the Survey Service – Talbot was a great friend until his death in the 1930s – Sir Gilbert Clayton and Sir Lee Stack, Wingate's personal secretary who succeeded him as acting Governor General in 1917.

Despite the view of historians who insist that he preferred military men as subordinates, Wingate knew that governing the Sudan exclusively with professional soldiers could not last indefinitely. Instead, he set about creating a Sudanese Civil Service, while recognizing that initially, it would be a modest enterprise, hardly comparable to the prestigious Indian example. For a start, it would not be able to offer attractive prospects for promotion. The most lucrative appointments would be those of governors of the various provinces, posts which would be broadly comparable with the headship of an Indian district. Another drawback was the extreme heat of the Sudanese desert where there were no hill stations to offer respite during the hot season, unlike in India. Further complications were caused by the fact that native candidates for the Sudanese Civil Service could not attain entry through the usual method via the British and Colonial Service, i.e. written examination and interview by the Civil Service Commissioners. Selection boards for British candidates were usually convened in London and always included a Sudanese official; Wingate himself served on these boards on at least two occasions. As with all selection and promotion boards, there were anomalies; for example, Lord Cromer once told Wingate that a board on which he served interviewed a candidate described as a man 'of sound physique but apparently feeble intellect'. The candidate in question turned out to be no less than the Senior Wrangler – a title given to a class of Cambridge University graduate who had obtained first class in the Mathematical Tripos, or honours list!

The terms and conditions of service of the Sudanese Civil Service were generous; three months' European leave and retirement on pension after twenty years' service. This was more attractive than the much-vaunted Indian equivalent whose conditions of service required more years in harness before a pension was paid. The main criticism levelled at the Sudanese Civil Service was that it was dominated by Oxford 'Blues', which was true to a great extent; the lower grades, the work-horses, were usually Egyptians or Sudanese. The indigenous recruits were also required to serve a minimum of fifteen years before they could qualify for a more senior post, such as that of assistant commissioner or assistant tax collector. In time, however, Sudanese men and women would administer their own country, a policy Wingate began in 1904; by 1923 the Sudanese Civil Service was offering attractive career prospects to native-born men and women.

During his seventeen years as Governor General, Wingate's administration was beset by constant problems. There were financial and political crises and periodic rebellions, which is hardly surprising given that the country's population was largely Muslim, oppressed by a minority rule of Christian 'infidels'. A crude benchmark of Wingate's success, however, is reflected in the financial situation between 1899 and 1920, by which latter year Wingate's association with the Sudan and Egypt had ended. In 1899 the Sudan's income was £126,000 with expenditure of £230,000; by 1920 the figures were respectively £4.4 million and £3.5 million, a net gain to Egypt of almost £1 million. During the rest of his life, Wingate continued to study reports on the state of both countries with personal satisfaction, the fruits of his earlier labours still paying dividends. Perhaps his greatest achievement was the cotton-growing schemes of the Gezira between the Blue and White Niles. For example, by 1951, two years before his death, Sudan's net income was £41 million and expenditure £23.5 million.[46]

Between 1899 and Kitchener's tragic death by drowning in 1916, Wingate kept in constant touch with his former Commander in Chief. He carried

Kitchener's vision of the future Africa in his head; like Kitchener, he foresaw that Africa was a country of promise, with its growing industries, mineral deposits and raw materials. Kitchener earnestly hoped that one day black and white would live in harmony and enrich both Africa and Britain. It was a fine dream which for a time did benefit Britain – but not without a price.

Meanwhile, in the early part of the twentieth century, the Wingates were acting as hosts to the great and the good, living almost in the style of minor royals. In April 1906 they entertained the Khedive of Egypt, Abbas Hilmi; he was so impressed by their hospitality that he made them a gift of his signed portrait which hung in the Residency at Khartoum, and later at Knockenhair. Kitchener also made periodic visits to the Sudan whenever he could. En route to India after the Boer War to take up appointment as Commander in Chief of the Indian Army, Kitchener made a stop at Khartoum to visit his old friend. He was back again in Egypt in 1911, serving as British Agent in Cairo until the outbreak of the Great War, when he was appointed Secretary of State for War.

The Wingates' guest list included the royals of Britain and Europe and several minor princes and princesses; Edward VII and Alexandra, the Princess Royal and her husband the Duke of Fife, Princesses Maud and Alexandra; Archduke Joseph of Austria and his wife were personal friends. Other visitors to Khartoum were Princess Henry of Battenberg, the Duke and Duchess of Schleswig-Holstein, Prince [later King] Leopold of Belgium, the King of Saxony and the Duke and Duchess of Connaught; the former was then the Commander in Chief of the British Army. Theodore 'Teddy' Roosevelt, the ex-President of the USA, also visited Khartoum on an occasion when Wingate was unfortunately absent. Formal dinners and balls were regular occurrences at the Residency in Khartoum, as were shooting parties organized by Wingate in the Upper Nile valley. These events were all part of the 'season'.

One of Kitchener's visits to Khartoum was not without incident. This occurred in February 1912 when Wingate was on his way to meet Kitchener at the railway station. The incident is frozen in a photograph. Apparently innocent, the photo shows a group of lancers milling around a hat lying in the road, looking for all the world like an impromptu game of polo, with the hat as ball. What is interesting is the inscription on the reverse, written in Wingate's distinctive hand:

Taken on 23 Feb 1912 (at Khartoum)
Enlarged snapshot of my escort (when Governor General of the Sudan) attacking the mad policeman who tried to brain me when I was on my way to the Railway Station to meet Lord Kitchener (High Com[missioner] for Egypt paying an official visit to Khartoum. I took the blow of a heavy club on my left wrist and in consequence my golf handicap has gone up at least a dozen strokes! ever since.
　Signed Reginald Wingate and dated Dunbar
　9 October 1935

Wingate's capacity for remaining friends with former colleagues is well documented by his son Ronald.[47] However, he was to lose one of his greatest and invaluable patrons in 1907, when Lord Cromer, after serving for several years as British Agent in Cairo, was forced to resign on the grounds of ill-health. At least that was the official – and, it has to be said, largely accurate – reason given for his departure. Although the Sudan was prospering under Wingate's diplomacy and understanding of its people, Cromer's steward-ship of Egypt was causing unrest. Cromer was out of touch and sympathy with the new generation of Egyptians. The British saw themselves as the benefactors of the Egyptian peasantry whom they had delivered from slavery and the lash. However, an incident in 1906 presented the British in an entirely different light. In June that year a fracas broke out between the villagers of Dinshaway and a party of British officers out on a pigeon-shoot. During the dispute, which became known as the Dinshaway Incident, two British officers were wounded, one of whom subsequently died. A special inquiry was set up to investigate the incident; the inquiry found several villagers guilty and, on Lord Cromer's orders, imposed excessive and brutal sentences, including four executions. An anti-British cloud hung over Cromer and, in the bitter aftermath, he decided to resign.

On 9 April 1907 Cromer sent the following telegram to Wingate in Khartoum:

> Decipher yourself. Very private. I have been obliged for reasons of health to resign. I shall be succeeded by [Sir Eldon] Gorst early next month. Keep absolutely secret until public announcement is made. This will probably take place in the House of Commons on Thursday. I need not say how greatly I regret the severing of our official relations. I thank you most sincerely for [the] invaluable loyalty with which you have co-operated with me. When the proper time comes, I shall send you a further telegram for circulation to your officers and officials.[48]

The following day Wingate replied that the news had come as a great shock and had made him 'thoroughly miserable'.[49]

Cromer and Wingate had been friends for twenty years and the former's departure from Egypt was a great blow. Cromer's illness was hardly life-threatening; he enjoyed ten years in retirement, dying at age sixty-six in January 1917. His successor, Sir Eldon Gorst, would be less well disposed to Wingate although, in the interests of solidarity and for the sake of diplomatic relations, Gorst reassured Wingate he would enjoy the same level of support as he had received from Cromer.

Gorst's brief period as Consul General in Cairo was the most vexing time during Wingate's tenure as Governor General of the Sudan. He and Gorst frequently disagreed over matters of financial policy; Gorst privately con-sidered Wingate administratively incompetent and that he had been part of a clique intent on blocking his succession to Cromer. In fact, in 1909, it was rumoured that Wingate would be replaced – in government circles then and now, there is a world of difference between being 'succeeded by' and being 'replaced' – the latter implying that an official has been sacked for incompetence. In 1909 the Egyptian Press reported objectively, stating that Wingate's ten-year contract as Governor General would come to an end in 1910 and that it would not be renewed. Possibly this was a reference to a bout of ill health he had suffered the previous year. Be that as it may, at least Gorst declared that he had no intention of replacing Wingate in the Sudan and even publicly expressed his confidence in Wingate, who at no time had hinted at his intention to resign from his position in the Sudan. Perhaps Gorst was simply protecting his back. It is always better to work with the devil you know than the one you do not. However, it has to be said in Gorst's favour that he endeavoured to diminish the growing power and number of the British Establishment in Egypt. He gave more responsibility and power to Egyptian political institutions although when he was succeeded by Kitchener, in 1911, he had achieved only limited success.

During the period 1907–10 Wingate had fallen increasingly out of step with his masters at the Foreign Office. He made no secret of the fact that he considered the conduct of many Army officers and senior administrators arrogant and insensitive to the Sudanese people. While stopping short of espousing the cause of Sudanese and Egyptian nationalism, he firmly believed that, in time, both countries should become independent nations. Wingate was farsighted enough to see that the continued and often brutal suppression of nationalism, particularly in India, was not only unforgivable but provocative as it encouraged new recruits to the cause.

In April 1909 Wingate was given an added responsibility; he was ordered to tour the British Protectorate of Somaliland, the peninsula in East Africa known as the Horn of Africa. France and Italy also possessed protectorates there; the British territory of 68,000 square miles extended over virtual desert inhabited by a few nomadic tribes beside the Gulf of Aden, with a port at Berbera, a virtually uncontrolled and inaccessible area. Wingate's mission was to restore order in the British zone, where a local brigand, Muhammad bin abd Allah Hussan (known to the British as the Mad Mullah) was terrorizing tribes loyal to the European powers, looting and destroying property and livestock. The British had sent three expeditions against the Mullah since 1899 but each had failed to capture or kill him. In 1905 the Italians had reached an agreement with the Mullah which was acceptable to Britain; he was placed under Italian protection. The ink was hardly dry on the agreement when the Mullah resumed his brigandage. Winston Churchill, then serving as Under-Secretary for the Colonies, visited British Somaliland and wrote a report that sparked off an acrimonious debate in the House of Commons, forcing the government to take action. Wingate was chosen as mediator.

The appointment was a poisoned chalice but Wingate selected his team carefully; Slatin, Gilbert Clayton as his Private Secretary and Charles H. Armbruster as his Military Intelligence officer. From the outset the mission was fraught with difficulty, not least caused by Captain Harry E. S. Cordeaux, Commissioner for British Somaliland and a member of the Indian Political Service; Cordeaux threatened to resign, complaining of Wingate's interference. Wingate, ever the peacemaker, persuaded him not to be so foolish. In July Wingate left Cairo, ordered to present a report on British Somaliland to the Colonial Office and recommend military action. His report seems to have languished in some official's in-tray, probably by design rather than by accident. It is almost certain that pressure was exerted by the Indian Political Service (possibly as a result of Captain Cordeaux's fit of pique) to do nothing. Wingate's recommendations for military intervention had to wait until 1920, when the RAF destroyed the Mad Mullah and his forces from the air. After delivering his report, Wingate departed for Dunbar to enjoy his summer leave.

A significant rift in Wingate's relationship with the Foreign Office occurred in 1910 when he rejected what he termed 'government by dictatorship' in the Sudan. Wingate was too astute to ignore the fact that the Christian minority in both predominantly Muslim Sudan and Egypt could not expect to dominate the political scene indefinitely, even if under that minority rule both countries were thriving as never before. To make matters worse, in the same year, against Foreign Office advice, Gorst introduced a Governor General's council to be run on the lines of the fashionable democratic model introduced by the Viceroy of India. The council would meet infrequently and did not affect or threaten Wingate's position – he actually welcomed and supported the idea as it would prove useful for promoting his views in Cairo and London.

In March 1910 ex-President Theodore 'Teddy' Roosevelt of the USA visited Khartoum. As Wingate was away on official business, it was left to Rudolf von Slatin to entertain him. Slatin was uncertain as to the extent of the entertainment; as he wrote to Wingate, 'I suppose he will stay only 2 or 3 days – I will show him Omdurman, the battlefield – the Gordon Memorial College and give him a dinner etc etc'.[50]

On 31 May 1910 Roosevelt attended a dinner at the Guildhall in London where, in a formal speech, he criticized certain aspects of British policy in Egypt, though he was fulsome in his praise of British achievements in the Sudan. Wingate was unable to attend the dinner as he was still recovering from his gallstones operation. Roosevelt did not refer to Wingate by name in his speech; he referred to the Sirdar who, with 'his lieutenants, great and small, have performed to perfection a task equally important and difficult'.

In April 1910 the Wingates embarked on a sea cruise to Venice, perhaps because Wingate was again in poor health. However, he deteriorated rapidly and was obliged to return to England where, on 3 May, he was admitted to the King Edward VII hospital in London, to be operated on for gallstones. By early June he was reported in good health and was able to leave hospital to convalesce at Number Nineteen, Bryanston Square, London, home of the Dr Acland who had treated him for typhoid in 1883.[51,52]

Perhaps as a direct consequence of his ready acceptance of the creation of Gorst's Governor General's council, rumours were again circulating that Wingate would relinquish his role in the Sudan and take up post of Master General of the Ordnance of the British Army Council. The Master General's Department was one of four responsible to the Secretary of State for War for the entire work of the War Department; in theory, it was an important position although in reality its main duties were to ensure British troops were adequately equipped for battle – the post was that of a kind of superior quartermaster. However, the rumour proved to be yet another press fabrication. Who was responsible for these rumours? Did it originate in the newspapers owned by press barons influential in Foreign Office circles? Were these rumours circulated in Whitehall by those hostile to Wingate? When he was hospitalized, the press speculated that he would be replaced as Governor General of the Sudan by General Sir John Grenfell Maxwell. It was a false rumour: things returned to normal. In September 1910 Wingate and his old friend Slatin were guests of King George V and Queen Mary at Balmoral; the foursome then went to Mar Lodge to visit the Princess Royal and her husband, the Duke of Fife.

In the first months of 1911 the British press was clamouring for the replacement of Sir Eldon Gorst; the newspapers were highly critical of Gorst's performance as High Commissioner and made no secret of their preferred replacement, Lord Kitchener. Wingate was faced with a dilemma; he and Gorst had at least formed a working relationship. Kitchener, although an old acquaintance, was remote, could be difficult and had little time for most of his subordinates. Gorst was a devil he knew, albeit a stuffy one. Sadly, Gorst would die of cancer that year. On a lighter note, Wingate in later life recalled an occasion during Edward VII's reign, when he and Gorst were invited guests at Balmoral and were required to wear formal court dress – knee breeches and tunics – displaying their honours. Gorst apparently wore his Knight of the Bath Order in an inappropriate manner, something frowned upon then and even now. Protocol required that the honour be suspended one quarter of an inch below the wearer's white bow tie; for some reason, Gorst pinned it to the top button of his waistcoat. This elicited a comment from the King, who studiously asked him, 'And where did you get your latest Masonic Decoration?'[53] Clearly the monarch, who was himself a Mason, was not amused by Gorst's gaffe. No doubt Wingate allowed himself a quiet smile as like Kitchener, he too was in the brotherhood.

Let us look back briefly to 1909, when Wingate had spent – or wasted – two months in British Somaliland during which time the Khedive of Egypt had formally opened the new trading harbour at Port Sudan. The harbour would prove invaluable to the Sudanese and Egyptian economies, the realization of one of Wingate's ambitions. The railway line at Atbara was extended to Port Sudan, thus linking it to the interior. Port Sudan itself not only facilitated trade within the Sudan but also opened up new trading possibilities with Arab states on the east coast of the Red Sea and to ships passing through the

Suez Canal. The seaport would also prove its worth during the Great War. The main commodities were millet, grain and cotton, exported to Arabia and Europe. The Atbara–Port Sudan rail link was the forerunner of an extensive rail system connecting towns such as Berber. During the construction of the Atbara line Wingate repeatedly urged Britain, as Egypt's co-partner in administering the Sudan, to contribute to its development. His arguments fell on deaf ears in Whitehall; the Egyptian Treasury was left to foot the bill.

Wingate had long harboured a dream of irrigating an area of the Sudan south of Khartoum between the Blue and White Nile known as the Gezira, where he believed cotton could be grown in commercially viable quantities. There were, however, problems, the main being that the summer flood of the Blue Nile was vital to the economy of Egypt; Wingate's proposal would divert water from Egypt though this did not sit well with the authorities and farmers there. The project would also require the construction of an expensive dam at Sennar, 160 miles south of Khartoum, with associated irrigation canals. It was an expensive scheme and there was virtually no prospect of financial support from the British Treasury, whose officials could see no direct benefit accruing from the investment; this was a short-sighted policy. Undeterred, Wingate sought support from sponsors; he persuaded two private companies to sink funds into what he was now calling his Gezira Scheme. The terms were that 80 per cent of the shares in the Scheme would be owned by the Sudanese government and the landowners in equal parts, the remaining portion being purchased by the private companies. Financing the Sennar Dam required £3 million which would be raised on the London Stock Market. The dam's construction became a defining moment in Wingate's career in the Sudan.

The chairman of the newly formed British Cotton Growing Association visited the Gezira and reported favourably on the project. Wingate had earlier secured the assistance of Sir William Garston, a competent irrigation engineer whose subsequent survey was favourable. And yet it seemed the scheme would never come into being despite the appointment in 1911 of a supportive Kitchener as Consul General in Cairo. There were delays in the development; natural and political obstacles made Wingate despair of the scheme ever being realized.

By the summer of 1910 Wingate was well enough to enjoy his summer leave and golf at Dunbar after his operation the previous year. The following year, the Wingates were guests of Dr Acland and his wife at their house in Bryanston Square, London, attending the coronation of George V at Westminster on 22 June 1911. The Wingates treated sons Ronald and Malcolm to the Naval Review at Gosport, Hampshire, then went on holiday in Europe, visiting Karlsbad via Nijmegen, Cologne, Mainz and Nuremberg. They were back in Dunbar on 1 August, united with all three children – a rare occurrence – during which Wingate renewed his acquaintance with the turf at Dunbar Golf Club. During that holiday Wingate learnt of the death of his sister Bessie and was thus in mourning when he, Kitty and Lord Kitchener visited Balmoral, where Wingate secured a promise from the King to visit the Sudan the following year. Wingate also managed to find the time to take Ronald to meet his old friend and benefactor Sir Evelyn Wood before leaving for Egypt in late September. He arrived in Egypt on 27 September, the day that Kitchener arrived to succeed Sir Eldon Gorst as Consul General of Egypt.

In 1911 Wingate was also successful in enlisting the financial support of various businessmen to invest in the Gordon Memorial College – Sir Henry Wellcome established pharmaceutical laboratories, Sir William Mather, a member of the British Cotton Growing Association, funded industrial work-shops and various schools were established by Christian missionaries. As for the Sudanese economy in general, the income from tourism, the export of animal products and gum-arabic was unlikely to attract sufficient revenue to make his Gezira Scheme viable, so Wingate began to examine other means of promoting it.

During his summer leave in Dunbar Wingate was again summoned to Balmoral, where he treated King George V to an in-depth report on the benefits to be had from the Gezira Scheme. As a constitutional monarch, George V could do little more than suggest that Wingate lobby Prime Minister Herbert Asquith and Chancellor of the Exchequer Lloyd George who were due to arrive at Balmoral. After several unsuccessful attempts to speak with Lloyd George, Wingate finally got his way, asking for only ten minutes of the Chancellor's time. He got an hour with Lloyd George. Impressed by the force of Wingate's argument, Lloyd George promised to guarantee a Treasury loan to construct the Sennar Dam but it would eventually take two years before the money was forthcoming. No matter, Wingate's energetic lobbying had convinced the Chancellor that creation of the Gezira Cotton Scheme would guarantee work for the workforce in the mills of Manchester and other cotton-spinning towns in the North of England.

Shortly after his visit to Balmoral Wingate in Dunbar was invited as a weekend guest at Whittingehame House, the country seat of the former Prime Minister and Leader of the House of Commons, Arthur J. Balfour. No doubt Wingate informed AJ of his recent discussions with Lloyd George. Balfour's sister, Lady Frances, commented that she had just returned from the Eisteddfod in Wales, where 'The Welsh Wizard' had made an impassioned speech in Welsh. She said the only words she recognized were 'Reginald Wingate'. She later asked LG to translate his speech and was told that Wingate had given him the inspiration for his theme which was to urge the Welsh people to speak their own language as well as English, as these languages would fertilize the barren lands of Britain just as the Blue and White Nile fertilized Egypt. One wonders if Wingate was impressed by the poetic metaphor; he was not known for an enthusiasm for poetry or great literature, detective novels and the Sherlock Holmes books of Conan Doyle being more his preferred choice of reading.

Despite Wingate's success in extracting promises of funds from the British Treasury for his pet project, the outbreak of the First World War put the

Gezira Scheme on the back-burner. His ambition would not be realized until 1925, when the dam and the irrigation system were finally completed. The venture paid dividends. By 1951 the Sudan's export trade was valued at £61 million, of which £54 million was raised from the sale of Gezira-grown cotton.[54]

Under Wingate's able and benevolent – if proprietorial – administration, the Sudan continued to prosper. He effectively made Khartoum a winter resort for wealthy tourists and VIPs. Even today, the journey from Cairo to Khartoum offers many attractions; the train proceeds by way of the temples and tombs of the Pharaohs – Luxor and Thebes – and thence to the impressive structure of the Aswan Dam. Next, a steamer with comfortable cabin accommodation takes visitors to the Nile's Second Cataract at Wadi Halfa, from whence passengers take the train to Khartoum, which offers steamer excursions to Fashoda.

After Wingate returned from his leave in Dunbar in 1911, he would face the most important state occasion in all his years as Governor General of the Sudan. In September that year, visiting the King and Queen at Balmoral, George V had accepted his invitation to visit the Sudan as part of a forthcoming tour of India. In mid-November Wingate met the Royal party in Alexandria; thereafter, he and Kitchener dined with the King and Queen on HMS *Medina* in Port Said. Wingate spent Christmas at Khartoum, joined by sons Ronald and Malcolm. Ronald recalls the morning rides across the Sudanese desert, the palace levees, or receptions, and balls. On Boxing Day the boys were taken to Dongola Province where they met Lord Kitchener. The two young men would shortly choose their careers, Ronald joining the Indian Civil Service, Malcolm enlisting as a subaltern in the Royal Engineers, Kitchener's old regiment. During his holiday in Khartoum, young Malcolm learnt that he had passed tenth in the Woolwich examinations, thus assuring him a posting to the Engineers.

After the Christmas festivities Wingate and his wife went to Port Sudan to entertain the royals on 17 January 1912. Wingate laid on a lavish range of ceremonies and entertainments, including dancers, whirling Dervishes, performing horsemen, sword dancers and military parades. It was all very colourful, possibly the high-water mark of Wingate's career in the Sudan. Some accounts maintain that Wingate deliberately set out to impress the Sudanese notables who were invited to the celebrations. Wingate himself admitted that his attempts to associate the British royal family with the Sudan were part of a policy to upstage Egypt and the Khedive and strengthen the British connection.

A month after the royal party's visit, Wingate was attacked by 'a mad policeman', an incident mentioned earlier. The attacker was safely disabled but not before he had inflicted a wound with a steel-pointed staff to Wingate's left wrist which the latter had raised to ward off the blow. Wingate never recovered fully from the injury.

However, let us return to the matter of Gorst in 1911. Wingate certainly had mixed feelings about Kitchener as Gorst's successor. Kitchener had intimate knowledge of the Egyptian Army and the Sudan and so would never allow himself publicly to be impressed by Wingate's expertise. Furthermore, Kitchener had taken on Lord Curzon, the Viceroy of India, the most powerful man in the Empire in a public debate on the running of India and won. Wingate, no longer enjoying the support of his former mentors Sir Evelyn Wood and Lord Cromer, was wary, knowing he would have to avoid confrontation with 'K of K', as Kitchener was known. However, to some extent, his fears were unfounded. Kitchener gave him a free rein in the Sudan. He only visited the Sudan on three occasions; the first for the visit of George V, the second to open the El Obeid Railway then a final visit in December–January of 1912–1913.

However, on the other hand, Kitchener's brief but autocratic rule as British Agent curbed the power and influence of the Khedive, thus serving the interest of the growing number of Egyptian Nationalists. Perhaps it was Cromer, Kitchener and, to some extent, Gorst who were the catalysts in the rise of nationalism; they hardly made Wingate's future appointment as High Commissioner of Egypt an easy one. When he was sacked in 1919 for attempting to placate the Nationalists, these three men, in their different ways, had unwittingly contributed to his career's demise.

Wingate reigned virtually supreme in the Sudan. He ran the country as if it were a feudal fiefdom, expecting the appropriate recognition of his position as Governor General and representative of His Britannic Majesty. He was a stickler for formal ceremony and proper dress, expected (and got) due deference from both Sudanese and British officials. He made it clear that even British tourists of the middling sort should pay him the appropriate respect. On at least one occasion, at a public appearance, a British tourist was approached by one of Wingate's aides who informed the innocent bystander watching Wingate's entourage proceeding through a Khartoum street that 'It is customary for all civilians to take their hats off when the Governor General passes [by]'.[55] This practice was insisted upon and enforced. Wingate never allowed anyone to forget who and what he was – the King's representative.

In 1912 the local newspapers in East Lothian continued to report on Wingate's summer leaves in Dunbar. These news items had become a regular feature over the past thirteen years and would continue for several more.[56-58]

The year 1913 was the last full year of peace before the outbreak of one of the worst wars in the world's history. In many respects the year was probably the happiest of Wingate's time in the Middle East, although it was marred by news of the death of his first escapee from Omdurman, Father Joseph Ohrwalder. At this time the relationship between the Sudan Plantations Syndicate and the Sudan government headed by Wingate was so interwoven that Wingate was moved to extol its virtues, saying it was an extremely interesting experiment, unique in the world 'For a Government and a Syndicate to combine on co-operative principles, and for a Syndicate to become, in some respects, a Government Department is an entirely new departure'.[59] The continuous round of social events in Khartoum entertaining esteemed British and European visitors seemed as if it would never end. The Wingates' guests included notably the Dowager Duchess of Roxburghe, from Dunbar.

In March that year Wingate embarked on a long and gruelling tour of Eastern Sudan, followed by a two-month stay at Kitty's Leap, as the hill station at Erkowit had become affectionately known to the family. In May the Wingates travelled to Europe, visiting Karlsbad for their annual 'cure' at the spa, where they celebrated their twenty-fifth wedding anniversary. They were back in England on 1 July where Wingate attended the annual Egyptian Army dinner. Three days later, they dined with the Princess Royal; the following day, they visited daughter Victoria at school, then left for Dunbar on 6 July. Wingate's summer of golf at Dunbar was interrupted by visits to London, where he continued to promote his proposals for the Gezira Cotton Scheme. In mid-August the Wingates were joined by daughter Victoria at Dunbar, then were guests of the Princess Royal and her husband, the Duke of Fife, at Mar Lodge. Kitchener visited Knockenhair in September and Wingate was joined there by Rudolf von Slatin who then accompanied him on the annual trip to Balmoral. After a weekend in London with Ronald and Malcolm, the Wingates left Britain for Egypt on 1 October. On 4 October Ronald announced his engagement to Mary Vinogradoff (Harpoth) with whom the Wingates had dined in London. Mary Harpoth was the daughter of a Danish banker who had died when she was aged just four. Her mother re-married Vinogradoff, Professor of Jurisprudence at Oxford University, Mary assuming her stepfather's surname.

In June 1914, the last peacetime summer, Wingate visited Rudolf 'Rowdy' von Slatin in Vienna, then he and Lady Wingate proceeded to Karlsbad. 'Old Rowdy' was about to marry Alice von Ramberg, an Austrian lady from a family whose male members were soldiers, sailors and artists. Her grandfather had been ADC to the Duke of Wellington at Waterloo and was ennobled in 1849. Slatin and Alice were duly married in July 1914; he was fifty-seven, she forty-one.[60]

As for Wingate, letters from friends congratulated him on yet another honour – the Knight's Grand Cross of the Order of the Bath, intimated in the King's Birthday *Gazette*. A few days later, the press reported the assassination on 28 June at Sarajevo of the Archduke Franz Ferdinand, heir to the Austrian throne, by a disaffected Serbo-Croat student, Gavrilo Princip. The event was hardly noticed in Britain, largely because few people knew where Sarajevo was, let alone appreciated the significance of the incident. In any case Britain was preoccupied with the threat of civil war in Ireland. The British people were soon to realize the profound consequences of that remote event in June 1914.

One wonders what, if anything, Wingate made of this news. No doubt he read *The Times'* account and dismissed it as a regrettable but minor incident in a distant European state. As far as he was concerned the Sudan was what mattered most. He was determined to make his name in the Sudan by being remembered for his achievements. It must be said that Wingate never received anything approaching the acclaim that Kitchener enjoyed after the re-conquest of the Sudan. Kitchener may be described as the sword who delivered it from tyranny, Wingate the ploughshare who developed it. In his time as Governor General of the Sudan, his stewardship of the country became progressively liberal; Wingate never set out to dominate or exploit the conquered people over which he was set. Today, however, he is hardly remembered in the land; the Sudan is a country suffering from the privations belonging to an earlier century – disease, malnutrition and political unrest, all of which Wingate strove to eliminate in his time.

Perhaps Wingate's achievements are ignored because today it is not fashionable to extol the virtues of Britain's imperial age. Modern revisionist historians are disposed to concentrate only on the shortcomings of the Empire. Even the irrigation system which Wingate introduced in the Gezira District to facilitate the growing of cotton has been criticized but modern agriculturalists consider Wingate's scheme an unqualified success. Hostile critics argue that his irrigation canals proved to be breeding grounds for the malarial mosquito. They also point out that, instead of providing food for the native population, the Gezira Scheme profited the Egyptian government by the export of cotton while the local population starved. At least these detractors concede that Wingate's scheme provided work for the Sudanese peasantry.

One has only to study the vast archive of Wingate papers held in Durham University Library to appreciate the extent of Wingate's commitment. There are papers on countless subjects ranging from matters of internal security, agricultural improvements, outbreaks of rinderpest in cattle, the spread and control of diseases injurious to human health – malaria spread by mosquitoes, the asal fly and other insects. There are documents on proposals for producing rubber from plantations in southern Sudan, the improvement of water supplies, the extension of existing rail and telegraphic links and a hundred and one other initiatives. And of course, the lavish arrangements made for prestigious visitors such as Edward VII, the Duke of Connaught and other notables.

As for Wingate's selfless dedication to the Sudan – genuine, albeit tempered by a sense of duty to Crown and Empire – one should remember that he went to Egypt to further his career. Egypt offered better rates of pay to British Army officers seconded to the Egyptian Army. No one can blame a man for seeking to improve his standard of living; after all, he had known poverty in the wake of the death of his father in 1862, and when marrying was still extremely poor. He had to pull himself up by his boot straps to make a living for his family. When he was appointed Governor General of the Sudan, his salary was £5,000 (£150,000 in modern terms). In 1900 a skilled artisan could earn £150 a year, respectable shopkeepers about £500. Wingate's salary was impressive but he spent it to the full, entertaining guests and friends during his time at Khartoum. There were, of course, grants and allowances to assist what was in effect (Egyptian) government hospitality; however, Wingate always seemed to be in the red, even demeaning himself to seek free railway passes when he came to Britain on official business.

Wingate's commitment to the Sudan was matched by that of his wife. It is certain that she added steel to his endeavours, ensuring that he accomplished all he set out to do. Kitty was devoted to her husband, sharing his professional and social life and backing him to the hilt. Who was it that once said that behind every successful man is a woman? Quick-witted, articulate and on rare occasions blunt, she nonetheless remained in the background. Her son Ronald described her as a strict disciplinarian, though that discipline was tempered with love. Lady Wingate took great pleasure in the role of hostess and helpmate. Her marriage to Wingate greatly improved her lifestyle. When Kitty Rundle met Reginald Wingate it had been love at first sight. Their subsequent courtship of two years grieved them as they wanted to be together as a married couple. In those early days Kitty knew her prospective husband was not rich, nor did his career at that time offer much in the way of a better lifestyle but she followed her intuition and became his faithful partner, confident that, one day, he would make good. Theirs was a love affair that would survive until her death in 1946.

Finally, let us return to events in the summer of 1914. The flurry of telegrams passing between the diplomats in Britain and Europe did not immediately affect the Wingates as they returned to London on 6 July. The following day Wingate attended a Gordon Memorial College board meeting, followed by the Egyptian Army annual dinner. On 10 July the Wingates met their future daughter-in-law, Mary Vinogradoff, Ronald's fiancée, for the first time.[61] They dined together and went to a performance of Oscar Wilde's 'The Ideal Husband' with Malcolm and the Princess Royal. Thereafter, they travelled to Dunbar on 11 July for the summer season. On 23 July, the day of the Austria-Hungary ultimatum to Serbia, the Wingates returned to London. The following day Wingate attended a meeting with Prime Minister Asquith to discuss the recent developments. The Wingates then visited son Malcolm at Chatham on 25 and 26 July and, on the 27th, Wingate visited his old friend and patron Sir Evelyn Wood. On the following day he had an interview with Sir Edward Grey, the Foreign Secretary, at which they discussed the impending crisis. Later that same day matters escalated as Austria and Hungary declared war on Serbia. Even so, the routine of life still continued; on 29 July the Wingates dined out again and visited the theatre with Malcolm and daughter Victoria, then took the overnight sleeper to Dunbar.[62]

In that last summer of peace in 1914 Wingate was in Dunbar for only a few days. His leave was terminated abruptly by a call from the Foreign Office, ordering him to return to the Sudan just before war was declared on Germany by Britain and France on 4 August 1914. Wingate left Dunbar on

2 August.[63] More than four years would elapse before the Wingates would again be able to return to Knockenhair.

Notes

1. *Not in the Limelight*, RELW.
2. *Ibid.*
3. *Ibid.*
4. *Ibid.*
5. *Ibid.*
6. *Ibid.*
7. *Sudan Tales*, Kenrick. As early as 1905 a detailed report on the suitability of Erkowit rather than Suakin as a hill station had been prepared (WP 277/6, 5 December 1905, SAD, DU).
8. *HC*, June 1899.
9. *Not in the Limelight*.
10. *Ibid.*
11. *Valuation Roll, 1900–1901, Dunbar*.
12. *HC*, 10 August 1905.
13. *Valuation Roll, 1910–1911*.
14. *Ibid.*
15. *HC*, 28 April 1905.
16. *Ibid*, 12 March 1920.
17. *Not in the Limelight*. When Wingate's daughter Victoria married Captain Henry Dane on 4 March 1922 in St George's Chapel, Hanover Square, London, the wedding reception was held at 31 Great Cumberland Place (*HC*, 10 March 1922).
18. *HC*, 15 June 1900.
19. *Ibid.*
20. Frederick Sleigh Roberts (known affectionately as 'Bobs'), Earl Roberts of Kandahar, Pretoria and Waterford was C-in-C of the British Army during the Boer War. He was awarded the freedom of the Burgh of Dunbar in 1893.
21. *HC*, 10 August 1900.
22. *HA*, 13 July 1900.
23. *Ibid*, 14 September 1900.
24. WP 270/8, SAD, DU.
25. WP 270/8, SAD, DU.
26. *HC, HA* respectively 7 and 9 September 1900.
27. *Not in the Limelight*.
28. In *The Sirdar*, (Daly) Captain George Miller Wingate is wrongly identified as being Francis Reginald Wingate's brother and dying in 1916. George in fact was FRW's cousin and died at Southsea in 1918. Confirmation of George Wingate's will was given at Haddington on 21 August 1918, the beneficiaries being his wife, Emily Livingstone Wood, living in Dunbar and his son Major George Frederick Wingate, residing in London.
29. Molly Marrow was the last of the immediate family. A well known figure in Dunbar, she was in charge of the Voluntary Aid Detachment (VAD) Nursing Association during both world wars. She lived at Westbarns, near Dunbar until her death.
30. *HA*, 12 July 1901.
31. *HC*, 26 September 1902.
32. *HA*, September 1903.
33. *Not in the Limelight*.
34. *Ibid.*
35. *HA, HC*, 8 November 1907.
36. *HC*, 4 December 1908. The Wingates resided in Stafford House, Bayswell Road in the summer of 1908.
37. *HA*, 9 July 1909.

38. *Ibid.*, 9 August 1912.
39. Sir Arthur Conan Doyle spent a holiday in Dunbar in 1906, staying in the Roxburghe Hotel, now demolished. He and Wingate probably enjoyed a round of golf (*HA*, 14 September 1906).
40. *HC*, 13 and 20 September 1907.
41. *Ibid.*, 16 April 1909.
42. *Ibid.*, 2 February 1912.
43. *Ibid.*, 29 March 1912.
44. *Al-Ahram*, 20 December 1899 (WP 269/12, SAD, DU).
45. *Dunbar Golf*, Harris.
46. *Wingate of the Sudan*, RELW.
47. *Ibid.*
48. Cromer to Wingate, 9 April 1907 (WP 280/4, SAD, DU).
49. Wingate to Cromer, 10 April 1907 (WP 280/4, SAD, DU).
50. Slatin to Wingate, 27 February 1910 (WP 290/2, SAD, DU).
51. *HA*, 29 April 1910.
52. *Ibid.*, 10 June 1910.
53. *Wingate of the Sudan.*
54. *Wingate of the Sudan.*
55. *The Sirdar.*
56. *HA*, 14 June 1912.
57. *Ibid.*, 21 June 1912.
58. *Ibid*, 19 July 1912.
59. Wingate to Phipps, 6 June 1913 (WP 186/3/9, SAD, DU).
60. *Slatin Pasha*, Hill.
61. They would be married in Lahore Cathedral, India in November 1916 (*HC*, 10 November 1916).
62. *The Sirdar.*
63. *HA*, 7 August 1914.

Chapter 5

World War

In the first decade of the twentieth century the Sudan, with its under-developed economy still suffering the devastating effects of the Mahdist rebellion, was ripe for reconstruction and reform. Reginald Wingate, appointed to a position which he had not sought, applied himself with vigour. He undertook his role as Governor General of the Sudan with the zeal that characterized many Scotsmen in the service of imperial Britain. During his first years of office Wingate introduced a legal system – which the Sudan had hitherto lacked – to deal with civil and criminal actions. Equally important were the administrative, social and economic reforms he intro-duced, measures long overdue. While Wingate in no way baulked at the prestige or the responsibilities of high office – he thoroughly enjoyed the trappings and the glitter of his position and made no bones about it – in a relatively short time he achieved more than his predecessors had thought possible. Untiring in his efforts to improve the lot of the Sudanese people, Wingate's name became a household word amongst those he governed in the Sudan and to a lesser extent, in Egypt. By 1910 he had gained a reputation that would survive long after his departure from the Middle East.

Before we examine the effects of the Great War on Wingate's administra-tion in the Sudan, it is perhaps appropriate here to offer a general view. The war certainly touched the Sudan, albeit in a superficial way; it was not until the outbreak of the Arab Revolt (see Chapter 6) that the Sudan and Wingate's role as its Governor General became prominent in the context of the war. It is one of history's ironies that Wingate's achievements in the Revolt have not been fully recognized, although he received a degree of praise from his masters in Whitehall for keeping peace in the Sudan while war swirled round its borders. At the outset of the Great War the question on everyone's lips was this: were Turkey to enter the war on Germany's side, to whom would Egypt and the Sudan show loyalty? Wingate and his administration viewed the prospect with alarm.

Let us revisit the closing page of the previous chapter. In May 1914 Wingate returned to Khartoum after spending the hot season at Kitty's Leap. On his arrival in Khartoum, he was visited by several messengers acting on behalf of Ali Dinar, the troublesome Sultan of Darfur Province.[1] It is certain that the meeting was arranged to discuss Ali Dinar's demands; he was a constant thorn in Wingate's side and would remain so until Major Huddleston, one of

Wingate's staff officers, defeated and killed Dinar in a short, sharp action in 1916. After dealing with this and other matters, Wingate went on leave to Dunbar, no doubt looking forward to a season on the local golf course. The holiday was interrupted by a telegram from London on 23 July, ordering him to the capital for talks with Prime Minister Asquith, Foreign Secretary Sir Edward Grey and Secretary of State for War Lord Kitchener. (It will be remembered that the day before war broke out on 4 August 1914, Sir Edward Grey, Lord Grey of Fallodon, had famously intoned, 'The lamps are going out all over Europe; we shall not see them lit again in our lifetime.')

After the war talk in London Wingate was back in Dunbar on the golf links, perhaps enjoying the company of James Hastie, the Cairo golf club's green keeper and professional who was also home visiting his family.[2] That summer, Wingate spent only three days in Dunbar; he was recalled to Cairo on 2 August.[3] Before Wingate set off, son Malcolm visited Knockenhair before joining his unit of the Royal Engineers, part of an expeditionary force that Germany's Kaiser Wilhelm would dismiss as a 'contemptible little army'; the veterans of that expeditionary force would become known as The Old Contemptibles. One likes to speculate that on some quiet August evening, when the swallows were wheeling and screaming round the spire of Belhaven Church and Knockenhair, their outlines softened by the setting sun, Wingate said goodbye to Malcolm. Kitty's favourite son returned to Knockenhair on leave in October 1915.[4] His parents were in the Sudan so he never saw them again after August 1914. Malcolm Roy Wingate would be killed during Operation MICHAEL, the Ludendorff Offensive in March 1918.

On 2 August 1914 Wingate set off for Egypt, leaving Lady Wingate at Knockenhair; it would be nearly five years before they would return to Dunbar. Lady Wingate joined him in Khartoum in November, following Turkey's entry into the war against the Allies.[5] Wingate boarded ship at Tilbury Docks, London, the first vessel to leave Britain at the war's outbreak. The ship called at Gibraltar, then Malta, where he was able to visit his brother-in-law Leslie Rundle who had been appointed Governor of the island in 1909.

Arriving in Cairo on 21 August 1914, Wingate found the administration there in a state of understandable confusion. As Kitchener had been hurriedly recalled to London to become Secretary of State for War, no one had yet been appointed in his place. The army commander, General Byng, was succeeded by General Sir John Maxwell who had been tipped to replace Wingate as Governor General of the Sudan in 1910. The Khedive of Egypt, Abbas Hilmi, was in Constantinople. The British government announced that Hilmi had defected to the Turks; in point of fact, the poor man was literally their prisoner and he decided to throw in his lot with Turkey. The British replaced him with his uncle Prince Hussayn Kamil who was given the new title Sultan of Egypt.[6] Abbas Hilmi was undoubtedly used as a pawn in Turkish propaganda which praised him for defecting from Britain in August, two months before Turkey entered the war.

Wingate spent nearly three weeks in Cairo, attempting to calm the panic-stricken Egyptian Council of Ministers, temporarily without a head of state and a British Agent or Consul General to advise them. Wingate discussed possible solutions, reassuring the Egyptian Prime Minister that Britain would not leave Egypt in the lurch; he also reviewed the troops in the Cairo garrison. Wingate was emulating the Duke of Wellington who always maintained that a review of his soldiers had a calming effect on them. Wingate was back in Khartoum by 9 September; like his masters in Britain, he had no idea as yet of Turkey's war intentions. However, he took the necessary steps to make the Sudan as secure as possible. German and Austrian nationals were expelled – men like Charles (or Karl) Neufeld, the Mahdist prisoner in Omdurman who could never make up his mind whether he wanted to be rescued and remained there until the town was relieved in 1898. It seems that Neufeld, outwardly a trading merchant in gum-arabic until 1914, was suspected of gun-running in the Sudan and stirring up anti-British feelings. Wingate certainly thought him a nuisance. Wingate also introduced censorship of all incoming and outgoing mail and orchestrated a press campaign stressing the loyalty of Egypt and the Sudan to Britain. He delivered impassioned speeches in Omdurman, El Obeid, Wad Medani and Port Said to ensure that loyalty, while avoiding criticism of Turkey. He laid the blame for the war solely at Germany's door.

As early as mid-August, concern was expressed about a pre-emptive Turkish landing at Aqaba (or Akaba) on the Red Sea; from there, it was believed that they might launch an attack on the Suez Canal. These British fears were not without foundation, as it was reported on 16 August 1914 that 'A Turkish ship, name painted out, left Suez yesterday and it is thought she may have gone [to] Akaba to transport this force'.[7] Added to this, Turkish mobilization in Arabia had raised 24,000 men. Despite these hostile moves, up to the very day that Turkey entered the war, Turkish diplomats argued that such a measure posed no threat to Britain or France. They insisted the measure was simply introduced to reassure the Turkish people and subject populations – the Arabs – that mobilization was necessary to counter possible aggression on the part of Christian Russia, supported by Syria. When British diplomats protested to Turkey that her war measure was considered a threat to Egypt, their Turkish counterparts responded, 'why are the British themselves sending such large numbers of Indian [Hindu and Muslim] troops to Egypt?'[8]

Like his contemporaries, Wingate was worried about the effect a hostile Turkey would have on the Sudan and Egypt, both being, like Turkey, predominantly Muslim. The next three months were fraught with nail-biting uncertainty. Wingate knew that if Turkey declared against the Allies, he might well be faced with a wider uprising in the Sudan. The Egyptian Army in the Sudan consisted of 14,000 troops led by a few British Army officers; the fear was that the native soldiers might decide to throw in their lot with the

Turks. In that event, there would be only a single British battalion in Cairo to oppose an uprising. During the month of September Wingate concentrated on restoring calm and confidence throughout the Sudan.

In an attempt to defuse the increasingly volatile situation, Wingate astutely called together the *ulemas* – the Islamic Learned Ones who guide and advise Muslims on religious matters. Wingate treated them to a stirring speech, delivered in his fluent Arabic:

> God is my witness that we [the British] never interfered with any man in the exercise of his religion. We have brought the holy places within a few days' journey of Khartoum. We have subsidised and assisted the men of religion. We have built, and given assistance for the building of new mosques all over the country ... The world policy of Great Britain will remain unchanged. She will ever maintain and enforce on others the maintenance and sanctity and inviolability of the Holy Places. As previously, she will shelter and protect all Mohammedans and mosques within her borders in the same way as, for over 150 years, she has guarded the interests of the 62 millions of Mohammedans of our Indian Empire – many thousands of which are now fighting alongside their fellow British subjects against the German army ... You in the Sudan have had bitter experience of the evils of Turkish rule ... but you may feel – and believe me, I sympathise with you truly in this matter – a certain sorrow at this war. You may fear, some of you, that the result of this war may in some way affect the situation of Mohammedans in other parts of the world. I assure you before God that your fears are groundless, and that in the British Empire the position of no single Mohammedan will be changed one iota and no single privilege granted to Islam will be repudiated.

He ended his impassioned words by advising the *ulemas* to carry his message to the people of the Sudan. He concluded thus:

> Now I ask you at this present time, you men of religion, learning and experience, to give wise and honourable counsel to the people who will listen to you; for here in the Sudan, as elsewhere in the world, the fools will listen to the wise, the ignorant to the learned, and the common people to men of wisdom and education.[9]

Pledges of loyalty to Britain were sent to Wingate from the four corners of the Sudan. Only in Egypt was there hesitation among those who were either pro-Turkey or harboured thoughts of independence from Britain. It is difficult to understand how the pro-Turkish and nationalist elements among the Egyptian population could have expected to achieve independence from both Britain and Turkey at the same time. For the moment, the war would have to be fought, Egyptian nationalist aspirations being put on hold. For his part, Wingate travelled throughout the Sudan, visiting remote outposts and garrisons to stiffen morale; his official correspondence records that at every place he visited, the officers of the Egyptian army expressed genuine loyalty to Britain.

In December 1914 the British government declared that Egypt would become a British Protectorate, without defining precisely under what terms. The British representative in Cairo, appointed in Kitchener's place, was Sir Henry McMahon, who was styled High Commissioner. In Khartoum, on 20 December, Wingate read out the proclamation of Protectorate status to the crowds of Sudanese assembled in front of the British Residency building. The following day he held a parade to mark the accession of the pro-British Sultan Hussayn Kamil of Egypt.

As far as the British government in London and McMahon in Cairo were concerned, the Sudan would be left to its own devices under Wingate's stewardship. British officials in Cairo were more preoccupied with the task of defending Egypt – in effect the Suez Canal – from Turkish invasion. Wingate now saw men subordinate to him rise to positions of power and prestige while he was virtually forgotten. As he confided to his diary, he felt isolated from the main theatre of the war, although that would change in 1916.

The initial effect of the first few months of the Great War on Wingate's personal life denied him the company of his wife. Kitty Wingate divided her time in Britain between Knockenhair and various friends in or near London until she was re-united with her husband in Khartoum on Christmas Eve 1914. Their son Malcolm, a subaltern in 26 Field Company, Royal Engineers had spent his twenty-first birthday at the Front on 28 August. Their eldest son Ronald, serving in the Indian Civil Service, was appointed to the British Commissioner's staff at Lahore. Ronald would marry his fiancée Mary Vinogradoff there in November 1916 although, because of the war, none of his family was present at the ceremony.[10]

A major disappointment to Wingate was the loss of the companionship of his old friend, Rudolf von Slatin. At the outbreak of the Great War the Austrian could not in all conscience remain as Inspector General of the Sudan in British service. Wingate felt the separation from his closest friend acutely. In one of Slatin's several hundred letters to Wingate, he once said that Queen Victoria, on being informed that her hero was with Wingate in Dunbar in the summer of 1900, had responded, 'Oh I know. He and the Sirdar are always together and each of them could hardly live without the other.'[11] Slatin wrote Wingate two letters, one formally renouncing his official position, the other a personal confession regretting the decision. The second letter addressed Wingate as his eternal friend:

My Dear Old Rex,
It is very sad – but let us say it is fate, and it [the war] had to come ... I did my best to join you before the declaration of war, but on account of mobilization it was impossible for me to leave the country [Austria] earlier. I returned from the way [sic] to Italy yesterday.

My personal friendship for you, my dear old Rex, shall not suffer though I condemn the decision of your government to fight against Austria, the traditional friend of England ... My wife [Alice] sends her best love. Goodbye.

From your affectionate

Old Rowdy.[12]

Accompanying this personal note was a formal letter tendering his resignation as Inspector General of the Sudan and relinquishing honours and decorations he had been awarded by the British monarchy, although the official renunciation of his British appointment and decorations was not reported until four months later.[13] The Great War did not prevent Wingate and Slatin continuing their correspondence through neutral channels. For his part, Slatin refused to take up a military appointment; he became involved in the Red Cross movement, caring for the prisoners of war of both Germany and Britain and her allies. It would be six long years before Slatin and Wingate, the 'Sudanese Twins', would meet again.

In late 1914 *The Times* in London reported that the bulk of the Egyptian Army was stationed in the Sudan. Wingate held a parade of those units of the Egyptian Army still in Cairo, then proceeded to Khartoum where he briefed first the senior officers of his staff, then the native sheiks and other notables. His next major public event took place in Omdurman, where he explained the causes of the war, after which he embarked on an exhausting tour of the country, holding similar meetings in various towns.

Wingate had always known that if Turkey entered the war on the side of Germany, his position in the Sudan would alter dramatically. Anxious to influence Turkey's decision, Lord Kitchener, Secretary of State for War, had taken what steps he could to reassure Turkey that the British were friendly towards the Ottoman Empire and that Britain's interests were solely concerned with the free passage of ships sailing under all flags through the Suez Canal. To this end, one of his measures was the publication of an archaeological survey of the Sinai Desert in which a young subaltern by the name of Thomas Edward Lawrence had participated. Kitchener thought that, by publishing the report, he might convince the Turks that British activity in the desert was purely scientific and in no way related to military map-making. Privately, Lawrence hoped that Turkey would declare war on Britain and her allies, giving them an excuse to expel the Turks from the Middle East and thus facilitate the establishment of an independent Arab Republic or kingdom in Syria and Arabia. At the same time, Kitchener had established contact with Hussein, Emir (the title Emir is given to the senior and most noble of all Sherifs) of Mecca, sounding him out on Arab reaction to Turkey's potential hostility towards Britain. In time, after almost two years of prevarication, Hussein would throw in his lot with the British. The result was that the subsequent Palestine campaign was triggered by what became known as the Arab Revolt in 1916; that campaign, British-led, was hardly altruistic in nature, the prime consideration being the security of Egypt, the Sudan and protection of the Suez Canal to allow the Royal Navy to operate freely.

When Sir Henry McMahon (1862–1949) succeeded Kitchener as High Commissioner of Egypt, he followed his own policy towards the Arabs, putting out feelers to ascertain how Sherif Hussein of the holy city of Mecca would react to a hostile Turkey. However, Hussein prevaricated and McMahon grew increasingly frustrated by Hussein's reluctance to declare one way or the other. In an attempt to encourage him to reach a decision, in October 1915, McMahon hinted broadly (see Appendix III) at the likelihood of creating an Arab kingdom or nation which would be self-governing were the Arabs to enter the war on Britain's side. The Foreign Office in London supported McMahon's aim but this would ultimately prove an empty promise.

On 29 October 1914 Turkey duly entered the war on the side of the Central Powers, giving assistance to a German bombardment of Russia. In Egypt the *Journal Officiel du Gouvernement Egyptien* contained a proclamation by Lieutenant General John Grenfell Maxwell declaring martial law on 2 November (see Appendix I). On 5 November, Britain and France declared war on Turkey. *The Times* of 6 November carried an article headed 'War with Turkey. Declaration by Great Britain', an extract from which reads:

Owing to hostile acts committed by Turkish forces under German officers, a state of war exists between Great Britain and Turkey as from today. Foreign Office, Nov. 5 1914.

T. E. Lawrence received the news with unconcealed delight. Turkish aims were to secure Suez and recover lost territory in Persia and Caucasia and once in possession of Persia, Turkey and her German ally could threaten Mesopotamia, with its prized oil wells, and perhaps even India. However, these ambitions depended on various factors. Not least was continuing Turkish control of the Arab states and Mesopotamia. As for Lawrence, his knowledge of the Middle East and his mastery of Arabic would be put to good use in the military intelligence unit in Cairo's Arab Bureau. In this, Lawrence was following in the footsteps of an older, wiser head in the person of Reginald Wingate, a man with whom the young idealist would soon be intimately acquainted.

It is appropriate here for the purposes of this and the following chapter to examine the role and nature of the Arab Bureau. In the second decade of the twentieth century, the British Middle East authorities became obsessed as never before with intelligence gathering. Before 1908, apart from Wingate's operations in the re-conquest of the Sudan between 1886 and 1898, there had been no formal espionage structure, no paid operatives in the Middle and Near East. The Foreign Office had relied on unpaid amateurs, adventurers and travellers such as Gertrude Bell, the famous Victorian explorer, and T. E. Lawrence, an amateur archaeologist, to report on their explorations and expeditions. The Great War would change all this. Gertrude Bell was actually recruited by the Foreign Office in 1915; she held the honorary rank of Major with the substantive rank of General Staff Officer 2nd Grade, the first female operative in the British Intelligence Service.

Among the small staff – numbering a mere fifteen – of the Arab Bureau were its head, Colonel Alfred Parker, Lord Kitchener's nephew, who was later succeeded by Sir Gilbert Clayton, Director of Military Intelligence of the Egyptian Army and extending his role as ADC to Sir Henry McMahon. Other key figures were the brilliant Oriental Secretary Sir Ronald Storrs; Dr David Hogarth, archaeologist, then serving as a Lieutenant Commander in the Royal Naval Volunteer Reserve; Kinahan Cornwallis (later Sir Kinahan Cornwallis who became Personal Secretary to Prince Feisal, the charismatic leader of the Arab Revolt); George Lloyd, a banker; Major (or Colonel) P. C. Joyce – of whom Abdullah, one of Hussein's sons and subsequent King of Trans-Jordan would write:

> Colonel Joyce, or Major Joyce, one of the most faithful people to both the British and the Arab Cause ... helped the Arabs more than Lawrence, suffering all kinds of calamities.

Other stalwarts in the Bureau were Stewart F. Newcombe who had been with Lawrence on the Sinai expedition in 1914, Charles Edward Wilson who was stationed in Jedda, Gertrude Bell and, last but not least, Lawrence, the scruffy but brilliant, self-absorbed junior officer who had joined the British Army to work in the Middle East map-making unit.

Of these Lawrence was the most unruly and charismatic member of the Bureau. Lawrence loved the desert and the Arabs; his interest in the Middle East was initially in the field of archaeology. As a student at Oxford he undertook a tour of Syria before the war; he was fascinated by the country, studying the terrain and searching for the ruins of crusader castles. He took part in a major dig at Carchemish under Dr David Hogarth; it was during this excavation that he first encountered Gertrude Bell, the daughter of the desert. They were well enough acquainted for him to refer to her in his letters as Gerty – but perhaps not to her in person.

Lawrence's involvement in the Middle East and Arabia would become an obsession. He championed the cause of the Arab tribes which for five centuries had suffered under the harsh rule of the Ottoman or Turkish Empire. In his classic book *Seven Pillars of Wisdom*, he wrote of past European attempts to stabilize the Middle and Near East:

> The efforts of the European powers in the Asiatic Levant had been uniformly disastrous ... Our successor and solution must be local [meaning an independent Arab nation] ... the competition would be with Turkey; and Turkey was rotten. [14]

In Cairo McMahon continued his exploratory correspondence with Sherif Hussein of Mecca. It was cloak-and-dagger stuff, worthy of John Buchan fiction. Messages were passed between Cairo and Mecca concealed in the hilts of daggers and soles of shoes, a correspondence that would continue from the outbreak of war between Britain and Turkey until June 1916, when Emir Hussein finally made up his mind.

On 1 January 1915, two months after Turkey's entry into the war, *The Times* praised Wingate's efforts to maintain order in the Sudan. The following is quoted from that newspaper:

> the existing security and the strong support which the whole population
> have [sic] offered to the British cause are very largely due to the results
> ... of Wingate, and of his many officers under his control

By then, the imperial troops in Egypt numbered 70,000, the bulk being stationed in or near Cairo. Throughout the war the Egyptian Army itself was largely engaged in the defence of the interior; rightly or wrongly, they were never trusted to guard the Suez Canal, nor did Egyptian soldiers play any significant part in the battles for the Middle East.

Wingate's administrative responsibilities as Sirdar and Governor General of the Sudan were increased as a result of the war. He had to make do with fewer staff, many of the army officers in his service being transferred to the British Army. Several served in the disastrous Dardanelles Campaign on the Gallipoli Peninsula. This was only one of his troubles; Wingate was faced with a rebellion in Darfur Province, orchestrated by its Sultan, Ali Dinar. Wingate crushed Dinar's rebellion in Darfur. The point was not lost on Ali Dinar, whose main sphere of operations was situated more than 100 miles west of Kordofan, its adjacent province. Darfur was a province containing 80,000 inhabitants, warlike people who were fanatical Muslims and well armed. Ali Dinar began his revolt by informing the government of the Sudan – in effect, Wingate – that he had repudiated his allegiance to the Sudan. No action could be taken against him as Wingate had few military resources available. In 1915 the Turks encouraged Ali Dinar to invade the Sudan interior at the same time as the Senussi tribe, friendly towards Turkey, were advancing through the western desert to invade Egypt. Wingate expressed the view that the Turks had 'got at' Ali Dinar as early as 1915. Ali Dinar could make little headway against the British until the rainy season arrived in July. He publicly proclaimed on 1 August 1916 that his religion required him to throw off his former allegiance to the Christians who ruled the Sudan. In his own words, he stated:

> If I now show my hatred and defiance of Christians, at worst they can kill
> me; in which case I gain the martyr's reward [seventy-two virgins in
> Paradise] and at best ... I may aspire, through my piety and hereditary
> prestige to greater things.[15]

His boast proved an empty one. Wingate, by now reinforced, took the initiative. Wingate's Darfur Field Force, led by Major J. H. Huddleston, defeated Ali Dinar near El Fasher in November 1916; during the skirmish,

Dinar was fatally shot through the head. A telegram dated 12 November 1916 informed Wingate of the event: 'Ali Dinar was killed 6 November during attack by [Major H. J.] Huddleston. Our casualties nil.'[16] Wingate wrote of him thus: 'As long as he [Ali Dinar] was in Darfur alive, Darfur would not have been allowed to develop in peace so he is good riddance.'[17]

Wingate knew that had Kitchener not been appointed Secretary of State for War, he might not have been allowed the funds to wage war on Ali Dinar which is why, privately, he gave the credit to Kitchener for the success of the campaign. Kitchener never forgot the Sudan, nor his debt to Wingate; he was acutely aware of the need to contain extremists like Ali Dinar who might have proclaimed himself yet another successor to the Mahdi. For this reason, Kitchener had supported Wingate to the hilt.

Surprisingly to modern eyes the Foreign Office and the India Office in London were not particularly disposed to consider Arabia as a vital theatre of operations to defeat the Turks. However, this would change under Wingate's perception of the importance of Saudi Arabia to the war effort; never given the due credit for his brilliant strategy, it was Wingate who organized and provisioned the Arab Revolt, although T. E. Lawrence was credited with its undoubted success. For his part, Wingate remained in the shadows, content to allow the younger man to make an everlasting, and controversial, reputation as Lawrence of Arabia. Perhaps Wingate was astute enough to realize that future historians might question the motives of crusading romantics. Or perhaps not ...

Turkey, the ruling power to which the Arabs were subservient as feudal subjects of the ancient Ottoman Empire, could not fail to appreciate the importance of the holy cities of the Hejaz, even if the British did not realize this until much later. The Amirate (or Emirate) of Mecca was an appointment in the gift of the Ottoman Sultan. The Arab leader who held the honour at the outbreak of the Great War was Sherif Hussein whose appointment dated from 1908. Hussein's second son Prince Abdullah virtually ruled the Hejaz; before war was declared, the Turks exerted pressure on Abdullah and his younger brother Prince Feisal to raise an Arab Corps to fight against Egypt and expel the British. This would change when Turkey entered the war against the Allies. Turkey lost no time in consolidating her position in the Islamic Middle East, calling for a *jihad* (holy war) against the infidel Christian British in Egypt and, more importantly, in India. Hussayn Kemal who succeeded Abbas Hilmi as Sultan of Egypt and was friendly to Britain, was condemned to death *in absentia* by the Turkish government in Constantinople. The British responded by reassuring the people of Egypt and the Sudan that war against Turkey would not mean war against Islam. Sense prevailed. The British government made it clear that Britain would keep open the holy cities of Mecca and Medina to allow pilgrims to visit them but the problem was that both were in Turkish hands. Well, perhaps that was a subtle hint to Hussein that if the Arabs expelled the Turks, they would regain control of their holy places.

Kitchener, now head of the War Office, urged the government to open negotiations with Emir Hussein to encourage his defection from Turkey. Kitchener, followed by his successor McMahon, promised assistance and military aid for Hussein who remained sceptical of British sincerity.

As noted earlier, the first step the British Cabinet took with regard to Egypt was to declare it a British Protectorate, the easy option usually taken by Britain when euphemistically agreeing to defend a country in her own interests. Sir Henry McMahon's appointment as High Commissioner of Egypt had no immediate effect on Wingate's position in the Sudan other than that the letters emanating from Cairo were signed in a new hand. Britain took the view that if her Allies – France, Russia and Italy – won the war, the Turkish, or Ottoman Empire, would be dismantled. Some in the Cabinet were in favour of annexing a major part of that empire, although the majority view was that there was nothing to be gained materially from greater involvement in the Middle East. How amateurish these politicians seem to modern eyes. One is tempted to speculate on how different the Middle East would look today if the legislators of 1914 had had their way ...

Turkish propaganda was directed at the Arab people (see Appendix II). As a Muslim nation, Turkey was clearly intent on expelling Christian and Western influence from the Middle and Near East.

One direct consequence of Turkey's entry into the war against the Allied Powers was to unite the Arab tribes to a degree previously unknown. In November 1914 Britain had no declared policy towards the Arabs in Mesopotamia, Syria, the Hejaz and Southern Arabia. In the initial stages of the war, the Arab nationalist leaders not unexpectedly demanded to know Britain's intentions in the event of a pan-Arabic revolt against the Ottoman Empire and the Turkish garrisons in the Arab states. These leaders hedged their bets from the outset, keeping an open mind regarding Turkey. They asked the vital question – would Britain offer assistance to establish a united Arab kingdom independent of all European powers (save its friendly relationship with Britain)? The Arabs had chafed under Turkish rule for centuries; they were hardly likely to exchange one tyrant for another, however enlightened. It was proposed that if Britain reacted favourably to an Arab revolt, she would provide only logistical and technical support, the Arabs themselves putting fighting men into the field. This was unrealistic; by no stretch of the imagination could the Arabs defeat the military might of the Turks without modern weapons and disciplined forces. The Arabs would require direct military assistance from Britain, with all that implied – Christian soldiers fighting on Muslim soil against other Muslims. As events would prove, it took professional British soldiers and resources to defeat the Turks, despite Lawrence's greatly exaggerated claims to the contrary, a fact which he himself later acknowledged.

Even if the extent of his initial role in the Arab Revolt is not well documented, Wingate supported the idea of an independent, self-governing Arab nation from the outset of the war. At the end of the war, when he was High

Commissioner of Egypt, he would remain faithful to this principle. However, that was in the future; in 1914, Britain was preoccupied with war and the need to defend the Suez Canal, vital to the Royal Navy and the free passage of Allied troop transports. British policy was aimed at clearing the Turks from Mesopotamia (modern Iraq) and protecting the Persian Gulf oilfields, oil being vital to the Navy. To this end, contingents of troops from the Indian Army were ordered to secure the important port of Basra in the Gulf, while British regular troops were concentrated in Mesopotamia. This achieved, Britain could then give serious consideration to establishing friendly links with the various Arab states, holding out a promise of independence. The irony in this stratagem was that the British government was prepared to support nationalism for the Arabs while continuing to resist the aspirations of the nationalists in India. Successive public demonstrations by Indian nationalists had been quelled, often ruthlessly. However, since Arabia had never been a British colony, there was no conflict of conscience

The Foreign Secretary, Sir Edward Grey, made no bones about Britain's position regarding the Arabs. He wrote to McMahon indicating his support for an Arab Revolt. At the same time McMahon was to make it abundantly clear to the Arab leaders that the price of British support for an Arab rebellion must in no way jeopardize existing British interests in Mesopotamia or the Persian Gulf. In point of fact, an Anglo-Indian administration already occupied Mesopotamia although the government was at pains to explain that this was simply a measure to protect the oilfields and should not be con-sidered in any other light. Most in the British Cabinet were able to convince themselves – if not the Arabs – that the Arab leaders would understand the reasoning behind British foreign policy and tamely accept a form of colonisation in everything but name. These men argued that the occupation of Mesopotamia was justified in the prosecution of war with Turkey and Germany. Seen through modern eyes, it is difficult to swallow this reasoning unquestioningly, although probably at the time, the Arabs – in some ways almost medieval in their thinking and with no experience of modern warfare – did not yet appreciate the formidable political weapon that oil represented.

The Hejaz, on the Red Sea coastline, had been dependent on Egypt for its food supplies for centuries, so its leaders were unlikely to alienate Britain and thereby threaten the region's survival. Wingate spent a good proportion of his time at Port Sudan on the west coast of the Red Sea, ostensibly acting as a go-between for the British administration in Cairo and the Arab leaders in the Hejaz and its neighbour, Syria. Few among the British staff in Cairo had knowledge of either until T. E. Lawrence arrived on 15 December 1914, eager to assist the Arabs; in his opinion, the Arabs offered a good chance of success in a possible war with the Turks, while at the same time preserving British prestige and interests. Lawrence zealously took up his appointment in the newly-formed Arab Bureau at Cairo; it freed him from the drudgery of army discipline which he detested, with its knee-jerk responses to those in command, men he considered his inferiors. His chief was Sir Gilbert Clayton who successfully combined the duties of ADC to the High Commissioner in Cairo, Director of Military Intelligence in the Arab Bureau, Assistant Director of the Sudan government's Intelligence Department (under Wingate) and intelligence officer for the British General Officer Commanding *Egypforce* – the ebullient Lieutenant General John G. Maxwell. Clayton's responsibilities gave him far too much power but he was diligent and efficient in these various roles.

Lawrence's first assignment for the Arab Bureau was to identify a suitable site for a British landing in Syria, which he opposed. In his view the Arabs should concentrate their energies on liberating their own territories from Turkish rule, though privately he knew this to be logistically impossible. It is perhaps appropriate here to expand on Lawrence's connections with the Middle East. In 1909 he embarked on a holiday walking tour from Haifa through the Lebanon and Syria, arriving in Carchemish. He spent nearly three months in Syria and promised himself a return visit as he was interested in the archaeological possibilities of the site. Educated at Oxford High School, then Jesus College, Oxford, a scholarship enabled him to return to Syria in 1910. During the next four years he learnt a great deal about the Arabs and was engaged in the excavations at Carchemish on the Euphrates in Syria, then Mesopotamia. As noted earlier, in Arabia he encountered the intrepid Gertrude Bell, who had gained an intimate knowledge of the area through her travels. Lawrence and Gertrude Bell would remain friends until her death in 1926. However, in 1914, he found himself side-tracked on to geographical work at the War Office when war was declared.

As early as 1915 Wingate sought to establish precisely where Britain stood in the event of a possible Arab Revolt. On 1 September he wrote to Clayton at the Arab Bureau, offering his view that 'we have need of our Arab friends'.[18] Then in October in a telegram to Clayton, he expressed more forthright views:

[Britain] should now unhesitatingly support the Sherif of Mecca ... we seem to be over-squeamish in not sympathising more readily with the aspirations of the Egyptian and Syrian Pan-Islamists ... the success of this policy requires the support of all parties ... the aspirations of a national idea ... should be combined with those of the Arabic, Syrian[,] Egyptian pan Islamism ... if the success of the movement is to be ensured.[19]

In 1915 Lawrence pondered the political situation. He knew that, for many years, France had aspired to territorial gains in Syria; when Wingate was informed of these aspirations he must have cast his mind back to the Fashoda Incident in 1898, when France had attempted to gain a foothold in the Upper Nile Valley. By now the British government took a different view of French ambitions in the Middle East; after all, France and Britain were now allies, fighting a common enemy, Germany. For their part, the Syrian Arabs were opposed to exchanging Turkish rule for that of France; however, in the early days of the war, they were ignorant of France's intentions regarding their country. The British government was anxious to please her ally; it was made clear to the French that even if Britain offered support for a possible Arab Revolt she had no territorial ambitions in Syria. Kitchener in London had no reservations about the creation of a united Arab nation, even if France went ahead with her plans to occupy Syria. In his view an Arab nation or kingdom which was friendly towards Britain would offer protection to Egypt, the Sudan, Mesopotamia and, most importantly, the Suez Canal. As for Wingate, it is ironic that in his years in the Sudan, fighting Mahdism with Kitchener, then supporting Arab nationalism with Lawrence and finally arguing the case for Egyptian nationalism, the first two of these policies would promote him but the third would precipitate his professional downfall.

In the summer of 1915 Wingate's personal life was no different from that of other British families whose husbands, sons and brothers were fighting in the trenches in Flanders. On 5 August he wrote to his cousin, George Miller Wingate in Dunbar, expressing concern about a relative, Alfred Wingate, son of Sir Andrew Wingate, who was feared killed or taken prisoner.[20]

Wingate made no secret of his support for an independent Arab nation. He openly encouraged that an Arab revolt be made from Port Sudan, where Arab and Sudanese trade was conducted. By no stretch of the imagination were the Arabs politically naïve, even if their culture seemed locked in the thirteenth century. In return for British support in the proposed revolt against Turkish rule, Hussein, the Sherif of Mecca made his position clear: he demanded nothing less than a united Arab kingdom comprising Syria, Mesopotamia and Saudi Arabia. In October 1915 he wrote to the Grand Cadi, an influential Sudanese leader, indicating that his fellow Arabs were still undecided as to how to act. Wingate received a copy of this letter on 5 October and immediately cabled its contents to Sir Gilbert Clayton:

> It would appear that the Sherif is in great perplexity regarding the course he should pursue ... The impressions I have received from this document are that the Sherif is increasingly apprehensive for his own position and in absence of news of our success [against the Turks] in Gallipoli, is probably inclined to turn a more willing ear to Constantinople than formerly.[21]

The Gallipoli campaign in the Dardanelles had been the brainchild of Winston Churchill, First Lord of the Admiralty. On the surface, his reasoning was sound; Churchill wanted to open a second front against Germany and her Turkish ally, thereby relieving pressure on the Western Front and Russia. Gallipoli proved a costly failure, both in terms of men and resources. The Sherif of Mecca watched these events with interest; his prevarication in joining the Allied powers was understandable as many Arab soldiers had been drafted into the Turkish army. A revolt in the desert against the Turks could mean the death of many Arabs then serving in Turkish regiments.

Clayton responded to Wingate's telegram of 5 October almost immediately. On 9 October he reported findings from his interrogation of an Arab officer who had recently deserted from the Turkish army in Gallipoli. Clayton quoted that officer's conversation in a telegram to Wingate:

> We [the Arabs] would sooner have a promise from England [sic] of half what we want than a promise from Germany and Turkey of the whole [of what we want] but if England refuses us, we must turn to Germany and Turkey.[22]

This was quoted from a lengthy letter bluntly informing Wingate that Britain's position in the Middle East was now in jeopardy. Clayton was never a man to pull his punches; he said that Egypt – and, by implication, the Sudan – was at great risk of invasion by the Turks.

And all the while there was Kitchener at the War Office, trying to be two things at once – Cabinet Minister and military strategist. In the latter capacity, he at first treated the war as if it were no more than yet another colonial confrontation but he warned that it would last at least three years. Prime Minister Lloyd George compared Kitchener to modern revolving lighthouses which 'radiate momentary gleams of light far out into the surrounding darkness and then suddenly relapse into complete darkness'. Kitchener was now in the exalted position of Secretary of State for War, still regarded as something akin to half-man, half-god by the British public. His reputation rested on Omdurman and the avenging of General Gordon, then the Boer War, another colonial conflict. (It was at Kitchener's instigation that the infamous concentration camps, first introduced by the Spanish in 1896 in Cuba during its war of independence, were created in South Africa at the end of the Boer War, terrible places where thousands of civilians perished.) Kitchener's prestige rested solely on the 'little' wars of Queen Victoria's reign, conflicts fought with modern weapons against natives possessing little or none. It was all very well to take on 60,000 fanatical warriors armed only with medieval weapons – spears, swords – and outmoded muskets. ('We have got the Maxim gun, which they have not.'). Kitchener rose to the occasion, creating volunteer forces, which became known as Kitchener Armies, until conscription was introduced in 1916. However, in less than two years of prosecuting the war, he reverted to type; ever more secretive, he made up policy as he went along and considered subordinates nothing short of nincompoops, especially those who disagreed with him. As he had often shown during the re-conquest of the Sudan, his violent temper which he increasingly failed to control – contemporaries described cold moments suddenly ignited by the blaze from behind his spectacles – clouded his judgement. Kitchener had no imagination and he fell considerably short of the resourceful qualities of, say, Robert E. Lee, the Confederate general who, supported by the able General Thomas 'Stonewall' Jackson ran circles round the largely incompetent Union generals until the death of the latter and the appointment of Ulysses S. Grant as Commander in Chief of the Union Army which brought him in direct conflict with Lee until the Confederate surrender in 1865. But, in 1914, in the mind of the British public, Kitchener was considered a Wellington. However, L. A. Carlyon's *Gallipoli*, perhaps the definitive historical account of the Gallipoli campaign of 1915, describes him as a man who 'preferred to be misunderstood than be suspected of human feeling'. For a good deal of his time at the War Office between 1914 and his death in 1916, Kitchener acted much in the manner of a late-nineteenth-century village schoolmaster, authoritarian, unloved, remote.

It was about this time that Sir Henry McMahon, High Commissioner of Egypt, penned his famous letter to Emir Hussein dated 24 October (see Appendix III). It made specific promises to the Arabs in return for their support against the Turks. Clayton's depressing account of the Arab officer who had defected from the Turkish army in Gallipoli came at the lowest ebb of the campaign there; British, French, Australian and New Zealand regiments had sustained unexpectedly high casualties from disease and battle and were reaching unacceptable levels even for the First World War. The Allies were making little headway against the Turks and the War Office had begun considering the evacuation of Gallipoli which, although a loss of British face in the war against Turkey, would release many British divisions for service elsewhere. There was, however, little prospect of any of these divisions being deployed to defend the Middle East. More worrying for Wingate was the fact that the evacuation of Allied forces from Gallipoli would facilitate the transfer of several Turkish divisions to Arabia and Mesopotamia, thus allowing the Turks to mount a serious campaign in the Sudan or Egypt and threaten the Suez Canal. The withdrawal of Allied forces from Gallipoli in January 1916 sent equivocal messages to the Arabs. At least for once, Kitchener appreciated the gravity of the situation, cabling Cairo and urging the British administration there not to alienate the Arabs. In Cairo, Sir John Maxwell, Commander in Chief of the British Army in Egypt, was solely concerned with protecting Suez. He was astute enough to foresee the danger to the canal if the Turks were able to mass in force in Arabia on the east bank of the Red Sea, a tactic which Wingate had also anticipated earlier than some contemporaries. Turkish aggression in Mesopotamia had been initially countered by Sir Charles Townshend with a division of British – mainly Indian – troops; however, in January 1916, his forces were besieged at Kut, near Basra. Despite several attempts to relieve Townshend, Kut was yet another disaster at the hands of the Turks. The town fell at the end of April 1916, the bulk of its 9,000 garrison dying in Turkish captivity. Gallipoli and Kut together proved that Turkey, 'the sick man of Europe' still had a lot of hostility to offer.

As the Gallipoli campaign concluded with the Allies' ignominious withdrawal, it became more important that the British administration in Egypt should secure the loyalty of any subject peoples of the Ottoman Empire and use them against their Turkish masters in the field. Wingate saw an Arab Revolt as a means to this end; he proved himself a shrewd politician in November 1915, when he wrote to Sir Gilbert Clayton expressing a practical, if cynical, view:

> After all what harm can our acceptance of his [the Sherif of Mecca's] proposals do? If the embryonic Arab State comes to nothing, all our promises vanish and we are absolved from them – if the Arab State becomes a reality, we have quite different safeguards to control it. In other words, the cards seem to be in our hands and we have only to play them carefully.[23]

The evacuation of Gallipoli in January 1916, then the fall of Kut, induced Hussein to reiterate his earlier demands that Syria and Mesopotamia be included in any future Arab kingdom. Hussein was nobody's fool. He recognized that if the British could not contain or defeat the Turks in Turkey or Mesopotamia, how could they protect his own homeland? And yet despite British reverses at the hands of the Turks, the pan-Arab nationalist movement and its disaffection with Turkey were gaining momentum. By now, Wingate was openly supporting the Arabs, backed by Clayton, Henry McMahon, Ronald Storrs, the Oriental Secretary in Cairo and, of course, T. E. Lawrence. However, France was making increasing demands of her own in Africa, demands which, as Britain's ally, could not be ignored. In Cairo, McMahon and his staff were well aware of French ambitions; he also knew that if those ambitions were made known to the Sherif of Mecca, negotiations on a possible pan-Arab revolt would wither on the vine.

After the Allied withdrawal from Gallipoli, a glut of weapons and ammunition was stockpiled in Port Sudan and placed under Wingate's control. The weapons were largely unserviceable but Wingate earmarked them for future use by the Arabs. With the fall of Kut in April, Cairo and London were anxious to convince the Arabs that Britain would support an Arab Revolt. As an interim measure, it was decided to send the young Lawrence, with his specialist knowledge of Arabia and its geography, to sound out the Arab leaders' intentions. (Before the surrender of Kut, an alternative to encouraging the Arabs was a dishonourable proposal made by the War Office to bribe the Turkish government – was it Kitchener's idea? – to release Townshend and his men. Lawrence and his colleague Aubrey Herbert were authorized to offer the besieging Turkish commander £2 million.) When Townshend surrendered on 29 April, Lawrence and Herbert returned to Cairo having achieved nothing other than to suggest that imperial Turkey was in decay, an impression which was naïve wishful thinking. Turkey was nowhere near throwing in the towel. Lawrence was of course totally committed to Arab independence and knew that nothing short of the complete defeat of the Ottoman Empire, by force or whatever other means, would be required. He was disappointed that he had been unable to encourage the Arabs to rise against their oppressors, although gratified to learn that several Arab officers in the Turkish army were now displaying open disloyalty to their masters. Lawrence took the view that if Britain had given him the means to harry the lines of communication between Baghdad and Kut, the town would not have fallen. He wrote as much in his classic account of the Arab Revolt, *Seven Pillars of Wisdom*:

> Time to develop such a scheme could have easily have been gained had the British headquarters in Mesopotamia obtained from the War Office eight more aeroplanes to increase the daily carriage of food to the garrison of Kut. Townshend's resistance might have been indefinitely prolonged. His defence was Turkishly impregnable; and only blunders within and without forced surrender upon him ... till the end of the war the British in Mesopotamia remained substantially an alien force invading enemy territory, with the local people passively neutral or sullenly against them, and in consequence had not the freedom of movement and elasticity of Allenby in Syria, who entered the country as a friend, with the local people actively on his side.[24]

Perhaps these are not unexpected words, given his sympathies for, and romantic view of, the Arabs.

After the debacle at Kut, McMahon continued his negotiations with Mecca, although few in Cairo believed that Emir Hussein would rise against the Turks. Nonetheless, the Arab Bureau in Cairo was devoted entirely to achieving this end. However, at the same time, secret negotiations between France and Britain on the future of Syria after the war had reached a conclusion. The outcome was the Sykes-Picot agreement. It is one of history's many ironies that by the time Emir Hussein declared himself and his people on the side of the Allies in June 1916, the ink had only just dried on the Sykes-Picot agreement, though, naturally, its contents were not revealed to him at the time. Under the agreement France would colonize Syria after the war and, for obvious reasons, the agreement was kept secret. It posed sticky problems for Britain, which could hardly encourage the Arabs to fight on its behalf, and support their Revolt, only to blithely hand over Syria to the French and conveniently ignore Sir Henry McMahon's promise to Hussein in 1915.

No matter, Wingate cabled Clayton in Cairo on 16 April 1916, informing him that recent intelligence had led him to believe that the Arabs were committed to action in Syria. His cable was direct and to the point:

> The first steps will be taken by Ali, the Sherif's son, who will cut the railway communication between Medina [in the Hejaz] and the Syrian frontier. Feisal [the Sherif's third and youngest son] will simultaneously raise the standards of revolt against the Turks in Syria, irrespective of whether or no [sic] the British troops co-operate by landing on the Syrian coast.[25]

Wingate was now in constant contact with Emir Hussein through Hussein's emissary, Sheik Oreifan. In the same cable, Wingate stressed the need:

To feed and equip the Arab levies [conscripts] who will join the Sherif's army, and to subsidise Chiefs of tribes who will be required to cut the lines of communication and on the line to Baghdad.

In Cairo McMahon was convinced that a revolt would never succeed without direct military assistance from Britain. This view was conveyed to an anxious Wingate by Clayton in a cable dated 16 April:

Feisal proposes to operate in a sphere which we have definitely left to the French ... how can we justify to the French our action in assisting to place in their sphere a force which will inevitably be violently opposed to their aims? ... The Sherif allows that Syria is useless for revolutionary purposes. Can we expect that the Hedjaz [sic] Arabs with their pro-verbial lack of organization, and far from their base, can do much more than waste our money and supplies in a series of aimless and indecisive raids in a country which they are too uncivilized ever to rule as it should be ruled? ...

The High Commissioner [McMahon] feels very strongly that at present the Sherif should be advised to confine himself to securing the Railway, and clearing the Turks out of the Hedjaz, and in conjunction with the Idrisi [Sayid Muhammed ibn Ali, leader in Asir] out of the Yemen.

We can safely back this for all we are worth with further funds and material as required in proportion to the results obtained. It is a definite plan which has a good chance of succeeding ... *We do not want to create a powerful and united Arab Kingdom either under the Sherif or anyone else, even were such a thing practicable* [author's italics]. It would be a danger and a cause of future embarrassment in view of our arrangements with France and Russia. We merely wish to keep the various Arab races and factions on our side and deny them to the enemy, which we have succeeded in doing so far without giving embarrassing guarantees.[26]

It was not what Wingate had hoped for, infinitely less so than had Lawrence. Wingate did not have to be a military or political genius to realize that this document made it abundantly clear that, in the British view, the Arabs were expendable. Such is the nature of politics. Wingate undoubtedly passed on a highly edited version to Hussein who wrote to McMahon requesting British troops be landed on the Mediterranean coast of Syria to encourage the Arabs there to rise up against the eight Turkish divisions holding the territory. McMahon knew that this was impossible but was unable and unwilling to give Hussein reasons for refusing his demands. His reply was couched in diplomatic terms, advising Hussein not to divide his forces but recall his son Feisal from Syria to the Hejaz, from where the Revolt proper should begin.

140

1. Wingate as a young army officer, 1890s. (*Author's collection*)

2. Slatin, Father Ohrwalder and Wingate meeting Baron von Egeregg, Austrian Consul General and his staff at Cairo Station, 19 March 1895.
(*Sudan Archive Department, Durham University Library*)

3. Slatin dressed in the patched *jibbah* worn by the Dervishes during his captivity in Omdurman.
(*Sudan Archive Department*)

4. Wingate interviewing Mahmud after the Battle of Atbara, 1898.
(*Sudan Archive Department*)

5. Sir Evelyn Baring, Lord Cromer.
(*National Portrait Gallery, London*)

6. Herbert Horatio, Lord, Kitchener.
(*National Portrait Gallery, London*)

7. General Sir Hector Archibald MacDonald.
(*National Portrait Gallery, London*)

8. The Wingates enjoying their first holiday in Dunbar, 1899. Seated left to right are Malcolm Roy, Lady Wingate with baby Victoria and Wingate; standing are Ronald Evelyn Leslie, Slatin, Sudanese servant and unknown.
(*Sudan Archive Department*)

9. Wingate's New Year Card c.1900; he is wearing the uniform of an officer in the Royal Artillery. (*Author's collection*)

10. Facsimile of a letter from Abbas Hilmi, Khedive of Egypt, to Wingate dated 11 April 1906. (*Author's collection*)

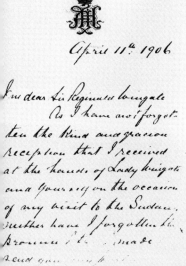

11. Wingate with daughter Victoria, Khartoum, 1907. (*Sudan Archive Department*)

12. Lady Wingate with Victoria, Khartoum.
(*Sudan Archive Department*)

13. Wingate in the uniform of Sirdar as
captain of Dunbar Golf Club, 1904 and 1905.
(*Dunbar Golf Club; GWS Photography, Dunbar*)

14. Captain George Miller Wingate, RA, as captain of Dunbar Golf Club 1909. (*Dunbar Golf Club; GWS Photography, Dunbar*)

15. Knockenhair House in final stage of completion, 1908. (*Author's collection*)

16. Knockenhair Lodge with Knockenhair House in the background. (*Author's collection*)

17. Photograph taken by Wingate on 27 February 1912 at Khartoum during the assassination attempt on him. (*Author's collection*)

18. Wingate and Slatin at Balmoral.
(*Sudan Archive Department*)

19. Slatin Pasha in the uniform of Inspector General, Sudan, pre-Great War.
(*Sudan Archive Department*)

20. Sir Henry Macleod Leslie Rundle, Governor General of Malta, 1914. (*East Lothian Council Museum Service*)

21. This is probably the last photograph taken of Lord Kitchener aboard HMS *Hampshire* which was sunk by a German mine off the Orkneys en route to Russia on 5 June 1916. (*Author's collection*)

22. Wingate in camp, Kordofan
Province, Sudan, 1916.
(*Sudan Archive Department*)

23. T. E. Lawrence in Arab dress.
(*National Portrait Gallery, London*)

24. A. J. Balfour in pensive mood.
(*East Lothian Local History Centre*)

25. Wingate in full dress with
all his honours and decorations.
(*National Portrait Gallery, London*)

26. Wingate in civilian life c.1920s.
(*National Portrait Gallery, London*)

27. Orde Wingate, clean shaven.
(*Private collection*)

28. Orde Wingate wearing the pith helmet which became his trademark from 1938. (*IWM, EA 21404*)

29. Wingate in military uniform, Marine Road, Dunbar, taken in his old age.
(*Sudan Archive Department*)

IN MEMORIAM

GENERAL SIR REGINALD WINGATE, Bt.
G.C.B., G.C.V.O., G.B.E., K.C.M.G., D.S.O., T.D., D.L., D.C.L., LL.D.
Colonel Commandant Royal Regiment of Artillery

Died 28th January 1953

TUESDAY, 3rd FEBRUARY 1953
at 12 noon

30. The cover of the Service sheet for Wingate's funeral on 3 February 1953. (*Author's collection*)

31. Wingate's grave monument, Dunbar Parish Church cemetery.
(*Author's collection; GWS Photography, Dunbar*)

To be fair to McMahon, Hussein and his intermediary, Sheik Oreifan, had made contrasting statements and estimates of Arab strength in Syria, a foretaste of equally wide variations in the number of combatants available in the Hejaz. It has to be admitted that the Arabs' partisan estimates of their capability in the field were somewhat over-optimistic and proved prescient. The Arab cat would however give the Turkish dog a bloody nose, even if it could not disable it.

After conferring with Sheik Oreifan, Wingate had written thus to Clayton on 16 April:

> It is considered certain that the Turkish troops in the Hejaz and other Arabian provinces are incapable of resistance and will be faced with surrender or extermination.[27]

Perhaps Wingate was over anxious to believe what Hussein's emissary had told him; either that, or he shared Lawrence's unshakeable faith in the Arabs' ability to mount a major campaign against the enemy. How could Lawrence be so certain of success? His belief was not shared by the civil and military powers in Cairo who remained sceptical of Arab success other than in local and minor incursions. That doubt had been justified by Gallipoli and Kut; Turkey was not the sick military man of Europe of popular opinion. Cairo's scepticism proved justified by the failure of the Arabs to act for a further month. On 22 May, Clayton wired Wingate:

> I hope we shall soon hear of the Sherif making a definite move – once he has openly and definitely declared himself against the Turks, we shall have scored an enormous asset, even though his operation may not have any great actual military effect.[28]

Clayton was nothing if not a realist. The 'enormous asset' rested solely in its value as a propaganda coup. An Arab uprising would serve as a public demonstration to the Muslim world that Emir Hussein of Mecca was determined to free his people from Turkish oppression, Turks being considered less than orthodox in their world. Clayton's cable left Wingate in no doubt as to what the powers in Cairo thought of Arab military effectiveness; it must have come as a disappointment to him, but Wingate was no romantic in the mould of Lawrence. He accepted the reality of the situation.

It is perhaps true to a certain extent that the Arab possesses certain feline faculties; he appears to be indolent, is independent and his mood can change suddenly from passive to aggressive hostile. Like the cat he also prefers to hunt his quarry alone, stealthily and by night. The comparison with cats goes further; cats are territorial creatures, manipulative and at times fawning to a sickly degree. However, when threatened, they are capable of extraordinary aggression and courage. Orde Wingate, Reginald Wingate's great-cousin, would later describe the Arab as 'lazy, feckless and, while not cowardly, sees no point in losing his life'. To some extent this can also be said of the cat. To pursue this analogy to its logical conclusion, the Arab cat had been playing with the British mouse for well over a year, hedging bets and making no secret of the fact that it would turn to Germany and Turkey to realize its aims if Britain failed to come up with the desired solution to its ambitions.

Two weeks after Clayton's cable, news arrived that Hussein had begun the Revolt on the second day of June, news which was welcomed in Port Sudan and Cairo. There had been grave fears that after the disaster at Kut and British opposition to a rising in Syria would have induced Hussein to postpone any action for an indefinite period, possibly even drive him into Turkey's arms. Now he demanded – and got – 60,000 gold sovereigns (about £1.8 million in modern terms). Hussein requested that Sir Ronald Storrs bring the money to a point somewhere on the Arab coast, where a meeting would be arranged with Sherif Abdullah ibn Hussein, another of Hussein's sons. Clayton cabled Wingate, welcoming the initiative because, in his eyes, Abdullah was considered a man of action who would provide the British with vital information about Turkish strength and movements. As he wrote to Wingate, 'For this reason [the meeting with Abdullah] I insisted on strengthening Storrs by sending [David] Hogarth and [Kinahan] Cornwallis.'[29]

Despite modern historical accounts and the mythology surrounding Lawrence, Wingate can, with hindsight, be seen as the real power behind the Arab Revolt. He made no secret of his support for the Arabs but, equally, he never documented or discussed his role in public. The talking and much of the writing came from Lawrence, General Edmund Allenby and the journalist Lowell Thomas, whose biography of Lawrence lionized him.

Notes

1. *HC*, 22 May 1914.
2. *Ibid.*, 17 July 1914.
3. *Ibid.*, 7 August 1914.
4. *Ibid.*, 6 October 1914.
5. *Ibid.*, 6 November 1914.
6. A signed photograph of the new Sultan of Egypt was displayed in the local bookshop; it was lent to Miss Downie, proprietor of the bookshop in Dunbar by Major William W. Carey of Seaholm (Church Street). Carey was a colleague of Wingate and also a golfing partner; he had enjoyed a fairly important position in Egypt and knew the Sultan well.
7. Director of Intelligence, Cairo, to Wingate, 16 August 1914, WP 193/1, SAD, DU.
8. Intelligence Report from Cairo to Wingate, 25 August 1914, WP 193/1, SAD, DU.
9. *Wingate of the Sudan*, RELW.
10. *HC*, 10 November 1916.
11. WP 270/8, SAD, DU.
12. Slatin Pasha, Hill.
13. *Ibid.*
14. *Seven Pillars of Wisdom*, p. 56.
15. Ali Dinar, 1 August 1916, WP 127/3, SAD, DU.
16. McGowan to Wingate, 12 November 1916, WP 139/7, SAD, DU.
17. WP 160/5, SAD, DU.
18. Wingate to Clayton, 1 September 1915, WP 135/3, SAD, DU.
19. Wingate to Clayton, 18 October 1915, WP 135/4, SAD, DU.
20. Wingate to G. M. Wingate, 5 August 1915, WP 196/2, SAD, DU.
21. Wingate to Clayton, 5 October 1915, FO 141/461/1188 folio 51.

22. Clayton to Wingate, 9 October 1915, WP 135/4, SAD, DU.
23. Wingate to Clayton, 15 November 1915, WP135/5, SAD, DU.
24. *Seven Pillars of Wisdom*, pp. 59–60.
25. Wingate to Clayton, 16 April 1916, FO 882/4 folio 90.
26. Clayton to Wingate, 16 April 1916, WP136/6, SAD, DU.
27. Wingate to Clayton, 16 April 1916, FO 882/4 folio 90.
28. Clayton to Wingate, 22 May 1916, WP 136/6, SAD, DU.
29. David George Hogarth and Kinahan Cornwallis were full-time members of the Arab Bureau in Cairo. Hogarth was already acquainted with Lawrence from the Carchemish archaeological excavations in 1909. Cornwallis would later become head of the Arab Bureau, then Personal Adviser to Prince Feisal.

Chapter 6

The Arab Revolt
(1916)

Britain had reluctantly committed herself to an Arab uprising, the decision being nothing more than a politically motivated move, a cynical necessity of war. Perhaps, with hindsight, the British authorities in India and Egypt were worried about the threat of a Muslim backlash; after all, Turkey was a largely Muslim country opposed to infidel Christians. The Sultan of the Ottoman Empire, the Commander of the Faithful, was mentioned in prayers each Friday, the Muslim holy day. The Arab leaders were prepared to overlook this convention in their bid for independence, but then war has always made strange bedfellows.

Negotiations with Emir Hussein had stumbled on inconclusively for more than a year until 2 June 1916. On that day Hussein fired a rifle from a rooftop in Damascus, signalling the start of the Revolt. From the British point of view, the main objective was to persuade Hussein to free the Hejaz from Turkish rule. In exchange Britain promised independence for the Arab nations, a promise it would not and – given the overriding need to co-operate with a French ally regarding its ambitions in Syria – could not keep. Wingate played no part in formulating British guarantees in exchange for Arab assistance against the Turks, nor did he have a hand in framing what became known as the McMahon Letters which defined guarantees and made promises to the Arabs. Wingate was, however, kept fully informed by Cairo and London on British policy and he provided the messengers who ferried government correspondence between Hussein and Cairo.

As indicated in the previous chapter, from the outset Wingate supported the idea of a Revolt. His remarkable organizational skills, his high-minded sense of duty and his energy would contribute much to the successful launch of the Revolt; he embraced the Arab cause with something akin to religious fervour. Zeal is a necessary ingredient for those who wish to remedy what they perceive as abuse and injustice but is a heady brew which must necessarily be diluted by sound judgement and a firm grasp of reality. Wingate possessed both, as he had proved time and time again; his obvious sincerity in support of the Arabs is clear from the many contemporary documents in his archive, despite T. E. Lawrence's later, unfair, criticism of his conduct during the Revolt. It must be remembered that Lawrence often allowed his intoxicating involvement in the Revolt to cloud his judgement; he made exaggerated claims about Arab successes and blamed failures on British bureaucracy and political chicanery, a degree of which was justified to a certain extent. Wingate was hardly in a position of power to affect the broader picture but, in Lawrence's view, he ran with the hounds in Cairo, making him equally culpable along with his masters when things later went wrong. Also, it has to be said that many politicians in England paid only lip service to the Arab Revolt; for example, the India Office in London was at best condescending about its success, at worst coldly dismissive of Arab effectiveness.

Despite his enthusiasm for the Revolt, Wingate knew that irregular Arab levies alone would be unable to defend a position or a line, let alone attack well-constructed fortifications defended by professional Turkish soldiers. Lawrence shared this view. Wingate, ever the professional soldier, recognized from the outset that the Arabs were at their best waging guerrilla warfare, tactics they had used for several centuries. For his part, Lawrence understood that the presence of British (Christian) troops in the Hejaz would not be welcome and might even lead to mass desertions from the Arab Army, especially the arm led by Prince Feisal.

Wingate saw a way out of this dilemma. He sent a contingent of Egyptian (Muslim) troops to Feisal who appointed his younger brother Zeid to command them. It would be a temporary solution to the problem, but all this was in the future.

On 16 April Wingate wrote in the following terms to the High Commissioner of Egypt, Sir Henry McMahon:

I have the honour to confirm my telegraphic summary of the contents of the latest communication from the Sherif of Mecca [Hussein] and to transmit originals and copies of the Arabic letters received. I also attach a copy of a further telegram giving information obtained in conversation with the Sherif's emissary.

I have little doubt that the Sherif now feels himself definitely committed to the movement for Arab independence and is merely awaiting the first favourable opportunity to declare himself openly [against the Turks].

He has secured promises of recognition and support by a great number of chiefs throughout the Arabian Peninsula and, provided that the necessary monies and arms are forthcoming, there appear to be strong grounds for believing that the rising will be successful in overthrowing the last shreds of Turkish authority in Arabia.

It is evident that the Sherif relies on the good offices of His Majesty's Government, having regards to the formal declarations of their friendly disposition towards the Arabs, to supply the money and arms which he requires; and that the success and scope of his movement depends largely on the extent to which his necessities in these respects can be provided.[1]

Again, armed with that invaluable scientific aid to historians known as hindsight, one could comment here that Wingate was indulging in a personal dream fired by his enthusiasm, albeit a dream which might advance his career. He was astute enough to realize that it would require professional soldiers to wrest Arabia from the Turks, not mere Arab irregulars totally ignorant of modern warfare and untrained in its weaponry. In addition, Wingate's optimistic telegram was sent exactly one month before the important and damaging treaty was signed between Britain and France, the Sykes-Picot Agreement, which would later undermine Arab aspirations to obtain independence.

The infamous treaty was named for the men who drafted it – Sir Mark Sykes and M. Francois Georges Picot, respectively a British MP and a French Foreign Office official. The Sykes-Picot Agreement, officially known as 'The Asia Minor Agreement', was signed on 16 May 1916; under its terms, France would assume control of most of the Syrian coast on the Red Sea and establish a protectorate in the interior of Syria, the capital being Damascus. Unfortunately, this was contrary to the McMahon Letters which, in 1915, had more than hinted at independence for the Arabs. The Sykes-Picot Agreement was nothing short of imperialistic political chicanery which would have disastrous consequences for Middle East-European relations in 1918–19. Even at this distance in time, the document reeks of sharp practice on the part of Britain but, at the time, the agreement remained a close secret, known only to a chosen few. Among those in the know was Lawrence, one of the self-styled 'Intrusives' in the Arab Bureau whose subversive intention was to infiltrate the corridors of power to 'foster the new Arabic world'. The Intrusives' first target was the gullible Sir Henry McMahon.

In practical terms, Wingate desired a clearer picture of the role expected of him in the Revolt. On 24 June 1916 he sent a member of his staff, Colonel C. E. Wilson, Governor of the Red Sea Province, to Jedda, intimating that Wilson would be his personal representative there. The chain of command from Wingate as Sirdar and Governor General of the Sudan through Wilson was clear; in the minds of those set above Wingate, however, it was not. Wingate exerted pressure on the War Office to clarify his position. In June 1916 McMahon asked Wingate to assume direction of military matters connected with Britain's assistance to Emir Hussein, intimating at the same time that he, McMahon, would retain overall responsibility for political matters arising therefrom. This was hardly a satisfactory situation for Wingate. He rightly asked if London would acquiesce to the Arabs' request for small arms and artillery, ammunition for both, aircraft, food and money. Finally, Wingate sought clarification of the respective functions of the High Commissioner of Egypt (McMahon), the Commander in Chief in Egypt (Maxwell) and the head of the Arab Bureau (Clayton). Clearly, Wingate wanted to know where he stood. This ambivalence was only partly resolved by McMahon; to be fair, the latter did not possess the authority to answer all Wingate's questions. Wingate made no secret of the fact that, in his view, had Kitchener or Cromer been High Commissioner, they would have long ago handed 'the whole affair stock, lock [sic] and barrel, over to the Governor General of the Sudan' [that is to say, to himself].[2]

The war presented the Allies – Britain, France and Russia – with a golden opportunity to dismantle the Ottoman Empire, the three powers intending to divide that empire among themselves. Russia desired a clear sea route to a warm water port which meant the annexation of Constantinople and the Crimea, ambitions which had brought France and Britain to the aid of Turkey during the Crimean War with Russia in 1854–56. Now it was proposed that Russia be allowed to achieve its 1854 ambitions as reward for supporting the Allies. In turn France would receive Syria as its reward. This was contrary to McMahon's promise to Emir Hussein the previous year; the Arabs had been led to believe that, after the war and the defeat of Turkey, an Arab kingdom embracing Syria would become a reality. The treaty between France and Britain is today rightly seen by historians as a betrayal, with Arab interests being forgotten.

The task of persuading Emir Hussein to rise against the Turks was fraught with difficulties. For one thing, the Turkish garrisons in the Hejaz were up to strength, adequately supplied with ammunition, artillery and aircraft. Coupled with this, the Allies had suffered a terrible defeat at the hands of the Turks on the Gallipoli peninsula, leading to the ignominious – if brilliantly executed – evacuation of British, Anzac and French troops in January 1916. In 1915 the Turks had even made a raid on the Suez Canal which, although a failure, proved that British forces were not invincible. Then came the ignominious surrender of Townshend at Kut in 1916. This series of Turkish victories caused Hussein to wonder whether he was wise to back the British. Wingate was given the unenviable task of persuading the Arabs to revolt against vastly superior Turkish forces and assumed the somewhat empty title of General Officer Commanding operations in the Hejaz. There was no British presence there and Wingate was based in Port Sudan, on the opposite shore of the Red Sea, facing Jedda; at least the Royal Navy ruled that sea.

Despite his enthusiasm for the Revolt, Wingate was beset with doubts about the Arabs' military ability to wage modern warfare. He was privately pessimistic about their chances of success and was under no illusion that the Hejaz would be taken from the Turks only with the support of professional British soldiers. He knew that the Arabs would reluctantly accede to the deployment of trained troops with modern weapons, as well as lots of gold sovereigns. The Arabs valued gold above all else; to be paid in paper money was considered an insult.

Wingate recognized that the main objective of the Revolt was to free the holy cities of Mecca and Medina. These cities were the emotional fulcrum of British propaganda; defeat of the Turks would ensure that Muslim pilgrims could visit these cities without hindrance. The Turks recognized it too; they made it clear that all Muslims would be allowed free and safe access to these holy places. So what could Emir Hussein offer to his people in justification for a revolt?

Wingate, ever the realist, embraced his new duties enthusiastically. As GOC of the Hejaz, he was fortunate in having as his assistant Colonel Wilson, then based at Port Sudan; Wilson was the Governor of the Red Sea Littoral, or province. He would later operate from the seaport of Jedda until illness forced him to take sick leave. Wingate was backed by the staff of the Arab Bureau in Cairo – staunch supporters such as Sir Gilbert Clayton, David Hogarth, T. E. Lawrence, Sir Stewart Symes, Kinahan Cornwallis, Gertrude Bell and Colonel Wilson about to be based in Jedda. His naval associates – also strong in their support – were Admiral Sir Rosslyn Wemyss and Captain William Boyle of the Red Sea Patrol; this last-named pair would prove invaluable to the success of the Arab Revolt.

From the outset Wingate had recommended that British troops be sent to the Hejaz but Cairo disagreed. A landing of Christian troops in Muslim Hejaz would provide the Turks with valuable propaganda. One can imagine the headlines in the Turkish newspapers of the day: 'Infidel Christians invade Muslim territory in the guise of setting it free, only to occupy it.'

Wingate was acutely aware of the dilemma. Using all his persuasive powers, he eventually obtained the agreement of the authorities in Cairo, recommending that only limited, logistical support be offered to the Arabs at the outset. He knew this would find favour in the initial weeks of the Revolt but he also knew that, sooner or later, British troops would have to be committed. No one believed that the Arabs could achieve more than local disruption of Turkish supply routes and communications with their incursions restricted to guerrilla warfare.

To understand Wingate's strategy and Lawrence's tactics in the Hejaz, it is necessary to describe the territory in question. The Hejaz consists of a narrow coastal plain running from the gulf of Akaba in the north to the straits of Bab-el-Mandeb in the south, between the Red Sea and the plateau of Arabia. Half way down the coast is the port of Jedda, less than 100 miles south of the holy city of Mecca. North of Jedda are the three small ports of Rabegh, Yenbo and Wejh. About 300 miles north of Mecca is the holy city of Medina, birthplace of the Prophet Mohammed and the terminus of the railway link to Damascus. Were Mecca and Jedda to fall into Arab hands, the next goal would be to take Medina; failing that, the Arabs would have to prevent the Turks advancing from Medina to recapture Mecca.

The Revolt which began on 2 June 1916 caught the Turks on the wrong foot, even if their intelligence units had been aware of negotiations between Emir Hussein and Wingate. At any rate, within days, Mecca and Jedda duly fell to the Arabs; Jedda was an easy acquisition, as it was within bombardment range of the heavy guns of Admiral Wemyss' flotilla of warships.

Events now moved rapidly. Sir Ronald Storrs arrived in the Hejaz on 6 June, his mission being to hand over funds to Hussein and assess the situation. That day he was surprised and no doubt gratified to learn that Hussein's son,

Sherif Abdullah, had begun operations against the Turks the day before. It was the first swipe of the cat's paw. The British delegation headed by Storrs also learned that Ali and Feisal, Hussein's other sons, had attacked Medina and the railway to the north. In the first months of the Revolt, Lawrence repeatedly requested that the Arabs be supplied with machine guns and heavy ordnance, stressing that tribesmen liked guns that made a lot of noise! Wingate responded by offering a few batteries of archaic artillery which, despite their age, proved effective against short-range Turkish targets. The Arabs managed to drag these to the walls of Jiyad, where they succeeded in disabling a few Turkish emplacements. After this successful bombardment, the Arab irregulars raced through the breached walls and captured or killed the entire Turkish garrison.

Encouraged by this success, Hussein moved on Mecca, while his son Abdullah menaced Taif, a few miles south of Mecca. Another force was directed towards Jedda, the port on the Red Sea west of Mecca. Things were happening at last even if, to the despair of the British in Cairo and the War Office in London, the Arabs were woefully ignorant of modern warfare, with no pre-arranged plans for conducting the Revolt. One member of Storrs' mission, Hogarth, criticized the Arab strategy which he said was left to the last moment, the Arabs relying on luck rather than tactics. Nevertheless, the Arabs' blood was up and Allah was with them. In view of these limited successes, Hussein was emboldened to demand an additional 20,000 gold sovereigns (about £6 million in modern terms) for Feisal and his brother Ali. In addition, Hussein asked for six machine guns, six mountain guns, 10,000 rifles and ammunition, and tons of food. Once more Hussein demanded that Britain land several divisions of troops on the Syrian coast, a move which would have contravened the Sykes-Picot Agreement, had he known about it. On their way back to Cairo, Storrs and his party learnt that Lord Kitchener, the demi-god of Omdurman, had been drowned while en route to Russia in the sinking of HMS *Hampshire* on 5 June 1916. The cruiser struck a mine off the Orkneys.

The Arabs enjoyed initial successes; they cleared the Turks out of Mecca and, with the help of the Royal Navy, captured Jedda and Taif, although the Turkish fort at Taif refused to surrender. The sole setback was at Medina, where Prince Feisal's forces were heavily outnumbered and, it has to be said, outclassed by the Turk commander Fakhri en din Pasha who employed his artillery batteries to good effect, terrifying the Arab tribesmen who had never before encountered such a deafening barrage. This apart, the Revolt had got off to a promising start.

To summarize Arab strength at the outset of the Revolt, Hussein had raised a force of about 50,000 under his four sons Ali, Abdullah, Feisal and Zeid. Few tribesmen possessed modern rifles and were facing a well-equipped and well-armed force of 15,000 Turks. In the attack on Medina, only 6,000 of Feisal's 30,000 followers had modern weapons and were easily repulsed.

It was at this time that intense rivalry grew between McMahon in Cairo and Wingate. To a great extent Wingate and his staff were in the front line, involved on a daily basis with Hussein, providing him with weapons and supplies. Tension between McMahon and Wingate began to increase during the summer and autumn of 1916. On the one hand, McMahon would advise the Foreign Office of the situation in Egypt and the Sudan without consulting Wingate, his immediate subordinate. Wingate, in tit-for-tat mood, began sending telegrams to the Foreign Office without consulting McMahon, despite the latter's protests.

Early in July, Colonel C. E. Wilson, one of Wingate's ablest subordinates, visited Jedda to advise Hussein on strategy. In time Wilson would become Wingate's invaluable representative in the Hejaz, keeping him informed about developments in the desert. His report to Wingate in July highlighted the problems of British supplies for the Revolt, largely caused by growing animosity between McMahon and Wingate. Wilson did not mince his words: '[Hussein] appears to have started his revolt without sufficient preparation and somewhat prematurely ...'

In the same communication Wilson argued that if there should be a serious reverse in the Arab initiative in Medina, Hussein would:

more than probably put the blame on the British government owing to supplies not being available when he expected them ... The seriousness of the consequences to the British government should the present Hedjaz [sic] revolt fail is too patent to call for remark.[3]

In point of fact, Hussein's hand had been forced by news of Turkey's troop movements in April, when he learnt that a force of 3,500 soldiers would pass through the Hejaz on their way to Yemen, a move he suspected was aimed at quelling any possible revolt there. In early May his son Feisal in Damascus contemplated the feasibility of a revolt when he had witnessed the execution of twenty-one Syrian nationalists by the Turkish commander there. A further message from Hussein was relayed to Wingate at Port Sudan on 27 May, explaining that he had recalled Feisal from Damascus as the Turks had gained knowledge of his plans. The Arab operations in the Hejaz – blowing up bridges, destroying rail tracks and derailing trains around Wejh (held by the Royal Navy) – were still seriously disrupting Turkish lines of communication.

Thus, in late July, following initial Arab successes in Mecca and its vicinity, the Red Sea ports of Rabegh and Yenbo fell to the Arabs, the latter chiefly achieved by the Royal Navy. However, in Medina, all was stalemate as Ali and Feisal were unable to feed and pay their men, let alone form them into a coherent fighting force. It seems that the arms, ammunition and food supplies landed at Rabegh were not being sent inland for some inexplicable reason, a fact of which Feisal complained bitterly. In addition, there was an increasing danger of counter-attack from Turkish units now being reinforced by troops from the northern provinces.

It was at this time that the British considered an operation in the Sinai desert, directed at Akaba on the Red Sea. Military thinking centred on the port of Akaba because its Turkish garrison would pose a threat to the right flank of any invading British force operating in northern Sinai. Besides, Akaba was only seventy miles from the German-built Hejaz railway link; a British presence there would be of strategic value to Hussein's activities in the south. Lawrence had considered Akaba of strategic importance as early as the spring of 1915, although originally he rejected its capture on purely logistical grounds, a fact he later admitted after the war. On the other hand, Colonel Wilson, Wingate's aide, had advocated a landing at Akaba in concert with Prince Feisal's forces; however, Feisal said this could not be achieved without a British landing at Rabegh, accompanied by air cover, mountain guns, machine guns and rifles for his ill-equipped army.

A major problem was religion – as so often. The prospect of Christian troops in Muslim territory would be unwelcome in the Arab world, even if Arab leaders knew that a professional army equipped with modern weapons was essential to their own success. Also, if the Turks were to attack Mecca, they would have to pass through Rabegh, at the time poorly defended by Feisal, who did not possess the strength or ordnance to halt a determined Turkish advance. He compromised by asking for a small contingent of British troops – about 300 in all – which seemed ludicrous to those in the British high command who believed nothing less than a brigade was required, British military thinking being that the Arabs would desert in the face of superior enemy numbers and weaponry. Clayton reported that his chief had suggested a way round the problem of Christian troops in the Hejaz; Wingate believed that if British troops were stationed in the Sudan, he could release several Sudanese – Muslim – battalions for service in Arabia. Though a shrewd proposal, it came to nothing.

By now Wingate had added a third string to his bow. In the autumn of 1916 he was again confirmed as General Officer Commanding in the Hejaz with responsibility for liaison with Hussein. It was yet another of the kind of decision made by the High Command during the Great War – that of appointing commanders remote from the centre of operations although, in this particular case, Wingate was without question the best placed man for the job.

Meanwhile, the Turkish garrison at Taif, beyond Mecca, continued to hold out against the Arabs; at the end of June Wingate had sent a small Egyptian unit to Taif with six mountain guns and six machine guns to dislodge the enemy. The fall of Taif on 22 September was achieved by Hussein's son Abdullah, whom the Arabs thought was the real brains behind the Revolt. Elsewhere the Arab initiative had stalled before Medina; at one point, it looked like the Turks might well advance via Rabegh and re-capture Medina which would have proved a serious setback. Wingate requested a British brigade from the Egyptian expeditionary force at Suez be detached and sent to Rabegh to forestall any possible Turkish threat. His request was denied by

Sir Henry McMahon whose persistent doubts as to the advisability of using Christian troops in the Hejaz were deepening. Why had he dismissed Wingate's earlier and acceptable solution of sending Sudanese troops into Arabia, with British forces taking their place in the Sudan? Surely it was not a case of professional rivalry between McMahon and Wingate – or was it?

Wingate subsequently switched to the idea of British troops in Arabia, but why? Perhaps having been rebuffed for his initial solution, he resorted to the second option, one he knew McMahon was reluctant to follow. Perhaps McMahon deliberately withheld British troops because he wanted the Arabs themselves to liberate their own territory. In fact, the way forward would depend entirely on the Arabs' ability not only to maintain but also to increase the pressure on the Turkish garrison at Medina. The key to success was to deny the Turks the use of the Hejaz railway and to close the Medina–Rabegh–Mecca road which would effectively prevent any Turkish advance on Mecca. The occupation of Akaba was also crucial since it would encourage incursions against the Turks by the Bedouin tribes in the northern Hejaz from towns like Yenbo, a vital seaport, and Wejh, rendering the Hejaz railway inoperable and denying the Turks at Medina reinforcements and supplies. However, without a British brigade, Hussein's forces would have to go it alone with whatever support Wingate could spare from his meagre resources in the Sudan. This support was limited to a few Egyptian and Indian Army personnel and specialist officers from the Sudan, a flight of aeroplanes sent to Rabegh in November and, most importantly, the Royal Navy presence in the Red Sea.

McMahon opposed Wingate's support for the Rabegh proposal. On 13 October he wrote to Lord Charles Hardinge, Permanent Under-Secretary at the Foreign Office, that in his view:

> The Sirdar [Wingate] ... is already agitating for the despatch of aero-planes with their British escort, and I fear that he will soon discover pressing needs for a brigade [of British troops] to follow. I will do my best to prevent it.[4]

McMahon was now decidedly hostile towards Wingate. He wrote to Hardinge:

> The Sirdar has lived so long in the limelight that it may prove physically impossible for him to conduct Hejaz operations without attracting to them a stronger blaze of limelight than is good for the Arab cause.[5]

Reading the extract, one cannot avoid regarding it as a proverbial stab in the back from an erstwhile friend, but what had been McMahon's reasons? Jealousy? Spite? Envy?

There had been criticism in London of McMahon's effectiveness in Cairo for some time. Perhaps he was a man who knew that his ability was under scrutiny and that by opposing Wingate he might save himself. The circumstances which led to McMahon's subsequent dismissal from Cairo were a lamentable organization of military supplies to the Hejaz Arabs and his animosity towards Wingate. In the early stages of the Arab Revolt, arrangements to meet its needs fell far short of what was required, a fact reported to London. On 3 October McMahon received a telegram from London informing him that:

> the question of military control and supervision of the arrangements for assisting the Sherif [Hussein] should be entrusted to Wingate, who should be instructed to take the steps necessary to keep himself in close communication and co-operation with the Admiral Commanding Naval Forces [Wemyss] in the Red Sea … [who] will be instructed to assist Sirdar in provision of stores and supplies so far as his own requirement will permit.[6]

McMahon's response did not directly criticize Wingate but reminded the Foreign Office that Wingate in Khartoum was too isolated from events to make an effective contribution to the Revolt. McMahon's arguments only served to convince the Foreign Office that Wingate should be moved to Cairo. On 11 October, Sir Edward Grey, the Foreign Secretary, cabled to Wingate indicating that:

> Lord Kitchener's death has made the consideration of an appointment necessary which can be substantive and continue after the war. In my opinion, there is no one so well fitted as yourself, by your special knowledge, experience and personal qualities to fill the post [of High Commissioner of Egypt].[7]

Wingate was not the only candidate being considered for the position. Ronald Graham, adviser to the Egyptian Ministry of the Interior, had also been considered but was 'passed over' in Civil Service parlance. Graham returned to the Foreign Office in London from where he was able to snipe at Wingate from a distance.

Wingate's appointment as High Commissioner of Egypt would prove something of a poisoned chalice. In time, Egypt became a career graveyard, not only for Sir Henry McMahon but also Reginald Wingate and his several successors. Later, Lawrence would write of Wingate as a man who:

> had complete confidence in his own grasp of the situation in the Middle East, foresaw credit and great profit for the country in the Arab development; but as criticism slowly beat up against McMahon, he disassociated himself from him, and London began to hint that better use might be made by an experienced hand of so subtle and involved a skein …[8]

Meanwhile, Lawrence was sent to Jedda to investigate and report on the situation there and the reasons for the failing Revolt. During his visit he would meet Prince Feisal for the first time; he was immediately struck by the man's noble bearing, a born leader of whom he would later write in *Seven*

Pillars of Wisdom, 'I felt at first glance that this was the man I had come to Arabia to seek – the leader who would bring the Arab Revolt to full glory'.[9]

Lawrence arrived in Jedda on 16 October, only four days after Grey's telegram to Wingate. McMahon had been fighting a cause already lost; not only his falling out with Wingate but also his mishandling of the Arab Revolt, had directly led to his dismissal. Grey's letter of 12 October effectively offered Wingate McMahon's post in Cairo. Grey then wrote to David Lloyd George, Minister for Munitions, informing him that 'I have decided in consultation with the Prime Minister that the Sirdar [Wingate] shall be appointed as High Commissioner of Egypt to replace McMahon. The appointment will be announced on 6 November and will take effect at the end of the year ...'[10]

Wingate was duly appointed High Commissioner of Egypt in December 1916. Sir Lee Stack, Wingate's Civil Secretary, was appointed as his successor in the Sudan. Interestingly, Wingate recommended Stack only as 'acting' Governor which implies that he hoped to return to the Sudan and resume his position at some point, particularly if his appointment in Cairo proved to be temporary, which he probably believed it to be at the time. Two days before the announcement was made in the newspapers, Emir Hussein proclaimed himself King (or Sultan) of Arabia, a hollow title as it transpired.

McMahon was summarily dismissed without any consideration for his feelings. There was no sweetener, nor was his dismissal softened by anything remotely resembling tact. His staff in Cairo were surprised and shocked, as there was considerable sympathy for him; many among his retinue thought that he had been sacked because he was not seen as one of the Foreign Office favourites. In the Arab Bureau, most sympathized with his position, particularly Lawrence. Few British observers blamed McMahon for the problems in Egypt and fewer thought that Wingate would be able to solve them.

It has to be said that the efficient, loyal but unimaginative McMahon had no desire for his career to be blighted by an unqualified support for the Arabs. Despite his unexpected and brutal sacking, he was privately relieved to be rid of his position as High Commissioner. The Arab Revolt apart, Britain had at the outset of the war assured Egypt that, at its end, she would honour her promise to accelerate the process of self-government, a false promise as it turned out and McMahon may have known this all along.

As for Wingate the poison in his chalice was added by the conduct of war and its effect on the Egyptian people. Despite assurances from Britain that she (and not Egypt) would bear the weight of the war – a euphemism for the considerable expense involved – ordinary Egyptian people were sucked into the war effort against their will. The vast engineering works connected with Egypt's defence and the plan to invade Turkish Palestine required vast numbers of labourers. Hundreds and thousands of *fellahin* (peasants) were conscripted into what was in effect forced labour. Draft animals were requisitioned and land devoted to growing cotton was put to growing grain to feed the armies. All these measures alienated the peasantry, abuses with which Wingate as High Commissioner would have to deal in future.

In January 1917 Wingate took up residence in Cairo in his new and exalted position. Before that, however, Lawrence was back in Jedda where he had a strained meeting with Sherif Abdullah; Abdullah had repeatedly requested an Allied brigade be sent to Rabegh along with a flight of aeroplanes. The planes were actually already on their way but Wingate's military advisers stressed the potential dangers of sending a unit of the Royal Flying Corps to the Hejaz without supporting troops. Negotiations were still continuing about the likelihood of a British brigade for Rabegh when, on the advice of Colonel Alfred Parker, the ship carrying the planes was recalled on 25 October, despite being within sight of the port.[11]

Confusion briefly reigned, much to Lawrence's ill-concealed disgust. Wingate's decision to cancel the landing of the aeroplanes could not have been an easy one. Now in complete control of the British mission which was supposed to co-operate with Emir Hussein, Wingate was in a difficult position. A Christian force landing at some point between Mecca and Medina would have dire consequences, not only for the Turks. At this point, Lawrence believed that the Arab Revolt was lost due to inept leadership on both the British and Arab sides. He made it his business to meet the Sherif's four sons, finding Abdullah 'too clever by half, Ali too clean and Zeid too cool' but he found Feisal had fire in his belly and a natural choice for the defence of Mecca; based in Jebel Subh, Feisal had the capacity to menace the Turkish left flank approaching from Medina.

It is perhaps appropriate here to briefly summarize Lawrence's role in the Arab Revolt. Much has been written of him but a précis of his aims and ambitions in the Arab cause is necessary. From the outset Lawrence had been an unswerving supporter of a pan-Arab revolt; he believed his unwritten duty – and destiny – was to support an Arab leader who could make effective use of British arms and gold. His mission to Jedda was purely diplomatic but when he met Feisal he rightly identified him as the only one of Hussein's four sons who possessed the necessary qualities of leadership and who might ensure the success of the Revolt. When they met, Feisal was aged thirty-one, Lawrence was twenty-six; both men had a great respect for each other. Lawrence made no secret of the fact that he considered himself more of an intellectual than a soldier; he was ill at ease wearing British Army uniform and instinctively knew that guerrilla warfare was the answer to the Arabs' efforts, recognizing them as brilliant light cavalry, more suited to hit-and-run tactics than to set-piece battles. However, the Bedouin tribesmen Feisal led were often little better than brigands, doing what they did for gold rather than freeing their country from the hated Turks. When Lawrence returned to Cairo after his first mission to Jedda, he expected to spend the rest of the war in map-making behind a desk; he even made that known to his colleagues in the Arab Bureau.

Lawrence referred to Wingate's intelligence department in Cairo as 'The Faculty' which implies that its interest in the Arab Revolt was academic rather than militaristic. He deliberately cultivated a protective outer shell, preferring to be considered an eccentric Oxford Don, which in many respects he remained, but he soon discarded his British Army uniform for Arab dress. His mastery of Arabic and appreciation of Arab culture brought criticism from his superiors in Cairo; to many, his association with Feisal from November 1916 to the end of the war had made him 'go native,' which to a certain extent was true. Lawrence certainly understood the mind of the Arab better than his military colleagues. He was steeped in medieval history, had conducted archaeological excavations in Carchemish before the war and revered the culture of the Arab people. This may have stemmed from his awkwardness in the company of women and an affinity with Arab men who praised overt masculinity and elevated male friendship above that of women. Such masculinity did not mean necessarily mean sexual congress between 'friends'; some historians consider that Lawrence's dedicatory poem 'To S.A.' in *Seven Pillars of Wisdom* was not addressed to Saudi Arabia but to a male friend.

Lawrence never considered himself a man of action nor even one with a desire to lead from the front. This probably explains why he and Wingate, with their mutual fluency in Arabic and their empathy with native peoples got on reasonably well. They did disagree about one aspect of the Arab Revolt: Wingate was convinced that only professional (Christian) troops could conquer the Hejaz and free it from Turkish domination; Lawrence was less sure but later conceded Wingate was right. As for the third member of this alliance, Feisal, he feared the presence of Christian troops would weaken Arab resolve and commitment to the cause. Feisal was astute enough to recognize that if the British fought and won battles in the Hejaz desert, Arab hopes of independence would recede to nothing.

The maze of politics began to grow ever more elaborate. A French military mission headed by Colonel Edouard Bremond in Jedda at the end of September confused matters yet further. The French were adamant that Arabs should not be allowed to take Medina and that, instead, Allied troops should land at Rabegh and take the initiative. They believed that the Arabs would return home with any booty, leaving Allied troops to finish the job. The French therefore proposed to capture Medina and hand it to Emir Hussein as a reward for his support. On the very day that Bremond met Lawrence, the former cabled Paris to the effect that if the Arabs managed to take Medina by themselves the French would then proceed to Syria. It was therefore imperative for France that Medina should not fall to the Arabs before the war ended. One has to ask the question – at this juncture, who was the Arabs' real enemy, Turkey or France?

Lawrence's next move was to make the 100-mile journey to meet Feisal whom he believed would prevent the Revolt from melting away. Feisal had scored a spectacular success against the Turks at Bir Abbas, some thirty miles south-west of Medina. This action relieved the pressure on Sir Archibald Murray's army (*Egypforce*) in the Sinai desert and also meant that perhaps foreign troops would not be needed after all. Hussein himself argued that

Muslim troops could defend the country without the assistance of the French and British, thus allowing his son Ali to capture Medina – hence the French concerns.

In Hamra, Lawrence found Feisal in a black mood. The Turks had recovered from their reverse at Bir Abbas and had driven Feisal back about thirty miles to Hamra. The problem was one of faulty strategic planning on Hussein's part in his failure to deliver supplies and ammunition to his more belligerent son, Feisal. Lawrence knew that Feisal was crucial to Arab success as he possessed the qualities of a true leader, qualities his father and three brothers, the Sherifs Abdullah, Ali and Zeid, woefully lacked. The other brothers were easy prey to French manipulation which aimed to keep them away from Medina and Syria. After several heated exchanges between Lawrence and Feisal, the former was convinced that Feisal, while brave and resilient, was too impatient for success and would be disastrous for the Arab cause were he to act precipitately. Lawrence's lengthy reports to Cairo are a model of clarity and detailed, accurate observation. Awaiting transport by sea from Yenbo was Colonel Parker, liaison officer to Sherif Ali, anxious to question Lawrence about the precise state of affairs in the Hejaz. He confided to his diary:

His Excellency the Sirdar [Wingate] should have first hand information of the nature of the country and the situation and I have advised Lawrence to proceed ... to Port Sudan, proceeding then to Khartoum.[12]

Wingate was still in Khartoum at this point; by the time Lawrence reached him, events had taken a dramatic turn in Rabegh; a Turkish column was only three days' march away. The British government had again authorized the despatch of a flight of aeroplanes to Rabegh and, as no military escort was available elsewhere, Wingate sent two companies of Egyptian troops from the Sudan under Major P. C. Joyce and Captain W. A. Davenport with instructions to assist in the training of regular Arab units being formed there.

On 2 November 1916 Wingate cabled the Foreign Office, stressing the seriousness of the situation. He made it clear that Hussein was repeatedly requesting guns and technical support to stiffen his forces. No weapons could be spared from the Sudan, so instead Wingate asked for support from the Royal Navy; he advised that a flotilla should anchor off Rabegh to protect the town and, if necessary, should the Turks break through, evacuate it.

After reconsidering the position in the light of Wingate's latest communication, the War Committee in London authorized Wingate to despatch to Rabegh 'whatever French, British and Sudanese military assistance which is immediately available'.[13] The fact that this telegram was sent on the same day as Wingate's must have given him much-needed reassurance that the government appreciated the danger but there was more than an element of buck-passing in this order. On the same day that Wingate received his instructions London cabled Sir Archibald Murray in the Sinai ordering him *not* to release any units from *Egypforce* if Wingate requested them. Poor

Wingate. At least the government had made an approach to the French to offer whatever troops they could spare – irrespective of whether they were Christian or Muslim – and the request was relayed to Wingate as a kind of sop. Ironically, on the same day that these decisions were taken in London, Wingate in Khartoum received advice that the reports of Turkish advance on Rabegh had been unfounded. Even so, Colonel Parker in Rabegh reported that conditions were so bad that he advised the British government to send a brigade of British troops in order to restore morale. It was at this point, when Wingate was considering how to proceed, that Lawrence arrived in Khartoum. He was informed that Wingate had succeeded McMahon as High Commissioner of Egypt, which Lawrence thought grossly unfair. In his view McMahon had been enthusiastic in supporting the Arabs; little did the young man know of McMahon's private feelings on the Revolt and the unlikelihood of its success. Lawrence did at least pay tribute to Wingate in *Seven Pillars of Wisdom*:

> The Arab revolt had been his [Wingate's] dream for years ... Sir Reginald Wingate, High Commissioner in Egypt, was happy in the work he had advocated for years. I grudged him this happiness; for McMahon who took the actual risk of starting it, had been broken just before prosperity began. However, that was hardly Wingate's fault.[14]

For his part, Wingate sponsored Lawrence; with his instinctive gift for perspicacity, Wingate saw the man beneath the skin, recognizing he was capable of great things. Wingate never dismissed Lawrence as a flawed genius, as his great-cousin Orde Wingate would in the 1930s and he appreciated that Lawrence was a man with a mission, possessed of great powers of endurance in the hostile desert, which his slight physical frame belied. Lawrence would later freely admit that, in supporting the Arabs, Wingate had risked his professional reputation, even his career. Furthermore, most members of the Arab Bureau in Cairo, while professing a high regard for McMahon, recognized that Wingate was more committed to the Arab cause. Many would later admit that the arrangements for supporting the Revolt in the Hejaz had been unwieldy and bureaucratic, which was hardly the fault of Wingate. No less a person than Admiral Rosslyn (Lord Wemyss) confessed in a letter to a friend dated 13 November 1916 that, under the new regime spearheaded by Wingate, affairs in the Hejaz would be better managed; he wrote this without animosity towards McMahon but because he hoped that Wingate would have a freer hand than before. Wingate and Wemyss were now the two most senior British officers directly involved in the Arab campaign, even if Lawrence, a subordinate officer, possessed the most up-to-date information on the situation in the Hejaz.

During their discussions in Khartoum Wemyss and Lawrence both argued against the despatch of a British brigade to Rabegh. Wingate disagreed with them, disappointed that the War Committee in London had failed to acquiesce to his demands. He wrote to Sir Archibald Murray to the effect in a telegram marked 'private and personal' on 23 November 1916:

> When I put ... the contingency of an advance in force on Rabegh by the Turks, and the possibility of arresting this advance by a brigade of British or French troops on the urgent appeal of the Sherif, I understand him to agree that in such an emergency the Arabs would welcome this help, and in spite of their religious objections, would cling to this hope of success rather than acquiesce in the certain defeat that failure to hold Rabegh would mean.[15]

As stated earlier, the Turkish advance on Rabegh proved to be mere scare-mongering. No matter, at the end of their discussions, Wingate drafted a telegram to the Foreign Office in which he appeared to accept the War Committee's decision. This author uses the word 'appeared' advisedly; Wingate was no fool and was abundantly aware of the political climate. Since no British troops would be made available, he would instead ask the French to send a Muslim contingent of troops already en route from North Africa. Wemyss and Lawrence were shown Wingate's telegram before it was despatched; Wemyss thought that Wingate's decision reflected a unanimous agreement, although Lawrence was still angered by the thought of a French presence in Rabegh. He salved his delicate conscience by assuming that neither British nor French troops would be sent to the Hejaz. For the moment, Wingate accepted Feisal should be the sole military obstacle to Turkish incursions and so proceeded to send guns, machine guns and air support to strengthen Feisal's forces.

If the foregoing appears confused to the reader it reflects the constantly changing attitudes of the government in London, Cairo and Khartoum. On the one hand we have Lawrence championing McMahon as a strong supporter of the Arab Revolt when he proved not to be so; Wingate comes in for some strong criticism from Lawrence, yet it was Wingate's painstaking groundwork which equipped the Revolt. In Cairo feelings were mixed as to the likelihood of Arab success; certainly, many of McMahon's supporters made no secret of the fact that the British government was throwing good money away in its support for Hussein and Feisal. Sir Archibald Murray, the Commander in Chief of *Egypforce*, refused to offer any military assistance to the Arabs, arguing that his prime responsibility was to protect the Suez Canal. Wingate, still in Khartoum but about to transfer to Cairo in January 1917, must have experienced feelings of doubt as to the backing he might receive as the new High Commissioner of Egypt. Wingate and Lawrence also knew that the principal objective of the Revolt would be to take Medina, the last Turkish stronghold in the Hejaz, a major operation requiring fine tuning. The tactics would consist largely of Arab hit-and-run attacks and the constant cutting of the railway line to prevent supplies and reinforcements reaching the Turkish garrison. These tactics were, of course, well within Arab capabilities but the British agreed to provide military and technical support; to this end, Wingate bolstered the number of Arab-speaking British officers in the Hejaz. He believed that an elite body of British military advisers was vital to the operation's success and informed the War Office in London accordingly:

> The necessity for the presence at Rabegh of a small expert military staff to superintend the organization of Arab trained bands and to advise on and appreciate the military situation is very urgent. Colonel Newcombe, an artillery officer and an engineering officer should be sent as soon as possible ... if possible, Colonel Newcombe's assistants should have previous experience of Arabs.[16]

These appointments would be in addition to those of Joyce and Davenport already in Rabegh and Major Garland, an engineer officer who was training the Arabs in the use of explosives. Newcombe's group would henceforth be known as the British Military Mission, a somewhat grandiose title for such a small group of officers. Lawrence admits as much, referring to Wingate as a British General while commanding the nominal expeditionary unit known as the Hejaz Force 'which in reality comprised a few liaison officers and a handful of storemen and instructors'.[17] On the other hand, the head of the French Military Mission at Jedda, Colonel Bremond, strongly urged the landing of Allied forces in the Hejaz. He had already brought to Suez some artillery, machine guns, cavalry and an infantry battalion of Algerian Muslims commanded by French officers. He further argued that, attached to British troops, his Algerian contingent would give the force an international flavour.

For the moment, Wingate knew he would have to rely on a small liaison staff to provide him with accurate information as intelligence from Arab sources was notoriously unreliable, especially on the estimated strength of the fighting men. A survey of the defensive preparations at Rabegh in October 1916 showed that these were practically non-existent or 'mere scratchings ... quite useless as they stand, against an army with any sort of artillery'.[18] On 11 November, just after Lawrence's departure from Khartoum for Cairo, Wingate received a cable from Sir William Robertson, Chief of the Imperial General Staff at the War Office containing welcome news:

> In view of the importance of establishing at Rabegh a military intelligence system it is suggested that an officer should be specially detailed to undertake as soon as possible the work of organizing such a system on the spot ... [It] might lead to our obtaining valuable military information about [the] Turks generally ... It is suggested that unless you have someone available in Sudan, you could obtain an officer from GOC Egypt. The names Lawrence or George Lloyd occur to me as suitable.[19]

Wingate immediately despatched a copy of Robertson's cable to Clayton adding that he proposed:

> sending Newcombe to Yenbo but in view of the possible delay of his arrival I think Lawrence would do this work excellently *as a temporary*

arrangement [author's italics]. George Lloyd [later 1st Baron Lloyd] might do well for Rabegh.[20]

Almost certainly, Wingate suspected Clayton would oppose his suggestion about Lawrence. He was right: Clayton argued that Lawrence was more valuable to the Arab Bureau HQ in Cairo. However, after some counter-proposals, Wingate got his way. Lawrence was sent to Yenbo to report on the situation and arrange supplies for Feisal. Wingate smoothed Clayton's ruffled feathers by promising that Lawrence would return to Cairo when Newcombe arrived in Yenbo.[21] For his part Clayton was gratified to learn that Lawrence strongly opposed sending Allied troops to Rabegh; he asked Lawrence to put his views on the matter in a report and Lawrence duly obliged. Clayton then circulated the report widely. Sir Archibald Murray, Commander in Chief of *Egypforce*, opposed to any Allied landing at Rabegh to assist the Arab rebellion, copied Lawrence's report to Robertson at the War Office, suggesting he study it carefully. Murray did this without informing Wingate, although Clayton informed him two days later that Lawrence's report had been sent to the Director of Military Intelligence in London 'as a matter of daily routine'. Clearly, Clayton was hostile to Wingate and his plans for assisting the Arabs which is why he deferred to London. Wingate expressed his view on this by adding 'OH!' in the margin of the telegram.[22] Given the tacit irritation expressed by that single word, one can only regret he did not add more for the benefit of future historians ...

Admiral Sir Rosslyn Wemyss, a staunch supporter of the Revolt, agreed with Lawrence's view on the advisability of sending Allied troops to Rabegh and wrote in such terms to Wingate on 19 November:

> As a general principle both McMahon and Murray are thoroughly in accord with your policy. Imagine therefore all our feelings when the telegram was received saying that the War Office were reconsidering the question of sending troops to Rabegh! [This rethinking may have been due to McMahon's recall for his tacit mishandling of the Arab rebellion, although it is difficult to understand why the War Office questioned Murray's advice not to send British troops since he was one of them]. I waited for nothing [meaning he acted at once] and telegraphed to the Admiralty ... telling them that I considered it would be most dangerous to the success of the Sherif's cause; and I found that Murray had done the same to the War Office. It is really heartbreaking to think that at last when everybody principally concerned has arrived at the same con-clusion, the War Council [now the War Committee] should be induced to consider other steps through the machinations of the French diplomats.[23]

So it appeared that it was the French, acting on Colonel Bremond's advice, who had swayed the British government which did not wish to put in jeopardy its prosecution of the war. Even so, Wingate still favoured sending a British brigade to Rabegh; he was sensible enough to temper his view in a cable dated 12 November to Robertson at the War Office. Perhaps he was protecting his position and career; we cannot censure him for that, given his continuing genuine support for the Arab cause:

> From the political and religious standpoint, it would be desirable to delay to the last moment the despatch of such troops. They should ... be held in readiness at Suez [rather than being sent immediately], as it is just possible the measures now being taken by Feisal may so threaten the [Turkish] advance as to cause the enemy to pause.[24]

The War Office in distant London must have been confused by these seemingly contradictory reports, struggling to make sense of the situation. The War Committee had little option but to assume that Wingate had received incorrect information on the situation at Rabegh; Wingate continued to argue for British intervention while Cairo opposed it. To modern eyes the military situation appears a shambles and it undoubtedly was; there were conflicting agendas and, to his credit, Lawrence saw that French diplomatic influence was beginning to prevail over British government policy.

Be that as it may, Lawrence was sent to Yenbo as Feisal's military adviser, a duty he did not relish as he believed that Feisal would resent outside interference and be 'very hard to advise' as Clayton reported to Wingate.[25] Wingate responded by supporting the decision to send Lawrence to Yenbo.[26] At this point, it has to be remembered that Wingate had not read Lawrence's vitriolic report on the inadvisability of sending Allied troops to Rabegh, a report which would put a strain on their future relations.

Clayton then summed up the whole view of the Revolt after discussions with Al Masri, an officer on Feisal's staff. He stressed that Yenbo, rather than Rabegh, offered better prospects for successful offensive operations. He reported this to Wingate on 19 November:

> The Hejaz is the key of [sic] the whole problem and it is the permanent cutting of the railway, or at least the dislocation of its running, which is the most important point to aim at.
>   The Turkish force at Medina can stay there as long as it likes, provided it is rendered incapable of a serious offensive and when eventually the railway is cut permanently, as a result of our activities further north, the Medina division [of Turks] is lost.[27]

It is perhaps true to say that the divergent views of Wingate and Clayton arose in part from their geographical separation. Wingate's chief responsibilities were still based in the Sudan and he had no influence over Murray's *Egypforce* in the Sinai. On the other hand, Clayton in Cairo was in constant contact with Murray and had access to wider intelligence resources than Wingate. Wingate had to rely on information about the situation in the Hejaz from his representative in Jedda, Colonel Wilson, who had very little contact with Feisal and whose advice was constantly questioned by Clayton.

Clayton's man, Lawrence, also disagreed with Wilson's view on many issues, putting Wingate at further disadvantage. These difficulties would be largely resolved when Wingate moved to Cairo to take up his post as High Commissioner in 1917. For the moment tensions increased, especially after Wingate was given a copy of Lawrence's hostile report arguing against the despatch of British troops to Rabegh. When he read it Wingate did everything he could to discredit Lawrence's argument. On 23 November he cabled Wilson in Jedda in an attempt to pour oil on troubled waters, describing the disagreement about the use or otherwise of British troops in the Hejaz as 'a storm in a teacup' and that, while he agreed with Lawrence's report, he felt that Lawrence had

> omitted the one and important essential [from his report] and that is that the Arabs have no more desire to come under the heel of the Turks again than has the Sherif himself, and when it comes to a matter of almost certain defeat, the Arabs will, in my opinion, welcome any steps taken to save them ...
>
> I have no doubt that Lawrence has done this [arguing against the landing of British troops in the Hejaz] in perfectly good faith, but he appears to me *to be a visionary and his amateur soldiering has evidently given him an exaggerated idea of the soundness of his views on purely military matters* [author's italics].

This was a view that would be later endorsed by his great-cousin Orde Wingate in the 1930s.

Wingate conceded that Lawrence's view of the French policy in the Middle East was close to the truth and he concurred with Wilson's own misgivings about French intentions. Wingate's cable of 23 November to Wilson continued:

> I am principally annoyed in all this matter, not so much on account of the apparent want [lack] of straightness on the part of certain people who should be above that sort of thing, but on account of the huge loss of time when I am working at very high pressure, morning, noon and night.
>
> It seems to me strategically absolutely unsound to abandon Rabegh for Yenbo, although I quite agree that Yenbo may be made quite a useful subsidiary base for helping Faisal [sic] and perhaps training some contingents there if the personnel is available.
>
> I am rather disappointed at the Arab Bureau being drifted about by any wind that blows.[28]

What should we make of this communication? Wingate was clearly under pressure to deliver the goods but his observations on Lawrence were sound. He also understood the politics and confusion in the communications passing between Cairo, the War Office and the Foreign Office. On the same day Wingate cabled Wilson, Clayton responded, attributing Lawrence's damning memorandum to pressure exerted on Lawrence by Sir Archibald Murray. However, Clayton's cable contained an outright lie; he informed Wingate that it was Murray, not himself, who had asked Lawrence to write the report. Here we see the devious bureaucratic mind in full flow. Was it not typical of a man like Clayton to blame someone else, as Wingate was about to be appointed as High Commissioner and become Clayton's superior? It was perhaps yet another example of self-preservation in public life. Clayton comes across as a duplicitous character, eager to please a proleptic boss.

As for Wilson in Jedda, who considered himself senior officer and ablest judge of the Arab situation, he was angered that a junior officer had impudently challenged his judgement, even if Lawrence's appraisal was accurate. He could not repudiate Lawrence's assessment, assuaging his bruised ego by criticizing Lawrence's decidedly unmilitary demeanour, untidy dress and rudeness. Wilson had already censured Lawrence for his habit of wearing Arab clothes, which in his view was scandalous behaviour on the part of a serving British officer. He wrote to Clayton on 22 November, insisting that Lawrence be disciplined and be made to clean up his image:

> Lawrence wants kicking and kicking hard, then he would improve. At present I look upon him as a bumptious young ass who spoils his un-doubted knowledge of Syrian Arabs by making himself out to be the only authority on war, engineering, running H[is] M[ajesty's] ships and everything else. He put every single person's back up I've met. From the Admiral [Wemyss] down to the most junior fellow on the Red Sea.[29]

Lawrence was eccentric, sensitive, an individualist and a scholar, not in the least a trained and disciplined soldier. For all his flawed character, he had principles and he could spot a fake at 200 yards. He was not a member of the Establishment though he knew he would have to endure its traditions, foibles and protocols to get his way. Any genuine, hard-working person who has made a career in public service knows that it attracts an abundance of bureaucrats, time wasters, egotists, sycophants, wafflers and incompetents. Wilson's cable to Clayton was hardly a propitious start for Lawrence's second mission to the Hejaz; what was worse, on this occasion, he was subordinate to Wilson. Certain geniuses are made of sterner stuff and can rise above petty jealousies. Unfortunately, Lawrence was not such a one. He undoubtedly possessed the skills of a guerrilla leader and understood the Arab mind, even if modern historians have come down hard on his often exaggerated claims about the effectiveness of the Revolt. The same historians give less credit to the contribution made by Lawrence's Arabs to the Allies' victory in the Middle East. It has to be said that, ultimately, it was the professional soldier who defeated the Turks.

In December genuine fear of a determined Turkish advance on Rabegh induced Wingate to ask the Foreign Office to re-open the question of a British landing in the Hejaz, a view backed by Wilson in Jedda. On 9 December the

Turks pushed back the remnants of Feisal's army – now only 1,500 strong – to Yenbo, which was at least protected by Royal Navy warships. As it appeared that the Revolt was in imminent danger of collapse, a nervous Wilson sent a telegram to Wingate on 9 December:

Following from Sherif Faisal [sic] to Sherif Mecca L37 [?]. Enemy stronger than I said. All forces identified in Hedjaz [sic] are now against me. Must resist any attempt of Turks to occupy Wadi or Yenbo. You should hold on Rabegh so I can act on offensive elsewhere.[30]

Wilson immediately followed this up the same day with comforting news, 'Turks tried to cut me off from sea. They failed and I have returned [to] Yenbo after slight engagement.'[31]

On the following day, Wingate cabled Clayton:

I am getting nervous about Wilson's health and feel that he may break down at any moment – he's altogether overworked … It seems almost inevitable that a [British] Brigade be sent to Rabegh – I much wish for General Murray's sake that such a course were unnecessary, but if the Turks really mean coming south after having pushed Feisal and Co aside, then an effort must be made to stop them – the question is can we do it in time?[32]

Wilson immediately followed up his two telegrams dated 9 December with the following sent on 11 December (Telegram from Wilson quoting messages from the Sherif of Mecca):

Owing to present war circumstances it is necessary to bring six battalions of regular troops. If it is possible for HM's government to bring Moslem troops it will be good; if not there is no objection if European troops are brought'.

To this Wilson added 'Battalion reckoned at 500 men by Sherif'.[33] The same day, Wilson despatched a second cable informing Wingate that:

Sherif … wishes British Brigade kept Suez or Port Sudan ready to proceed immediately on his request. His present urgent need is 1,500 troops Rabegh and 500 Yenbo. Can French be persuaded [to] support? Have explained situation and danger fully and Sherif thoroughly understands situation. His great fear is effect on Moslem opinion if Christian troops are landed in Hedjaz [sic].[34]

The subsequent flurry of telegrams from Wilson gave details of Turkish troop movements and operations. The Egyptian troops stationed in Yenbo were becoming disaffected, so it was recommended they be moved to Rabegh. Hussein continued to voice his concern about the prospect of a possible landing of Christian troops in the Hejaz, believing that the majority of the Arab tribes would go over to the Turks. He worried that anti-Christian propaganda generated by Turkey would accuse him of having given Arabia to the British.

On 14 December, Wingate cabled the Foreign Office:

Our efforts to train and organize an Arab force capable of meeting the Turks in the field have been unsuccessful, mainly owing to the inertness and ignorance of the Arab leaders: and the conduct of Arab levies in recent skirmishes affords little or no grounds for believing that they will be able to withstand a sustained advance by the Turks ... The immediate question for decision by H. M. Government is whether we shall make a last attempt to save the Sherif and his Arabs in spite of themselves.[35]

Wingate based his request on reports of conditions in the Hejaz from Colonel Bremond of the French Military Mission in Jedda and George Lloyd who had arrived in Khartoum on 14 December. In Lawrence's view, Wingate had been taken in by Bremond and had been over-eager to embrace the French solution to the problem – that he, Bremond, would command a mixed brigade of French and British troops in a landing. For his part Wingate allowed himself to be persuaded that Emir Hussein would accept Christian troops if he were pressured; he next sent a telegram to Wilson in Jedda for transmission to Hussein:

I fear in view of the doubts expressed by Your Highness regarding the political wisdom of sending Christian troops, that H. M. Government will refuse to send them. If however the urgent necessity of preventing the failure of Your Highness's and the Arab cause induced H. M. Government to accept an inevitable risk and to send these troops, I am confident that Your Highness will accept them, and will try everything possible to prevent any misunderstanding [of British intentions], or false suspicions on the part of Your Highness's military commanders and Arabs generally.[36]

In addition to this diplomatic arm-twisting, Wingate then sent Wilson a covering note instructing him to 'induce the Sherif to send me a satisfactory reply'.[37]

Wilson cabled back on 15 December to the effect that Hussein had rejected Wingate's suggestion out of hand and that the presence of Christian troops in the Hejaz would imperil his cause.[38] Wilson's attitude to the Rabegh question was shifting as he had learned from Arab sources that Hussein's anxiety about a British landing was well founded; his view of Lawrence's earlier hostile memorandum was also changing, as was his attitude to Lawrence himself. Wilson helpfully suggested a middle course as alternative; two Muslim battalions together with Bremond's North African contingent should be sent instead of British (Christian) troops.

Wingate, unimpressed by Wilson's response, decided to exert more pressure on Hussein. He telegraphed the Foreign Office on 16 December intimating that he intended to send the Sherif an ultimatum to the effect that no Muslim troops were available and that the British force on standby at Suez could not be retained indefinitely. His telegram did not mince words:

> If his [Hussein's] reply is in the negative [to the offer of Christian troops landing at Rabegh within a fortnight] he must understand we shall regard his refusal as final, and that our present offer will not be repeated.[39]

It was a standoff. Wingate's ultimatum was successfully acceded to and Sir Archibald Murray in the Sinai was authorized to despatch troops as soon as Hussein indicated his agreement. However, events in the Hejaz had now taken an unexpected turn as the Turks had withdrawn from the vicinity of Yenbo, thus allowing the Arabs to advance from Rabegh.

The Arab Revolt was now about to take new direction. By the end of 1916, when Wingate left Khartoum to take up his appointment as High Commissioner of Egypt, Feisal, to whom Lawrence was temporarily attached, decided that he must take aggressive action. His initial steps were to make a determined attack on the railway, so he advanced on Wejh to divert Turkish attention from Rabegh, his aim being to bottle up the Turks in Medina. Assisted by Admiral Wemyss' warships anchored off Wejh, Feisal led an undisciplined but successful attack on the Turkish garrison there. The initiative in the Hejaz was now turning in favour of the Arabs, the Turks being obliged to place troops at intervals along hundreds of miles of railway track, their sole link with the main force at Medina. The British Military Mission was now headed by Newcombe as Lawrence, his stand-in, had been recalled to Cairo but Feisal was reluctant to release Lawrence, as he knew that he, more than any other British officer in the Hejaz, was wholly committed to the Arab cause. He pulled a few strings and, although Lawrence embarked for Cairo on 27 January 1917, Clayton had little choice but to accede to Feisal's request that he be returned to the desert. Much to his unconcealed delight, Lawrence almost immediately returned to the Hejaz on an indefinite liaison posting as Feisal's adviser.

In writing a biography of Reginald Wingate and his career in the Middle East, hopefully this author has put into perspective his part alongside that of T. E. Lawrence in the Arab Revolt. Wingate had dreamed of an independent kingdom of Arabia and wholly supported the Revolt from the outset, his chief role being to provide logistical and political support. It was hardly a glamorous role and Lawrence took the acclaim for Arab successes but Wingate was the unsung hero. Lawrence documented his part in the Revolt; Wingate never did and, unlike Lawrence, was a realist, strongly believing the Arabs alone would never defeat the Turks, a view with which most modern historians agree. Nevertheless, Lawrence's Arabs did make a considerable contribution to the eventual outcome, scoring spectacular successes against a modern Turkish army, principally in the capture of the seaport of Akaba.

Lawrence's *Seven Pillars of Wisdom* offers a summary of the political dealings preceding the Revolt:

> The Arab Revolt had begun on false pretences. To gain the Sherif's help our Cabinet had offered, through Sir Henry McMahon, to support the establishment of native governments in parts of Syria and Mesopotamia, 'saving the interests of our ally, France.' The last modest clause concealed a treaty (kept secret until too late, from McMahon, and therefore from the Sherif) by which France, England and Russia agreed to annex some of these promised areas ... I had had no previous or inner knowledge of the McMahon pledges and the Sykes-Picot treaty, which were both framed by war-time branches of the Foreign Office ...[40]

In writing this Lawrence was not being entirely honest; he *was* aware of Sykes-Picot at the time the agreement was promulgated. No matter, his other comments are apposite; he knew only too well that the Arabs were being used. He wrote that he 'assured them that England kept her word in letter and spirit. In this comfort they performed their fine things; but, of course, instead of being proud of what we did together, I was continually and bitterly ashamed.'[41]

As always, French intrigue in that part of the Middle East was never far away. When Feisal took Wejh, Colonel Bremond, the head of the French Military Mission, was determined to ensure that Arab influence would not predominate in Syria – action in Wejh was a shade too far north for his liking – where French interests after the war would be assured under the Sykes-Picot Agreement. Bremond was content to support the capture of Akaba which would effectively satisfy Arab nationalist aspirations without threatening France's ambitions in Syria. Bremond had hoped to restrict the Arab movement at Rabegh by introducing Christian troops there but from his perspective the taking of Akaba would achieve the same result. An Anglo-French force advancing inland towards Damascus would convince the local tribes that the Sherif's European allies were interested not simply in occupying Arabia but in liberating it. Bremond was not only a military man he was also a political animal. His aim was to contain the Arab movement to the Hejaz and, to this end, he set about deliberately poisoning the mind of Feisal against British intentions.

By now the British High Command was convinced that a British landing of troops was necessary to liberate the Hejaz, whether Emir Hussein wanted it or not. One wonders whether this was decided by Bremond's sabre-rattling and a desire to conquer territory in Saudi Arabia and was probably the sole determining factor in convincing Britain that she should intervene alone in the Arabs' rebellion. However, the astute Feisal was one step ahead of Bremond and he was unconvinced by the Frenchman's proposals, much to Lawrence's relief. By 1917 Lawrence was aware of the Sykes-Picot Agreement and he was faced by a quandary: should he take Feisal into his confidence and divulge Sykes-Picot or remain silent? He knew that, sooner or later, the truth would emerge and he was concerned that the trust he had built up with Feisal would come to an end. Conscience got the better of him as it would have in any man with Lawrence's idealistic temperament. He finally told Feisal in the autumn of 1917 that the McMahon-Hussein correspondence offered no guarantees of an independent Syria and that the Sykes-Picot Agreement had been accepted by Britain and France. Under the agreement, France, he confided, would be certain to gain the Lebanon and take over the administration of Syria as well – unless of course, the Arabs took Damascus, Homs, Hama and Aleppo, the four towns identified in the Sykes-Picot Agreement. His decision could not have been undertaken lightly. Lawrence had betrayed a confidential state secret and, technically, while not guilty of actual treason, could have been court-martialled. His crisis of conscience resolved, Lawrence was left with only hope of mending fences; for his part, Feisal would have to recast his plans. He now knew that his Arabs would have to capture Damascus and the other three towns before the war came to an end. Lawrence advised him that an Arab success might force France to reconsider her ambitions and that Britain would support the Arabs in their desire for an independent Arab state in Syria and elsewhere. Like McMahon, he hoped that parts of the agreement would thus become unworkable.

The key to success was the capture of Akaba, which Lawrence rightly believed would end the war in the Hejaz and allow British troops to invade Syria; the Arabs under Feisal would act as the right flank of the British advance under General Allenby who replaced General Sir Archibald Murray after the latter suffered a reverse south of Gaza on 26 March 1917. By now even Lawrence admitted that the Arabs alone could not take Damascus and as a consequence Feisal's army came under the command of Allenby.

In the build-up to the attack on Akaba, Lawrence and his fellow officers were instructed to encourage and assist the Arabs in disrupting the Hejaz railway which they did effectively, starving the Turkish garrisons of supplies, ammunition and reinforcements. The culmination of Lawrence's activities in the desert came in July 1917 when he and some 500 Arab irregulars undertook the arduous trek through the hostile and unforgiving Negev desert, one of the worst areas in the Hejaz and known as the Sun's Anvil. It was a brilliantly planned and executed operation; Akaba was the last Turkish stronghold in the Hejaz. It fell with the loss of only two Arab casualties and 300 Turkish dead and 160 prisoners. To the British, success at Akaba meant that any advance into Syria would be protected on the right flank by Feisal's Arabs; to the Arabs, Akaba meant money, guns and food.

Before Akaba was taken, Lawrence tells us of an amusing anecdote concerning Auda abu Tayi, chief of the Howeitat tribe and one of Feisal's more capable allies in the attack. To Auda, Feisal was 'Our Lord, the Commander of the Faithful', the comparison to feudal service in medieval times being entirely appropriate. When Auda joined Feisal at Wejh he was eating in Feisal's tent one evening when he suddenly scrambled to his feet shouting

'God forbid!' and rushed from his master's tent. Lawrence recounts the incident in *Seven Pillars of Wisdom*:

> We stared at one another, and there came a noise of hammering outside. I went to learn what it meant, and there was Auda bent over a rock, pounding his false teeth to fragments with a stone. 'I had forgotten,' he explained, 'Jemal Pasha [a Turkish officer] gave me these. I was eating my Lord's bread with Turkish teeth!' ... he went about half-nourished till we had taken Akaba, and Sir Reginald Wingate sent him a dentist from Egypt to make him an Allied set.[42]

Akaba was to be Lawrence's crowning glory, proof positive of his belief in Feisal's Arabs' capacity to wage successful war. Out of touch with developments in Cairo and the events in Egypt and the Hejaz for two months, Lawrence returned to Cairo on 10 July to report dramatically that the Arabs had taken Akaba. It was welcome news after Sir Archibald Murray's reversal in the Sinai Desert. His replacement, General Sir Edmund Allenby, reclaimed British prestige by capturing Beersheba and Gaza, then in December 1917, accepted the surrender of Jerusalem from its Turkish mayor.

Allenby and Lawrence took to each other from the outset. They met in Cairo where the older man congratulated Lawrence on his success at Akaba and questioned him about Arab strength and further initiatives. (Even Colonel Wilson, who only seven months previously had called Lawrence a bumptious young ass, was fulsome in his praise. He magnanimously cabled Wingate in Cairo, recommending Lawrence for a DSO.) For his part, Wingate described Lawrence's capture of Akaba as 'nothing short of marvellous' and cabled him as follows:

> The Chief of the Imperial General Staff has requested me to convey his congratulations on your most recent exploit and I do so with the liveliest satisfaction. It was a very gallant and successful adventure which it has been my pleasant duty to bring to the notice of the higher authority for special recognition ...[43]

Lawrence pondered whether Wingate had sufficient political clout to transfer Feisal to Allenby's command at this high point in Arab success. He admitted that Wingate did not hesitate to agree; in *Seven Pillars*, Lawrence wrote 'it would be both his [Wingate's] duty and his pleasure to give him [Feisal] up for the good of the show'.[44] Thus the war in Saudi Arabia entered a new phase which would do much to bolster Lawrence's reputation and Britain's prestige in the face of French domination in the Middle East.

Notes

1. *Wingate of the Sudan*, RELW.
2. Wingate to Parker, Arab Bureau, 8 July 1916, WP, 138/4, SAD, DU.
3. C. E. Wilson to Wingate, WP, 138/5, SAD, DU.
4. McMahon to Hardinge, Lloyd George Papers E/3/12/1 House of Lords.

5. *Ibid.*
6. FO to McMahon, FO 141/238.
7. Grey to Wingate, 11 October 1916, WP 160/43, SAD, DU.
8. *Seven Pillars of Wisdom*, p. 62.
9. *Ibid.*, p. 64.
10. Grey to Lloyd George, Lloyd George Papers E/2/13/12 House of Lords.
11. Wingate to Lieutenant General Sir Archibald Murray, Chief of *Egypforce* assigned the task of defending the Suez Canal. The cable read 'You should instruct [Colonel] Parker on the arrival of the officer commanding the flight to notify him that pending further orders, he should not land the flight'. WO 158/627, FO to Wingate via Sir Archibald Murray, WO 158/603.
12. *Lawrence of Arabia: The Official Biography*, Wilson.
13. FO to Wingate via Sir Archibald Murray, WO 158/603.
14. *Seven Pillars of Wisdom*, pp. 113, 172.
15. Wingate to Murray, WO 158/602.
16. Wingate to Arbur, WO 158/627.
17. *Seven Pillars of Wisdom*, p. 113.
18. WP, 141/6, SAD, DU.
19. Robertson to Wingate, WP 143/2 SAD, DU.
20. Wingate to Clayton, WP 143/2, SAD, DU.
21. *Ibid.*, 143/2.
22. Clayton to Wingate, WP 143/2, SAD, DU.
23. Wemyss to Wingate, 19 November 1916, quoted in Wingate to Murray WO 158/627.
24. Wingate to Robertson, quoted in Wingate to Murray 18 November 1916, WO 158/627.
25. Clayton to Wingate, 19 November 1916, WP 143/3, SAD, DU.
26. Wingate to Clayton, 19 November 1916, WP 143/3, SAD, DU.
27. Clayton to Wingate, WP 143/6.
28. Wingate to Wilson, 23 November 1916, WP 143/6, SAD, DU.
29. Wilson to Clayton, Clayton Papers 470/4, SAD, DU.
30. Wilson to Wingate, 9 December 1916, WP 160/6, SAD, DU.
31. *Ibid.*
32. Wingate to Clayton, 10 December 1916, WP 160/6 SAD, DU.
33. Wilson to Wingate, 11 December 1916, WP 160/6 SAD, DU.
34. *Ibid.*
35. Wingate to FO, 14 December 1916, FO 158/64.
36. Wingate to Wilson, 14 December 1916, FO 882/6.
37. *Ibid.*
38. Wilson to Wingate, 15 December 1916, FO 882/6 folio 44.
39. Wingate to FO, 16 December 1916, FO 158/604.
40. *Seven Pillars of Wisdom*, pp. 282–3.
41. *Ibid.*, p. 229.
42. *Ibid.*
43. Wingate to Lawrence, 14 July 1917, FO 882/7 folio 29.
44. *Seven Pillars of Wisdom*, p. 332.

Chapter 7

High Commissioner of Egypt (1917–1919)

On 12 October 1916, to his great surprise, Wingate was informed by Sir Edward Grey of his appointment to the post of High Commissioner of Egypt, with Grey's telegram from the Foreign Office adding:

> In my opinion there is no-one so well-fitted as yourself, by your special knowledge, experience and personal qualities, to fill the post ... The absence of trouble in the Sudan is attributable to your personal influence and policy ... I consider it would be in the public interest that you go to Cairo.[1]

Wingate had been happy in the Sudan, enjoying the perks and benefits of the office of Governor General. Now that he was elevated to High Commissioner, he possibly harboured doubts about the promotion, acutely aware of the fate of his predecessors in the office. As for his personal life, he and Lady Wingate received the happy news that their son Ronald had married Mary Vinogradoff in Lahore, India in November 1916.[2]

The post of High Commissioner of Egypt was second only to the Viceroy of India in responsibility and power. Wingate had never in his wildest dreams entertained hopes of the position; he saw his mission as being Governor General of the Sudan, dedicating himself to the welfare of the Sudanese people. He had steered the Sudan through a difficult time, repairing fences destroyed by the Mahdi's uprising. However, being an astute statesman and given the recent problems arising from the British involvement in the Arab Revolt, he may have been relieved to be offered the career change. He had, perhaps, expected to retire from the Sudan and public service after the Great War, like his eminent close colleagues Lords Cromer and Kitchener. Wingate was a soldier and distrusted politicians; politicians and soldiers have always been at odds, but he brought personal attributes to the role of governor-administrator. However, he would use his great capacity for watching, listening and taking in every snippet of information to come his way to advance his knowledge of Egyptian affairs. After all, he had been Kitchener's Intelligence Officer during the re-conquest of the Sudan. Old habits would die hard.

172

During the recent bickering between the civil and military authorities in Cairo and London, a less tolerant man than Wingate might have refused the appointment. In his carefully and respectfully worded telegrams from Khartoum, Wingate defused the internecine squabbling and hypocrisy that passed for diplomacy in Cairo, a testament to his abilities as an administrator in a veritable wolves' den. One has to ask the obvious question: whom might Wingate trust in Cairo? His staff consisted of many who had been and were still loyal to Sir Henry McMahon, a man sent home for his incompetence – real or imagined – and for his fumbled handling of the Arab Revolt. At least Wingate's appointment would give him the edge on Sir Gilbert Clayton, head of Cairo Intelligence. This must have been an advantage in Wingate's book, considering the overheated political atmosphere that existed in Cairo.

At first, all was sweetness and light. Those who knew Wingate well, men like George Lloyd, said that Wingate was possessed of 'administrative ability ... [with] a thorough knowledge of Egypt and her ways, and a sound judgement'.[3] Others were equally fulsome in their praise; Gertrude Bell and Brigadier General Sir Gilbert Clayton – the latter at least on the surface – both then serving in the Arab Bureau.

Wingate's knowledge of Arabic stood him in good stead. He was also acquainted with all the important people in Cairo. Subsequent events would, however, find him wanting in administering the complex bureaucracy which existed in Cairo, a far cry from the relatively simple demands of Khartoum. Wingate would be indirectly accused of failing to handle successfully his British colleagues in Cairo; his Whitehall masters would criticize him for not acting in the way they desired regarding the subject of Egyptian nationalism. His chief critics in the Foreign Office were Foreign Secretary A. J. Balfour – a golf partner and nearby neighbour in East Lothian – Lord Robert Cecil, Sir George Curzon, Sir Ronald Graham and, disappointingly, Lord Charles Hardinge, the Permanent Under-Secretary of State at the Foreign Office whom Wingate considered a friend. Another hostile critic was Lord Edward Cecil, Robert Cecil's brother, both cousins to Balfour; Edward Cecil and Wingate had been comrades-in-arms in the Sudan campaigns and colleagues in the diplomatic missions to Abyssinia and Fashoda. Edward Cecil informed his brother that he despised Wingate, considering him vain and ruthless with anyone who challenged his authority:

> He will stop at practically nothing to get rid of anyone whom he fears as a competitor ... As you know, my ambition has always been to be at the head of Egyptian affairs, as I should have been if Lord Kitchener had lived.[4]

Of course, Cairo was a different world for the new appointee; in the Sudan, Wingate had virtually ruled as uncrowned king, exercising personal authority in a country many considered a backwater. While he seems not to have been particularly effective in handling his British colleagues, his relations with native people were rarely in question. Perhaps these facts marked him as a target for his political masters in London, particularly the *cabal* which ran the Foreign Office. Wingate could and did get away with much in the minor bureaucracy and convivial atmosphere in what was almost medieval rule in Khartoum. Even there he had his detractors; his private secretary Lee Stack, who succeeded him in 1917, criticized 'Master', as Wingate was affectionately known to the Sudanese. Stack would later find fault once more with his former chief, implying that Wingate was indecisive as High Commissioner in Egypt; writing to Clayton on the future political status of Egypt, he cynically asked if 'Master had any views of his own?'[5]

Yet Wingate still earned praise from some colleagues for his sympathy, never-failing courtesy and his fair and kind treatment of them, possessing the knack of doing and saying the right thing at the right time. These are hardly qualities found in a vain and even incompetent individual. Some nevertheless were irritated by certain character traits, his voluminous memoranda and lengthy telegrams – not for nothing was Wingate known as 'Father of the Ink' by his Egyptian staff, as he often followed his telegrams with even lengthier explanations. He was seen as fussy and pedantic – traits frowned upon in bureaucratic organizations, being indicative of a lack of confidence. Almost from the outset Wingate's detractors in Whitehall began to accuse him of alarmism in the face of rising Egyptian nationalism or that he was failing to put his case across adequately. Why was his advice to the Foreign Office on this and other important aspects of Egyptian politics persistently ignored or disregarded? Was his advice not couched in sufficiently robust terms or did it fail to adequately stress the dangers facing the British government? Was it not the case that those in Whitehall, particularly Robert Cecil and Ronald Graham, were dismissive of him? Wingate, of lowly origin, was regarded as somewhat limited in his talents, something of a *petit bourgeois* by Balfour, his cousins Robert and Edward Cecil and others in high office. The Cecils certainly entertained such thoughts; Wingate was considered unsophisticated and therefore not capable of effective political dealing. A particular instance of this occurred in 1918 when Balfour sent a telegram intended for Sherif Hussein, and in the name of T. E. Lawrence, via Wingate but over the heads of both Wingate and Allenby. Wingate took it upon himself to withhold the onward despatch of the telegram, thinking Balfour's procedure irregular. Instead, he checked matters with the Foreign Office; after all, he was still GOC of the Hejaz operations and should have been consulted beforehand. He was shocked to receive a rebuke from Balfour for withholding the telegram and was ordered to despatch it at once. Was Wingate right to act as he did? He clearly thought so. Perhaps he saw the writing on the wall ...

Wingate's position as High Commissioner had been confirmed in the British Press on 6 November 1916. His appointment took effect from 1 January 1917 and so he made arrangements to journey to Cairo in December. During the interim period, Wingate learnt of the fall of Herbert Asquith's government to that of Lloyd George. Sir Edward Grey was replaced by Arthur J.

Balfour. Lord Charles Hardinge, Viceroy of India until 1918, would return to the Foreign Office as Permanent Under-Secretary of State that year; a friend of Wingate during his Sudan years, he would prove less than supportive in the final years of Wingate's incumbency in Cairo.

Wingate left Khartoum by steamship on 27 December 1916. Changing from steamer at Aswan to complete the journey to Cairo by rail, he received an urgent invitation from the Sultan of Egypt, Kamil Hussein, to visit him on his private yacht. Hussein was fulsome in his praise of Wingate, regarding him as a deliverer from the ill-concealed hostility and strained relationship between the British and the Egyptians in Cairo, relations that had reached breaking point. The Sultan complained that, for over a year, he had been isolated and ignored by the British and was virtually alone in his continued support for the British government; he believed his people were fast moving towards nationalism as a result of the policies Britain was foisting on his government.

Wingate, ever the patient listener, promised he would do all he could to restore cordial Anglo-Egyptian relations; he assured Kamil Hussein that the promise was his highest priority as agent of His Majesty's Government. He then proceeded to Cairo, immediately immersing himself in his new duties. On 24 January 1917 Wejh fell to the Royal Navy and a force of 400 Arabs commanded by Captain Bray, facilitating Feisal and Lawrence's entry to the town. Feisal's elder brother Abdullah then made a wide encircling movement north of Medina, crossing the railway line and making his base at Yenbo. This put Feisal and Abdullah in excellent positions to menace the Hejaz railway, a fact which must have brought some comfort to Wingate. Sherif Hussein's four sons now had 4,000 trained Arabs based at Wejh, Yenbo and Rabegh, supported by a few mountain guns and machine guns. In addition, 10,000 Bedouin irregulars were ready for battle. Against this force were ranged 9,500 Turks in Medina, commanded by Fakhri Pasha, more than half of which had field experience. Some 2,500 Turks were also distributed in blockhouses set up to guard the Hejaz railway. Wingate's response was to despatch several British officers to Colonel Wilson in Jedda, the most experienced being Colonel S. F. Newcombe, a sapper who, with Lawrence, established a demolition training school in Wejh. Raids against the Turkish lines of communication met with considerable success. Prince Zeid, the youngest of Hussein's sons, intercepted a large convoy of Turks en route to Medina, killing some and capturing another 250; a subsequent raid by Newcombe and a mixed demolition party of Egyptians and Arabs destroyed five kilometres of the Hejaz railway. A month later, Colonel Joyce, with his mixed force of Egyptians, Algerians and Arabs, wrought further havoc. The campaign in the desert was now gathering momentum, much to Wingate's and Lawrence's satisfaction.

Wingate's strategic plan was now largely achieved; even if Medina was still held by the Turks, he was assured that they had little or no offensive capability. In London, the government studied the advance of the Arab forces and that of General Allenby. Allenby took Jerusalem in December 1917 and the way was now open for an assault on Damascus and Aleppo, with the anticipated destruction of the Turkish forces there. In July Feisal and Lawrence had been removed from Wingate's command and attached to Allenby. In some respects Wingate must have been relieved, although now that the Arabs were making a valuable contribution to the war effort, and given his steering of the Revolt through its early days at great risk to his reputation, he was being asked to relinquish command on the very brink of Arab success. Lawrence himself had suggested Feisal's transfer from Emir Hussein, convincingly arguing that Feisal's forces in Akaba would act as a shield to Allenby's right flank during the advance on Jerusalem. In *Seven Pillars of Wisdom*, Lawrence pays tribute to Wingate for agreeing to relinquish his role in the Revolt after having assumed responsibility for it in its 'darkest hours', then handing over the Arab forces to Allenby's command.[6] Wingate had contributed much to the success of the Revolt; the Turks had been driven out of Mecca and were now effectively isolated in Medina. The Hejaz was under virtual Arab control and the Revolt now stood on the threshold of further successes. After his father's death, Sir Ronald Wingate wrote that Wingate 'was delighted that they [Feisal's Arabs] could be of use to Allenby'.[7]

Was Ronald Wingate gilding the lily? His father surely breathed a sigh of relief that the sometimes troublesome and unorthodox Lawrence was now no longer his direct responsibility. Wingate had always believed that winning the war was the first priority; although he had backed the Arab uprising it was only a means to an end. Ronald Wingate argued that the transfer of Feisal and Lawrence to Allenby was arranged with the best of motives but it was, in his view, a serious error. It was one thing for the Arabs to operate in a restricted area such as the Hejaz but something altogether different to move Arab forces into a wider sphere of military – and political – intrigue.

It is perhaps now appropriate to examine the relationship between Prince Feisal and Lawrence in the light of these and other recent developments. After the war Ronald Wingate once asked his father to define that relationship and this is reputedly what Wingate had said 'Feisal was a man of the world, a diplomat and a politician ... it seems more probable that Lawrence *was used by him* [author's italics]'.[8] Looking back on that time, we now know that Lawrence was aware of the Sykes-Picot Agreement under which Arabia would be carved up after the war. When Lawrence admitted its existence to Feisal, which of the two men came out of the situation with honour? Surely it has to be Lawrence, the romantic. Feisal acknowledged Lawrence's commendable honesty, even if it had come late; however, he later dismissed Lawrence as a romantic idealist. For his part, Lawrence did the Arab cause no service when, in 1919, he turned up at the Paris Peace Conference wearing his colonel's uniform but with Arab head-dress, thus earning the opprobrium of his military and political colleagues. There was always more than a touch of the theatrical in Lawrence's make-up.

In *Seven Pillars of Wisdom*, Lawrence recognizes Wingate's dedication – albeit qualified – to the Arab Revolt. Lawrence almost missed his destiny in November 1916 when he was a junior officer and argued strongly against Wingate's proposal to send Christian troops to the Hejaz. Wingate rightly concluded that:

> L[awrence] has done all he has in perfectly good faith, but he appears to me to be a visionary and his amateur soldiering has evidently given him an exaggerated idea of the soundness of his views on purely military matters.[9]

Wingate's view enshrines the wisdom of many years as a public servant over the relative inexperience of a young, romantic idealist but Wingate recognized Lawrence's potential and gave him as much free rein as he dared. As for Lawrence, he would earn a reputation of sorts, although along the way he would discover that dealing with Arabs was an art, not a science.

When Wingate took up what would prove his last appointment in the Middle East, he knew that the task was a delicate one, requiring tact, skilful negotiation and empathy. The burden of being High Commissioner of Egypt was somewhat alleviated by trust in both his Cairo and London colleagues, a mistaken trust as it would turn out. Almost immediately after he arrived in Cairo, Egypt's Financial Adviser, Lord Cecil, was recalled to London, throwing Wingate in at the deep end. He immediately set about restoring good relations with the Sultan of Egypt, his Council of Ministers and the British advisers. Cecil and Wingate were long-standing friends from the Sudanese campaign in Dongola and the Rodd Mission to Ethiopia in 1897; Wingate had also supported Cecil's secondment to the Egyptian Army in 1901 as 'someone to be trusted'. By 1904 Wingate's confidence in the man had grown to such an extent that he entrusted Cecil with supreme command of all Egyptian troops stationed in Sudan during his absences. Despite this Wingate was perfectly aware of the fact that two men cannot, metaphorically speaking, ride the same horse. If and when Edward Cecil returned to Cairo, Wingate realized he would have to tread carefully in his relationship with the politician. He said as much in a letter dated 31 January 1917 to Lord Hardinge, Permanent Under-Secretary of State at the Foreign Office:

> It is not that I am in disagreement with Cecil [and his relationship with the Egyptian government] as to any given measures, but his relations with the Sultan and Ministers are not in my opinion satisfactory and I think I ought not to be hampered by this fact in dealing with the Egyptian Ministers ...[10]

Perhaps the statement was ill judged, given Edward Cecil's powerful relatives in the British government. Wingate concluded by suggesting that Cecil be given some other role more directly linked to the war effort or, failing that, if he returned as Financial Adviser, his relationship to Wingate must be made clear. Put bluntly, Edward Cecil was envious of Wingate's promotion, having had high hopes of being appointed High Commissioner himself 'as I would have been if Lord K[itchener] had lived'.[11] Wingate was asking the Foreign Office to impress upon Cecil who precisely was boss in Cairo. This development did not augur well for Wingate's future and Cecil would almost certainly have known Wingate's view of him also.

Despite his busy schedule Wingate took time to visit wounded British soldiers hospitalized in Cairo. On 12 May 1917 he made an official tour of the YMCA's Esbekieh Soldiers' Club, where it had been decided to entertain the convalescing troops. Tea was laid on for 3,000 men and Wingate, as patron of the YMCA in Egypt – its HQ was housed in St David's Buildings, Cairo – gave a short address in which he paid tribute to the sterling work of the Association in providing comforts and 'healthy' activities for the men.[12] Wingate was only too aware of the temptations in the city; Cairo was a notorious hotbed of brothels and street prostitutes, venereal disease rife and too many taverns where drunkenness abounded. Apparently, a further benefit event was held on 24 May – Empire Day – when Wingate played host to another 1,000 convalescents.[13] That same year, he wrote to his son Ronald, informing him that he was kept very busy, meeting hundreds of people, touring war hospitals, attending Red Cross events and charity functions. He was so heavily engaged in war work that he barely had time for golf, playing only nine or eleven holes a week.

The YMCA of course worked closely with the Red Cross, organizing outings for the wounded men. Wingate attended at least one such outing, arranged for 2,000 troops in Alexandria, an occasion which was reported in *The Egyptian Gazette*:

> The High Commissioner on Saturday last was present with Lady Wingate at the YMCA Convalescent Outing Fete at Nuhza Gardens, Alexandria.[14]

Wingate made yet another speech, expressing pleasure at the honour bestowed upon him by the YMCA in Egypt. He made specific reference to the work of W. Jessop, the Association's able secretary, paying tribute to his energy and contribution to the welfare of every British soldier in providing for

> the social side of his [the soldier's] make-up ... The first consideration [of the British government] is to turn out a well-trained and physically fit fighting machine ... but ... unless his leisure is also provided for, he is apt to go stale and his efficiency becomes greatly impaired.[15]

These activities no doubt took Wingate's mind off a by now growing feud with the Cecils, particularly Lord Edward who was determined not to give way to Wingate without a fight. At the end of August 1917, on his own initiative and with the support of his brother Lord Robert Cecil, then serving as A. J. Balfour's Secretary at the Foreign Office, Cecil submitted a memorandum to the War Cabinet outlining his proposals for the future government of Egypt. Cecil intended to sideline Foreign Office influence in the running of Egypt and when this was made known to Wingate he was enraged. The War Cabinet created a committee to consider Cecil's proposals; not unexpectedly, the membership of this committee included Foreign Secretary Balfour, Lord Curzon (former Viceroy of India and now Lord President of the Privy Council and future Secretary of State for Foreign Affairs) and Lord Milner (a member of the War Cabinet who would become Secretary of State for War in 1918). Ronald Storrs, Wingate's very capable Oriental Secretary in Cairo, was appointed Secretary to this high-powered committee, which heard evidence including that of Sir Milne Cheetham, Wingate's councillor. Lord Edward Cecil made no secret of the fact that he considered the brilliant Storrs 'an ass', a remark which tells us much about Cecil.

The main thrust of Cecil's argument was that the conduct of Egyptian affairs should be removed from the Foreign Office and placed under the control of a separate department; he also proposed that the post of High Commissioner be strictly controlled by the same department. Cecil's proposals came to nothing on this occasion but his memorandum would be dusted off in 1919, when the Middle East Department of the Foreign Office was formed. Ronald Wingate is scrupulously – one is tempted to say naively – fair about these somewhat shady dealings which, had they been implemented in 1917, would have considerably weakened his father's position in Egypt. Perhaps in doing so, Ronald Wingate knew of the long association between his father and Cecil and perhaps did not wish to upset Cecil's living relatives.[16] As it turned out, although Edward Cecil returned to Cairo as Financial Secretary, he fell seriously ill; he was diagnosed as suffering from tuberculosis and was sent to a sanatorium in Leysin, Switzerland, where he died on 15 December 1918.

In 1917 Cairo was a city fraught with intrigue and conspiracy where no one could trust anyone else. Wingate was assiduous in keeping Whitehall informed of the political unrest fomented by the nationalists. He constantly reminded his masters that the Egyptians wished to return to the relative self-governing principles enshrined as far back as 1883. In March 1917 he wrote to Sir Ronald Graham, his rival for the High Commissionership in 1916, seeking clarification of the precise terms of the Protectorate (a euphemism for 'colony' in imperial Britain's parlance) which had been introduced in 1914.[17] On 21 March he received a less than satisfactory reply from Graham:

> The higher authorities here did not take up your suggestion to adopt the opportunity of formulating changes of policy required owing to the establishment of a Protectorate ... Indeed, no one here has any very clear ideas on the subject ...[18]

A reply such as this would not have been out of place in an episode from the popular television series *Yes, Minister*.

Three days later Wingate reported to Lord Hardinge at the Foreign Office, drawing his attention to several points he had discussed in a lengthy interview with the Sultan of Egypt:

> I have no sort of doubt in my own mind that he [Kamil Hussein] and his Ministers hope the Egyptians may be given more freedom in the *Interior* [Wingate's italics] government of their country than exists at present.[19]

These were the words in the writing on the wall and the subsequent – albeit tacit – besmirching of his reputation. As early as 1917 Wingate had politely but firmly warned the British government that the nationalist cause in Egypt was gathering momentum, and that it was imperative to defuse the time-bomb ticking under an increasingly restless Cairo.

In his two years as High Commissioner Wingate established a reasonably friendly working relationship with the Sultan and his ministers. During that time he was obliged to address what he saw as two main problems. The first was to obtain the precise terms of the British Protectorate agreed in 1914 and the consequences arising therefrom. On the surface, the agreement had provided for the defence of Egypt and the protection of her people and interests in the war. The second, and directly related, question was the future nature of the relationship between Egypt and Britain at the end of the war. In Wingate's view, these issues were inseparable, although the first was more important, given Britain's overriding aim of winning the war.

Perhaps a brief summary of Egypt's contribution to that end is appropriate here. The Egyptian Expeditionary Force under the command of General Sir Archibald Murray looked to Egypt as its main provider of supplies and manpower. As the war progressed, the British government considered that Egypt would have to contribute much more in terms of money, supplies and men than she had in the war's early stages. Up to 1916 Egypt had made a substantial contribution to the war effort in the defence of Suez, maintaining a free Sudan, then in supporting the Arab Revolt. In 1917 Murray demanded yet more from Egypt, arguing that the cost of supplying the Egyptian Expeditionary Force (*Egypforce*) with food and animal transport should be borne by Egypt, especially in the years 1917–18, when a German U-boat campaign had intensified, seriously curtailing the flow of supplies. Cotton production was also directly affected by the U-boat campaign, as more land had to be given over to agriculture to feed the populations of Egypt and the Sudan. When the supply of raw cotton from the Middle East shrank, the Lancashire cotton mills also began to lay off workers; the War Office was besieged by appeals from the Lancashire textile mill-owners – many of whom were influential in government circles – concerned by the loss of income.

Wingate was the meat in this sandwich, the buffer between the Army's needs on one hand, and the financial and political stability of Egypt on the other. These demands were difficult to juggle, so he chose to give priority to the Army which, not surprisingly, enhanced Wingate's reputation, first with General Murray, then Murray's successor, General Allenby. Meeting both these demands was a tribute to his skill in the administration of Egypt, and neither of these decisions seriously impaired his relations with the Sultan and his ministers. The year 1917 brought at least one consolation; in June, Wingate was appointed a Colonel Commandant of the Royal Artillery.

Now let us return to the war and its prosecution. In June 1917, following Murray's unsuccessful attempt to capture Gaza and his subsequent dismissal, Allenby took the city from the Turks with comparative ease. In July Lawrence's brilliant capture of Akaba also allowed Allenby to plan an advance on Jerusalem.

It was when Feisal was in Akaba, preparing for the march on Damascus, that he learnt of the Sykes-Picot Agreement of 1916. A copy had fallen into Turkish hands, becoming a weapon to disrupt Arab support for the Allies. Feisal had suspected some kind of agreement had existed, although he had no idea of its precise terms. Sykes-Picot went against the 1915 promises made by Sir Henry McMahon to Feisal's father regarding Arab independence. Feisal knew of the McMahon Letters but his father refused to let him study them. The revelation of Sykes-Picot very nearly ended the Arab Revolt; London was contacted and replied that the Agreement was nothing more than Turkish propaganda but Feisal confronted Lawrence, who had to come clean. He would later write thus:

> So the Arabs, having tested my friendliness and sincerity under fire, asked me, as a free agent, to endorse the promises of the British Government. I had had no previous or inner knowledge of the McMahon pledges and the Sykes-Picot treaty, which were both framed by wartime branches of the Foreign Office. But, not being a perfect fool, I could see that if we won the war the promises to the Arabs were dead paper ... So I assured them that England kept her word in letter and spirit. In this comfort, they performed their fine things: but, of course, instead of being proud of what we did together, I was continually and bitterly ashamed.[20]

Were Lawrence's words entirely honest? Many historians believe that he had known about Sykes-Picot at the outset, a view with which this author agrees. At least the air had now been cleared and Arab support for Allenby was secured despite this development.

As for Wingate in Cairo, his relations with Sultan Hussein Kamil remained cordial. Kamil continued to confide in and trust him implicitly and went as far as to say that, if the Allies won the war, Britain must take the place of Turkey as the military protector of Islam as she was the supreme power in India with its Muslim regions. Kamil even expressed the view that in the post-war world, Egypt would become the centre of Islamic culture and that closer integration with the British Empire would be in Egypt's best interests. This was surprising, hardly the ambition of a committed nationalist – or was Kamil simply playing the British at their own political game? Perhaps he was being diplomatic in order to achieve his real ends – complete independence from Britain. In the event, these were the dreams of a man with only a few months to live. Kamil died on 9 October 1917. Who might succeed him?

By the law of primogeniture, the succession in Egypt would pass to Kamil's son, Prince Kamal-al-Din; next in line was Prince Ahmad Fu'ad, the late Sultan's brother. Kamal-al-Din was a *bon viveur*, sybarite and pro-Turkey and was possessed of an independent mind which unfortunately often strayed into flippancy. Furthermore, he made no secret of his distaste for politics; Kamal was the exact opposite of his uncle Fu'ad who had been educated in Italy, knew little of Egypt and did not even speak Arabic.

Wingate thought that Kamal-al-Din should succeed his father; the ruling class in Egypt, including the Prime Minister, preferred Kamal to the virtual stranger Fu'ad. The Foreign Office disagreed as they believed Kamal to be virulently anti-British. Wingate persisted in lobbying on behalf of Kamal, advising London that the succession should pass to the legitimate heir; however, should Kamal renounce his claim to the throne, he would have to do so formally and publicly. Wingate had made it known on several occasions that, as far as he was concerned, either claimant was acceptable to him although, privately, he probably thought neither was equal to the task of government.

In the event, Kamal bowed out and Fu'ad became Sultan, which suited a Foreign Office which believed him the lesser of two evils; in time, the FO would come to regret Fu'ad's succession. Although his relations with Fu'ad were cordial, Wingate privately thought that an acquiescent ruler with pro-British sentiments would not necessarily be of lasting benefit to the British government. His reasoning was based on long experience of the Muslim mind which brought him to the conclusion that a frank, open and honest Sultan was preferable to a mere puppet ruler. As it turned out, Fu'ad proved the FO wrong and Wingate right. On the surface Fu'ad was outwardly loyal and eager to co-operate with his British masters but his pro-British overtures proved to be front; behind his dilettante, cosmopolitan exterior, Fu'ad harboured a burning ambition to obtain greater sovereignty for his country. Such was the extent of this ambition, he confidently expressed as much to Sir Edwin Montagu, the Secretary of State for India. Montagu of course knew that Egypt already possessed a greater degree of self-autonomy than India and told Fu'ad so. Fu'ad turned to his Prime Minister, Hussayn Rushdi Pasha, and pointedly remarked 'Listen to this Rushdi, Mr Montagu thinks we have autonomy in Egypt'. Then he laughed loudly, not exactly the response of the puppet ruler the FO believed it had backed. From the outset of his appointment as Sultan, Fu'ad began formulating plans to stir up anti-British feelings which would ultimately lead to full-scale public agitation across Egypt.

Wingate was too perspicacious a statesman to be fooled by Fu'ad for long. He lost no time in informing Lord Hardinge at the Foreign Office of the Sultan's intrigue and reported that Fu'ad had sought changes in the composition of the Egyptian cabinet. These changes included Sa'ad Zaghlul, the middle-class son of a farming family and fine orator who would become

Minister for Justice, and Abd al Aziz Fahmy, a leading lawyer and Zaghlul's close friend, also becoming a minister. Fu'ad announced to the British government that these men would replace two pro-British Egyptian ministers. Wingate warned Whitehall that both men were well-known in Egypt as agitators; their appointment would give the Egyptian cabinet 'a somewhat nationalist flavour'. He added, however, that he was not altogether averse to this. A month later, worried by developments in Egypt's political circles, Wingate changed his mind, warning the Foreign Office that the nationalist cause was gathering momentum and, in his view, would increase at the end of the war. Hardinge instructed Wingate to inform Prime Minister Rushdi that the government did not consider the two ministerial candidates wholly satisfactory. Then, in an unexplained *volte face*, the Foreign Office backed down, withdrawing opposition and endorsing these appointments without qualification.

By August 1918 Wingate was again warning Hardinge that, at the close of the war, Sultan Fu'ad would press his claims for home rule for Egypt. For nearly two years, London had turned a deaf ear to Wingate's repeated requests for a definition of the British Protectorate status agreed in 1914. Surprisingly, nobody in Whitehall professed to know the precise nature of protectorate status; this suggests that political chicanery was behind such a lame admission. By November 1918 the stage was set for the beginning of the end of Wingate's career.

However, in November 1917, a month which saw Allenby scoring success after success in Gaza, a small cloud appeared on the horizon. In time it would create a storm which would rumble on to the present day. In that fateful month Foreign Secretary Arthur James Balfour issued his famous Declaration, the wartime pledge of British support for a national home for the Jews in Palestine. (The Balfour Declaration has been described as the *Magna Carta* of Zionism.) Palestine's population was 90 per cent Arab and, with the benefit of hindsight, the Declaration was arguably one of the most disastrous and controversial decisions ever taken in twentieth-century British political history. It is appropriate here to examine the reasoning behind the decision.

Some historians have argued that the main motive for Balfour's action was financial; Britain had received and was continuing to receive substantial amounts of Jewish money and support for the war effort. However, before the war, the leading Zionist, Dr Chaim Weizmann, had made his views known to several influential British Jews – Lord Rothschild and Sir Edwin Montagu among them – in seeking support for a Jewish state. Weizmann, a reader in biochemistry at Manchester University, had invented a process for manufacturing acetone, essential in the production of explosives, of which there was a shortage at the outbreak of the war. Weizmann did not seek financial reward for his invention; he made it clear that all he wanted was British government support for the Zionist cause and his dream of a home in Palestine, formerly biblical Canaan, the last Jewish kingdom. The kingdom had been annexed by the Roman Empire, then claimed by Islam in the seventh century. Thereafter, it became Christian until the twelfth century, when hardships wrought on the Christians gave rise to the ill-fated Crusades. Palestine and Egypt finally fell to the Ottoman Empire in 1517, remaining in Turkish hands for the next four centuries. By the time of the Great War there were already in fact a few thousand non-Zionist Jews settled there, living in peaceful co-existence with their Arab neighbours. All would be changed by Balfour's Declaration ...

Weizmann, a man of infinite charm and persuasion, had set about cultivating the help of Lord Robert Cecil who persuaded Balfour, Winston Churchill, Lloyd George and Sir Mark Sykes, among others, to support his aims. The idea struck a romantic chord in the Foreign Secretary's imagination; Balfour drafted his declaration inspired by history and the Old Testament perspectives, convincing himself that it was a just and righteous cause. More realistically, he was committed to creating a British sphere of influence in the Middle East after the war and Palestine offered an ideal opportunity to this end. He announced that when the Holy Land was freed from Turkish yoke, Britain would create a homeland for 'the wandering Jew'. The Declaration contained a blatant contradiction which is obvious to us today:

> His Majesty's Government view with favour the establishment in Palestine of a national home for the Jewish people, and will use their best endeavours to facilitate the achievement of this object, it being clearly understood that nothing shall be done *which may prejudice the civil and religious rights of existing non-Jewish communities* [i.e. Arab] *in Palestine* [author's italics] ...

How hollow the words sound to modern ears, after nearly a century of conflict in that unfortunate region. Some modern historians maintain that Balfour was interested in the Jews as long as they did not occupy his backyard; others go further, suggesting he was anti-semitic. Whatever the truth, the Balfour Declaration was promulgated; its most vehement critics at the time even included Sir Edwin Montagu, himself a Jew, who stated that Zionism was a 'mischievous political creed, untenable by any patriotic citizen of the United Kingdom'. Other vociferous critics included Reginald Wingate and Gertrude Bell. Wingate, in particular, voiced his opposition to Balfour's proposal. Wingate and Balfour were not only near neighbours in East Lothian but were friends and golfing partners. Wingate stated his concerns to Sir Mark Sykes, warning him that both Christian and Muslim Egypt would view the prospect with alarm. Balfour would not easily forget Wingate's opposition. (As a footnote, when A. J. Balfour died in 1930, the Jewish community is said to have mourned him with honours never before accorded a Gentile.)

Wingate was of course right to voice concerns about Palestine and history has vindicated him. His cousin Orde would echo the same sentiments in the 1930s. The Balfour Declaration would prove an unwholesome cake whose bitter ingredients were smothered in sugar coating. Like the separation of the Lebanon from Syria by the French, it would become another obstacle in the path to achieving an Arab kingdom after the war. The declaration would cause monumental problems for Britain, then later for the Palestinians, problems which today seem no closer to a solution.

Meanwhile, the war in Palestine was progressing successfully. On 11 December 1917 Allenby entered Jerusalem, to much public acclaim in Britain. By then, the Bolshevik October Revolution had taken Imperial Russia out of the war, leaving Britain alone to continue the war against Turkey. It is interesting to note that when Major T. E. Lawrence was in the north, Dr Chaim Weizmann, head of the Jewish Council in the Middle East, visited Feisal's camp to discuss the possibility of Jewish settlement in Palestine on the lines of Balfour's proposals. Feisal was not hostile, although he was probably non-committal at that time.

After the fall of Jerusalem, Cairo became a focal point for distinguished visitors, among them Weizmann and his delegation putting out feelers regarding Palestine. Wingate entertained Weizmann and confessed that he thought him a reasonable man with modest ambitions for his people. However, in a cautionary letter to the Foreign Office, Wingate informed Lord Hardinge that he had urged the Jews to proceed cautiously in their ambitions for Palestine, taking care to demonstrate their sympathy for, and goodwill towards, Palestinian Arabs. He stressed the need for Weizmann to be particularly circumspect in his delegation's discussions about the acquisition and occupation of land in that country.

The British campaign against the Turks gained momentum. With the desert war entering its final, successful stage, Wingate paid a brief visit to Jerusalem to join in the celebrations. It is not certain if he met Lawrence (now holding the substantive rank of colonel) on that occasion but it is a distinct possibility. Allenby went on to win yet more territory as well as personal accolades. Lawrence was never far away from the fighting nor, for that matter, from Wingate's mind. However, the year of 1918 was barely three months old when the Wingates received the tragic news of the death of their son, Malcolm Roy. Major Wingate, DSO, MC, Croix de Guerre had been killed on 29 March 1918 in the final desperate German campaign to win the war before the army of the United States of America could make an impact. The Wingates were devastated, particularly Lady Wingate; she made no secret of the fact that Malcolm had been her favourite. In Wingate's many letters to friends informing them of the loss of their son, that to Wingate's old friend in Dunbar, Major W. W. Carey, was expansive:

He was killed instantaneously by [a] shell splinter ... as he and his Field Company (the 459th Royal Engineers) were moving up from billet to battle position and was buried where he fell ... He could have had no suffering and was saved all the anguish of having to retreat. [Field Marshal Haig had issued an order that no British soldier would retreat in his famous 'backs to the wall' command at the height of Ludendorff's campaign.] We know that in his short and strenuous career, he gallantly did his duty and his leaving his [safe] Staff billet at GHQ was, I know, a matter of conscience – he wrote me very fully about it, but the upshot of it all was he thought a less able-bodied man could do his staff work and that he ought to return to the fighting line. When I knew and understood how much he was worrying, I did my best to help him, though we all realized what it might mean – but neither his mother nor I – nor he – would have wished it otherwise ... he has left behind him a fine example of a good British officer – sans peur et sans reproche [without fear and reproach]. God rest his soul.[21]

A further blow followed. On 9 April 1918 Wingate's cousin, former comrade-in-arms and golf partner, Captain George Miller Wingate (Royal Artillery, retired) died while on a visit to Southsea, Hampshire. As a young lieutenant in the RA, George Wingate had been present on the field of Tel-el-Kebir under Sir Garnet Wolseley against the nationalist army led by the dissident Egyptian Army officer, Arabi Pasha, in 1882. It is possible the Wingate cousins met there when Reginald was posted to Egypt. Captain Wingate's death was reported in the *Haddingtonshire Courier*,[22] a brief obituary describing him as having taken a keen interest in the local golf club and that he had been a vestryman at St Anne's Episcopal Church in Dunbar. Captain Wingate also lost sons-in-law in the Great War. The same issue of the *Courier* recorded a memorial service held on 10 April at St Anne's Episcopal in honour of Malcolm Roy Wingate. The service was attended by officers from the various regiments stationed in the district, Colonel Walter Wingate Gray and NCOs of the Dunbar Volunteer Company and representatives from the Town Council. In the closing moments, the 'Dead March' from 'Saul' was played, then the 'Last Post' was trumpeted by a party of Regular Army buglers.

The same issue of the newspaper also reported that His Excellency [Sir Reginald Wingate] had sent £50 to his friend Major Carey with instructions to distribute the money as follows:

St Anne's	£10
Dunbar Parish Church	7
Local Red Cross	10
Dunbar Prisoner-of-War Fund	10
Dunbar men serving on minesweepers	3
Coal for the Poor	10

It was a typical gesture from a noble, caring man. After the war the Wingates made regular visits to their son's grave in Lagincourt Cemetery. Lady Wingate's ashes were also buried there at her request in 1946.[23]

In the summer of 1918 Wingate received a telegram from Emir Hussein's agent in Cairo angrily demanding to know the precise and present status of the Sykes-Picot Agreement. Not surprisingly, Wingate was concerned that this confusion was endangering future co-operation between the Arabs and the British, so he drafted a reply for Hussein, but also cabled the Foreign Office for guidance asking if he might 'add that we regard the [Sykes-Picot] Agreement as dead for all practical purposes'.[24] On this occasion he got an unequivocal, if untruthful, response. Wingate's reply to Hussein's agent made it clear that the British government had confirmed that Sykes-Picot was dead in the water. The words were conveyed to Hussein and copied to the Syrians via David Hogarth at the Arab Bureau on 25 June. Lawrence was also relieved to learn of the decision; however, Sykes-Picot had in reality only been put on the back burner.

In the autumn of 1918 a memorandum prepared by a few Syrian residents in Cairo claiming to represent the majority view of the Syrian people protested at a proposed division of Arabia into British and French zones. On receiving the memo, Wingate sent a copy to London with his comments, his view being that it would be inadvisable to either reject the document out of hand or to respond negatively. In his opinion, an unsatisfactory response might lead the signatories

to modify their pro-Allied inclination and ultimately ... to enter into communications with the enemy [the Turks] ... I feel strongly that we should be ill-advised to ignore the aspirations towards independence and eventual political union ... which are held, I believe, by the majority of the Moslem and a large proportion of the Christian Syrians: and I think it would be very advantageous to supplement, if possible, the very general – and in native eyes, vague and consequently unsatisfactory – lines of our declared policy in regard to the future of the Arab people.[25]

In London, Sir Mark Sykes drew up a four-point plan for the future of what would become Saudi Arabia; the areas of Syria, Lebanon and Mesopotamia which had been free and independent before the war and those areas liberated from the Turks by the Arabs themselves would be given complete sovereignty; the other two categories, i.e. those areas occupied by the Allies and those still under Turkish control, would be governed on the principle of the consent of their governors. This mish-mash of proposals, suitably and deliberately vague, would have confused the Arabs had they known of them. Did Sykes mean that any *further* areas of Syria and the Lebanon liberated from Turkish rule by the Arabs would fall into the first two categories above? No wonder Lawrence was disillusioned by the political wheeling and dealing that would emerge during the peace negotiations in Paris in 1919.

In the Middle East, there was now increasing dissent among the Arab leadership, Feisal quarrelling with his father about the future. The closing stages of the Revolt, with its victories in battle and defeats in politics, are history. In the end Palestine and Syria were conquered by the professional soldier, although Feisal's forces protected Allenby's right flank all the way to Damascus, thus ensuring his success. In point of fact, Feisal's Arabs were the first to enter Damascus on 1 October 1918, something which Lawrence gleefully reported to the British High Command. All that remained was the apportioning of the spoils of war. Who would benefit from the conquest of this last vestige of Turkish territory? The answer would be determined at the Peace Conference in Versailles in 1919 and the process was completed with the Treaty of Sèvres the following year.

As for Lawrence, he remained loyal to Sir Henry McMahon, to whom he gave credit, rather than Wingate, for bringing the Arabs into the war. He wrote of McMahon in the following terms:

> [McMahon] was sacked (largely for it) when things got bad in the early days of the rising. Now Wingate says he did it [the Revolt]. It was really McMahon, advised by [Sir Ronald] Storrs, Clayton and perhaps myself.[26]

It is incredible that Lawrence, an intelligent and sensitive individual could dismiss Wingate's role as he had always supported the Revolt and given Lawrence himself a chance to prove his worth as a guerrilla leader. Wingate had organized the Arab Revolt but never broadcast the fact. Those who talked and wrote about it – Lawrence, Allenby and Lowell Thomas, the journalist at *The Strand* magazine, who later wrote Lawrence's biography, claimed all the credit and glory. Wingate was virtually ignored, even forgotten.

Lawrence did later pay grudging tribute to Wingate's role in the Revolt but friendly relations between the two men did not survive beyond the end of the war. Like many men of his temperament, Lawrence could be peevish and even vindictive. He accused Wingate of having taken the glory for the Revolt, which Wingate merited while never disclosing in print his role, nor seeking any personal accolade for it. It is to Wingate's credit that he bore no grudge towards Lawrence. When Damascus fell to Allenby in December 1918, Wingate recommended Lawrence for the Victoria Cross in recognition of what he termed a magnificent achievement, one of the finest of the war. His recommendation was refused as Lawrence had not fulfilled the conditions for such an award, which are that operational activities must be witnessed by other serving British Army officers, which of course was nigh impossible, given Lawrence's undercover guerrilla activities. Lawrence did however receive a medal for his exploits – the Military Companion of the Bath.

Lawrence expressed the view that

> The dismissal of Sir Henry McMahon confirmed my belief in our essential insincerity [towards the Arabs]; but I could not so explain myself to General Wingate while the war lasted, since I was nominally under his orders, and he did not seem sensible of how false his own standing was. The only thing remaining [to me] was to refuse rewards for being a successful trickster.[27]

It is interesting to note that when Lawrence was writing *Seven Pillars* in 1922, he commissioned portraits for the book. He paid a popular artist, William Roberts, to paint McMahon, whom he still believed – with some justification – had been badly treated by the British government. He also asked Roberts to execute a portrait of

old General Wingate – Sir Francis Wingate, ex-Governor of Sudan, High Commissioner of Egypt etc. Do you think you could draw a courtly old man, broken and disappointed because his career ended badly? A man who was no more than a butter-merchant and great-man's friend, even in his best days, but whose administration was so successful that it gave him confidence, and for a while he believed himself great ... please be very gentle with him, if you do him. He's not so much a butterfly as a ghost of one, a thing by no means to be broken on a wheel.[28]

Lawrence here is at his most ungracious and the above letter is unworthy of him. His comparison of Wingate with a butterfly is odd and undeserved, as it suggests one who is ephemeral. In February 1923 Lawrence told Roberts that Wingate who had 'proved very elusive until now ... will write to you shortly and suggest a time [for his portrait'.[29] Perhaps Wingate was being deliberately evasive and un-cooperative, aware of Lawrence's opinion of him. Tellingly, the final version of *Seven Pillars of Wisdom* contained not a single portrait or photograph of Wingate.

Wingate acknowledged Allenby's prosecution of the war in Arabia with unstinting praise; he was also generous in his recognition of Lawrence's contribution. But the fact remains – and it needs to be stated now over fifty years after Wingate's death – that his role in the Arab Revolt is to this day unrecognized. He was upstaged by more colourful figures and official recognition of his achievements was suppressed by a small-minded, mean-spirited government in the wake of subsequent events in Egypt.

The military outcome had at last been resolved in the Middle East; well, that is to say, the Turks had at least been ejected from the last vestiges of their Ottoman Empire. Now the politicians took over; one is tempted to compare them with chefs carving up a turkey or a baron of beef. However, on his appointment as High Commissioner of Egypt, Wingate encountered problems of a different kind. He was still General Officer Commanding the Hejaz and responsible for the Arab Bureau, the Egyptian frontier district, the political purview of Aden and the tribes in the Yemen, as well as general supervision of the Sudan and all matters relating to Abyssinia and Somaliland. It was a mammoth task and it was his unenviable lot to keep in touch with every shifting aspect of Egypt's situation. Aware that there was a strong current of disaffection with the status and intent of the 1914 British Protectorate – to many Egyptians, this appeared to be the end of Egyptian autonomy – Wingate was strenuous in his attempts to insist otherwise while repeatedly seeking a precise definition of the document's status from London.

After Lawrence's fatal motorcycle accident in 1935, Wingate privately wrote that he was in no doubt of the man's personal attributes and resourcefulness, his brilliance as an irregular soldier. However, he tempered this view by reminding historians that the gold sovereigns with which he had provided Lawrence had as much to do with the success of the Arab Revolt. The war in the Middle East was won by Allenby and his professional soldiers, not Arab irregulars.

Perhaps Lawrence's sad words about his disillusion with Britain and her government apply in some respects to Wingate who, in 1919, was effectively (but never formally) sacked from his appointment as High Commissioner of Egypt:

> The Cabinet raised the Arabs to fight for us by definite promises of self-government afterwards. Arabs believe in persons, not in institutions. They saw in me a free agent of the British Government, and demanded from me an endorsement of its written promises. So I had to join the conspiracy, and, for what my word was worth, assured the men of their reward. In our two years' partnership under fire they grew accustomed to believing me and to think my Government, like myself, sincere. In this hope they performed some fine things, but, of course, instead of being proud of what we did together, I was continually and bitterly ashamed ... I began in my reports to conceal the true stories of things, and so to persuade the few Arabs who knew to an equal reticence.[30]

Lawrence is being frank and honest here. Despite his respect for, and grudging acknowledgement of, Wingate's commitment to the Arab Revolt, he felt that he and others like him had let the Arabs down. As for Lawrence's personal contribution to the Revolt, he suffered the privations of the desert, enduring waterless days and freezing nights, disease, wounds and stresses that taxed his slight physical frame; the final blow came with the shoddy treatment his beloved Arabs received at the Peace Conference of 1919. As for Wingate, he was still keen to develop Egypt, making it a country fit for its inhabitants. When sacked in 1919 Wingate was in the process of planning yet another vital rail link through the desert, thus demonstrating his enduring commitment to the welfare of the Sudan and Egypt. It is hard to think of any other man who did as much to bring civilization to the inhospitable terrain of the Sudan, a country he clearly loved. Today, if Wingate is remembered at all by modern historians, it is as an arch-imperialist, a mere footnote in the history of the British Empire. Of course he believed in the civilizing aspects of British rule as a means of bringing prosperity to both the Sudan and Egypt, thereby improving the lot of their indigenous populations. This proved correct in the case of the Sudan, which today has disintegrated into a worse state than ever, in some respects comparable to the years of the Mahdist regime's tyranny.

Notes

1. Grey to Wingate, paraphrase of telegram dated 11 October, 1916, WP 177/2, SAD, DU.
2. See Chapter 4, note 61.
3. *The Lion and the Sphinx; the rise and fall of the British in Egypt 1882–1956*, Keown-Boyd.

4. Edward Cecil to Robert Cecil, 5 November, 1917, *The Sirdar*, Daly.
5. Stack to Clayton, 5 November 1917, SAD 470/7 DU.
6. *Seven Pillars of Wisdom*, p. 332, Lawrence.
7. *Wingate of the Sudan*, RELW.
8. *Not in the Limelight*, RELW.
9. WP 237/1, SAD, DU.
10. *Wingate to Hardinge*, 31 January 1917, WP 164/3, SAD, DU.
11. *Imperial Marriage; An Edwardian War and Peace*, Cecil, Hugh and Mirabel.
12. *The War Work of the YMCA in Egypt*, Barrett.
13. *The Sirdar.*
14. *The War Work of the YMCA.*
15. *Ibid.*
16. *Wingate of the Sudan.*
17. Wingate to Graham, 20 March 1917, WP 164/3, SAD, DU.
18. Graham to Wingate, 21 March 1917, WP 164/3, SAD, DU.
19. Wingate to Hardinge, 24 March 1917, WP 164/3, SAD, DU.
20. *Seven Pillars of Wisdom*, pp. 282–3.
21. Wingate to Carey, 6 April 1918, WP 168/2, SAD, DU.
22. HC, 12 April 1918.
23. *The Sirdar.*
24. Wingate to FO, FO 371/381 folio 7–8.
25. Wingate to Balfour, FO 3780 folio 558–559.
26. Lawrence to G Dawson, editor of *The Times.*
27. *Seven Pillars of Wisdom*, p. 24.
28. Lawrence to Roberts, 21 October 1922, Bodleian Library.
29. Lawrence to Roberts, 7 February 1923, Bodleian Library.
30. *Seven Pillars of Wisdom*, p. 24.

Chapter 8

Peace at a Price
(1919–1921)

The concluding two months of 1918, following the armistice, brought relief to millions of people, civilians and soldiers alike who survived that most terrible war. It was a euphoric time for the survivors when hostilities ceased at the eleventh hour of the eleventh day of the eleventh month of that year. Millions were dead; yet more millions would succumb to the Spanish influenza epidemic which swept across Europe like a medieval plague between 1918 and 1920. It was as if the gods were punishing civilization for its appalling behaviour.

The conflict in the Middle East was regarded then, and to a certain extent still is today, as a sideshow. However, it saw the utter rout of the Turks and the passing of a corrupt Ottoman Empire. With practically no remaining effective army in the field, Turkey signed an armistice with the Allies on 20 October, three weeks before the cessation of world hostilities, although Germany still possessed a formidable army, capable of inflicting casualties on the Allied nations.

When the Armistice was declared, in Egypt, as elsewhere, the mood was one of exhilaration; the nationalists of Egypt saw the war's end as a means to obtain full independence which Britain had vaguely promised at the outbreak of hostilities in 1914. The Egyptian National Party believed the political propaganda of 1914 would gather momentum and bring about independence. The war had imposed unacceptably severe casualties upon the populations of Europe; some asked themselves if the price paid in human blood had been too high, given that the war was prosecuted largely to preserve the European dynasties and monarchies. There were other, abstract casualties – truth, honour and humanitarian concepts had been debased – a fact evident to British artists like Siegfreid Sassoon, Robert Graves and Wilfred Owen, serving soldiers and three of the finest British war poets. Perhaps the waste of human life was quicker to reach the common people who made the ultimate sacrifice in giving fathers, sons, brothers and uncles to the bitter, bloody killing fields on the Gallipoli beaches and the Somme, then in the mud of the trenches at Third Ypres, also known as Passchendaele. Despite the terrible loss of life, in Britain, Lord Kitchener, dead for over two years, was still revered, despite never having lived up to the expectations of those who had placed their faith in his military capabilities. The people of Britain looked up to men like him and later, Haig; the incompetent amateur was succeeded by the dedicated professional. In fairness to Haig, his tactics in the closing years of the war retrieved his reputation for being unjustly described as a callous butcher to a considerable degree, although he is still reviled by many in his native country, Scotland, for his callous squandering of many fine Scottish regiments. Haig has been compared with Ulysses Grant of American Civil War fame who ground down Lee's Confederate armies by waging a war of attrition. Grant is also still considered a butcher in the States by historians in the Southern States of the USA yet Haig has been reinstated by modern historians who admit that he was justified in strategies the effectiveness of which critics still debate.

In the Egypt of 1918 the attitude to Britain was changing rapidly. The country had not provided troops in any significant quantities for the military campaigns but its people had been subjected to strict martial law and its legislative assembly was suspended, thus curbing the activities of the middle-class politicians and those who championed the cause of nationalism. Added to these restrictions was the imposition of forced labour regulations on the peasantry, put to work on defence projects.

How did Wingate view events in Cairo in 1917, almost two years before the end of the war? From the outset of his appointment as High Commissioner, Wingate had repeatedly sought a precise definition of the status of Egypt as a British Protectorate but his requests had fallen on deaf ears. His aim was simple enough; he was anxious to allay the fears of the Sultan Ahmad Fu'ad, his Council of Ministers and the growing body of aggressive nationalists who were haranguing their more moderate colleagues as well as inciting the general public to give voice to their opposition to British rule. The year of 1917 passed with Wingate attending to his sometimes mundane duties. At the end of 1918 he counted the cost of the war on his own family. The Wingate family suffered their fair share of war casualties. Among the war dead listed by the Commonwealth War Graves Commission are thirty-two Wingates; some were close relatives such as his son, Malcolm. Wingate also lost relatives – Alfred Douglas Wingate (Second Lieutenant, Black Watch, 1915), Alexander (Sandy) Wingate, (Second Lieutenant, Glasgow Highlanders, 1915), Reginald (Rex) C. Wingate (godson of Wingate, son of his cousin George Miller Wingate, 1915) and other relatives through marriage such as John Congreve Murray (Lieutenant, Royal Scots, 1917), husband of George Miller Wingate's daughter Muriel.

Along with countless other families, Wingate and his wife coped with their grief as best they could. In the last year of the war Britain desperately desired peace but it took most of 1918 to achieve it. By the autumn everyone anticipated a cessation of hostilities but, on 1 November 1918, a political bombshell burst; the Anglo-French Allies declared that the Arabs and those countries freed from Turkish rule would be granted self-determination. Well, most would be. Wingate received no prior warning of this shift in policy and so the man who arguably understood Egypt, the Sudan and possibly the Arab world in general better than many, and was most directly involved in the politics of the region, was kept in the dark. This cannot have been an over-sight on the part of the Foreign Office; more likely, it was part of a calculated policy, the man behind it being the Foreign Secretary, Arthur J. Balfour, and his relatives the Cecils and others of the inner circle hostile to Wingate.

Wingate struggled to make sense of it all. On learning of the government's proposals for the Middle East, he followed the only course open to him; he cabled the Foreign Office to seek clarification of British policy regarding Egypt. He was acutely aware of the immediate effects of the news and its repercussions in Egypt, not only among the growing nationalist faction but also among all classes of Egyptians who regarded themselves as equally deserving inclusion among those countries considered capable of self-government. Wingate received no reply to his cable.

This treatment of Wingate seems a deliberate act on the part of the Foreign Office, not so much a sin of omission as one of commission. The Foreign Office's silence surely must have raised in Wingate's mind the question of his future as High Commissioner of Egypt. The war had been won and men like Wingate and Lawrence now seemed expendable. The former was becoming a thorn in the side of the Foreign Office on account of his radical views on the future government of Egypt. The latter was a nuisance, his romantic vision of an independent Arab kingdom being seen as disruptive and an embarrassment.

Who were Wingate's detractors? First, he had antagonized Balfour in his opposition to the Balfour Declaration; second, there was no love lost between Wingate and Edward and Robert Cecil, Balfour's cousins. Let us briefly re-visit the political landscape of 1916, when the Conservative government was replaced by a coalition led by Lloyd George. The powerful position of Foreign Secretary went to Balfour, a champion of Lord Edward Cecil, who was Financial Adviser in Egypt. Edward's brother Lord Robert was Permanent Under-Secretary of State at the Foreign Office. Despite having been comrades-in-arms in the Nile Campaign of 1886–98, Lord Edward and Wingate had disagreed about the way to rule Egypt over the succeeding years. Cecil had been Wingate's assistant during his time as Governor General of the Sudan, entertaining hopes of succeeding Sir Henry McMahon as High Commissioner of Egypt in 1916. By then, Cecil made no secret of the fact that he despised Wingate. When Wingate was appointed High Com-missioner, Cecil took every opportunity to criticize Wingate's handling of Egypt's financial matters. For his part Wingate committed a grave error in recommending Cecil's return to London, as he could have kept a closer eye on his opponent in Cairo. Sir Ronald Graham, who had also served with Wingate in the Sudan, returned to the Foreign Office in 1917, where he appears to have been both counsellor to Wingate and the Cecils, playing a double game to further his own ambitions. Perhaps this interpretation is unfair to Graham but it must be said that he did not emerge from Wingate's subsequent sacking with entirely clean hands.

It is clear that, by 1918, a *cabal* determined to discredit Wingate had formed in the Foreign Office. The principal members were Balfour, the two Cecils and Lord Hardinge, aided and abetted by Sir Ronald Graham. To Graham's credit, it must be said that, as early as 1917, he had tipped off Wingate that Robert Cecil had suggested to the Cabinet that responsibility for Egypt be transferred from the Foreign Office to the Colonial Office, a move which Wingate would have welcomed. On the surface, the proposal might have been construed as Cecil's support for Wingate, who detested the FO. Robert Cecil was not, however, motivated by such sentiment; he simply wanted to get rid of Wingate, preparing the way for brother Edward's appointment as High Commissioner. In 1917 Balfour sent a communiqué to Wingate advocating the return of Lord Edward Cecil to Egypt. In his telegram Balfour candidly referred to the strained relationship between Wingate and Cecil but expressed the hope that

> personal difficulties would not stand in the way of [their] working together and that any intractable divergence of opinions on Egyptian affairs would be referred to [and resolved by] the Foreign Office.

One has to assume that Balfour intended to use Cecil as a 'plant' who would eagerly grasp any opportunity to inform on Wingate's supposed shortcomings.

Wingate must have viewed the prospect with concern; it was certainly an ominous development. It was also no secret that there was a considerable degree of muted hostility between Wingate and the pro-Foreign Office bureaucratic regime in Cairo. For Cecil's part, there was more than a whiff of intrigue directed at Wingate for his criticism of the Finance Ministry (and by extension, of Edward Cecil) in Cairo at the time. It is almost certain that Wingate endured complaints from Egyptian ministers, keen to support Wingate's rivals in the spirit of 'my enemy's enemy is my friend'.

Wingate's track record was not entirely squeaky-clean; he was forced into decisions to cover his back, as well as a doubt in his own ability to handle the delicate political situation in Cairo. In the Sudan he had ruled supreme, using his position to increase his standing in London, if not necessarily advancing his career. He had been content with his life in the Sudan where he enjoyed a fairly free hand. (It should also be remembered that he had never sought the position of High Commissioner of Egypt; it had been unexpectedly thrust on him by Sir Edward Grey when Sir Henry McMahon was recalled to London.) In Cairo, many of Wingate's policies were consistent and well thought out, even if some were necessarily motivated by self-preservation.

Who could blame Wingate for being confused when the wolves were beginning to bay at his heels? At least he could offer plausible explanations for his opinions and motives; these were based on his knowledge and experience, justified by his assuring Whitehall that his primary aims were to advance Egypt's development and maintain cordial relations with the Sultan and his ministers.

Wingate had his eye fixed on the future during his brief time as High Commissioner. He predicted accurately that when the Great War ended the position of Egypt would have to be re-assessed, probably by a British Royal Commission. Royal Commissions are appointed by governments of whatever political persuasion to defer taking decisions on difficult matters. Wingate was proved right, as a Royal Commission was later appointed under the chairmanship of Sir Alfred Milner. The feuding between Wingate and the Cecils continued; they sniped at, rather than directly confronted, each other. Lord Edward Cecil's stay in Cairo in 1917 was brief; diagnosed with tuberculosis in that year, he was forced to resign his post in Egypt and died shortly afterwards. The *cabal* against Wingate had lost a valuable member but the vacancy would soon be filled by a more powerful man and a greater threat to Wingate – Lord George Curzon, former Viceroy of India, the jewel in the crown of the British Empire.

Wingate was too intelligent, too perspicacious not to read anything other than a likely recall to Britain into the Foreign Office's continued silence. On 8 November 1918 he received a visitor at his Cairo residency. The Nationalist Sa'ad Zaghlul Pasha, the Vice President of the Egyptian Legislative Assembly, whom in 1917 Wingate had recommended to the Foreign Office as a minister in the Egyptian Cabinet (better in than out, as the saying goes) but whom the Foreign Office had rejected. The Legislative Assembly had been suspended since 1914 and Zaghlul urged Wingate to lift the suspension, arguing that it was no longer appropriate now that the war was over. On 13 November 1918 Wingate received three Egyptian politicians, headed by Zaghlul Pasha who demanded nothing less than autonomy for Egypt, informing Wingate of his intention to lead a *Wafd* [Arabic for delegation] to London where he would argue for independence.

Wingate listened carefully to Zaghlul's arguments but, without Foreign Office authority, he could only advise patience, quoting from the Koran 'Allah ma es Sabairin, izza Sabiru' (God is with the patient, if they are patient).[1] Wingate, rarely a cynical man, had no response to Zaghlul's demands. How could he react to the Egyptian? He had been ostracized by Foreign Office officials and abandoned by his masters in Whitehall. A few days later, he and his ADC, Captain Ulick Alexander, were accosted in the Mohamed Ali Club by Zaghlul, who asked for a further interview but would not be drawn on the specific matters he wished to discuss. In his subsequent conversation with Wingate that night, Captain Alexander was not far short of the truth; he speculated that Zaghlul's request for an interview would simply be a re-iteration of Nationalist demands about the future government of Egypt.

Wingate had always felt more comfortable in the role of mediator than of ruler; he was keen to accelerate the metamorphosis of Egypt from British

Protectorate (Colonial) status into a free-standing, self-governing, independent country. So with his hands tied by the Foreign Office, all he could offer the Nationalists was to suggest a visit to London to state their case. Zaghlul was demanding nothing less than complete autonomy, arguing forcibly that Egypt was more capable of governing herself than the Arabs, Syrians and Mesopotamians who had already been promised a measure of self-government less than two weeks previously in Paris.

Privately, Wingate must have wished that his masters in the Foreign Office could have been present to witness at first hand the fall-out from their ill-judged declaration regarding the future of Egypt. But they were far away, faceless, unapproachable and seemingly lacking in anything close to common sense, let alone constructive imagination. It is perhaps true that most politicians fall into one of two categories – the reckless gamblers and the subtle chess-players. Wingate belonged to the latter; as an administrator, he knew his duty was to anticipate, to be one step ahead, as a good chess-player must be. He was also astute enough to know that the politicians and civil service mandarins in England were sheltering safely in the wings, scrutinizing his every move and speculating about the way he might jump.

Wingate listened patiently to Zaghlul's arguments and demands; how Egypt had remained loyal to Britain during the war, had provided valuable resources for its prosecution and successful outcome. His impassioned pleas were not lost on an empathetic Wingate; now that Turkish rule was over, why should Egypt not receive its reward? Zaghlul promised that Egypt would remain loyal to Britain and assured Wingate that he considered the British to be his closest friends. Zaghlul larded his argument further with promises of a peaceful alliance, adding that Egypt would continue to accept a degree of British financial control. He ended his supplication with a request for permission to travel to London to put the Egyptian case. Wingate, ever the patient listener, was convinced that Zaghlul was sincere in his expressions of goodwill but was powerless to accede to Zaghlul's demands, unable even to arrange a meeting in London. He could only stall for time, advising Zaghlul and his delegation not to advance their case too vigorously.

Major criticism of Wingate's handling of the Egyptian question appears in Lord Lloyd's book *Egypt Since Cromer* but it is weak criticism at that. Lloyd argues that, in agreeing to meet Zaghlul Pasha and his deputation, Wingate had compromised the constitutional position of Sultan Fu'ad's Council of Ministers; in his view, Wingate should have referred Zaghlul to the Council rather than entertained him at his official residence. Let us examine the character of Sa'ad Zaghlul Pasha, who today is revered as the father of Egypt's independence. Reviled by his British contemporaries as a political agitator, he appears to have been a popular leader who appealed to the cupidity of the masses. Trained as a lawyer, he became a civil judge who was respected for his honesty and moderation. In 1913 he was elected to the Egyptian Legislative Assembly. In 1917 the Sultan chose not to include him in his Cabinet, perhaps as a political gesture which he thought would be well received by the British government. Wingate had advised the Cabinet in London that, while Zaghlul's appointment would have given the Egyptian Cabinet a somewhat stronger Nationalistic tendency, he was not averse to this, a view which perhaps sealed Wingate's fate.

Who can say with impunity that Zaghlul was acting independently of Sultan Fu'ad? Modern historians might question such a notion. Wingate harboured the impression that the delegation headed by Zaghlul was known to the Sultan although he was unsure if he had approved it. Lloyd's account and criticism of Wingate in his handling of Zaghlul seems no more than a slap on the wrist for a departure from the protocol of the day. Protocol is all very well but when you are menaced with the sharp end of circumstances by superiors several thousand miles away and who cannot – or deliberately refuse to – appreciate the conditions on the spot, how do you respond? Wingate was repeatedly left in the dark by Whitehall – or, perhaps more accurately, denied clear advice on how to proceed. What is more, Lloyd signally fails to mention that the Sultan Fu'ad and his Prime Minister Rushdi Pasha *were* in fact privy to Zaghlul Pasha's interview with Wingate and had given their approval for that meeting. Others who could have saved Wingate remained conspicuously silent. Some historians have argued that Wingate was not up to the job of High Commissioner; among his contemporary critics was Lord Edward Cecil, who remarked that Prime Minister Rushdi was 'running circles round poor little W[ingate] the whole time and we shall come off very second best'. Cecil's contempt grew; in a letter to his wife Violet he asked, 'what can you do with a weak frightened man of inferior intellect?' – hardly a fair assessment of Wingate.

Prime Minister Rushdi met Wingate shortly after his interview with Zaghlul Pasha. Rushdi stated bluntly his intention to go to London and discuss the matter of Egyptian independence with the Foreign Office and that he would be accompanied by prominent representatives of the Egyptian Nationalist Party, which would obviously include Zaghlul. Wingate dutifully wrote to Lord Hardinge, Permanent Under-Secretary at the Foreign Office, giving him a full and frank account of his meetings with Zaghlul and Rushdi. His cable of 13 November pulled no punches:

> If those burning questions are not settled now, we are likely to have con-siderable difficulty in the future. The general spirit of self-determination to which the war has given birth has taken a firm hold on Egypt, and I think it is only just that the Sultan, his Ministers and the Egyptians should know how they stand.[2]

At least one modern historian accuses Wingate of having been 'surprised' by the rise of Nationalism in Egypt but this is difficult to accept, given Wingate's track record in the Sudan and his natural genius for intelligence-gathering. How in all conscience could he have been surprised? He was well aware of the political situation in Cairo and elsewhere; Nationalist activities were hardly secretive; these were regularly reported in the Egyptian press. Besides, it was Wingate's duty to know what was going on in the political hotbed that was Cairo, in its European clubs, bazaars and *souks*.

Wingate cannot be faulted for his accurate assessment of the situation, bluntly expressed as it was. He gave London prompt and ample warning of the political climate prevailing in Cairo. It is a historical axiom that nationalism is the most immediate response to an overweening regime imposed from without. As with other countries like India, Egyptian Nationalism began in the form of a cultural and linguistic revival, galvanized into a political and social movement. The term nationalism is used by ultra-patriotic parties and groups which claim to represent a national resurgence or awakening, something of which Wingate had long been aware, even if his masters in London dismissed it as political mischief-making. Egyptian reaction to the imposition of Britain's imperial might is patently apparent to any student of political history. For her part, Britain considered nationalists an affront to sound government and those who supported them as little more than agitators.

It has also to be remembered that no constitutional parliament existed in Cairo at that time. The Sultan appointed his ministers, although Britain reserved the right to veto any individual appointment; Wingate was at pains to remind the Sultan of that right. Despite this, a significant body of intellectuals and businessmen in Cairo were supported and encouraged by a powerful – and increasingly pejorative – press. Added to this broth was a strong religious movement hostile to Western (Christian) morality and ethics. In Egypt, since 1883, there had existed the distinct possibility that demonstrations against a minority ruling power would fire the imagination of the masses. Lords Cromer and Kitchener had fully appreciated the sensitivity of the situation and appreciated the need to keep the British government informed about Egyptian public opinion, certainly during the long campaign to reclaim the Sudan. Wingate was simply following their example, although the political goal posts had shifted considerably since Omdurman.

Wingate must have been deeply dismayed by the Foreign Office's response to his cable of 13 November the following day. Its response was typical of the stalling tactics familiar to those who study or work in government. It was an ostrich-like head-in-the-sand reply:

> We have had up to now no indication of such Native aspirations nor of the form they are likely to take. You should keep me fully informed of any developments on lines you mention.[3]

Had not Wingate repeatedly done precisely that very thing? Or had he been less direct, less forceful than the situation demanded? It is clear from surviving correspondence that Wingate had been warning the Foreign Office since 1917 of Nationalist pressure in Egypt and that it would reach a crucial point after the successful termination of the Great War. It would appear that some civil service mandarin in the Foreign Office thought Wingate a scaremonger at best, at worst an administrator who was 'windy' and had lost his political nerve. That same mandarin perhaps delegated the task of drafting a reply to Wingate's cable to a junior so as to enjoy an undisturbed lunch at one of the fashionable clubs near Whitehall. A less compliant, less tolerant man than Wingate would have responded quickly by reminding the Foreign Office that he had in fact kept it informed of 'native aspirations' for the past two years! Furthermore, these aspirations had been brought to Whitehall's attention by Sultan Kemal, and his successor, Sultan Fu'ad.

What was going on at the Foreign Office? The answer must surely lie with Balfour, Wingate's supposed friend of many years. Surely Balfour understood the gravity of the situation, or had the lunatics taken over the asylum? The drafter of the astonishingly naïve telegram had perhaps enjoyed a more than usually convivial liquid lunch. Such things are regular occurrences in bureaucratic circles, the British Civil Service being no exception. It is an old trick for senior staff to absent themselves from their desks at moments of crisis so that they are 'unavailable' for comment or a decision. It smacks of the classic syndrome, 'Bloggs can deal with this, it is a matter of little importance,' Bloggs being a minor official; Wingate must have felt a chill wind was now blowing his way. He wanted to know – and asked his Whitehall masters to advise yet again – on 'the line to take' when the Nationalists demanded an audience 'as they undoubtedly will'.[4]

On 20 November Wingate patiently and scrupulously telegraphed Balfour, informing him yet again of the political situation in Egypt. He pointed out that there were no outward signs of an armed uprising, nor were there any obvious signs of hostile activity on the part of religious fanatics or anti-British demonstrations in the streets, but he knew perfectly well from the undercurrents that a storm was brewing. Four days later he followed the cable to Balfour with another to Lord Hardinge, recommending that the Egyptian Ministers and Nationalist leaders be allowed to visit London to plead their case, adding,

> If possible, let it [the Egyptian question] be settled once and for all. And I repeat my own convictions that the present appears to me a favourable time to grasp the nettle'[5]

Permission would be granted for the visit but not in the foreseeable future; the nettle would not be grasped for several months. On 3 December Wingate received a Foreign Office telegram to the effect that his decision to entertain the Nationalists in November had been 'unfortunate'. This was blatant criticism; he was being accused – albeit blandly – of gross incompetence. At about the same time, Robert Cecil informed Balfour that, if Wingate were to be recalled, Allenby would be a suitable successor as 'everyone to whom I have spoken about W. is confident he is not up to the job'.[6] So Wingate – ever the man of principle – offered his resignation. The reply from Whitehall assured him that was unnecessary: HM Government had unqualified confidence in his administration and that the word 'unfortunate' had been imposed or inserted by 'a [unidentified] higher authority'. Was Balfour that authority? Wingate's subsequent advice to the Foreign Office was to take a constructive line with the Nationalists led by Sa'ad Zaghlul, a suggestion rejected out of hand. He had struck a sensitive nerve with a proposal which had little or no currency in Whitehall.

It was a time of intense activity in Whitehall; preparations were well advanced for the proposed Peace Conference in Paris. The British delegation included Balfour, Lord Milner and Lord Hardinge, who arrived in Paris in December. The Conference did not begin its deliberations until 18 January 1919 however, the delay being caused by the Liberal Prime Minister Lloyd George who deemed it politically expedient that his mandate be under-written by the British public; the General Election of 14 December 1918 duly provided this, returning him to power in a coalition with the Conservatives.

Lloyd George's arrival in Paris was followed by a preliminary meeting of the British, French, Italian and US political leaders, respectively Lloyd George and Balfour, Georges Clemenceau and Stephen Pichon, Vittorio Orlando and Sydney Sonnio, Woodrow Wilson and Robert Lansing. These formed them-selves into a Supreme Council, or Council of Ten, subsequently reduced to a Council of Four. Egypt was not included among the thirty-seven nations which had declared war on Germany, nor was it represented by any Egyptian official at the Conference. As for the Arabs, only Prince Feisal, accompanied by T. E. Lawrence, was there to support the Arab cause; Lawrence arrived on 9 January and remained in Paris until May.

In January 1919 Paris hummed like a beehive. Delegates from several countries attended, both victors and the vanquished. Representatives waved petitions and submitted applications seeking independence, while others sought clarification of national boundaries re-drawn as a result of the Great War. Accompanying the *Prominente* nations of Britain, France, Italy and the USA was a vast army of political advisers, clerks, typists and archivists; among the latter was Victoria, Wingate's daughter. The delegations of prime ministers, foreign secretaries, diplomats, kings and princes were plagued by the world press, minor lobbyists and hangers-on. As the editor of *The Times*, Wickham Steed, wrote, 'all the world is here.' This hectic activity elicited statements of opprobrium from Lord Milner and Lawrence who both thought the conference was no better than a circus. They were right: for all the comings and goings between the Paris hotels and the conference hall, few there accomplished anything of use.

The quartet of most important delegates were those who represented all the Allies; the American President Wilson, Britain's Prime Minister Lloyd George, France's Clemenceau and Italy's Orlando. The statesmen met twice a day, usually in Wilson's study, men from very different backgrounds and with strikingly different temperaments. Wilson was stiff, formal, resembling a college professor criticising a student's thesis; Clemenceau 'Le Tigre' was passionate, bellicose and did not suffer fools gladly; Lloyd George was his charming self, dazzling colleagues with his eloquence and ready wit; Orlando, the fourth member of the Council of Four, was highly strung, with an embarrassing tendency to shed tears when decisions went against him.

The British delegation had taken up residence in several nearby hotels, the main being the Hotel Majestic – where else for an Imperial power? – in Avenue Kleber, near l'Arc de Triomphe. The resident French hotel staff were dismissed, replaced by a team of British caterers recruited from British railway companies – the mind boggles at the likely catering standards in the heart of a city renowned for its cuisine. The British government had insisted that the food must be prepared by British caterers to prevent the restaurant being taken over by spies and other hostile 'foreigners'.

Let us examine the detailed proceedings of the Conference. Certain countries like Egypt, the Sudan and Palestine were not officially represented at all. As British Protectorates, or Mandated territories, the British delegation had previously agreed, importantly without consulting these countries, that their interests would be best represented by the British government. One must draw an obvious conclusion from this: Egypt and the Sudan were considered side issues and Palestine did not even figure in the equation. Arabs who lived in areas neither protected nor mandated by Britain would be represented by their own leaders. In the case of Syria, Prince Feisal, son of the Emir of Mecca, supported by Lawrence, would advance the Arab cause but Feisal and Lawrence would be ultimately, and shamefully, ignored by the British delegation.

The delicate negotiations were not helped by the ignorance of the Council of Four, whose grasp of detail was irresponsibly weak and, on occasion, comically lamentable. British diplomat Harold Nicolson described a meeting between the British and Italian delegations as an instance of pure farce, an incident worthy of *Monty Python's Flying Circus*, the popular British TV comedy. One day the two delegations were seated round a table studying a large map of Western Turkey. Prime Minister Orlando demanded that Italy should occupy a particular area. Lloyd George countered by pointing out that such a demand could not be met as the area was largely occupied by Greeks. In an aside, Nicolson informed Lloyd George that there were hardly any Greeks in the area under discussion. Lloyd George was adamant the area *was* Greek as it was coloured green and that the areas coloured brown were occupied by the Turks. The delegates thought they were studying an ethnological rather than a geographical map which identified the forests and the mountains!

When Feisal and Lawrence docked at Marseilles on their way to Paris, they were badly treated by French officialdom. The authorities there informed Feisal that he had been 'badly advised' in making the journey. To their credit, the British delegation intervened on Feisal's behalf and his name was subsequently added to the list of recognized delegates. Lawrence was treated with even more diffidence and open hostility; he was subjected to rude and insulting stares from the French. On being informed he would only be allowed to attend the conference hall wearing the uniform of a British Army officer, he compromised by wearing his colonel's uniform with a *keffiyeh*, or Arab headdress. Lawrence, ever the theatrical player, refused to comply; to some, his headgear was at best considered a petty gesture, at worst an insult to his countrymen. He was of course cocking a snook at the British Establishment which he detested. The British delegation responded by denying him a room at the Hotel Majestic; to allow him to reside there would have been seen as official recognition of his standing. Lawrence had to make do with one of the poorer quality hotels; he knew he was being snubbed but went along with the charade.

From the outset France dominated the talks; the French delegation demanded excessively harsh reparations from Germany, obstructed British claims in the Middle East and generally acted as if France had won the war single-handedly. Their Prime Minister Clemenceau and his team of ministers demanded Syria – and would get it. The Egyptian Question was not even discussed by the British, although the Palestine Question was prominent on the British agenda. Dr Chaim Weizmann, the leading Zionist of the day, buttonholed Feisal for a second time, seeking his agreement to a Jewish settlement in Palestine.

Weizmann, a man of infinite charm, persuaded Feisal to lend his support to the Balfour Declaration. Feisal was somewhat dismissive of Palestinians, regarding them as less than true Arabs. In an unguarded moment, probably preoccupied with his own problems, Feisal accepted Weizmann's persuasive argument for a Jewish settlement, saying there was enough land to go round and (mistakenly) admitting there could be benefits for Arabs in a Jewish-Palestine partnership. In Feisal's eyes, the Jews, with their Western education, business acumen and energy, might be able to turn infertile desert into productive agricultural land, which of course they subsequently would. It was one of the worst decisions after the Great War. Wingate had argued against it, as had Lord Curzon, who wrote that the country given the mandate over a Palestine containing Jews would forever 'have [a] rankling thorn' in its side. History has proven Wingate and Curzon right.

On 3 January 1919 Feisal and Weizmann signed an agreement. In exchange for Jewish settlement in Palestine, Weizmann promised Feisal Zionist support in his campaign for an independent Arab state. The Palestinian people, unrepresented at the Conference and not even consulted about the implementation of the Balfour Declaration rioted in Jerusalem. Their representatives also wrote in protest to Balfour but, apparently, the voluminous correspondence never reached his desk; it is said that his private secretary consigned every letter to the fire.

In the preliminary discussions at the Conference Lord Robert Cecil was at the epicentre. Lloyd George admitted he was a formidable debater. Cecil repeatedly advised Lloyd George to resist French demands for excessive reparations from Germany, urging moderation in the treatment of a fallen foe. The French would have none of this view. Britain had made a supreme sacrifice on the Somme in July 1916 to save the French at Verdun which should have given Britain an edge in these negotiations. It did not. Cecil demanded that Lloyd George stand up to the French. He did not. Cecil even saw a way to draw French teeth by siding with President Wilson's proposal to establish a League of Nations which would work towards securing long-term peace in Europe.

As for Feisal, his shabby treatment by the British induced him to leave the Conference in April; on his way home he visited the Pope in Rome. A disappointed man, he had learnt of the full extent of the Sykes-Picot Agreement giving the French a mandate for governing Syria. As mentioned earlier, Feisal's father, Emir Hussein, had refused to let him see the McMahon Letters of 1915, so he had been unable to argue from a point of strength at the conference against Sykes-Picot. Lloyd George did at least allow Feisal to read the infamous document and Feisal immediately realized the extent of Britain's promise – not to his father but to the French. It has to be said in Britain's favour that the minutes of the Peace Conference's Supreme Council show that Britain made strenuous efforts to honour the McMahon pledge but it is difficult to see how Lloyd George could have squared the circle in the light of Sykes-Picot. The French defended the agreement by stating that whatever deal the British had struck with the Arabs before Sykes-Picot, it had nothing to do with the French government; that was Britain's problem, Britain's muddle. Lloyd George advised Feisal to seek the support of President Wilson, as the USA was the only nation strong enough to stand up to the French; in doing so, the British Prime Minister was conceding defeat, an admission of failure. Wilson was known to sympathize with the plight of the colonial and mandated nations as his own country had once been a British colony. Feisal took Lloyd George's advice and approached Wilson to plead his case for Syria but Wilson was non-committal. When the American delegation pulled out of the negotiations shortly afterwards the Arab cause was dead in the water.

When Feisal met his father in Mecca in April 1919, the old man, jealous of his son's wartime successes, bluntly informed him he would never accept the terms of the Treaty of Versailles which gave Syria to the French. Estranged from his father and brothers, Feisal was ultimately ignored by the French and castigated by his own people. For years after 1919 Syria would be plunged into chaos.

One now has to ask the obvious question: how did Wingate view the proceedings in Paris? The answer must be with disappointment and even disgust. Not only had his support of the Arab Revolt and its contribution to the war been ill rewarded, his advice against the creation of a Jewish homeland in Palestine had been ignored. A third disappointment was to see his advice on the treatment of the rise of Egyptian Nationalism being rejected. Wingate, a Scot whose ancestors had been at Bruce's side at Bannockburn in 1314, knew full well that countries seeking independence from a mightier power discover that is rarely given – it must always be taken by force or other means. Scottish and world history had taught him that lesson. In every struggle for independence, there is rarely any recourse to democratic electoral systems, even if they exist. One has to admit that 50,000 swords or rifles can be more effective than 50,000 favourable ballot papers. In urging Whitehall to make concessions to the Egyptian Nationalists in 1918–1919, Wingate had his eye on history; he was also determined to avoid unnecessary bloodshed. His replacement as High Commissioner, Viscount Edward Allenby, shared this view and said as much to Wingate.

The Middle East question had been badly handled and unsatisfactorily resolved in Paris and the world still suffers the consequences. Today, one has to ask the question, albeit informed by hindsight – would the Arabs in Syria and Palestine have been better off had they thrown in their lot with the Turks? The answer has to be in the negative, for Turkey 'was rotten' in the words of T. E. Lawrence. And yet ...

In the light of the decisions taken in Paris and enforced by the Treaty of Versailles, how could Wingate have possibly hoped to succeed in his recommendations regarding Egypt where charismatic men like Feisal and Lawrence had failed? The pragmatic Gertrude Bell had written in 1911 that 'We people of the West can always conquer, but we can never hold Arabia – that seems to me to be the legend written across the landscape.'

As for Wingate and his representations on behalf of Egypt, who was he to presume to advise the British government? He was both regarded and treated as a minor official. Balfour saw him as a small cog in the wheel of state; Andrew Bonar Law, the future Prime Minister, considered him inefficient. Wingate attended the Conference in Paris to plead the case of the Hejaz Arabs and that of Egypt but his views were studiously ignored. Wingate was not one of the *clique* who held sway in the Foreign Office of the day.

Let us briefly consider the nature of those in power in the Foreign Office. Many like the Cecils and A. J. Balfour were Old Etonians, sons of aristocrats. Eton was the most famous public school in England and Wingate had not attended it; he was educated in an obscure Channel Island establishment. In those times, where you were educated invariably determined your career. In Wingate's day, the Cecils' father, Lord Salisbury, appointed his relatives – whatever their abilities – to key government posts. Salisbury's sons Hugh and James and his sister's son, A. J. Balfour, were given sinecures to buttress his rule. This was blatant nepotism but in no way detracts from the achievements of men like Balfour who did great things; the observation is here to illustrate the fact that some men are destined to succeed by birth, while others have to earn their place through dedication and hard work. The Cecils were the nearest that Britain had to an imperial family but, despite their Eton education, with its emphasis on classical and modern languages, the Cecil sons were woefully deficient in both. This did not prevent their elevation to positions of great power. By comparison, Wingate was fluent in several languages including French and Arabic, the latter being especially difficult to master. The Cecils and their cousin Balfour may have resented Wingate for his Arabic fluency; perhaps his achievement reminded him of their own shortcomings and damned him in their eyes.

The Old Guard in the Foreign Office were hardly likely to be well disposed to Wingate's limp, to their eyes, warnings of a rise in the Egyptian Nationalists' demands for independence and his advice on how to take the heat out of the situation. The Etonians of Whitehall's old guard were more preoccupied with the rise of nationalism in India and Ireland to give much consideration to Egypt.

Let us briefly examine the consequences of the Paris Peace Conference. The most significant result was the establishment of a Covenant of the League of Nations, the brainchild of Woodrow Wilson and one of his famous fourteen points for the future of Europe. (Woodrow's detractors commented that God had only required Ten Commandments to rule the world.) The concept of the League was the most ambitious and greatest peace movement in modern times. The League's aim was laudable: by substituting arbitration and forming an international code of law to settle disputes by discussion rather than military aggression, its *raison d'etre* was to eliminate the possibility of future wars. It was an honourable concept but sadly never lived up to its expectations, failing because some members, notably Japan with its aggressive policy toward China in Manchuria, Italy with its invasion of Abyssinia and Germany's manipulation in the 1930s rendered the League impotent. The support given by both Italy and Germany to the reactionary General Franco during the Spanish Civil War, and the failure of Britain and France to recognize the democratically elected government in Spain, sounded the League's death knell. As it turned out, the League proved to be about as effective as a Boy Scout jamboree, reviled by Germany, Italy and other Axis powers who later brought about the Second World War. By 1939 the organization had become discredited, having lost any remaining vestige of control over Europe, thus allowing Hitler and Mussolini an ominously free hand.

The Treaty of Versailles, drafted during the Peace Conference, was presented to the Germans on 7 May 1919; it was signed under extreme protest on 28 June. The League of Nations was established on 16 January 1920, its formation bringing the conference to an end. Germany had been humiliated, prostrated by French demands for financial reparations and the return of Alsace-Lorraine, which the Germans had annexed after the Franco-Prussian war of 1870. The seeds of the Second World War had been sown.

During that period of intense political activity on a world scale, the Arabs and the Egyptians were largely forgotten. Disillusioned by the factionalism among the Arab tribes and despite Prince Feisal's efforts to resolve the problem, Lawrence ruefully admitted they would never be capable of forming a united Arab nation. Years later he described the period from January to May 1919 as the worst in his entire life. Sir Gilbert Clayton, his erstwhile colleague in the Arab Bureau in Cairo, now political adviser to Allenby, drafted a memorandum on 11 March 1919 which highlighted the incompatibility of

British policy in Arabia with Sykes-Picot, that cynical agreement which detached Syria and the Lebanon from a hoped-for Arab Kingdom.

Let us return to Lawrence the man rather than the idealist guerrilla leader. In October 1918 he was suffering from wounds, disease, physical and emotional exhaustion. Summoned to Buckingham Palace on 30 October to receive his honours – the Order of the Bath and the DSO, he refused both, leaving a perplexed George V 'holding the box [containing the awards] in my hands'. Lawrence's psychological make-up and inner personal conflicts – his loyalty to Britain and to the Arabs – may have been the root causes of his poor health. In Arab eyes, Lawrence's prime loyalty was to imperial Britain, despite his repeated protests that it was a love of the Arabs which had motivated his support for the Arab Revolt. It has to be said that while his conviction was genuine, Lawrence privately believed that a self-governing Arab nation would become a dominion of the British Empire, like Canada.

During his time in Paris during the Peace Conference, Lawrence, ever the actor and romantic adventurer, lobbied in vain against French demands in the Middle East. Disillusioned and depressed, he made himself ill writing his account of the war in the desert, the brilliant, if flawed, masterpiece *Seven Pillars of Wisdom*, privately printed in 1926. Perhaps Lawrence's words at the end of the book sum up his disillusionment with the war and the treatment of his beloved Arabs afterwards: 'I knew how much I was sorry.'[7] However, his involvement with the Arabs did not end in 1918 or 1919. He was invited to the Middle East to advise on Arab affairs but merely as a private citizen. Wingate was also asked to prepare a memorandum on the way forward, a manuscript he would write in the draughty library at Knockenhair, with its impressive view over the North Sea. Lawrence and Wingate were treated shabbily by the British government; they had been friends and confidants during the war but were now ostracized. Completely different in temperament and character, they nonetheless harboured a mutual, if grudging, respect for one another. Wingate, the loyal imperialist, happily married and a father, a shrewd detective-cum-espionage officer, with little or no recorded interest in literature other than the novels of Conan Doyle (with whom he had played golf in Cairo); Lawrence, the idealist, crusader, classical student, masochist, liar and failed actor. These opposites were flung together by one of the worst wars the world had ever known.

During his stay in Paris Lawrence learnt of the deaths of his father and that of Sir Mark Sykes. Both had succumbed to the virulent Spanish Flu which claimed more lives than the war itself. In 1921 Lawrence was acting as adviser to Britain on Egyptian affairs and was able to redeem some of his seemingly unrealistic promises to the Arabs, but this came too late, as did Wingate's memorandum on the way forward in Egypt. Lawrence sought anonymity as a humble RAF mechanic under the assumed surname of Ross, then as a soldier in the Royal Tank Corps as T. E. Shaw, a surname he appropriated from George Bernard Shaw, his near neighbour at Cloud's Hill in Dorset. His destiny was to be abruptly resolved in a fatal motorcycle accident on 13 May

1935. One can but speculate how Wingate received the news of his tragic death; being the gentleman he undoubtedly was, it is certain that he mourned the passing of a young man he had known and respected.

President Woodrow Wilson's pledge to support the Arabs' claim to self-determination was probably applauded by Wingate, albeit quietly. In March 1919 Wilson suggested that an inter-Allied commission be sent to Syria to gauge the wishes of the Syrian people on their government. Prince Feisal left Paris for Syria to prepare for the commission's arrival. Lawrence, still in Paris, learnt of Wilson's mission and cadged a lift in one of the RAF's Handley-Page bombers flying to Damascus on 18 May. En route, he was injured when his plane had to refuel in Rome; the plane crashed into a tree and Lawrence suffered a cracked shoulder blade which hospitalized him for a month. He finally arrived in Cairo on 18 June 1919. In the intervening period, he learnt that the French would participate in President Wilson's commission to Syria only if the British troops stationed there were withdrawn and replaced with French soldiers. Lloyd George solved the problem by cutting the Gordian knot – he simply withdrew the British representatives who were to have accompanied the commission. Ultimately only American delegates went to Syria; arriving on 25 June, they stayed ten days, their mission rendered impotent, no more than an ineffective diplomatic gesture. Syria was ceded to France without fuss; there was no powerful enough Arab voice in Paris to challenge the decision, Feisal and Lawrence both being in Damascus. The British officials who opposed an independent Arab nation were in the majority; Sir Arthur Hertzel in the influential India Office wrote to Lord Curzon, Secretary of State at the Foreign Office bluntly stating that there would never be peace in the Middle East until T. E. Lawrence's 'malign influence' was removed. The unofficial campaign to discredit Lawrence intensified, driving him into the anonymity of lowly positions, first in the RAF, then in the Tank Corps.

The decisions of the gathering of vultures in Paris – how else could it be described? – laid the foundations of the Second World War. Woodrow Wilson, arch-architect of the plan to prevent future world wars, never succeeded in having his famous fourteen points adopted. Lofty idealism blinded him to his own political weaknesses; an inability to listen to the advice of his own Democratic Party turned his political career into a tragedy of world politics and he died a broken man in February 1924. At least the Arabs did not come away from Paris entirely empty-handed; Feisal was given part of Mesopotamia, now known as Iraq; his brother Abdullah received the newly formed state of TransJordan. France was given Syria and Lebanon while Britain acquired the poisoned chalice of Palestine. Balfour steered the Foreign Office ship of state through the shoals and reefs of international politics, stubbornly refusing to adjust course until a wind of change altered it; Wingate had repeatedly given London clear warning of the storm that was brewing in Egypt.

A postscript to the Paris Peace negotiations was that Prince Feisal, denied the throne of Syria, was crowned King of Iraq in 1921. The following year, after tortuous and lengthy negotiations, he signed a treaty with Britain giving recognition to Iraq as an independent state, thus ensuring it a seat at the League of Nations in 1932.

In Cairo in 1919 Wingate assiduously reported to Lord Hardinge at the Foreign Office the unfolding political situation in Egypt. He had learnt that petitions were being circulated in the provinces, with anti-British propaganda being taught openly in the schools. (Wingate would later write that there were campaigns denouncing the Protectorate and that he had subsequently banned all public meetings and demonstrations.) As mentioned earlier, Wingate had been instructed to keep the Foreign Office 'fully informed' which implied he had not hitherto done so. On 2 December 1918 Balfour had wired him:

> I note that Extremist leaders are exploiting [the] fact of your having received them at [the] Residency *which was unfortunate* [author's italics]. You will of course make it perfectly clear that you view this agitation and all those who participate in it with extreme disfavour ... I understand leaders of [the Nationalist] movement do not carry much weight but it might become mischievous and even seditious ... if [this] is left un-checked. You will no doubt adopt all ... measures to prevent such developments.[8]

The assumption that the Nationalists did not carry much weight is unbeliev-able; on what planet was Balfour living?

It later transpired that the words 'which was unfortunate' were, according to Sir Ronald Graham, who had drafted the telegram, added by 'a higher authority'. The authority was not Balfour, as Wingate might have surmised. The words had been added by Sir Eyre Crowe, a Foreign Office protégé of Cecil, who described Wingate as 'incredibly weak'. Graham informed Wingate of this and, with breathtaking hypocrisy, ended his letter of 19 January 1919 to Wingate as follows: 'The government continue [sic] to have every confidence in your skill and judgement.'[9] At the same time, Graham informed Lord Hardinge that he personally considered Wingate's 'private interviews' with the Nationalists 'irregular'. Hardinge passed this information to Balfour in Paris, adding that he endorsed Graham's view. Wingate's interviews had not been private, nor were they irregular. After all, as High Commissioner, it was part of his duty to receive deputations of Egyptians from all walks of life who had grievances they wished to make known to the British government. They could only do this through the obvious British representative, the High Commissioner.

Before Graham's hypocritical letter, Balfour sent Wingate a cable dated 1 January 1919 – in the UK at that time, only Scotland celebrated New Year as a holiday – offering a compromise to defuse the political unrest in Cairo. In a remarkable u-turn, Balfour informed Wingate that Egyptian ministers should come to London if Wingate thought:

> this would have a pacifying effect in Egypt ... I have no objection to their arriving during the course of February ... [but] in no case can they be permitted to go to Paris during the sessions of the Peace Conference.[10]

What had changed? The Foreign Office was determined to maintain the status quo of the British Protectorate – still undefined in its purpose and intent; perhaps the impact of Wingate's cables was finally getting through. On occasion the persistence of the far-sighted can make even the blind see. Had Wingate argued his case strongly enough? Possibly not, as he was astute enough to realize that, in politics, a positive stance is made more effective by the constraint exercised in its delivery.

At last Wingate believed he had succeeded in convincing his masters in Whitehall of the political situation in Egypt. The Foreign Office invited him to visit London ten days before the Egyptian delegation arrived in February or March 1919. This must have given Wingate some reassurance; his assessment of the situation was a necessary prelude to any future discussions with representatives of the Egyptian government. Wingate left Cairo on 21 January for Paris, he and Lady Wingate arriving on 29 January. The following day Wingate had lunch with Balfour who gave him the impression that he was in general agreement with Wingate's policy in Egypt. However, Balfour advised him to go into more detail with Lord Curzon in London, Curzon then acting as Foreign Secretary. Before leaving for England, the Wingates took time to see their daughter Victoria who was working as an archivist for the British delegation to the Peace Conference. Then, on 2 February, they went to Lagincourt to visit the grave of their son Malcolm, killed in March 1918.[11] Wingate then proceeded to London to meet Lord Curzon whom he hoped would support him and smooth the path of the visiting Egyptians, many of whom were personal friends. It proved a forlorn hope.

Let us briefly examine the career and character of Lord George Curzon. By nature more of an efficient administrator than politician – he shared that much with Wingate – he was a stickler for detail, striving for perfection and obsessed by time-keeping – anyone turning up late for meetings irritated him, incurring an unconcealed displeasure. Curzon was hard-working; he had effectively ruled India for several years and devoted much of his energy to the development of that vast nation, albeit in the interests of imperial Britain. His less attractive personality traits were an overweening indulgence in self-pity and the belief that he was badly served and even betrayed by his colleagues. These traits, along with a neurotic obsession with punctuality, suggest someone prone to paranoia. As Viceroy of India, Curzon rightly felt he was more important than any Cabinet Minister, the equal of any Prime Minister. After leaving India he was put in charge of the Foreign Office while his superior, Lord Balfour, attended the Paris Peace Conference. He would later succeed Balfour as Foreign Secretary, serving in that capacity until 1924.

In February 1919 Wingate was about to endure the unpleasantness of a typical Curzon interview.

When Wingate arrived in London on 3 February he did not expect to stay long; the purpose of his visit was simply to inform government ministers of the political mood in Egypt. He would soon learn that, in the grand scale of things flowing from the Peace Conference, his recommendations on Egypt were seen as peripheral, even irrelevant. The finer points of the implications of the Peace Conference and how they would be played out among British subject peoples in countries like Egypt and the Sudan were, as far as Balfour and Curzon were concerned, marginalized and even irrelevant in the overall picture.

Wingate waited two weeks before being granted an interview with Curzon, a man of whom it must be said that he was capable of considerable charm and acts of kindness. He was, however, noted for severe treatment of subordinates; junior staff in the FO suffered frequent rebukes, which mark him as something of a bully. Wingate was hardly a subordinate but Curzon treated him as such. Who gave a jot for Wingate's concerns about Egypt? Apart from the stout, dapper little Scotsman sitting patiently in the Whitehall corridor where Curzon occupied an office, there was no one else to exert pressure on the FO and mollify the Nationalist faction in Egypt. In Curzon's view, it was better to maintain the status quo, to wait, to observe, to do nothing, than succumb to the demands of a few crackpot Egyptian ministers who had no appreciation of the benefits flowing from imperial Britain. Surely in view of the time he had to wait for an audience with Curzon, Wingate must have harboured the feeling that he was a lone voice, crying in a political wilderness and pushing a heavy boulder up an incredibly steep hill.

At last Curzon deigned to see him. In an unpleasant interview Wingate was left in no doubt that, in Curzon's view, he had lacked conviction in his dealings with the Egyptian Nationalists – a conviction which would ensure imperial British rule continued over Egypt. Wingate argued that the difficult situation in Egypt would be resolved to some extent if the British government would invite the Egyptian Ministers and the Nationalist leaders for talks in London. Curzon dismissed the proposal out of hand, saying that the government could not allow the Nationalists to 'hold a pistol to our head'.

Despite Curzon's stance, on 17 February Wingate prepared a draft telegram for Curzon to send to Sultan Fu'ad, intimating that his Council of Ministers would be well received in London. Wingate was trying to pave the way for a peaceful settlement but, at the same time, he warned Curzon that if his (Wingate's) draft proposals were unacceptable he could not be answerable for the pressure the Egyptian nationalists would exert on the Sultan and his ministers, effectively rendering them impotent.

Curzon was incensed by Wingate's advice which he regarded as nothing short of impudence. Curzon had lost the plot, failing to appreciate that Sultan Fu'ad and his Ministers were powerless to oppose the Nationalist Party in Egypt, even if they had wanted to, which they did not. Not surprisingly,

Curzon considered the Nationalists as little more than extremists, who were putting Egypt's economy, well-being and interests at risk, (Curzon meaning Britain's interests). An intractable Foreign Office was confronted by an equally stubborn Sultan of Egypt. Curzon and Wingate had reached impasse; at least Curzon promised to resolve the difficulty by forwarding Wingate's views to Paris along with his own assessment of the situation in Egypt, a country of which he had little or no knowledge. This was of small comfort to Wingate, acutely aware that he was a lesser minion in the hierarchical scale. It was inevitable that, as Wingate's senior, Curzon's view would be accepted. After all, Curzon made no secret of his opposition to Wingate's arguments – he told him as much – and, in a subsequent cable to Cairo, made no bones about his distrust of the Egyptian Nationalists.

Wingate's draft telegram of 17 February was accepted, with significant and anti-Wingate amendments, by Curzon and sent to Paris on 26 February 1919. Curzon did at least inform Balfour of Wingate's suggested solution to the problems in Egypt but added that he would argue against it. Curzon acknowledged the fact that the Sultan of Egypt's Council of Ministers would not agree to come to London without the Nationalist leaders. Curzon described the Nationalists as men of 'doubtful standing' and accused them of organizing 'a disloyal movement' against HM Government, their protecting power. Then came the final condemnation; if the British government were to allow the Nationalists to visit London, the government would be seen to be conceding defeat, or at very least granting them a recognition 'to which they were not entitled'. When the contents of Curzon's telegram were made known in Cairo, the Sultan's ministers including Prime Minister Rushdi resigned *en masse*. The Sultan's subsequent attempts to form a new Council of Ministers brought threats of civil disobedience from the Nationalist Party. Those threats were so strong that Sultan Fu'ad was obliged to ask the British Residency for protection. The ringleader, Zaghlul Pasha, was arrested by the British authorities along with three of his closest associates; the four men were deported to Malta. The Egyptian propaganda machine kicked in immediately; Egypt was to be subjugated. The gloves were off and civil disobedience escalated; there were riots and widespread demonstrations in the streets of Cairo and elsewhere, resulting in the loss of several lives. Despite Balfour's rejection of Wingate's proposed solution, he reluctantly agreed to meet a deputation of Egyptian Ministers in London.

All that Wingate had predicted in repeated memoranda and cables to the Foreign Office was now coming to pass. For now, the riots were put down in less than three weeks by troops under General Bulfin. As early as 3 January 1919 Lord Robert Cecil had informed Balfour that General Allenby, liberator of Damascus, would be a suitable successor to Wingate 'if he were called home'. Cecil sowed a seed with these words; nonetheless, the Foreign Office continued to reassure Wingate that the government had every confidence in him. Curzon's telegram of 26 February 1919 to Balfour effectively sealed Wingate's fate as High Commissioner; one man's obstinacy had created an avoidable political situation, but then the history of the British Empire is strewn with many such incidents, the casualties being those who dared to challenge the prevailing view. The choice had been between the advice, wisdom and practical experience of the government's man on the spot – Wingate – and the views of a powerful cabinet minister known for his intractability in granting any form of self-government to India. Curzon the puppetmaster, flying the imperialist, right-wing banner, had strayed into territory he clearly did not understand. His blunt refusal to recognize the Egyptian Nationalists simply strengthened their resolve and would result in Egypt's full independence in 1924 (even if British troops continued to occupy the country until 1936). Under the subsequent Anglo-Egyptian Treaty of Alliance, British occupation was limited to the Suez Canal Zone and Ismailia: other matters reserved at the discretion of the British government were the security of imperial communications and the protection of foreign interests and of minority peoples like those of the Sudan. (Sadly, this accommodation did not prevent relations between Britain and Egypt further deteriorating after the Second World War when, in 1952, the control of Egypt was seized by a group of young army officers led by Colonel Nasser. Nasser declared Egypt a republic, pressing for British withdrawal from the Canal Zone and precipitating the Suez Crisis in 1956. British restraint finally snapped under the premiership of Anthony Eden who mounted an Anglo-French expeditionary force to counter the 'piracy' of Nasser. Nasser responded by blockading the Suez Canal, stopping the flow of oil to Europe and outwitting the British and French who insisted their presence in Egypt was to prevent war between Israel and Egypt. The expeditionary force was replaced by a United Nations peace-keeping force to guarantee the security of the Suez Canal.)

As for Wingate, like others of his generation and position in government, he never forgot that his prime duty was to serve the British Crown. He cannot be faulted in his devotion to duty but he was years ahead of his time, recognizing that Egypt and the Sudan would have to be granted independence and that British officials could play a useful role in bringing this about peacefully. This may strike modern critics of British imperialism as somewhat naïve but we must judge Wingate both by his own writings as well as by the conventions of the time.

Early in 1919 Wingate's position was weaker than ever. He was *persona non grata* not only in the FO but also in the Cabinet. Pressure to remove him was mounting; the eggshell fragility of his situation could not withstand the weight of the forces ranged against him.

Wingate's career in the service of Egypt and the British Army effectively came to an end in February 1919. In his last month as High Commissioner he was perhaps consoled by a letter he received on 19 January 1919 from W. Jessop, secretary to the YMCA in Egypt. Jessop thanked Wingate for sending a photograph of himself and acknowledging the interest 'you have always shown in my work ... and your personal support'. On 20 April 1919

Wingate sent a dictated letter from his flat in Queen Anne's Mansions, London to Sir James W. Barrett's representatives thanking him for receipt of a gifted copy of Barrett's book on the work of the YMCA in Egypt during the Great War.

Wingate's days as High Commissioner in Egypt numbered but a few pages on the calendar. In February 1919 he was recalled to London; his first request was to be given permission to return to the Middle East, a request which was refused. The reason given was that he was needed in London, where he was directed to prepare a memorandum on the political state in Egypt. This direction was given with superficial civility, the hallmark of bureaucracy. Lloyd George and Balfour would later admit that Wingate's assessment of the political situation in Egypt had been accurate and that Curzon's was wrong. A telegram from Paris to London dated 18 March 1919 reversed Curzon's policy; it came too late to save Wingate. As High Commissioner, Wingate should have received a copy *ex officio*; at least, his position entitled him to that courtesy. With a cynical disregard for his feelings and position, the Foreign Office sent Wingate a bowdlerized version of the telegram a few weeks later. The upshot was that Wingate's suggested solution to the Egyptian problem – one which he had been advocating diplomatically for two years, then vociferously for the previous four months – was adopted. The stable door had been shut after the horse had bolted. At least order was restored in Cairo when a competent government was formed and the Foreign Office signalled that HMG would be prepared to receive a delegation of Egyptian ministers and Nationalist leaders in London. It was a humiliating U-turn, one which could have been avoided if the Foreign Office had listened to Wingate. The climb-down seemed to add more bargaining power to Egypt.

After his ordeal with Curzon, Wingate was virtually ignored by the Foreign Office but, while in London, he devoted much of his time to winding up his late son Malcolm's affairs and collecting his personal belongings. The visit to London in February 1919 was not without compensation. On 16 February he lunched at Clarence House, home of the Prince of Wales; on 25 February, he and Lady Wingate were guests at a party at St James' Palace and on the 27 February, the Wingates attended a royal wedding. In the spring of that year there were violent riots in Cairo, Alexandria and towns in Upper Egypt; many Europeans, including both British civilians and soldiers, were killed by mobs. On 19 March Wingate was recalled to London.

On the very same day as Wingate's return to London, General Allenby arrived in Paris to attend the talks on the future of Syria. The British government was in complete disarray but acknowledged that a strong hand was needed in Cairo. That hand could not be Wingate's as his recall to London had signalled to Egypt that the government no longer had any confidence in him. It was clear that someone else would have to fill Wingate's chair, someone hitherto unconnected with Egypt. Allenby was duly appointed Special High Commissioner with full military and civil powers. Allenby must have considered his new role a poisoned chalice; professional soldiers rarely transfer from soldiering to politics with ease, Wellington being another classic example. Even so, Allenby insisted that concessions be made to the Nationalist faction in the hope that a peaceful settlement could be reached and so Zaghlul Pasha was released from custody in Malta. The Nationalist Wafd was by now a countrywide organization dominating Egyptian politics. At least Allenby appreciated the gravity and sensitivity of the situation in Cairo, although he still implemented the policy now being advocated by Whitehall – Wingate's earlier advice. He made concessions to the Nationalists in the hope of reaching a peaceful settlement, informing Whitehall that he intended to issue passports to any Egyptians wishing to visit Europe, regardless of their political persuasion. In his final, characteristically thoughtful postscript, Wingate had shared his view of the Egyptian situation with his successor. Allenby then wrote a comforting letter to Wingate: 'I wish this had been done when you first advocated it. We are some months too late ... I wish your advice had been taken.'[12]

On 20 March 1919, Balfour cabled Wingate stating that Allenby's appointment as Special High Commissioner 'makes no technical change in your position'. He followed this with a sanctimonious and insensitive letter which was tantamount to informing Wingate he had been dismissed, even if not stated in so many words:

Allenby's appointment as Special High Commissioner leaves the position of the existing High Commissioner [Wingate] untouched.' [But then came the crunch.] 'Two great officials cannot exercise their functions simultaneously ... So long therefore as General Allenby is dealing with the existing crisis, your services will hardly be required.

Within that single sentence is compressed Balfour's cynicism, callousness and injustice. He continued thus:

In the meantime I can do no more than thank you for the great services which you have performed in the Soudan [sic] and Egypt, and for the administrative skill which has done so much for the well-being of their inhabitants.[13]

In modern day parlance, Balfour might have added 'Have a nice day', that totally meaningless and insincere mantra. It was clear that Wingate had, in the eyes of his masters, not been firm enough in his dealings with the nationalists. Balfour had previously told him in yet another u-turn that no useful purpose would be served by allowing Nationalist leaders to come to London to advance their 'immoderate demands for independence'. Wingate was so incensed by this that, in a rare moment, abandoning usual tact, he instructed his Private Secretary to convey Balfour's decision to the Wafd. Wingate's carefully composed memoranda had been written with the best of intentions, aimed at preserving the interests of the Crown in Egypt but he was rewarded with the door being slammed in his face. Wingate would no longer pursue a civil career and was too old to serve in the Army. From now on, the Foreign Office would studiously ignore him. Perhaps a stronger or more determined man might have appealed to the House of Commons, seeking to enlist the support of backbenchers to plead his case, but that was never Wingate's way. In the final analysis, he fell victim to the consensus politics of the time. While in Egypt he had forced through complex and far-reaching diplomatic changes and decisions in his attempts to maintain peace while upholding British interests. However, the issue of the Nationalists whom he had tried to placate was not confined to Egypt; Indian nationalism had become a burning issue by 1919. This was of little help to Wingate however; the trajectory of his career across the sky had now dramatically turned earthwards.

Allenby's comforting and conciliatory letter to Wingate would have incensed Curzon. By now Curzon had been apprised of the government's intentions regarding Egypt and, officially at least, was obliged to acknowledge Wingate's accurate assessment of the Egyptian problem, now reflected in government policy. The Conservative's Andrew Bonar Law, Scottish 'hard man' in Lloyd George's coalition government and acting Prime Minister, returned from Paris and interviewed Curzon and Wingate together; Curzon made no attempt to conceal his displeasure regarding the government's decision, while Bonar Law simply listened to the argument. Curzon made no bones about it, stating that the decision reached in Paris had been a mistake, taken against a background of Egyptian threats and intimidation. Then Curzon made a threat of his own; if his policy was to remain on the shelf, he would feel obliged to consider his own position as Foreign Secretary. Bonar Law responded firmly; he reminded Curzon that he was a member of the Cabinet and that

> when you talk of considering your position [ie his resignation from the government] you are talking about a Cabinet matter which can only be in the purview of the Cabinet. Sir Reginald Wingate is not a member of the Cabinet and I must ask you to say no more.[14]

This blunt statement silenced Curzon for the rest of the meeting. On the other hand, Bonar Law informed Lloyd George that he had formed a poor impression of Wingate and had no faith in his judgement, damning words from a fellow Scot. Most sensitive people party to this knowledge would have urged Wingate to retire to his Edwardian house in Dunbar and await the official verdict on his fate. The Wingates remained in London, having by then rented a flat in Queen Anne's Mansions. From there Wingate wrote to his old friend Sir Francis Grenfell informing him that he was 'very much occupied with Egyptian affairs and ... constantly in consultation with the Foreign Office'.[15] He clearly wanted to give Grenfell the impression that he was still in charge, still in the thick of the political morass that was Egypt. In point of fact, his consultations with the Foreign Office were with underlings, not Curzon.

Meanwhile in Austria, Wingate's friend Rudolf von Slatin learnt that his old comrade-in-arms would not be returning to Africa and wrote to him in sympathetic terms which would have brought a few crumbs of comfort. To his credit, Wingate never betrayed any bitterness towards his successor, Allenby, accepting that his sacking as High Commissioner was inevitable. Post-Victorian politics were a veritable minefield for men of foresight who, in the often narrow vision of the Foreign Office, were dismissed either as cranks or politically unsound. Slatin commiserated with his old friend but was of course powerless to affect the outcome. In time Wingate would accept his enforced retirement and a baronetcy, with the honorific First Baron Dunbar and the Port Sudan, but was denied a peerage, a clear indication that he was out of favour. That year of 1919, Wingate's *annus horribilis*, was mitigated by the award of an honorary doctorate from Edinburgh University in July.[16] (The honour had actually been bestowed in 1915 but Wingate had been unable to attend the ceremony in Edinburgh on account of the war.) In making the award, the Dean of the Faculty of Law was fulsome in his praise; his speech highlighted the fact that Wingate 'had delivered the Sudan from an oppressive tyranny and that he had laid the foundations for that country's security and well-being'. The Dean went on to describe Wingate's achievements as High Commissioner of Egypt and that his statesmanship there 'had brought tranquillity [sic] to that country, thus crowning "the civilized labours of Lords Kitchener and Cromer"'.[17]

Wingate returned to Dunbar after an absence of nearly five years, only to be summoned to London once more to comment on the disturbances reported from Egypt.[18] The following week, he left for London to meet the delegation of Egyptian ministers and Nationalist leaders who would present their case to the British government. The Wingates returned to Dunbar in the first week of August,[19] when Zaghlul Pasha was again banished to Malta. Zaghlul was held without trial in a military prison, his only consolation being that his case would soon become a *cause celebre*. In the summer of 1919 he was accused of inciting the Egyptian people to rebel against the ruling power (the Sultan, in theory, the British government, in effect) and of stirring up civil strife and bloodshed.

Back in Dunbar, Wingate was no doubt enjoying a few rounds of golf, meeting James Hastie, the Dunbar-born greenkeeper and professional at Cairo's Gezira Sporting Club, also on a visit to Dunbar.[20] In the same week, through his contacts in the Coldstream Guards, Wingate arranged the presentation of a captured German field-piece to the Burgh of Dunbar, a gift gratefully accepted by the Town Council.[21]

On 15 May Lord Curzon announced to the House of Lords that the Colonial Secretary, Lord Milner, would head a special mission to Egypt to enquire into the causes of the recent disturbances and report back on the form of constitution which, under the British Protectorate or mandate, would secure stability and prosperity for the country. He also intimated that the mission would examine self-governing institutions while at the same time protecting British interests. After months of pretence, the Foreign Office hinted that Wingate should resign. By now Wingate knew that certain criticisms had been levelled at his administration and he was determined to go down fighting. He demanded that the nature of these criticisms be made known to him as well as an opportunity to refute them; he also insisted he be given the names of those who had voiced these criticisms. He was never afforded the satisfaction.

The Milner Commission (1919–20) – in effect a Royal Commission – was boycotted in Egypt. However, Milner was subsequently able to have private talks in London with Zaghlul Pasha, released from custody in Malta. Milner recommended a form of independence for Egypt that was rejected by the British government in 1920. During this fiasco – no more than an exercise in papering over cracks in Anglo-Egyptian relations – Allenby pressed the government to promise independence, thereby hoping to out-manoeuvre Zaghlul by creating a faction of pro-British sentiment in Egypt which would weaken the Nationalists' case.

It is perhaps appropriate here to examine the situation when Milner arrived in Cairo. Apart from the boycott by all non-official Egyptians, the hostile atmosphere in official circles was ill-concealed. Though some officials did co-operate by placing certain evidence before the Mission, there were no discussions. No amount of coaxing or cajoling would convince the Egyptian press that the Mission was anything other than an instrument of British imperialism – which, of course, it was – with an agenda that would deprive Egypt of its rights. In fact, the more the Mission declared its intentions the less creditable it appeared. Returning to Britain in 1920, the Milner Commission had at least gathered some information, unfortunately proving to be of little practical value. Having said that, the Mission completely reversed Lord Curzon's policy towards Egypt; it recommended that Britain should recognize Egypt's independence and form an alliance under which British troops would support Egypt in the defence of its borders. Troops would be stationed at pre-determined places solely for safeguarding Egyptian territory and British interests – meaning Suez – but the troops should not be regarded in any way as an occupying force. This plan must have caused more than a few raised eyebrows in Egypt's political and social circles.

The Milner Commission's fact-finding memorandum was received with some trepidation throughout Britain and her dominions. Curzon confessed that he had only the dimmest idea of what was going on, a shocking admission which must have elicited a wry smile from Wingate. The Milner Report was officially sanctioned and published in February 1921 and declared, on the surface at least, to represent British government policy in relation to Egypt. The Report still did not satisfy the Nationalists, who were now scenting blood. Further agitation inspired by Zaghlul Pasha occurred in May, resulting in further loss of life. The new Prime Minister Ali Pasha headed a second delegation to London in July, where talks with the Foreign Office continued until November, the sticking-point being the location of a British garrison somewhere in Egypt.

In 1919 the uncertainty of his position took its toll on Wingate's health although the Wingates remained in London for much of the year. It was a stressful time although Wingate remained 'on the strength' – meaning retained on full pay – until October, when he was placed on half-pay as a general in the British Army. During that period he prepared a memorandum on Egyptian affairs which would shape part of the Milner Commission's remit the following year. In July 1919 a deputation of Sudanese officials visited Britain and Wingate was given the honour of presenting them to George V.

Being nobody's fool, Wingate was by now acutely aware that he had been made the scapegoat for what was happening in Egypt, particularly the March riots in Cairo. These claimed the lives of 800 people and had prompted London to replace Wingate with Allenby, the professional soldier. No attempt was made to defend Wingate; in vain, he protested to the government that his reputation should be safeguarded. He received a bland response to the effect that, if he were attacked directly in the British press, the government would stand by him. It never did; in the public mind and in the press, Wingate was made to appear at fault, albeit obliquely. The government took the convenient view that what was hinted at in the British newspapers did not constitute a direct attack on Wingate. It was a familiar example of the government tacitly laying the blame for its own shortcomings on a seemingly incompetent individual public servant.

To his credit Wingate took his fall with exceptional grace. For four decades he had faithfully served king and country in the Sudan and Egypt. In Egypt itself many Nationalists and their sympathizers considered Wingate a man of honour. He was never formally sacked but he knew his career was effectively over. Visiting Knockenhair in 1919, his son Ronald described his father as 'inconsolable'.[22] Even so, Wingate felt that his personal misfortune should not detract from British policy in the Middle East. Some men would have gone down with all guns firing but it was not in Wingate's character so to do. However, he did detest the Foreign Office for the rest of his life. Perhaps with hindsight, one might say, at his worst, Wingate had been weak and, at best, he remained the quintessential gentleman.

Wingate was ruined professionally; it was a blow from which he never recovered. He would never again be employed in any capacity by the government. Curzon, perhaps nursing a bruised conscience, offered him the post of Governor of the Straits Settlements, a Crown Colony of Malaya in 1919, an unhealthy posting for a younger man, let alone one in his fifty-eighth year. Curzon then attempted to secure a government directorship on the Suez Canal Board for Wingate but as the appointment was exclusively in the Prime Minister's gift, it was filled by Lloyd George's own Private Secretary. Wingate might have been offered a lucrative post in the Foreign Office's Diplomatic Service, given his mastery of Arabic and other languages and he was more than qualified for an overseas posting, perhaps to Turkey, although that was probably out of the question in view of his support for the Arabs during the war. There were no vacancies on offer, nor were there likely to be; in the FO's eyes, Wingate had shot himself in the foot.

In his detailed and excellent account[23] of High Commissioners McMahon, Wingate, Allenby and Lloyd, the writer C. W. R. Long lists the charges, real or imagined, against Wingate and examines the shortcomings which appear to have directly influenced the government's decision to sack Wingate. Wingate was perceived in turn as stubborn – which he could on occasion be – and weak in his keenness to receive the nationalists in the Cairo Residency. Furthermore, over the years, Wingate had lost his fresh, succinct writing style of the Sudan years. In Cairo, he was guilty of long-windedness – a trait the mandarins of the public service view with suspicion, regarding it as cover for woolly thinking, lack of conviction and indecision (the contrast in writing styles is borne out by the evidence of his papers in the Sudan archive at Durham University). Most astonishing of all the criticisms laid at his door was the accusation that, from 1917, he had failed to put his case forcefully enough to the Foreign Office of the danger signs evidenced by the rise of nationalism. His critics went so far as to suggest that Wingate had been taken by surprise as to the extent of the agitation. That and the fact that he had entertained Zaghlul and his colleagues in November 1918 were seen as proof of Wingate's weakness, that of giving official sanction to the nationalist movement. Furthermore, he had informed Zaghlul and company that they were 'free agents' and could go anywhere, which of course was denied them under the terms of the British protectorate. All these ills were later laid at Wingate's door, thereby guaranteeing his ultimate removal.

Wingate had implacable enemies in the Foreign Office, Sir Ronald Graham perhaps being the most devious. A serious charge of Graham's was that Wingate had neglected his relations with the Sultan and of course he accused Wingate of being weak when confronted in person by the nationalists. Graham also accused Wingate of holding private interviews with the nationalists, despite Hardinge's endorsement of Wingate's belief that it was important to keep the door of the Cairo residency open to Egyptian people. The most serious charge used by his detractors at home and in Egypt was that by receiving the nationalists Wingate had sold the pass, giving credence and official (HMG) sanction to their cause.

Wingate was now permanently resident in Dunbar. In late July or early August 1919, he attended peace celebrations in London.[24] He fretted in Knockenhair until October, when the *Haddingtonshire Advertiser* made a brief announcement that Field Marshal Viscount Allenby had been 'appointed His Majesty's High Commissioner in Egypt in succession to General Sir Reginald F. Wingate [sic].'[25] On 2 October Curzon informed Wingate officially of Allenby's appointment as High Commissioner. He took pains to describe Allenby as Wingate's successor – not his replacement – in Egypt. Curzon, the arch-imperialist, knew that 'replacement' was a derogatory word in the diplomatic jargon of the day. In imperial language, to be replaced meant you were incompetent, a reflection on the credibility of the government which had appointed you in the first place. Curzon assured Wingate that his succession implied 'no reflection whatever' on Wingate, whose services had been 'of no common order', especially in the Sudan. Wingate's services to Egypt were not mentioned.[26] He returned to Khartoum in the autumn of 1919, presumably to wind up affairs there.

Incredibly, it took Balfour nearly three months to contact Wingate; his telegram dated 15 December 1919 is addressed to 'Sirdar, Khartoum' and had this to say:

Private. Your private letters of November 1 and November 23 [presumably suggesting that Allenby remain in control of the military situation with Wingate as the civil administrator in Egypt]. Your proposal has received my careful consideration and I quite understand the present position must entail a certain amount duality. On the other hand, to combine civil and military powers in the hands of the High Commissioner would be attended by distinct disadvantages and might give rise to misconception. Existing system seems on the whole to have worked smoothly and well and I can trust you to ensure its continued success. As regards your personal status, I think there will be no objection to your name being retained in the Army Active List for the present and you have been authorized to arrive at Cairo in [the] uniform of a British General. But you should bear in mind that the High Commissioner is a civil post and you should wear the uniform of a Minister in His Majesty's Diplomatic Service on all full dress occasions excepting those of Military Ceremonial. This was a practice to which Lord Kitchener conformed when he was Agent & Consul-General in Cairo.[27]

A copy of this telegram is filed in Wingate's papers at Durham. In the margins, in Wingate's own hand, is added an asterisk to the words 'High Commissioner' where they first occur in the document; it reads as follows:

*When the trouble broke out in Egypt in March 1919 – and R [eginald] W [ingate] was at home – he applied to return at once to his post but Gen. Sir E Allenby who was in Paris, was sent out as "Special High Com [missioner] and R W was kept at home "to advise" – Mr Balfour's teleprint to Sir R Wingate (dated Paris 20 March No 542) was as follows "Condition of affairs in Egypt requires prompt action and Allenby leaves Paris for Cairo tomorrow night. Prime Minister [Lloyd George] and I think that in addition to his military rank, he ought to be given complete civil authority, and he will be appointed Special High Com^m with supreme civil and military control. This makes no technical change in your position, but on this subject I am writing at length.
S[igne]d A. J. Balfour.[28]

Clearly, Wingate had been writing for posterity.

There were many who thought Wingate had been disgracefully treated, especially as he had been thrust into an appointment he had not sought and which, in the view of some, he had ably filled. Balfour tried to lay the blame at Curzon's door; at least he was honest in describing Wingate in a letter to the Lord Privy Seal as

A good fellow, and has been a very valuable and distinguished public servant. He gave specific advice on a difficult problem, warning us that if his advice was not followed, trouble would ensue. Thereupon we practically tell him that he is not the man most competent to deal with the situation thus created, and that somebody else must be put in his place! This, I take it, is the skeleton of the story and it is not one very easy to clothe in attractive flesh and blood. [29]

By December 1919 Wingate's sacking was public knowledge. At the end of the year he attended the funeral of Field Marshal Sir Evelyn Wood,[30] another of his former colleagues in the Sudan.

The year 1920 began on a lighter note. The Wingates were among the guests of Major William W. Carey at his Guernsey holiday home. A local newspaper intimated that 'Since his retiral as Sirdar of the Egyptian Army and later High Commissioner of Egypt, the distinguished general is spending most of his time at Dunbar'.[31] Carey, a golfing partner, resided at Seaholm in Church Street, Dunbar and was an old friend from Wingate's Sudan days. Behind that brief press statement is concealed the great personal loss Wingate was suffering. At least in July that year his family received yet another accolade: Lady Wingate was awarded the OBE by George V at an investiture ceremony in Holyrood Palace, Edinburgh on 3 July.[32] Then on 6 July 1920 Wingate received his baronetcy, being created First Baron Dunbar and Port Sudan. Denied the peerage he believed to be his due, he complained to his cousin, Sir Andrew 'Dan' Wingate, a long-serving Indian civil servant, that Curzon had personally countermanded the suggestion of a peerage. Wingate attributed this to the unpleasant interview he suffered at Curzon's hands in February 1919. In the end, after Allenby's appointment, the Lloyd George administration was implicitly convinced that, all along, Wingate had been right and Curzon wrong. It was small consolation to a broken man.

Three weeks later the Wingates suffered the loss of a Dunbar friend, Mrs Marrow, widow of his golfing partner Major Peter Marrow, at Belhaven Hill House.[33] In that same month the Wingates were visited by Rudolf von Slatin, 'Old Rowdy', of the Sudan years. It was their first meeting since the Great War but it was hardly an unqualified success; while the 'Sudanese Twins' were as friendly as ever, Lady Wingate was mildly hostile to the little Austrian. Her coolness was probably due to a mother's feelings at having lost her favourite son Malcolm for a cause in a war in which Slatin was on the opposing side.

Another matter which soured Wingate's relationship with the Foreign Office was the payment of his retirement pension. Throughout his career Wingate had been on the Active List of the British Army but he had been paid out of the Army Estimates Vote only during his few years as a subaltern. For most of his time in the Middle East, his salary was met by the Egyptian government except for the period 1917–19 when his salary came from the Foreign Office Vote. (Wingate held different ranks in the Egyptian and British Armies which accounts for the sometimes seemingly contradictory references to his rank made by the author.) On his retirement, the British government offered him £600 a year, which he refused to accept, rightly considering it a paltry sum for all his years of distinguished service. Others took up his case, including George V – discreetly, as he was a constitutional monarch who could not intervene directly. This shameful episode was at last resolved by the intervention in 1922 of the Army Council; surprisingly, Lord Curzon's suggestion that Wingate should receive a pension equivalent to that of a Minister in the Diplomatic Service was adopted. Wingate was awarded £1,300 a year, £100 short of the award a General in the British Army with the same length of service could have expected. Did Curzon support Wingate's award out of conscience? Government officials are not usually noted for their magnanimity towards superannuated colleagues.

Surprisingly – or perhaps not – Wingate had always skirted the fringes of bankruptcy, or at least near insolvency, because of a lifestyle to which he had grown accustomed since 1900 as Governor General of the Sudan. In 1920 he attempted to repair his parlous financial situation by applying for a company directorship in Burmah Oil, Persia, one of many applications which were politely turned down. Wingate then applied for a seat on the Board of the Suez Canal Company – an appointment in the gift of Prime Minister Lloyd George, who gave it to his Private Secretary as mentioned earlier. Then Wingate asked to be considered for an ambassadorship in Constantinople, an Indian Governorship and then Governor of Gibraltar; in this last application, the then Colonial Secretary, Winston Churchill, offered no hope of success.

In 1920–21 the Wingates spent most of the autumn, winter and spring in London, returning to Dunbar in May 1921, where they were guests of the Duke of Roxburghe at a soiree held at their country seat of Broxmouth House, a mile east of Dunbar. This occurred on the night of 16 May. Perhaps it was common knowledge that Knockenhair would be unoccupied that night, as the property was burgled. It appears that eight soldiers stationed at Castlepark Barracks, Dunbar, committed the offence. A local newspaper gave a detailed account of the theft of several valuable articles which included the following:

A gold pencil case, a gold necklace, three medals, a gold ring, two silver boxes, a gold-mounted box, a silver paper knife, a silver tray, a silver trowel [probably that used by Wingate's daughter Victoria when she laid the foundation stone of Knockenhair in November 1907] a silver waist-belt, an Oriental cup, a silver shield, silver inkstand, an Egyptian gold sovereign, sets of Abyssinian and Egyptian coins and seven Dervish dollars.

The culprits were caught, tried and sentenced but remarkably lenient sentences of between two and eight months were imposed.[34]

In 1921 the Great War, with its horrific casualties, was kept fresh in the public mind of every city, town, village and hamlet in the United Kingdom, each with its memorial to the fallen. Most communities followed the example of the London Cenotaph (Greek for *empty tomb*), designed and erected by Sir Edward Landseer Lutyens and unveiled by George V on Armistice Day 1920. In Dunbar a War Memorial Committee was formed with the remit of creating a monument to the twelve officers, 108 Other Ranks and one woman (Sister Violet Fraser, a nurse in Bosnia) from the parish and burgh of Dunbar who gave their lives. The memorial was erected in 1921; it was originally situated on the clifftop promontory at the entrance to the West Promenade, and later moved to its present site in Bayswell Park. It is an impressive monument; surmounted by a Celtic cross, it was constructed by local builder and stonemason, George Cunningham, whose descendants are personal friends of the author. Consisting of a broad base of local Catcraig stone and Aberdeen granite, the monument is 16 feet high and dominates the park, overlooking the North Sea. On Sunday, 3 July 1921, Reginald Wingate unveiled the memorial and made the following brief but moving address:

In the faith of Jesus Christ, I unveil this memorial cross to the glory of God and in proud and loving memory of those of the burgh and parish of Dunbar who gave their lives in the Great War 1914–1918.

He then read out the beautiful and indescribably poignant lines from Laurence Binyon's 1914 poem *For the Fallen* which had won immediate recognition as the ultimate expression of the grief of an entire generation affected by the war: *At the going down of the sun and in the morning, we will remember them*. The names of the fallen were then read out;[35] Wingate, the steadfast gentleman, probably did not pause when he came to that of his younger son, Major Malcolm Roy Wingate, DSO, MC and Croix de Guerre, Royal Engineers.

In the immediate post-war years the Wingates filled some of their time officiating at public events in Dunbar's social calendar. Wingate was of course a keen member of Dunbar Golf Club and President of the local British Legion & Comrades' Club and the Royal National Lifeboat Institution. He sponsored Dunbar Rugby Club, Dunbar Swimming Club, taking part in gala events at the (today demolished) open-air swimming pool where he usually judged the fancy dress parade. He presented a Sirdar Medal to the golf club and a competitive Swimming Medal, both of which are competed for to this day. One notable event was the visit of a team of New Zealand bowlers, whom Wingate was invited to welcome as guests of the local bowling club. No doubt he paid tribute to the thousands of Australians and New Zealanders – the Anzacs – who had fallen in the Gallipoli Campaign of 1915. Strangely – or perhaps understandably – he never stood as a candidate in Burgh Council elections, possibly because he had endured enough of public service to last the rest of his life.

During 1921 the Wingates spent most of May in London, arriving back in Dunbar in early June; Wingate had been ill but was now reported as being 'well'.[36] In July he attended the funeral of Lord Balfour of Burleigh in Alloa.[37] Wingate's association with Alexander Hugh Bruce of Kennet, 6th Lord Balfour of Burleigh, may have been through Balfour's son, George Gordon Bruce. It is thought that Wingate had known George, a captain in the Argyll and Sutherland Highlanders in the Boer War. George Bruce subsequently served in the Egyptian Army from 1910 to 1914 and was stationed in the Sudan in 1912, where he would have met Wingate.

In November Wingate went to Manchester to inspect the 7th Manchester Regiment, of which he had been Honorary Colonel since his Sudan days. He took the salute at the march-past, recalling that the battalion had entered Khartoum in October 1914 wearing heavy clothing more suited to a chilly European climate. He remarked that, despite the oppressive Sudanese heat, not a single Tommy fell out of parade. At that cold autumn Armistice Day parade in Manchester, 10,000 Territorials and war veterans marched past the saluting base.[38]

Without doubt, the Wingates followed events in Egypt and the Sudan for many years, especially from 1922 onwards. Wingate felt bitter for a long time and while he never lived to see the 1956 Suez Crisis, had he been alive, he would have been entitled to say 'I told you so nearly forty years ago'. The lack of understanding of the Egyptian situation at senior political levels in the British government of Wingate's day explains to some degree how Egypt came to play a troublesome role in the British Empire after the Great War. Allenby, apprehensive of further rioting in Cairo, was forced to deport Zaghlul Pasha once again. His concern was such that he went to London in February 1922 to establish the extent of his power and jurisdiction under the British Protectorate agreement. Wingate had done the very same three years earlier; like him, Allenby was fobbed off with vague responses time and time again. But Allenby was a Field Marshal and peer of the realm, a public hero in the same class as Kitchener and rightly believed that he possessed more clout than Wingate and therefore was entitled to an unequivocal answer to his requests. In exasperation, he laid a letter of resignation on the tables of his four principal advisers, bluntly informing Lord Curzon and Lloyd George that they would have to make up their minds regarding Egypt's future administration. He called their bluff; on 28 February 1922 the government rescinded the Protectorate, replacing it with a declaration which recognized the sovereignty and independence of Egypt, subject to certain conditions. The conditions were the security of imperial communications, especially the canal, defence, protection of foreign interests and minorities and of the Sudan; these were not unreasonable demands. On 15 March 1922 the Sultan was elevated to the position of King Fu'ad of Egypt, a constitutional monarch in the mode of George V but Egyptian constitutional monarchy would prove as elusive as Egyptian independence. A political struggle would continue between the three main protagonists – King Fu'ad, the Wafd and the British government. This state of affairs was only finally resolved by Colonel Gamal Abd-el Nasser, the leader of a group of young army officers who toppled the Egyptian monarchy in 1952.

Many in Egypt felt that the country was on the road to freedom and Wingate must have derived some comfort from the fact, illusory though it was. Perhaps he recalled the statement made at the Peace Conference in 1919 which praised him – albeit in a low key – for his sterling work in the Sudan: 'The Governor Generalship of Sir R Wingate [sic] is one of the richest pages in the history of British rule over backward races.' How patronizing that seems today to Wingate, but even more so to the 'backward races'.

Egypt's position in 1922 was hardly one of peace and prosperity. Over the next three years events there would complicate relations with the British government. Wingate's evidence to the Milner Commission of 1919–20 had advised its members on the future of the Sudan, which was yoked to Egypt. In his memorandum, Wingate defined the relationship between the two countries – the defence of the Sudan and its balance of payments – which would not improve for many years. Wingate also highlighted the importance of the Upper Nile Valley and the cultural, linguistic, religious and economic ties which bound the two countries. And, true to his knowledge of the region, he prophesied that the cry would be 'Sudan for the Sudanese', a view he wholly endorsed through his connections with Sudan's Military College and the Gordon Memorial College in Khartoum.

Enter Sir Lee Stack, whom Wingate had recommended as his temporary replacement in the Sudan in 1916; Stack faced different problems in 1922, after Egypt had gained a measure of independence. He drafted a long memorandum – almost a carbon copy of Wingate's of 1920 – pointing out Britain's responsibilities in relation to the future of the Sudan and the dangers posed by an independent Egypt. In 1924 Zaghlul Pasha was Prime Minister of Egypt, his Nationalist Party enjoying a comfortable majority in the Egyptian parliament. Although it is difficult to prove, Zaghlul appears to have ordered the assassination of Stack in 1924. Why? Perhaps Stack had shown less sympathy to the Sudanese population – and by extension, to that of Egypt – than Wingate. Viscount Allenby responded to the murder of Stack by delivering an ultimatum to Zaghlul, demanding an apology for the murder and the arrest of those responsible. Allenby shared much of Oliver Cromwell's characteristics; he sought not only 'the heads of the assassins' but also the cessation of public riots against British rule. He demanded a fine of £500,000 be paid to the British government, warning that failure to comply with these demands would bring 'retribution'. The retribution, never specified, was enough to encourage Zaghlul Pasha to resign and be replaced by a moderate eager to placate Allenby.

Egypt apart, the Sudan gradually achieved self-government. In 1924 it happily became a British Mandated territory. It would be many years before the Sudanese would choose Egypt as its protector. Today, the Sudan is a country devastated by drought, famine, civil war and unrest; the province of Darfur in particular is a hotbed of insurrection. The country is in tragic turmoil, with corruption and barbarism rife among its rulers. Were he alive today, Wingate would be deeply disappointed by the current regime.

Ultimately, Wingate had sacrificed himself to the wolves of Whitehall. His assessment of the political situation in Egypt had been accurate in 1919 even though he knew the strength of Whitehall's opposition to his recommendations and the Foreign Office's power to overrule him. So why had he persisted with what amounted to professional suicide? Perhaps this is best answered by his approach, virtues and a natural inclination to tell the truth; Wingate was a man who tempered his idealism with a sense of honour and a desire for justice, which had their roots in the Celtic culture of his native Scotland. He cannot be accused of naivety, nor of being some twentieth century Don Quixote on a crusade. Many who came into contact with Wingate in his professional and private life were impressed by him; he was a gentleman through and through, a man who won hearts and minds with his simplicity, courtesy, loyalty, warmth and sincerity. He made friends for life but such men do not often carry much weight in the corridors of power in Whitehall, where the mirrors of bureaucracy can distort images. Like T. E. Lawrence, Wingate was in a way a casualty of his own success.

Notes

1. *Wingate of the Sudan*, RELW.
2. *Ibid.*
3. *Ibid.*
4. Wingate to Grahame, 6 November 1918, WP 170/3, SAD, DU.
5. *Wingate of the Sudan.*
6. *The Sirdar*, Daly.
7. *Seven Pillars of Wisdom*, p. 683.
8. FO to Wingate, 2 December 1918, WP 237/10, SAD, DU.
9. Graham to Wingate, 19 January, 1919, WP 177/2, SAD, DU.
10. Balfour to Wingate, 1 January, 1919, WP 237/10, SAD, DU.
11. *The Sirdar.*
12. *Wingate of the Sudan.*
13. Balfour to Wingate, 20 March 1919, WP 237/2, SAD, DU.
14. *The Sirdar.*
15. Wingate to Grenfell, 6 April 1919, WP 151/4, SAD, DU.
16. *HC*, 18 July 1919.
17. *Ibid.*
18. *Ibid.*, 8 August 1919.
19. *Ibid.*, 15 August 1919.
20. *Ibid.*
21. *Ibid.*

22. *Not in the Limelight*, RELW.
23. *British Pro-Consuls in Egypt 1914–29; the Challenge of Nationalism*, Long.
24. *HA*, 8 August 1919.
25. *Ibid.*, 24 October 1919.
26. Curzon to Wingate, 2 October 1919, WP 238/1, SAD, DU.
27. Balfour to Wingate, 15 December 1919, WP 160/5, SAD, DU.
28. *Ibid.*
29. Letter dated 9 June 1919, *Chatham House*, Kedourie.
30. *HA*, 12 December 1919.
31. *Ibid.*, 13 February 1920.
32. *Ibid.*, 9 July 1920.
33. *Ibid.*, 30 July 1920.
34. *HC*, 24 June 1921.
35. *Ibid.*, 8 July 1921.
36. *HA*, 3 June 1921.
37. *Ibid.*, 15 July 1921.
38. *HC*, 25 November 1921.

Chapter 9

Private Citizen and Businessman (1922–1929)

After his ignominious dismissal from public service Wingate was obliged to seek an alternative career in business. When his public career came to an end he was treated with respectful, if distant, politeness by subsequent British governments and consulted occasionally on Sudanese – but never on Egyptian – matters. There should have been ample opportunities open to a man of sixty-one years who had spent most of his adult life in the service of his country, first in the Army, then in colonial administration. Others in his position were usually awarded directorships, which were in the gift of the government, in what today would be called quangos, or quasi-autonomous non-governmental bodies. In 1921 his main source of income was an Army pension of £1,300 a year, a comfortable enough sum for the time, allowing him to maintain his mansion at Knockenhair and enjoy his golf on Dunbar's East Links course. After a stint as Captain of the Dunbar Club in 1904 and 1905, he continued to play until old age and ill health prevented him. But time lay heavily on his hands.

It may come as a surprise to the young, modern mind that the end of the Great War came as a great shock to the privileged young men of Britain – sons of aristocrats and minor titled classes who had joined elite regiments. Their lives radically altered in 1914. Many were students at Oxford and Cambridge with careers mapped out for them by their parents. After four years of bloody trench warfare, those who survived and who had hereditary family pedigrees were abruptly thrown on the heap of the unemployed. However, coming from privileged backgrounds, they were spared the indignity of selling bootlaces and matches on street corners. At least Wingate did not suffer the same fate but knew that it was unlikely he would remain on the Army Active List. The dictates of financial necessity drove him into a business career at an age when many would have been looking forward to comfortable retirement.

In 1921 the Princess Royal, Louise, Duchess of Fife, invited Wingate to fill a vacancy on the Board of Trustees for her Fife estates, a position he would occupy until 1936. By all accounts the appointment was tedious, as trusteeships invariably are, being involved with the trivia and minutiae of estate life. At least there were some lighter moments; in 1927 Princess Louise was the

Wingates' guest at Knockenhair, ostensibly to attend the opening of the new Cottage Hospital in East Links Road, Dunbar which had replaced the Victoria Harbour Battery Isolation Hospital for contagious diseases. The formal opening was performed by the Duchess of York – hence its name, York House. Among the guests that day were Sir Reginald and Lady Wingate and their daughter Victoria (Mrs Henry Dane), Mrs Hay of Belton, president of the hospital, and the vice-president, ex-provost Robert Aitken, a Dunbar High Street chemist.

In 1924–25 Wingate's friends made a last ditch attempt to win a peerage for him. The Sennar Dam on the Blue Nile would be opened the following year, realizing Wingate's and others' dream to irrigate the Gezira Plain south of Khartoum. This enterprise alone might have ensured his elevation to the Lords but the government stood firm. Wingate was invited to the opening ceremony inaugurating the dam but declined, pleading pressure of business.

Wingate never completely severed his association with the British Army; he was appointed a Colonel Commandant of the Royal Artillery, his old regiment; he was also Honorary Colonel of the 7th Battalion the Manchester Regiment which had served under him during the Great War.

At Wingate's age, most men might have looked forward to retirement, devoting the remainder of their lives to hobbies. Wingate was not satisfied with merely golf or his inveterate love of detective novels. His transition from public servant to private citizen could not have been easy; after a lifetime of imperial service with its almost regal trappings and sybaritic lifestyle, he must have been easily bored.

In February 1922 Wingate took great pleasure in announcing the forth-coming marriage of his only daughter, Victoria, to Captain Henry Dane;[1] sadly, Captain Dane would die in a Japanese prisoner-of-war camp in 1943. In the same month, the local newspaper announced that Wingate had been appointed Honorary Colonel of 2nd (Lowland) Medium Brigade,* Royal Garrison Artillery (TA).[2] His daughter's wedding took place in London on 6 March. Among the guests were Sir Henry and Lady McMahon, Princess Maud (the future Queen of Norway), General Sir Archibald Hunter and Lady Hunter, along with Lady Frances Balfour, A. J. Balfour's sister. Victoria Wingate's five bridesmaids included Alison Marrow of Belhaven Hill, a friend of the Wingate children in Dunbar during the 1900s.

In May 1922 Wingate unveiled a roll of honour dedicated to 137 Brethren connected with Dunbar Castle Lodge No 75, some of whom had given their lives in the Great War.[3] At the close of the ceremony he presented the Lodge with an ancient masonic relic discovered in Egypt. About a week later he presided over a meeting of the Comrades Club in the Assembly Rooms in Church Street, Dunbar; at the meeting, it was proposed that the Club be affiliated to the British Legion. Afterwards he and Lady Wingate took a summer holiday in the south of France, remaining there until late July.[4] At

*Redesignated as 57th (Lowland) Medium Brigade in 1921.

this time he was filling his days in the social circuits in England and Scotland, as well as entering the business world of the City. In August he inspected 57th Lowland Brigade at their summer camp at Buddon Ness, near Broughty Ferry.[5] In his capacity as President of the Dunbar branch of the British Legion, he attended the Armistice Day Memorial Service at the recently inaugurated war memorial on the West Promenade.[6] In London Wingate had joined an 'old boy' network which would bring him added financial rewards in due course. Life in the City was reasonably comfortable; the hectic pace of the modern businessman, with its long, exhausting hours chained to a desk or jet-setting all over the world was virtually unknown to men of Wingate's generation. He spent a good deal of time in the fashionable and exclusive London private clubs, especially the two of which he was a member, the Army & Navy Club and the British Empire Club.

It was possibly while dining in one of these clubs that Wingate had an unexpected stroke of luck. He met a mining engineer, Robert Williams, who had discovered and developed extensive copper fields in Katanga in the Belgian Congo. Williams had been hired by the Belgian government and invited Wingate to join the Board of Management, the *Board de Union Minière du Haut Katanga*. (The Company was officially known as the Rhodesia–Katanga Junction Railway and Mining Co.) Other offers came from the African Railways Finance Company; the British (Non-Ferrous) Mining Corporation and the Allihien Copper Mines Ltd and membership of the Benguela Railway Company which involved annual trips to its headquarters in Lisbon. (For some unspecified reason, possibly on health grounds, Wingate declined a trip to Angola in the Belgian Congo for the official opening of the Benguela Railway line in 1929.) In December 1922 the local newspaper reported that Wingate had been appointed chairman of the British mining company Tanganyikan Concessions Ltd, which had a substantial stake in the Congo Free State.[7] In 1921 the output of copper from the territory had been 30,000 tons and there were commercially-viable deposits of gold, tin and iron in the 200-square-mile area. The company would further flourish under Wingate's chairmanship.

During the period December 1922 to July 1923, apart from a weekend in Dunbar in March, the Wingates spent most of the winter and spring seasons in London, meeting friends and attending social functions. Wingate was also visiting the Continent, partly on business in Brussels, partly on pleasure to visit his old friend Rudolph von Slatin. The Wingates also took the annual 'cure' in one of the spa towns in the south of France, possibly Vichy. Despite his fall from grace Wingate and his wife still moved in the upper stratum of society. For example, in May 1923, the Wingates were the guests of the Duke of York – the future George VI – and his wife-to-be, Lady Elizabeth Bowes-Lyon, at Buckingham Palace on the eve of their wedding; they were also among the wedding guests attending the ceremony at Westminster Abbey the following day.[8]

From 1919 until 1940 the Wingates' London residence was a small flat in Queen Anne's Mansions, a property they had unsuccessfully tried to sell in 1921; the flat was destroyed during the London Blitz. During their stay they had Sir John – later Lord – Reith, Director General of the newly-formed British Broadcasting Corporation as a neighbour. It is not known if the two Scotsmen ever met.

The social round continued; Wingate was a guest at the Egyptian Army annual dinner held on 8 July 1923, after which the Wingates attended Prime Minister Stanley Baldwin's garden party on 12 July.[9] Such was the flurry of social events that summer in London that the Wingates were unable to return to Dunbar until late July.[10] In August he returned to London to be re-elected chairman of the increasingly prosperous Tanganyikan Concessions Ltd. Addressing the shareholders at a dinner, Wingate remarked that he had delivered the *coup de grace* to the notorious Khalifa in the Sudan twenty-three years before, in November 1899. He then went on to describe the creation of the Gezira Scheme – not by name – which he had personally planned and hoped would produce a viable commercial cotton crop to boost the Sudanese economy. He also spoke of the Sennar Dam – again not by name – then under construction, expressing the hope that Tanganyikan Concessions Ltd would in time become involved in the production of cotton.[11]

In the autumn Wingate was lionized in the American magazine *Standard Union*, published in Brooklyn, New York. According to the article, the Brooklyn Library had recently received copies of his two books on the history of the Sudan.[12] Thus were his exploits brought to a whole new range of readers. In November he took part in the now annual Armistice Day parade to the Cenotaph in London, representing the Dunbar branch of the British Legion. After that the Wingates were able to enjoy a holiday in Lisbon, returning to London for the winter season.

As for the government, then as now, it had within its gift several director-ships. Wingate lobbied Whitehall on several occasions, offering his services to various government-sponsored regulatory bodies without success. He must have felt an outcast, even if he maintained and enjoyed a wide circle of friends and influential people.

In 1924 Wingate represented the Dunbar and Skateraw stations at the centenary celebration of the founding of the Royal National Lifeboat Institution at a dinner held in the Mansion House, London and presided over by HRH the Prince of Wales.[13] By now he was heavily involved in his expanding business interests. In April 1925 he presided over the annual general meeting of Tanganyikan Concessions Ltd which was now worth £5.5 million (£154 million in today's money) in assets. He was re-appointed chairman in 1926, so clearly his contribution had been considerable; the company would continue to prosper for many years.

Wingate's membership of the board of the Belgian Congo Mining Company required him to live in London for a considerable part of each year. In 1925 he was only able to spend a few days with Lady Wingate at

Knockenhair. In June that year he was remembered in the late Lord Grenfell's will, one of several army officers who had served under Grenfell as Sirdar and Governor General of the Sudan in 1886, then Commander in Chief of British Army forces in Malta and in Ireland. Wingate's inheritance was the volume known as Grenfell's *Mementoes*. In August that year the Wingates were the guests of Princess Maud and Lord Carnegie at Mar Lodge, Aberdeenshire for the shooting season.[14] The Wingates returned to Dunbar in early autumn but left Knockenhair for London almost immediately in October. On 10 December 1925 Reginald attended the dedication ceremony for the Kitchener Memorial Chapel in St Paul's Cathedral.[15]

The Wingates remained in London until the early summer of 1926, the year he received a glowing tribute in the *African World*, a magazine which extolled his success as Governor General of the Sudan. The occasion was the official opening in January that year of the Sennar Dam at Marwar, Egypt and the Gezira Scheme which would produce cotton in commercial quantities and thus contribute to the Sudanese balance of payments. The then serving Governor General, Sir Geoffrey Archer, paid tribute to Wingate for his forward thinking in the creation of both dam and cotton-growing scheme. As a result Wingate was subsequently awarded the gold medal of the Royal African Society for these initiatives and also the vice-presidency of the Gordon Memorial College in Khartoum in 1927. However, in late August 1926, the Wingates returned to Dunbar after yet another visit to the Princess Royal at Mar Lodge, no doubt for the shooting season.[16]

By 1926 the Wingates had established a regime of spending late autumn and winter in London, visiting the Continent in spring and spending the summer and early autumn at Knockenhair. In March 1928 Wingate was one of six pallbearers of the rank of general in the British Army who, in full-dress uniform, carried the coffin of General Sir John G. Maxwell, who had been present on the field of Omdurman in 1898 and who, in 1909, had been tipped as Wingate's successor as Governor General of the Sudan.[17]

In 1929 Wingate presided over the first Sudan Dinner Club which he attended regularly thereafter. At the end of the year Wingate was appointed Deputy Lord Lieutenant of the County of Haddington, the last public office he would hold. In 1930 he declined an invitation to meet a delegation from Egypt and Arabia, having disassociated himself from Egyptian affairs for good. He had been happiest in the Sudan where he had achieved much in his dual roles of Governor General and Sirdar.

Now in his late sixties, Wingate was experiencing the inevitable consequences of longevity, not just in terms of failing health. More and more of his contemporaries were passing away and he was constantly attending the funerals of old friends and Army colleagues. On 24 May 1929 he was present at the memorial service held in St Margaret's Chapel, Westminster, for Lord Rosebery, the former Foreign Secretary and Prime Minister.[18] St Margaret's Chapel had become familiar to Wingate, it being the chosen venue to celebrate the lives of men and women who had served the British Empire.

Rosebery had been a particular friend as Foreign Secretary during the years of Dervish domination in the Sudan between 1892 and 1894, then Prime Minister from 1894 to 1895, crucial years for Kitchener and Wingate in the reconquest of the Sudan. Perhaps with Rosebery's passing, Wingate sensed that a page of history – one with his own name inscribed upon it – had been turned.

Notes

1. *HC*, 24 February 1922.
2. *Ibid.*
2. *Ibid.*, 5 May 1922.
4. *HA*, 7 and 23 July 1922.
5. *Ibid.*, 5 August 1922.
6. *HC*, 17 November 1922.
7. *HA*, 8 December 1922.
8. *HC*, 4 May 1923.
9. *Ibid.*, 13 July 1923.
10. *Ibid.*, 3 August 1923.
11. *Ibid.*, 17 August 1923.
12. *Ibid.*, 19 October 1923.
13. *Ibid.*, 14 March 1924.
14. *Ibid.*, 21 August 1925.
15. *Ibid.*, 18 December 1925.
16. *Ibid.*, 27 August 1926.
17. *HC*, 22 March 1928.
18. *Ibid.*, 31 May 1929.

Chapter 10

Orde Wingate: A Family Affair

Francis Reginald Wingate is often confused with Orde Charles Wingate, the son of his cousin, Colonel George Wingate, one of several Scottish Wingates to serve in India and live much of their life in England. Although Reginald and Orde met occasionally in London when the former's business interests and the latter's army leaves coincided, much of their contact was conducted through correspondence, most of which concerned Orde Wingate's military career. For his part, Reginald Wingate, or 'Cousin Rex' as he was known to Orde and his siblings in Colonel George's family, used his considerable influence and contacts in the Establishment to further his great-cousin's career in the British Army. (Throughout this chapter, Reginald Wingate is referred to as Cousin Rex, or Rex Wingate, in order to distinguish him from his younger kinsman.)

Born on 26 February 1903 in Naini Tal in the United Provinces of North India, Orde Charles Wingate was the third child and first son of Colonel George Wingate (19th Foot, later The Green Howards, and India Staff Corps) and his wife Ethel Stanley, daughter of Captain Charles Orde-Browne, Royal Horse Artillery, a man who sprang from a Gloucestershire family with a long tradition of military service. Orde Wingate appears to have enjoyed a happy childhood, although he inherited the brooding temperament of his father. Throughout his childhood and youth Orde displayed no marked proficiency, no unusually intellectual alertness, no sign of exceptional gifts. He was not a particularly outstanding scholar, a fact which sometimes prefigures the career of those destined for greater things. Those who enjoy fame in adult life are often found to have been educationally limited in their formative years. Many examples of this are scattered throughout history; perhaps it is best illustrated in the case of John Muir of Dunbar, the father of conservation. Muir was an average student at school but used his eyes and let the environment he loved as a boy enter and inform his mind in a way no teacher could. The John Muirs and Orde Wingates of the world rise to the top despite their lack of educational achievements, a fact sometimes lost on the teaching profession.

One or two of Orde Wingate's contemporaries at school recalled him as a dour, unsociable and unlikeable student who did not fit the accepted mould of the English private school. In his teenage years at Charterhouse he joined the Officers' Training Corps, obtaining the requisite certificate to enable him to enlist in the Army. After leaving Charterhouse he followed Rex Wingate's footsteps by entering the Royal Military Academy at Woolwich ('The Shop') as a Gentleman Cadet, or Cadet Officer, in 1921. It is more than likely that Cousin Rex had not yet met his great-cousin, nor had they corresponded at that time. Orde passed out of Woolwich placed fifty-ninth out of seventy cadets in his intake, hardly an auspicious beginning. As a result of his dismal showing in the exam, he was gazetted as subaltern in the Royal Garrison Artillery at Larkhill, Salisbury Plain, a somewhat ignominious posting. Those students who excelled were posted to more prestigious units of the British Army.

The Army which Orde Wingate joined in 1923 hardly differed in tone – if not in armaments – from that in which his father, Colonel George Wingate, and Cousin Rex Wingate had served during the last two decades of the nineteenth century. Rex Wingate would offer invaluable support through his Army contacts in furthering his young kinsman's military career.

It was not until 1924 that Cousin Rex and Orde began a correspondence that would last for the next two decades, ending only with Orde's death in 1944 at the age of forty-one. As far as can be established, they first met face-to-face in 1927 in London, where Rex Wingate was residing at Queen Anne's Mansions. One can but speculate on the older man's initial impressions of his younger relative; perhaps he saw something of T. E. Lawrence in him. By an irony of fate, Lawrence and Orde Wingate were distant cousins; Orde's great-great grandmother Maria Chapman was the sister of Thomas Chapman, an Anglo-Irish baronet and Lawrence's father. Maria Chapman married Thomas Browne, from whom Orde's mother Ethel Orde-Browne descended. T. E. Lawrence and Orde Wingate were not only connected by blood but possessed similar characteristics. Even more ironic was the fact that Rex Wingate knew both men. It is perhaps appropriate here to remind ourselves of Lawrence's background, as Orde Wingate would repeatedly denigrate his distant kinsman during his professional life.

Thomas Edward Lawrence was born in Tremadoc, Gwynedd, in North Wales, a fact which assured him a place at the Welsh-only Jesus College, Oxford. Unlike Orde Wingate, Lawrence was illegitimate, a stigma which undermined his confidence and embittered him all his days; Lawrence never came to terms with the circumstances of his birth. His father, Sir Thomas Chapman, was of Anglo-Irish stock, belonging to a family that had owned a substantial house and many acres of land in County Westmeath. Sir Thomas was something of a *roué*; he had an affair with one of the family servants, reputedly a governess who presumably was dismissed from service by Chapman's cuckolded wife, Edith. A second governess, the Scots-born Sarah Junner, subsequently became his mistress and, this time, Chapman did the honourable thing, absconding with her to Wales and changing his name to Lawrence. In the process he renounced his title. T. E. Lawrence was the first of five sons born to the 'Lawrences' who never married as Lady Edith Chapman refused to grant her wayward husband a divorce. When Lawrence learnt of his beginnings, he regarded himself a tainted outcast for the rest of his life.

Orde Wingate had much in common with his distant relative, although he was more virile and less unstable than Lawrence. Both Orde and Lawrence were possessed of impressive talents; such men rarely grow up in an atmosphere of what psychologists would describe as 'normal'. The childhoods of men of destiny tend to fall into two categories; one is marked by precocious behaviour, where the child prodigy astonishes and often dismays his elders with a premature display of distinctive personal qualities; Johann Wolfgang Amadeus Mozart falls into the first category. The second type is often a shy, withdrawn loner whose destiny is hidden from view, lying dormant until adulthood. Lawrence and Orde Wingate belong in the second category.

Both men were possessed of exceptional talents; they also shared certain physical characteristics and psychological traits. They had penetrating blue eyes and both had the unique gift of inspiring and leading others. In adult life their attitude to their military careers was also similar; they adopted conventional military uniforms only reluctantly, or when making grudging concessions to the British Army when forced to wear them, doing so untidily. They both eschewed army traditions and were regarded as misfits which marked them as irregular, or unorthodox, soldiers. Both were touched with genius and became experts in guerrilla warfare – Lawrence in Arabia and Orde in Palestine, Abyssinia and, finally, Burma during the Second World War. Men of similar dispositions sometimes disagree with, and dislike each other. Lawrence championed the cause of his Arabs, first against the Turks in battle, then against predatory European powers. Orde Wingate supported the Jewish colonists against the Arabs in the years following the Balfour Declaration of 1917 and the Paris Peace Conference which endorsed Balfour's plan for Jewish settlement in Palestine. This alone would have ensured hostility between the two men had they met. It is not known whether Lawrence ever made any direct comment on the Jewish question; by the time Orde Wingate declared himself for the Jews, Lawrence was dead. However, we know that Orde not only avidly studied the books and correspondence of T. E. Lawrence but also literature written about him before and after his death. Orde was scathing in his criticism of his distant relative, both as soldier and private person. He vehemently denounced Lawrence's military claims, believing the achievements to be flawed and fallacious and that he had overstated the Arabs' contribution to the defeat of Turkey in Saudi Arabia. He deplored the cult and mystique surrounding Lawrence during and after the war, largely created by Lawrence himself. Modern historians tend to agree with Orde Wingate's view; Lawrence was a flawed genius who did not hesitate to tell downright lies or half-truths when it suited his purpose.

Whether he recognized or admitted it, Orde, like Lawrence, was driven by a burning sense of mission. After the Great War Lawrence sought anonymity, adopting two aliases and serving as a lowly other ranker in the Tank Corps, then the RAF. His desire for obscurity undoubtedly stemmed from a sense of failure, lack of self esteem and, inevitably, even his illegitimacy. These self-indulgent lapses into anonymity – perhaps pseudonymity would be more apt – were short lived however; eventually, Lawrence's sense of self-importance would drive him to reveal his true identity, usually to an acquaintance in the barracks. Both he and Orde Wingate desired to be somebody, neither being content to remain a time-serving army officer in the conventional sense. The difference between them was that, while Lawrence professed a craving to escape from the world, Wingate was, in his own view, often fenced in by army bureaucracy which vexed and fretted him.

Orde Wingate's intense dislike of Lawrence was also personal; during one of his visits to Cousin Rex, the latter revealed the facts of Lawrence's illegitimacy and that he and Orde were distantly related. As a result Orde disliked the man even more. Nor did he care for the nickname given to him during his support for the Palestine Jewish settlers – 'Lawrence of Judea'. This sobriquet, coined by journalists and fellow officers, often provoked him to violent outbursts. His prejudice towards Lawrence was no more bitterly expressed than when he described him as 'that unfortunate charlatan' and referred to *Seven Pillars of Wisdom* as 'that unfortunate masterpiece'. As far as Orde Wingate was concerned, Lawrence had untruthfully represented the Arab, making him seem an almost mythical being; for his part, Orde Wingate considered the Arab 'lazy, ignorant, feckless, and without being particularly cowardly, sees no point in losing his life'. Lawrence would have vehemently disagreed with this view, even if it bears a ring of truth. Orde Wingate confessed that he harboured no prejudices against the Arabs; his criticism of them dates from the 1930s, when he began to take an interest in the plight of Jewish settlers in Palestine. He was impressed by Jewish industriousness, their successful transformation of desert into productive land; besides, he had a broad religious streak, believing that in Palestine the 'wandering Jew' had come home at last. It must be remembered that in the first fifteen years after the Balfour Declaration of 1917 – which Cousin Rex had opposed – Jewish emigrants from Britain and Europe had been but a trickle; by 1935, the trickle had become a flood when the Nazi regime began widespread persecution of the Jews. However, almost from the outset, Jewish settlers were subjected to Arab terrorist attacks.

Whatever their differences in opinion on Lawrence and his beloved Arabs, Orde Wingate was on cordial terms with Cousin Rex from their first meeting. For his part, Rex was either motivated, or bound by, family ties to champion the progress of the younger man. He came to Orde's rescue on several occasions during the latter's career in the Sudan, Libya, Palestine and Abyssinia. Rex Wingate may be rightly accused of favouritism to Orde and giving him unfair advantages over his contemporaries; the world that the elder Wingate had known and served in was rapidly disappearing, the British Empire was teetering and would finally collapse when India gained independence in 1947. Perhaps Rex Wingate saw in his younger relative a means to exact revenge on other servants of that Empire which he felt he had loyally served but who had treated him shabbily.

As we saw, the two Wingates met for the first time in London, in March 1927, when Rex Wingate was on City business; perhaps he invited young Orde to lunch or dinner to one of his clubs – the Army & Navy Club or the British Empire Club. Their first meeting was fruitful; the younger man confided in his famous and still influential relative from the outset. Orde Wingate informed Rex that his plan was to gain qualifications to enable him to become an army interpreter in Arabic. Rex Wingate strongly advised him to continue his attendance at the London School of Oriental Studies which he duly did, with the agreement of the War Office. Rex urged him to polish his Arabic in Egypt and the Sudan and recommended that he apply for a posting to one of these countries. After all, the family name was still a byword in that part of the Middle East and Rex Wingate intended to milk it for all it was worth. Initially, the plan foundered. After passing his examination with flying colours in March 1927, Orde failed to obtain the necessary leave to travel to the Sudan; his commanding officer considered him too young and inexperienced. Orde, the indifferent scholar at Charterhouse, had proven his worth at the School of Oriental Studies. He had worked hard, voraciously devouring books on Arabic, passing his exam with almost casual ease and feeling he had earned an overseas posting which would enable him to further his knowledge.

After intervention by Cousin Rex, Orde's second application for leave in June 1927 was successful. In September 1927 the young man spent a few days with Cousin Rex and Lady Wingate at Knockenhair, Dunbar; the visit appears to have been the only occasion he came to Scotland, even if he was proud of his Scottish origins. Perhaps as he viewed the blue, misty Lammermuir Hills from the lofty eminence of Knockenhair, Orde Wingate sensed that his future career was assured, supported by his relative. The two men may have sat in the draughty library overlooking the North Sea one evening, discussing the options open to the young man. At length, it was proposed that Orde should seek a posting to Cairo and report to the Sudan Agency, from where he would have to obtain transport documents authorizing his journey to Khartoum. There he would apply for permission to join the language classes on offer to officials of the British administration. Finally, while he was studying, he should seek a secondment to the Sudan Defence Force, commanded by Cousin Rex's old friend General Huddleston. From this time, Orde's career was mapped out largely as a result of his famous kinsman's influence. He never hesitated to enlist Cousin Rex's support whenever he encountered any setbacks.

Throughout his brief but brilliant career, Orde Wingate's official dealings with authority invariably contained more than a seed of trouble, such was his unconventional character. When his superiors agreed to one of his proposals – often on the surface routine and innocent – he would reveal the real reason behind his request. He usually got what he wanted, which caused resentment among his older and more conventional military colleagues. When in temperate mood, he was not above massaging egos, fawning and playing the sycophant to achieve his ends. He knew only too well how the bureaucratic mind of the British Army worked and that firing point-blank demands at senior officers was fruitless. Thus his relationships with those set above him were almost always correct but rarely cordial. If his oft-repeated requests were denied he could turn cold and bitter.

As for Cousin Rex, he was never backward in responding to Orde's requests for help; he used his many and varied contacts in the War and Foreign Offices and even his acquaintances at Court. To modern eyes, Rex Wingate's repeated intervention on Orde's behalf smacks of cronyism or nepotism. However, it must be said that, at the time, there were few opportunities for rapid promotion in the British Army without either possessing family prestige or displaying an outwardly lavish lifestyle, both indicative of a man's influence and affluence at this time. Orde Wingate possessed neither. By way of illustration, young men regarded as potential officer material were expected to own horses for hunting, racing and playing polo. The young cadets and junior officers who took a keen interest in horsemanship impressed the curmudgeonly senior military staff, especially those who had served in cavalry regiments before and during the Great War. Another reason for the lack of promotion prospects was that, after the war, the British Army was considerably reduced in size, its role limited to policing the British Empire in distant places like the North-West Frontier of India. (The author's father joined the Army in 1929 and spent nearly ten years in India, his soldiering allowing him to play polo and hockey.)

Despite Orde Wingate's high pass in his Arabic examination, he fell foul of the army system; he had only been commissioned for four years and War Office regulations stipulated that young officers should serve for five years in a line [infantry] regiment. Reasonable though that may have seemed to most young subalterns, Orde Wingate was no ordinary junior officer. He was aware that his next career move was crucial; a contemporary brother officer recalled that when he first wrote to Rex Wingate in 1924, and for the next three years, Orde had never considered any posting other than Egypt or the Sudan and was determined to get his way. Having been turned down by his commanding officer for a posting to Egypt, he approached Cousin Rex, who, he hoped, would be able to pull a few strings.

Although he had retired from public service in 1919, Rex Wingate could still occasionally wield influence in Establishment circles. In 1927 the name Wingate was still revered in Whitehall among senior military and political men and even some ageing civil servants. Rex Wingate was probably sympathetic to Orde's desire to obtain an overseas posting, having himself been refused a position in Sir Evelyn Wood's administration of Egypt in 1882, under the same five-year rule.

Orde Wingate's second request for leave in June was granted. His official biographer Christopher Sykes does not say that this was due to Cousin Rex's intervention but it is entirely likely. At any rate, the second application for leave was granted although, due to some administrative error, Orde's posting was to Aden. This muddle was ultimately sorted out; having secured six months' leave to travel to the Sudan and study the language, his next step was to visit Cousin Rex in Dunbar.

During his brief visit to Knockenhair, Cousin Rex agreed to furnish Orde with a letter of introduction to General J. H. Huddleston, officer commanding the Sudan Defence Force. (Huddleston had commanded Wingate's Darfur force in 1916, killing Ali Dinar, the despotic Sultan of Darfur Province in November that year.) Like Orde, Cousin Rex was not put off by trifling army rules although his letter quoted below makes no secret of the obvious obstacle:

> He [Orde] will not have completed five years service until 1928, and *unless exceptions are made with regard to length of service* [author's italics]. I suppose any application he might make to join the Sudan Defence Force could not be considered until he has completed the specified period.[1]

No doubt Huddleston took the broad hint. Rex Wingate had stuck his neck out in support of his young relative, a man he scarcely knew, hoping that the family name would carry the appropriate weight. The five-year rule was conveniently forgotten.

Before proceeding further it is perhaps appropriate to comment on the Sudan Defence Force (SDF) and how it came into existence. Huddleston had formed the SDF in 1925, after the murder of Sir Lee Stack, Governor General of the Sudan. Stack had been assassinated by Egyptian Nationalists as a response to the reparations imposed on the Egyptian government by Viscount Allenby.[2] The SDF was created to police the Sudan; its Other Ranks were recruited from native Sudanese clans and Arabs who had settled in the country. It consisted of 4,500 men officered by British Army regulars although, in time, Sudanese officers would assume command. Application to join the SDF posed a problem for Orde Wingate. Apart from the five-year rule, officers had to be sponsored. The SDF leadership was fussy about its officer recruits since they were expected to lead and train the native levies; also, the *lingua franca* was Arabic. Selection depended almost entirely on the old boy network. Being fastidious about its choice of officer on grounds of experience and proficiency in Arabic was one thing; being dependant on who you knew was another. Few candidates were accepted unless they were acquainted with and recommended by a serving SDF officer, or one who had recently served in the Force. This presented no problem for Cousin Rex, despite the fact that he had never served in the SDF. He and Huddleston were comrades-in-arms and Rex Wingate was confident that the family name in the Sudan would be sufficient to ensure the success of his young relative's application. In a frank second letter to Huddleston after Orde had left Dunbar, Cousin Rex wrote thus:

I may say that until I saw him in Dunbar where he stayed with us for a few days, I had little or no knowledge of him, and although I think he is a fairly strong character, I do not know that I was altogether impressed by his savoir faire, but then I am a bit out of touch with the modern young officers and perhaps he is only one of a type but I do believe he is a good sportsman and a hard worker.[3]

What should we make of this? In the opinion of Rex Wingate, Orde was naïve, a good sport on the field but (tacitly stated) not a genius. To his candid and honest description of Orde, Rex Wingate might have added that he saw certain aspects of T. E. Lawrence in his character. Perhaps the comparison was best left unsaid; by 1927 Lawrence's star was descending rapidly, largely due to his histrionics over the plight of the post-war Arab nation.

Rex Wingate's second letter to Huddleston did the trick. Orde set off for the Sudan, armed with a letter of introduction to Huddleston Pasha. The Sudan was still a hostile environment for Europeans but offered better pay and allowances than the British Army; it was also a country where reputations could be made.

On 1 November 1927 Orde wrote to Cousin Rex from the Sudan Club, recounting the details of his trip through Europe. He had cycled most of the way, was robbed in Czechoslovakia, arrested as a vagrant in Vienna, took ship in Genoa for the Middle East and finally stepped ashore at Alexandria. From there he went to Cairo, where he was fortunate to meet several natives who were personal friends of Cousin Rex, 'Syrians who had served under you and they all said they would never forget you and send their salaams to yourself and Cousin Kitty'.[4] Another of the *prominentes* in Cairo to whom Rex Wingate provided a letter of introduction for Orde was Ibrahim Bey Dimitri, who had been his Arab Secretary and who would introduce Orde to a circle of influential Egyptian and Syrian politicians and businessmen in Heliopolis that year.

During many of his sojourns in the Sudanese Desert, Orde was more often than not the only European at his station. The rather grim anecdote recounted in Chapter 3 is worth telling here a second time. Orde was very much attached to one of his troop leaders, a tall, majestic Arab who was somewhat gloomy and haughty. One day, Orde and the Sudanese troop leader were talking about the early days of British rule. During the conversation Orde drew from his wallet a photograph, explaining it had been taken by his relative Rex Wingate in November 1899 after the Battle of Um Dibaykarat and showed the corpses of the Mahdist Khalifa and his Emirs lying on their sheepskin *firwas*. The young man examined the photograph for a few seconds then handed it back to Orde Wingate saying 'I am the Caliph's [Khalifa's] youngest son'. It was a dreadful moment but the two men remained friends.[5]

Rex and Orde Wingate exchanged letters during the next eight or nine years. Orde never forgot the debt he owed his relative, nor did he hesitate to seek his advice and support whenever coming up against the immovable bulwark of army bureaucracy. This was especially true in 1932 when, yet again, Orde used his elder relative's influence to plan an expedition into the Libyan Desert – the 'Great Sand Sea' as it is known – in an attempt to locate the lost oasis of Zerzura.

In 1932 Orde diverged from his custom of taking three months' leave in summer in England; that year, he went on holiday from February to May. The reason for the change of plan was simple; he wanted to prove his mettle by exploring the desert and thereby enhance his reputation. His secondment to the SDF would come to an end the following year and he was determined to finish his African service with a flourish. Again, we see similarities between himself and T. E. Lawrence who tested his powers of endurance on long trips across the desert. British Army officers are renowned for tasking themselves in hostile climates and environments. The Libyan Desert offered a challenge as it remained largely uncharted between the two world wars. In Orde Wingate's case, he had only six weeks to complete the planned expedition.

Orde Wingate considered two possible projects he felt worthy of his time and energy. Being at heart a romantic, he chose two of the fabled legends of the region – the lost army of a Persian king, Cambyses and the lost oasis of Zerzura. His first choice was Cambyses and his army of 50,000 men which, according to legend, were literally swallowed up by a fierce sandstorm in the sixth century BC, the bodies of his men being preserved – it was believed – in the Libyan Desert. The tale was untrustworthy then and remains so today, so we need not be detained by it. The second project offered more scope for success – the oasis of Zerzura, a mythological place whose existence was equally doubtful, although it was widely talked about in the bazaars, coffee shops and *souks* in Cairo.

Zerzura is first mentioned in Arab literature of the thirteenth century. It was supposed to have existed far to the west of the Nile, a place of sweetness, thronged by thousands of fluttering songbirds, home to a tribe of sturdy black giants, the abode of a sleeping king and queen and the site of a vast treasure. It is somewhat ridiculous that professional archaeologists in Britain of the time gave the myth credence. The Libyan Desert was then one of the least known regions and encouraged belief in the possibility of the fabled 'Oasis of the Blacks'.

Orde Wingate was captivated by the story but he was not the only European interested in the legend. A reasoned argument for the existence of Zerzura had been posited by a Hungarian adventurer, Count Ladislaus de Almasy. Almasy's exploration of the Libyan desert was fictionalized in Michael Ondaatje's poetic and romantic novel *The English Patient*, a story of love, betrayal and war in the hostile desert landscape; the novel won the Booker Prize for literature and was subsequently made into an Oscar-winning film, featuring Ralph Fiennes and Kristin Scott Thomas, two very fine actors.

The true story behind *The English Patient* is much more dramatic and compelling, stranger than any fiction. It is about rivalry during the inter-war years between Britain, Italy and Germany – centred on the strategic importance of the Libyan Desert which offered an opportunity for Italy, then Germany, to invade the Sudan and Egypt. The story concerns the Zerzura Club – not a club in the normal sense with rules and protocol – a collection of mainly British, Hungarian and Austrian members determined to find the lost oasis. Almasy was among the core members of the Club which included Major R. A. Bagnold and Wing Commander H. W. G. J. Penderel, RAF, a Great War air ace, and Dr Richard A. Bermann, a Viennese anthropologist. Almasy's expedition was not the first attempt to locate Zerzura; Major Bagnold (brother of Enid Bagnold who wrote the best-seller *National Velvet*) had made an attempt to find the site in 1929–30. Bagnold was unsuccessful but was awarded the Royal Geographical Society's gold medal in 1935 'for journeys in the Libyan Desert'.

Almasy and Penderel had been investigating the hostile terrain from the air; the Hungarian Count had identified several places in Libya where greenery emerged in profusion even after only normal rainfall, surviving in pockets until the vegetation withered and was 'lost'. The most likely area for Zerzura, he argued, was the Gilf Kebir Plateau, about 450 miles west of the Aswan Dam. A friend and regular correspondent of Rex Wingate, Dr Bermann (real name Arnold Hoellriegel, which he changed to obscure his Jewish antecedents) wrote to inform him of Almasy's aerial reconnaissance. Orde Wingate had not heard of Almasy's theory, nor did the two men meet. However, Orde did encounter a seasoned traveller of the Libyan Desert, Colonel Wilfred Jennings-Bramly. Young Wingate stayed with him on two occasions in the latter half of 1932, in Jennings-Bramly's small walled town of Burg el Arab, which he had persuaded the nomadic tribes in the region to build and serve as a market centre.

In August 1932 Orde wrote to Rex in Dunbar, informing him of the preparations he was making for his expedition and promising to keep in touch about his venture. For his part, Rex offered what assistance he could (the ensuing Bermann-Almasy-Wingate correspondence is held in Rex Wingate's private papers at Durham University Library). As mentioned above, six months before Orde's expedition, Wing Commander Penderel of the RAF and Count Almasy had taken aerial photographs of Gilf Kebir which on closer examination, showed a *wadi*, or dried-up watercourse, with traces of plant and animal life together with what appeared to be ancient rock carvings. This, they concluded, was surely the lost oasis of Zerzura. The pair then sought and were promised finance for a desert expedition by motor car until the backer died, leaving the expedition without support, even though the necessary vehicles had been purchased. Almasy began to look for other backers. Dr Bermann contacted Rex Wingate to enquire if someone else might take up the challenge and decided to put forward Orde's name. Rex Wingate wrote to Orde on 27 October 1932; his letter is quoted in part below:

My Dear Orde,

Although I have not written to you very recently ... I have not been idle in the matter of your proposed journey in the Western Desert and things are developing in rather a curious and interesting way.

You will remember my speaking to you of Dr Bermann[6] who is an Austrian ... political correspondent in Vienna of the Berliner Tageblatt [a newspaper] and a man of considerable European influence – he was a very staunch friend to my dear old friend Slatin up to the end of the latter's days, and he and I have been in constant correspondence.

Only yesterday I received a long letter from him a copy of which I now enclose and which shows he is joining an Expedition which, to some extent, is a rival of your own and evidently he is going largely with the idea of writing a book.[7] All this may be good from your point of view – for it means that whatever may be the success of the Expedition he contemplates, it will be given wide publicity and this may be a good thing for you should you decide to join it.

Immediately I got Bermann's letter I sent it to de Lancey Forth[8] postehaste as I wanted to lose no time in getting his reply (especially as he is leaving almost at once for Egypt to stay with [Colonel Wilfred] Jennings Bramly and his views, for I look on him as quite the most reliable, trustworthy and experienced traveller in the Western Desert that I know ...[9]

He ended the letter by advising Orde to contact Bermann and wished him the best of luck. There was no mention of Almasy in his letter which was but one piece of a five-sided correspondence between Colonel de Lancey Forth, Dr Bermann, Rex and Orde Wingate and Almasy.

Orde Wingate decided to go it alone. Unwisely and erroneously – he believed that motorized transport was impossible in the desert terrain – he chose camel transport; the Almasy expedition used motor cars. Rex Wingate, a keen motorist himself, had first suggested camels, then was converted to Almasy's preferred mode of transport. Rex Wingate, after all, had tested a desert motor car at Belhaven Beach, near Dunbar, more than two decades before. The two explorers were determined to succeed, both Orde Wingate and Count de Almasy wishing to be remembered as the discoverer of the fabled lost oasis.

At first, both expeditions experienced difficulties. Orde was refused permission to embark on his expedition by the Sudan Defence Force on the grounds of risk to his life. As for Almasy, the Egyptian authorities made claims on the fleet of motor cars he had assembled and so delayed his start. In Orde's case, his first reaction was to write to Rex Wingate, seeking help; the latter immediately responded by writing to the Military Secretary at the War Office, who in turn sent a telegram to Khartoum approving the expedition.

Yet again Rex Wingate and his contacts had bailed out the young man. At about the same time Almasy seems to have resolved his difficulties and both expeditions were able to proceed. At Qasr Dakhla, on the verge of the Libyan Desert, Orde met up with his camel train of thirteen animals and four Arab cameleers.

Typically, Orde imposed a harsh regime on his small caravan as it lumbered through the desert. It was accepted practice to rest during the greater part of the day to avoid the hot sun, starting off near sunset and travelling through the night, then halting to make camp an hour or so after sunrise. However, Orde was impatient and insisted on travelling through the heat of the day, much to the consternation of his company. (One immediately is reminded of the famous Noel Coward song about mad dogs and Englishmen in the midday sun.)

The expedition took five weeks. Orde found no trace of Zerzura. All he discovered was the carcass of a camel, the skeleton of a bird, a single egg and a prehistoric flint tool. His party was also caught in a violent sandstorm (shades of the dramatic sandstorm which Ralph Fiennes in *The English Patient* describes as the *gibli* to Kristin Scott Thomas) during which one of the Arab camel drivers optimistically declared that storms of such ferocity usually occurred near the fabled oasis, which must have caused Orde Wingate to question the Arab's sanity; storms are a constant occurrence in the Libyan desert. During the course of the expedition, Orde was surprised – and somewhat disillusioned – when he came across a motor car in the desert. He probably thought of his rival Almasy at that moment, although uppermost in his mind must have been the realization that his journey of two weeks by camel could have been achieved in a day by a car, which he thought impossible. (The car actually belonged to Patrick Clayton, a member of the Egyptian government's Desert Survey Department who was conducting an exploration of the region. Clayton actually encountered Orde one day in the desert; the eccentric Wingate was seen rolling a single bicycle wheel with an attached milometer across the sand.)

It has been robustly – and accurately – suggested that the real reason for the Almasy expedition was to map out the desert for the military, either British or Italian; this is certainly highlighted in the film *The English Patient* and is historically accurate. Both Britain and Italy were engaged in mapping activities, the British aiming to protect Egypt from invasion by Italy and its leader Mussolini who made no secret of the fact that he desired to create a Roman (Italian) empire in Libya and Abyssinia. Particularly interesting is the subsequent career of Count Ladislaus de Almasy, the eponymous hero of the film. In real life Almasy fared no better than Wingate in the discovery of Zerzura although, in exploring the Gilf Kebir Plateau on foot, he and his group found three wadis which bore traces of vegetation, the closest any explorer ever got to finding Zerzura. In temperament, Almasy resembled Wingate in one respect – a compulsive determination to succeed. However, in most other respects, Almasy was different in character. A smooth, well-mannered cosmopolitan, he loved intrigue and was frivolous save for his dedication to exploration.

Let us now briefly compare the real Almasy to the character portrayed by Ralph Fiennes. Almasy was not particularly fussy from whom he received help or who he helped in turn. In the mid-1930s he appears to have been financed by Hitler's Nazi Germany to chart the desert, as is suggested in the film. However, fact and fiction part company at that point; the film makes it clear that the fictional Almasy gave information – maps – to the Germans in exchange for an aeroplane to rescue his injured lover from a cave in the desert. The factual Almasy's motive was less altruistic and had nothing to do with love. The Germans needed his maps in the coming war with Britain but Almasy was genuinely attached to Britain, as he had been partly educated in England; at the outbreak of the Second World War, he was in Cairo and sought employment as a desert adviser to General Sir Archibald Wavell. His application was refused, possibly because he was suspected of collaboration with the Germans or, at least, having Nazi connections. He left for Hungary but returned to Egypt two years later, this time as desert adviser to Field Marshal Erwin Rommel. He joined the *Afrika Korps* with the rank of Captain and was later promoted to Major; he was awarded the First and Second Class Iron Cross for mapping services to the German Army in Libya.[10] Curiously, or perhaps to throw the British off the scent – Almasy was by now known to the intelligence services – the Germans reported him killed in action in 1942, possibly at El Alamein. After the war he turned up very much alive (and certainly not in any way burnt to toast, as depicted in the film) in Cairo as a tourist. In March 1950 he was appointed as Director of the Desert Institute of Egypt by King Farouk; later that year, he renewed his acquaintance with some of his former Zerzura Club associates including Major Bagnold who along with other dignitaries, including his rival in the desert, Pat Clayton of the Survey Department, were invited to Cairo to celebrate the founding of the Institute.[11] Almasy's new-found and more respectable fame was brief; he contracted amoebic dysentery and was invalided to Salzburg, Austria, where he died of an untreatable abscess of the liver on 22 March 1951, the very day he learnt that he had been elected Honorary President of the Desert Institute. Almasy was a society man, something of a playboy, with – as evidenced in Michael Ondaatje's novel – a taste for beautiful women. He was reputedly bereft of seriousness, world affairs holding no interest for him, at least not outside his professional ambitions. He was an interesting and entertaining raconteur, a lover of women (although some contemporaries claimed he was a practising homosexual) and a beguiling enigma.

In 1934 Orde Wingate's account of his Zerzura expedition was published in the *Journal of the Royal Geographical Society*. His time in the Sudan came to an end in March 1933; in the five years spent there, he had gained considerable and valuable experience and the venture into the interior of Libya had proved, at least to his own satisfaction, that he had a great gift for leadership.

It was on his sea voyage home to England in January 1934 that he met his future wife, Lorna Elizabeth Margaret Paterson, a sixteen-year-old schoolgirl; he was almost thirty-one. She was the only child of Walter Paterson, director of a trading company in Ceylon, and Alice Ivy Wigmore of Australia. In 1920 the Patersons returned to Scotland to live in a house called The Place of Tilliefoure, Monymusk, Aberdeenshire. In 1933 the family had been visiting Alice's relatives in Australia and were en route home; the ship docked at Port Said to pick up passengers, among them Orde Wingate. It was love at first sight, as Lorna would admit later in life, 'I marched up to him and said you're the man I'm going to marry; we both felt the same way about it.'[12] They were married on 24 January 1935[13] in Chelsea Old Church, the day before Lorna's seventeenth birthday. However, the marriage had not been without some opposition. Cousin Rex again came to Orde's aid; he wrote to Lorna's father recommending Orde as a suitable husband and son-in-law despite their difference in ages.

By 1936 Orde considered himself qualified to enter the Army Staff College at Camberley. He wrote to Cousin Rex on 10 June saying as much but realistically added, 'It remains for me to get there.' Entrance to the Staff College was by nomination from the Army Council. In the same letter to Cousin Rex, Orde listed his reasons for thinking he should be nominated – his service record, his skill as an Arabic interpreter and the desert expedition in search of Zerzura. He ended the letter light-heartedly:

> Well, Sir, I show some audacity in again asking for the help you have so adequately and generously given me in my past enterprises. But if you would like to see me treading in your footsteps (somewhat tardily!) and the name of Wingate with fresh prospects of greatness in the service of the country; [sic] then I hope you may find some way to assist me towards this nomination – the turning point in my life.[14]

Once again, Rex Wingate took up cudgels on his behalf. On 11 June, the same day he had received Orde's letter, he wrote to the Military Secretary, recommending that Orde be nominated for the Staff College. Despite this intervention, Orde was not accepted; he was devastated. Perhaps by now Cousin Rex's influence in Whitehall was exhausted, or perhaps a new generation of civil servants felt him to be an interfering nuisance consigned to the pages of history. There was one consolation however; Orde was soon promised the first available posting as a staff officer overseas. The promise was kept; he wrote to Cousin Rex on 7 September 1936, informing him that he was about to be sent to Palestine as an intelligence officer. It would prove to be a crucial posting, one which set his career on the road to success in championing the Zionist cause in Palestine.

As we have seen, Rex Wingate had opposed A. J. Balfour's Declaration in 1917 which, with hindsight, proved to be a wise course, given the strife which has existed in that part of the Middle East for almost a century. What is less understandable is Orde Wingate's support for the Jewish settlers; one can only guess at the strain that must have placed on the Orde-Rex Wingate relationship.

Perhaps a brief revisiting of the Balfour Declaration and its consequences is appropriate here. Balfour's intention was somewhat obscure. In his lifetime he was considered a Zionist inspired by the Old Testament, which he read avidly. He was also a personal friend of Dr Chaim Weizmann, the British scientist and leading Zionist during the Great War. Several British politicians were opposed to Balfour's Declaration; they argued that Palestine could never accommodate more than a third of the world's Jewish population. Balfour countered by arguing that his measure was intended to create a Jewish *homeland*, not a country for all Jews. The Arabs had occupied Palestine since the fifth century; opposition to a Jewish state there was understandable on both religious and cultural grounds. The Declaration proved a disaster for Britain, which became the mandatory power; in time, both Jewish settlers and Arab inhabitants alike grew to detest the British presence in the area.

The Paris Peace Conference which redrew the boundary lines of countries in the Near and Middle East previously governed by Turkey incorporated the Balfour Declaration in its plans. As a result of the Franco-British disposal of those territories, a new country, Transjordan, came into being under the Hashemite leader, Emir Abdullah, one of the sons of Emir Hussein, Sherif of Mecca, who had joined his father in the Arab Revolt. Transjordan was excluded from the terms of the Balfour Declaration but not Palestine, which became a British Mandated territory. In 1921 Winston Churchill, as Colonial Secretary, attended the Cairo Conference whose main objective was to consider the future of the Middle East. Churchill was faced with virtually irreconcilable issues, not least the British wartime pledge for a Jewish homeland while honouring a promise to 500,000 Arabs living in Palestine that they would obtain self-determination.

In discussions, Churchill instructed Sir Herbert Samuel, High Commissioner for Palestine and a Jew, to restrict his responsibilities to an area west of the river Jordan, where the Jews were to be allowed to settle. He also gave Samuel a Jewish force to defend the territory. Rex Wingate, one of the early and unswerving opponents of the Declaration, was joined in his opposition by Lord Curzon, the Zionist Sir Wyndham Deedes, Gertrude Bell, the famous desert explorer, and many others. These critics had rightly argued that to allow Zionist Jews to settle in Palestine was guaranteed to stir up trouble between the Arabs and the existing small number of Jewish settlers. Opponents of the Declaration looked to the future, knowing full well that the political situation would deteriorate in the next decade and they were to be proved right.

At first Palestine posed few problems for the Colonial Office, or for the indigenous Arabs, largely due to an effective local government and moderation on the part of Dr Chaim Weizmann, the leading Zionist of the day. Then, in 1922, the Arabs refused to recognize the Declaration and, for good measure, the Mandate given to Britain by the League of Nations. Jews were subsequently massacred in their settlements by Arab mobs. The Arabs defended their homeland, insisting that there would never be peace in Palestine until the Jews were removed, which of course stiffened the resolve of the Zionists to obtain not just a homeland but ultimately the state of Israel. The legacy of the Paris and Cairo Peace Conferences is with us to this day.

While Transjordan influenced the course of events until 1935, it was Nazi Germany which added additional fuel to an already burning fire. In November 1935 Adolf Hitler passed the Nuremberg Laws which deprived Jews of German citizenship, and triggered a Jewish exodus from Europe. In 1931 there had been about 4,000 Jewish settlers in Palestine; by 1936 the figure was nearly 62,000. What had been an annual trickle of a few hundred settlers now became a flood as the immigration increased rapidly. Weizmann and his staff at the Jewish Agency were faced with demands for the purchase of land in both Palestine and Transjordan. Such were the demands that many Arab lands were sold off to the new settlers, thereby dispossessing Arab small-holders. It was a recipe for disaster. Naturally, the Arabs grew increasingly concerned that they would be pushed out of what had been their homeland for centuries.

By 1936 the Palestine Arabs rightly feared that a Jewish state was being formed and that they would soon be in the minority. (This came to pass in 1948, when the British abandoned the mandate following a wave of Jewish terrorism, the worst being the extensive bomb damage to Jerusalem's King David Hotel with the loss of many British lives. In May that year, the state of Israel came into being.) However, in 1936, a general strike by Arab workers was followed by a series of attacks on Jewish property and several Jews were murdered. The British attempted to restore order by using minimum force but threatened to impose martial law. As a result, the Peel Commission was set up to investigate the roots of the problem – as if such a thing were necessary. In 1936 Orde Wingate was posted to Palestine as an intelligence officer; paradoxically, but perhaps true to his nature, Orde's sympathies were with the Jews and the powerful Jewish Agency. He befriended Dr Weizmann and privately admitted in 1937 that he had adopted Zionism 'as a religion'. For Orde Wingate, the Old Testament was not just a religious tract but an inspiring record of the Jewish people and their struggle for existence. He had read the Koran and, having compared it to the Old Testament, denounced it as 'pompous verbiage'. (The eminent philosopher and writer Thomas Carlyle had come to a similar conclusion.)

It was against this background that Orde Wingate's support for the Jewish settlers began. Orde Wingate wrote to Rex Wingate from Jerusalem on 12 January 1937.[15] It was a long letter, professing to bear no prejudices against the Arabs in Palestine. As mentioned above, William Robert Wellesley, Lord Peel, the Lord Privy Seal, had been appointed chairman of a Royal Commission to resolve the Palestine Question. Peel recommended that Palestine should be divided into three zones – one for the Arabs, one for the Jews and one for British subjects. (Lord Peel died that year, possibly as a result of stress brought on by his duties.) The Peel Commission's recommendations were ratified by the British government.

The Jewish settlers had turned vast tracts of Palestine desert into productive *kibbutzim*, which the Arabs believed would act as inducements for yet more Zionists to come to Palestine. The British government viewed the growing unrest with a divided outlook; many politicians declared their support for the Arabs and demanded that the injustice to Arab nationalists be addressed. Britain's main preoccupation in the Middle East continued to be centred on the Suez Canal and the continuation of trade with India by sea. Despite the massacre of 300 Jews in Palestine in 1936, British foreign policy was directed at appeasing the Arabs. It was at this point that Orde Wingate arrived in Jerusalem to espouse the cause of the Jewish settlers.

In 1937, Lord Peel's recommendations on the partitioning of Palestine were accepted. It was against this background that Orde Wingate's support for the Jewish settlers began. His first act in 1936 was to form Special Night Squads of Jewish men and women to protect their communities and property from Arab terrorism. In his lengthy letter dated 12 January 1937, Orde explained his position to Rex Wingate. His assessment of the Arab world in general and Palestine in particular appears naïve to modern eyes; his letter included statements like 'Islam ... cares little for the Arabs of Palestine. Islam today has no strength, England continues to think it has the same influence as in pre-war [Great War] days. That is a fallacy.'[17] He maintained that Transjordan intervention on the side of the Palestine Arabs would provide the excuse for Britain to remove corrupt Arab leaders. He believed that a possible Arab revolt in Palestine would lead to the arming of Jews, the proclaiming of martial law and the arresting and exiling of every Arab of note. It was also his belief that the calibre of British officers sent to administer Palestine was poor, anti-semitic and pro-Arab. He criticized the then High Commissioner of Palestine, Sir Arthur Wauchope, who, in Orde's view and despite some favourable qualities, had lost his grasp of Palestinian affairs. This view alienated him from the Foreign Office and a Wingate family quarrel with a recalcitrant Foreign Office was thus perpetuated.

Orde's assessment of the Jews was perhaps the more accurate. He believed they would be loyal to HM Government and prove themselves worthy soldiers. In his letter to Cousin Rex, he continued:

The Jews are loyal to the Empire. The Jews are men of their word – they have always been so – in fact it is the Gentiles' main complaint against them. There are 15,000,000 Jews in the world. Palestine will take over a million in seven years. You can have no idea of what they have already done here. You would be amazed to see the desert bloom like a rose; intensive horticulture everywhere – such energy, faith, agility and inventiveness the world has not seen. I have seen the young Jews in the

Kvutsots [kibbutzim]. I tell you that the Jews will provide better soldiers than ours. We have only to train it [sic]. They will equip it [sic].[18]

He further maintained that Britain had 'the chance to plant here in Palestine and Transjordan a loyal, rich and intelligent nation'.[19] His strategy was to arm and equip the Jews to take over both the internal and external defence of Palestinians. Lastly, he predicted that the coming war with Germany required Britain to 'redeem our promises to Jewry and shame the devil of Nazism, Fascism and our own prejudices'.[20] He ended the letter by boldly informing Cousin Rex that Palestine was more important than Egypt and that 'I shall hope to identify myself with it [Palestine]'.[21]

The letter is complex, a mixture of perspicacity, naivety and prejudice. Perhaps we may excuse it on the grounds of inexperience although, when written, Orde was thirty-four, hardly a callow youth. His summing up of the response of non-Palestine Arabs to the Palestine Question was undeniably accurate. But his idea that Transjordan intervention should be encouraged in the hope that it would expose the corrupt Hashemite regime is nothing short of cynicism, a trait that Orde Wingate never lost. He was also unfair about the qualities of the British officers in Palestine; at that time those who were responsible for administering the mandated territory of Palestine were capable men who served admirably, even if Orde's contention that they were pro-Arab was later proved correct. His criticism of the High Commissioner, Sir Arthur Wauchope, is however accurate; Wauchope was out of his depth and failed to interpret properly the admittedly confused and confusing policy dictated by London.

Orde could only guess at Cousin Rex's response to his complex letter – if there ever was one. Orde knew that Cousin Rex had spent his entire public life serving the Sudan, then Egypt and, by extension, the Arabs. Whatever Cousin Rex's feelings about his young kinsman's attitude to the Arabs, his relationship with Orde does not seem to have suffered although they corresponded less frequently over the next three years. Perhaps that tells us something.

It must be said that Orde Wingate's declared support for the Jewish settlers was premature, insubordinate and irresponsible, given his obligations to the British government. In a letter to Dr Chaim Weizmann, he offered support before the findings of the Peel Commission were made public, advance knowledge of which he had received in his capacity as an intelligence officer. He was guilty of leaking the contents of a classified state document which had not yet been debated in the House of Commons. In this respect, a comparison with T. E. Lawrence is hard to resist; both men championed causes of those in which they believed, without regard to official policy. There is nothing intrinsically wrong in such action – it may be excused on the grounds of excessive zeal – but the Establishment has never felt comfortable with men of vision, idealists who consider themselves above what to them are grubby politics. Orde Wingate and T. E. Lawrence were both guilty of irresponsible and even dangerous indiscretions.

The next two years in Palestine and Orde Wingate's assistance to the Jews are well documented. With typical enthusiasm and efficiency, Orde organized the Jewish Night Squads to defend Jewish settlements from the incursions of Arab terrorists. It was during this period that the Orde-Rex Wingate correspondence appears to have waned; the older man had always espoused the cause of the Arabs and was one of the last of the Empire builders of the Victorian Age. He tacitly criticized his young kinsman's new-found faith in Zionism although he never lost his affection for the young man. The relationship between the two men grew warmer in 1938 when Orde was posted to Ethiopia (Abyssinia), a country with which Rex Wingate was familiar. Rex and Orde met in London and discussed the future of Ethiopia which had been invaded by Mussolini who boasted he would found an Italian empire in Africa. At first Mussolini was successful and, in the first year of the Second World War, Orde was sent to Abyssinia to assist Emperor Haile Selassie, 'The Lion of Judah', in expelling the Italian Fascists. Orde's role in that conflict restored him to his older kinsman. Rex Wingate was in London in 1940 and was entertained to lunch by Orde and Lorna. The day after their lunch, Rex Wingate wrote this to his young relative:

> I do indeed congratulate you most heartily. You may be sure we are all proud of the lustre you have so honourably and so gallantly added to the family name. Go on and prosper and 'more power to your elbow' ...[22]

Rex Wingate was not slow in spreading an account of his young kinsman's exploits in Abyssinia. Now that the former warm relationship had been re-established, Cousin Rex hoped for yet greater glory for his young relative during the Second World War.

In the autumn of 1940, Orde was impressed by the exploits of the Long Range Desert Group (LRDG) created by Major Bagnold, one of the core members of the Zerzura Club. The LRDG, or 'Bagnold's Boys', as it was known, had operated first against the Italians, then the Germans in the Libyan Desert. Orde, the irregular soldier, praised the success of the hit-and-run tactics of Bagnold's small force. He proposed that a larger and fully mechanized desert force be formed, consisting of 10,000 British troops, 1,000 RAF personnel and a contingent of Nigerian troops. His original aim was to create an expanded force consisting of the Jewish soldiers he had led in his Night Squads, formed to fight Arab terrorism in the 1930s. Although the then Secretary of State for War, Anthony Eden, supported his suggestion, it was dismissed by Sir John Dill, Chief of the Imperial General Staff, who put forward an alternative agenda. He proposed to deploy Orde in Abyssinia to raise a revolt amongst the Abyssinian tribes against Italian rule, which Orde Wingate did with considerable success, acting as Emperor Haile Selassie's military adviser and ultimately achieving freedom for the country.

In June 1941, Rex Wingate wrote to Orde in Cairo advocating the creation of a Jewish homeland in Ethiopia:

> You know better than I do how much traditional connection there is between the two countries [Palestine and Ethiopia] and having regard to the fact recent events have shown that you have joint sympathies with the future of the two countries, you might perhaps be instrumental in sounding Heile [sic] Selassie and if he is agreeable, the suggestion might come from him (through you) to HMG and through the latter to the American Zionists with whom Weizmann has close relations.[23]

This idea had been suggested by others, with Uganda also proposed as a possible Jewish homeland. However, Orde rejected his relative's suggestion, even if agreeing with him that Britain was handling the situation in Ethiopia badly. (Rex Wingate also suggested that a solution might be to repeat the Condominium arrangement which had been introduced in 1899 for Egypt.) A further letter from him to Orde in November 1941 advocated the provision of experienced staff from the Sudan Civil Service to provide Ethiopia with firm administration before power was handed back to the Emperor.[24] Orde responded in December, intimating that Cousin Rex's idea would only work if it were supported by the Ethiopians and only if it appealed to 'their higher human qualities: humanity, faith and courage'.[25]

The fact of the matter was that Rex Wingate had circulated certain documents containing these suggestions to the Foreign Office, Buckingham Palace and Number Ten Downing Street; his proposals were considered out of touch with the contemporary situation and he was accused of meddling in politics. By now, Britain had lost interest in formulating any further mandated territories. Emperor Haile Selassie was eventually restored to his throne in 1941 but only with British help.

After his time in Abyssinia Orde Wingate endured poor health for almost two years; he fretted until a medical doctor pronounced him fit for active service in September 1943, the last time he was in the company of Cousin Rex. That month Orde left England for India, from where he would conduct a campaign against the Japanese in Burma. Before his tragic and untimely death in March 1944, yet again, Orde Wingate, by now holding the rank of brigadier, demonstrated his genius for guerrilla warfare. He formed a formidable organization which became known as the Chindits – so called from a soldiers' corruption of the word *chinthe*, the mythical beasts that guard Burmese temples. Sadly, the Chindits ceased to operate as a coherent formation after Orde's death. Some modern historians have argued that Wingate and his Chindits were yet another of Winston Churchill's errors of judgement. The author disagrees with this view; the Chindit force was as effective as were Lawrence's Arabs in the Great War nearly three decades earlier, even if Orde would have hated the comparison. Orde's audacious exploits behind the Japanese lines in Burma have become legendary and, in the history of modern guerrilla warfare, Orde Wingate ranks alongside T. E. Lawrence and others of similar stamp.

One can but speculate about the state of his mind at the time of his death. That day, 23 March 1944, a clean-shaven Orde Wingate (he was usually bearded) dressed in fatigues and wearing his familiar Wolseley tropical helmet, took off from an airfield in Imphal. He never reached his destination. En route to Lalaghat, the USAAF B-25 bomber in which he was travelling plunged in flames into a hillside ridge near the village of Thilon at about 8.30pm. There were no survivors. In his tribute to Orde Wingate in the House of Commons on 2 August 1944, Winston Churchill had this to say:

> There was a man of genius who might well have become a man of destiny. He has gone, but his spirit lives on in the long [range] penetration groups.[26]

Churchill might well have been referring to T. E. Lawrence. In life Orde Wingate was variously described as an egomaniac, a muscular Christian, a genius in unconventional warfare and possessed of great reserves of physical and mental energy, moral courage and self-confidence; on the other hand, he could be rude, abrasive and certainly unorthodox in his military dress, sharing many character traits with Lawrence. Even after his death, the mention of his name in government military circles could cause controversy. His official biography was written by Christopher Sykes, second son of the diplomat Sir Mark Sykes, co-drafter of the Sykes-Picot Agreement. The book was published in 1959 but the family, particularly Orde's wife Lorna, were displeased by some of its content.

Even Orde's final resting-place generated a great deal of ill feeling and displeasure within the family. Lorna Wingate wrote to Churchill requesting that her husband's remains be returned home; Churchill informed her that Orde's remains would be disinterred from the crash site and re-interred at the British Cemetery, Imphal in 1947. They were subsequently exhumed and re-interred at the American Military Cemetery at Arlington, Virginia, where they remain beside other famous soldiers such as General Robert E. Lee, whose family owned Arlington House whose grounds now form the cemetery. News of this also caused bad feeling in the Wingate family, although the government pointed out that it was obliged to comply with an agreement with the USA that the final resting place of remains buried in communal graves should be determined by the country whose dead were in the majority.

Orde Wingate was a man who took no theories on trust, no matter how well tried and tested they were. It can justifiably be said that he was an unusual man who was destined for fame, but at a price. He was prepared to pay that price. How many of us in our youth entertain visions of greatness and renown, visions which thankfully disappear when, in the light of experience and common sense, we mature. As Orde matured, he never abandoned his vision.

Ten years after Orde Wingate's death, Lorna Wingate married John Smith, a prosperous East Lothian farmer; ironically, they farmed near Cockburnspath, a small village only seven miles south of Rex Wingate's adopted home in Dunbar.

In later life Orde Wingate confessed that he wanted a cause to fight for, that he considered himself fated to lead a country, adding with a burst of laughter that 'any country would do'. His five years in the Sudan, a bold but brief expedition into the Libyan desert in search of Zerzura and his guerrilla exploits in Palestine and Abyssinia and Burma proved to his own satisfaction that he possessed the gift of leadership. He was half afraid of the power that he possessed, suspicious of his own ambitions because he knew himself to be capable and ruthless enough to achieve them. Like T. E. Lawrence, he once said he only wanted peace, to escape from the world and yet, like Lawrence, he still desired to be at the centre of the struggle. Orde Wingate had the courage to follow his instincts and brave the unknown, unable to resist the call of his destiny.

Notes

The papers and private letters of Orde Wingate are lodged in the Imperial War Museum, although some of his private papers remain with his family. Only a few letters between Orde and Rex Wingate are catalogued in the Sudan Archive Department, Durham University Library under file ref 243/7 (Wingate Papers).

1. *Orde Wingate*, the Official Biography, Sykes.
2. Field Marshal Viscount Edmund Allenby (1861–1936), who defeated the Turks in 1918 and was appointed Reginald Wingate's successor as High Commissioner of Egypt in 1919, serving in that capacity until 1925.
3. *Orde Wingate.*
4. *Ibid.*
5. *Ibid.*
6. Bermann was a Viennese anthropologist, novelist and journalist who reputedly spoke ten languages.
7. Eventually published as *Historical Problems of the Libyan Desert* in 1934.
8. Colonel de Lancey Forth, Commander of the Camel Corps.
9. *Orde Wingate.*
10. *The Hunt for Zerzura*, Kelly.
11. *Ibid.*
12. *Orde Wingate* and *Orde Wingate Irregular Soldier*, Royle.
13. *Ibid.*
14. Orde Wingate to FRW, 10 June 1936.
15. Orde Wingate to FRW, 12 January 1937.
16. *Ibid.*
17. *Ibid.*
18. *Ibid.*
19. *Ibid.*
20. *Ibid.*
21. *Ibid.*
22. *FRW to Orde Wingate*, 12 December 1940, WP 243/7 SAD, DU.
23. *FRW to Orde Wingate*, 20 June 1941, WP 243/7 SAD, DU.
24. *FRW to Orde Wingate*, 11 November 1941, WP 243/7, SAD, DU.
25. *Orde Wingate to FRW*, 15 December 1941, WP 243/7SAD, DU.
26. *Orde Wingate.*

Chapter 11

Wanderers
(1930–1945)

In the immediate years after the Great War, the Wingates spent more time at Knockenhair, Dunbar. Increasingly, however, Wingate's inactive life soon palled. As we have already seen, the Wingates adopted an almost nomadic lifestyle from 1921 until 1939, when the outbreak of the Second World War confined them to Britain. During the war much of their time was spent between London and Dunbar and by 1946 Kitty Wingate's failing health had brought them back to Dunbar for good. By then she was suffering from a weak heart and other complications; Wingate's own health was also in decline.

From 1930 the Wingates had continued to fill their days with their respective interests – he in his various business ventures, she entertaining relatives, friends and the dwindling number of contemporaries they had known in public life. During the inter-war years, the Wingates' long association with the royal family continued and became more intimate. They were not only invited regularly to state functions but were guests at royal lunches and dinner parties. Kitty developed a close friendship with Edward VII's daughter Louise, the Princess Royal, Duchess of Fife, who had visited the Sudan during Wingate's time as Governor General. Wingate continued to act as trustee of the Fife estate until the Princess died. One of the consequences of longevity is that friends disappear at an alarming rate and loneliness beckons.

In 1929 the Wingates had delayed their annual visit to Dunbar until August when, yet again, they were house guests of Princess Louise at Mar Lodge.[1,2] In the same year, Wingate was no doubt saddened to learn of the premature death of James Lees Hastie, the Dunbar man he had recruited as golf professional to the Gezira Golf Club whose course he founded. Hastie died on 17 May 1930 aged only forty-eight; he was buried in the local parish church cemetery where his monument survives.

The Wingates reciprocated the Duchess of Fife's hospitality by inviting her to Knockenhair on several occasions. Her last visit occurred in 1930 when, aged sixty-three and in failing health, she thanked the Wingates for her stay in Dunbar; she maintained that the bracing sea breezes had improved her health. (Among the various social events laid on for her by the Wingates was a visit to York House, better known to the local people as the East Links

Cottage Hospital which, until demolished, was situated near the present day Lammermuir House, a private nursing home.) At the end of her visit, Princess Louise said that the sea air at Dunbar had done her a power of good. It is often said that Dunbar, known locally as 'Sunny Dunny,' with its fresh North Sea breezes, either cures or kills. In 1930 the salt air failed to restore the ailing lady. Not long after the Princess' visit, her health rapidly deteriorated and she died in January 1931; Wingate was among the chief mourners at her funeral in Windsor.[3]

The year of 1931 was one of seemingly endless funerals for the Wingates. On 31 March, Arthur J. Bigge, Lord Stamfordham, died at St James' Palace in London. Bigge, former secretary to Queen Victoria, then King George V, had been a regular visitor to Dunbar, where he enjoyed many rounds of golf partnered by Wingate. It is entirely possible that Bigge had long ago suggested Dunbar as a summer resort to Wingate in 1899. It is not known whether Wingate attended Bigge's funeral but it is probable, given his frequent visits to London.

In the same year Wingate was devastated to learn of the death on 4 October of his old friend from the Sudan days, Rudolf 'Rowdy' von Slatin, his 'Sudanese Twin'. Despite the Great War the two men remained friends and regularly corresponded via neutral Switzerland between 1914 and 1918. In 1920 Slatin had visited the Wingates in Dunbar, where Wingate held a dinner in his honour at the Hotel Belle Vue. Wingate and Slatin had continued to correspond and meet regularly in London and Austria between 1920 and 1930. Another friend from the Sudan days, Colonel the Hon. Milo Talbot, an old comrade-in-arms, also exited the stage that year.

By now the Wingates were spending long periods in London, Belgium and France. Between October and June each year they resided in Queen Anne's Mansions, occupying a tiny flat which consisted of a simple living room, kitchen, lavatory and small bedroom. They returned to Dunbar in July, staying there until September. In 1933 they were only able to spend the month of June in Dunbar, probably due to the distractions of Wingate's business commitments in the City and Europe.[4] In 1935 they delayed their annual visit until August, again no doubt on account of Wingate's business activities.[5] Perhaps, by now, the seventy-four-year-old Wingate was less able to negotiate the golf links at Dunbar, possibly due to an inveterate love of large cigars and whisky, the latter being preferred to the dinner table claret, the conventional libation of the middle and upper classes. No true Scotsman would dream of finding fault with his preference!

For many years, the Wingates took the annual – and fashionable – 'cure' at the spa towns of Karlsbad and Marienbad in Bohemia, once part of the Austrian Empire and, later, Czechoslovakia. No doubt they combined their trips with visits to Rudolf von Slatin and his wife Alice. Sadly, Alice had died in 1921 after only seven years' marriage; 'Old Rowdy' was consoled by their only child, Anne-Marie. Wingate's business commitments to *Union Minière* took him to Belgium in 1930 and 1931, then to Austria; after the death of

Slatin, he probably 'took the waters' in Vichy, in the south of France. On his visits to Belgium, Wingate was able to renew acquaintance with King Albert and his consort, Elizabeth of Bavaria, whom he had entertained on several occasions at the Residency in Khartoum between 1899 and 1914. Wingate and Albert remained friends until the latter's tragic death in a mountaineering accident in 1934.

On one memorable visit to Vichy, Wingate's past caught up with him in an unexpected and embarrassing way. While he was taking the 'cure' he arranged to have physiotherapy on a troublesome wrist injured by a fanatic in Khartoum in 1912 (see Chapter 4). The Vichy physician treating him was noticeably lame and had lost an eye. Assuming the doctor had sustained his wounds during the Great War, Wingate engaged him in small talk, commiserating with him for what he thought were honourable war wounds. He was taken aback when the doctor turned on him with ill-concealed bitterness, 'No, these wounds were the result of fighting against your man, Rabeh, in West Africa. You are responsible for them, not the Germans.'[6]

Wingate was staggered. The doctor was referring to an incident from the Sudan of 1892 when Rabeh Zobeir, a Sudanese tribal chief, had led a force of irregulars against the French near Lake Chad in French Equatorial Africa (modern-day Nigeria). Rabeh had written to Wingate, promising to hand over to Britain any territory he conquered in French West Africa. (At that time, Wingate was a brevet Major in the Egyptian Army with little clout; even so, he had clearly made an impression on Rabeh.) That day, sitting in the French doctor's surgery, almost forty years after Rabeh's incursion into Chad, Wingate felt it incumbent upon himself to apologize to the doctor, protesting his innocence. The doctor was unmoved. He bluntly informed Wingate that, when the French defeated and killed Rabeh, they found correspondence on his body which mentioned Wingate's name. In his surgery that day the doctor did not mince his words:

> We knew of your service to the Sudan, and it was obvious to us that Rabeh's advance in West Africa was connected with British activities. So you see, I have some reason for saying you are responsible for my wounds.[7]

Did Wingate suffer a twinge of conscience? We shall never know.

In addition to his annual trips to Belgium and France, Wingate visited Lisbon each year to attend meetings of the Benguela Railway Company which provided the main outlet for the copper extracted by Tanganyikan Concessions Ltd for the benefit of the Belgian government. These European visits were the sum total of Wingate's travels abroad; he never visited Egypt or the Sudan, though both countries were uppermost in his memory. His sole remaining link to these countries was through the London-based governing body of the Gordon Memorial College in Khartoum and his chairmanship of the annual Egyptian Army dinner held in London. Even this contact was tenuous; in the 1930s he resigned from the governors' board of the Gordon College after writing an account of its achievements.

In 1925, Wingate's daughter Victoria, known to the family as Catherine, the wife of Captain Henry Dane, had borne Wingate his first grandson, Paul Malcolm Henry; granddaughter Josephine was born in Poona, India in 1928, followed by Louis Martin Henry in 1938.

In 1933, Wingate invested in a scheme to turn the farm fields between Knockenhair and the sea, an area known as Winterfield, into what subsequently became Winterfield Golf Course. (In 1935, he was appointed Hon. President of the Club.) In 1934 the Wingates suffered yet another sad loss with the death of Lady Wingate's brother, Sir Leslie Rundle. Wingate and Rundle had been brother officers in the Sudan for seventeen years; Rundle had risen in the ranks and was appointed Governor of Malta in 1909, serving in that capacity until his dismissal in 1915.

In 1937, *Burke's Peerage* listed Wingate's hobbies as golf, cars and collecting Dervish weapons. He was still involved with several organizations in Dunbar, notably as president of the local Royal National Lifeboat Institution station. In that capacity he officiated at a ceremony in Eyemouth to inaugurate the reception of a new motorized lifeboat, the *Frank and William Oates*; the donor of the lifeboat was the late C. G. Oates, whose nephew, the gallant Captain Lawrence Oates, had perished in Scott's doomed polar expedition of 1912. (It will be remembered that Oates sacrificed his life in an honourable but futile attempt to save his comrades; crippled by frostbite, he left the tent and deliberately walked into a blizzard to make the task of his colleagues easier.)[8]

One by one Wingate's former comrades were passing away. In April 1937 he published a tribute in the magazine *East Africa and Rhodesia* to his friend and golfing partner Sir James Currie, the first principal of the Gordon Memorial College in Khartoum and Director of the Sudanese Education Service. Currie had visited Knockenhair on at least one occasion. An extract from Wingate's obituary to him was published in the local newspaper:

> By the sudden death of Sir James Currie on 17 March while visiting Cambridge [to establish a vetenary [sic] education in the Sudan] ... the British Empire has lost a truly great and loyal public servant, and one who can be ill-spared – especially at a time when the vast problem of co-ordinating education, scientific research and agriculture throughout the Dominions, Colonies and Protectorates are receiving a [sic] belated and much-needed attention, and for which Currie was in large measure responsible and an able pioneer and efficient exponent ...[9]

At the end of 1936 Wingate learnt of the death of his cousin, Sir Andrew 'Dan' Wingate. The eldest son of the Reverend William Wingate, Sir Andrew had gained great distinction in the Indian Civil Service and was deeply religious. His obituary in *The Times* of 4 January 1937, described him as an ardent supporter of the Balfour Declaration of 1917. In 1919 he published

Palestine, Mesopotamia and the Jews: The Spiritual Side of History, a book which voiced his high hopes for the restoration of Jewish influence in Palestine and what he held to be other fulfilments of prophecy.

Between 1937 and the outbreak of the Second World War, the Wingates continued to spend part of the summer and early autumn each year at Dunbar. In July 1939 Lady Wingate played host to her son Ronald, who had not been home since 1919 on account of his employment in the Indian Civil Service. The Wingates made few visits to Knockenhair during the Second World War, spending much of their time in London. One wonders if Wingate was at home when Churchill and the American President Franklin D. Roosevelt met at nearby Archerfield, near North Berwick, to discuss the war. Churchill and Wingate were friends and former comrades-in-arms, both having been present on the field of Omdurman in 1898. Might we speculate that the two men met at Knockenhair at a crucial phase of the war? There is nothing to support the supposition. However, we know that Wingate offered Knockenhair as a lookout point to the local ARP and Royal Observer Corps throughout the war.

When war broke out in 1939, Wingate, aged seventy-eight, was too advanced in years to serve in any official capacity in the conflict. Surprisingly, he never joined the Dunbar Home Guard. He pursued his private and business activities with the usual zeal, visiting his London watering holes – the Army & Navy and the British Empire Clubs. On 26 January 1941, as its patron, he represented the East Lothian Boy Scouts' Association at the memorial service held in London for General Lord Baden-Powell, founder of the Boy Scout movement in 1908; yet another of Wingate's friends from the Great War, Baden-Powell had died in 1937.[10] In 1941 Wingate was appointed Honorary Colonel of a Territorial Army unit, the 7th Manchesters, raised in 1939 as a duplicate of 6th Manchesters (The Ardwick Battalion) which became 65th (Manchester) Heavy Anti-Aircraft Regiment. This appointment stemmed from his close association with a Regular Army battalion of the Manchesters. Twenty-seven years earlier, as Sirdar and Governor General of the Sudan, he had welcomed the battalion, then part of 42nd (East Lancashire) Division, to Egypt in 1914, where it undertook training before taking part in the Gallipoli campaign.

In 1941 the Wingates' flat at Queen Anne's Mansions took a direct hit during a German air raid; fortunately, they were in a nearby underground air-raid shelter at the time. They were obliged to seek alternative accommodation at the Goring Hotel, Grosvenor Gardens, Ebury Street, as confirmed by facsimiles of envelopes addressed to Wingate in 1943 and 1944 in the possession of the author.

During the war years one wonders if Wingate knew of the spy school in Dunbar, located at Belhaven Hill, which was set up by the Special Operations Executive (SOE) to train operatives dropped into France and forge links with the *Maquis*, or French underground movement. The SOE unit was but a few hundred yards from Knockenhair where his young sons had played with the children of Major Marrow, a golfing partner before the Great War. It is unlikely that Wingate was aware of this clandestine operation, being well past the age of serving the British government. The SOE at Belhaven remained a closely guarded secret for many years, details of its existence being withheld until the elapse of the government's thirty-year rule.

In 1944, Wingate fell seriously ill, requiring admission to a London hospital; he was apparently suffering from a prostate complaint and was prescribed a course of penicillin – a drug whose use was still in its infancy. It had been administered to human patients only two years before; according to Wingate's son Ronald,[11] without penicillin, his father would have died.

The Wingates sat out the war in London, which says much for their courage; they would have been safer at Knockenhair. In March 1944 Wingate learnt of the death of his kinsman Orde in an aeroplane crash on his way from India to mount an offensive against the Japanese in Burma. The Wingates were devastated; Orde had proven his worth in several theatres of conflict.

No doubt after participating in the tumultuous celebrations of Victory in Europe (VE) Day in London on 8 May 1945, the Wingates returned to Dunbar where they would spend their remaining years. Sadly for Lady Wingate she had only a year to live; her last days were spent in the isolated and draughty rooms of Knockenhair. She died in the month of June, at the height of summer. Wingate was inconsolable, devastated at her passing. Three years older than him, she had been his constant companion since 1888 in a happy marriage which had lasted fifty-eight years.

Notes

1. *HC*, 16 August 1929.
2. *Ibid.*, 22 August 1929.
3. *Ibid.*, 16 January 1931.
4. *Ibid.*, 23 June 1933.
5. *Ibid.*, 9 August 1935.
6. *Wingate of the Sudan*, RELW.
7. *Ibid.*
8. *HC*, 27 August 1937.
9. *Ibid.*, 2 April 1937.
10. *HC*, 31 January 1941.
11. *Wingate of the Sudan.*

Chapter 12

Final Years
(1946–1953)

Francis Reginald Wingate and his wife and kindred spirit Kitty spent their final years in Dunbar. After an absence of over six years, their eldest son Ronald visited Knockenhair and found both parents in poor health. Wingate was so ill that as Honorary President of the Dunbar branch of the British Legion he sent his apologies to the serving secretary for absenting himself from the Annual General Meeting.[1] But by far the worst blow in his long life came with the death of his beloved Kitty at the age of eighty-seven at 3.45pm on 10 June 1946. Kitty had been suffering a weak heart for some time; the cause of death entered on her death certificate by their family doctor (and, by a coincidence, this author's), Dr William Anderson of Templelands Surgery in Dunbar, was senile cardiovascular degeneration; the certificate records her full name as Catherine Leslie Wingate and those of her parents as Joseph Sparkinhall Rundle and Renira Catherine Rundle, *nee* Leslie. Wingate was so deeply grief-stricken that Ronald, then living at Number Eight, Chelsea Embankment, London, had to register his mother's death, his father being too distraught and frail to do so.

At their meeting on 12 June, Dunbar Town Council recorded their condolences, the provost instructing the Town Clerk to send a letter of sympathy to Sir Reginald. Unusually, the funeral service was conducted in the dining-room at Knockenhair on 13 June; at her request, Kitty Wingate's remains were cremated in Edinburgh; again at her request, the ashes were scattered over her beloved son Malcolm's grave in Lagincourt Cemetery, France.[2]

By all accounts Kitty was a pretty, gracious Victorian lady, a brilliant linguist, accomplished pianist and a witty, if occasionally caustic, conversationalist. During her lifetime she had been awarded honours in her own right – Dame Commander of the British Empire (DBE), Dame of Grace of the Order of St John of Jerusalem, Grand Cordon of the Order of Kemal, the Khedive of Egypt. Throughout her married life she had been a devoted wife, a loving, if strict, mother to three children and an attentive and imaginative hostess supporting her husband in the Sudan and Egypt, both in his official capacities and in their private lives.

Reginald Wingate never recovered from the loss; the death of his helpmate, supporter, cherished lover and companion left him a bereft and lonely old man in the cold and draughty mansion of Knockenhair. During the last few years of his life he heard the clocks ticking loudly through its empty rooms. Time hangs heavily on the old; the minutes seem like hours yet, paradoxically, the years flash past. What were his thoughts and preoccupations during these final years? He remained bitter to the end about his dismissal as High Commissioner of Egypt by the Foreign Office; for him, Egypt had hardly been the Promised Land; however, he was consoled by his service in the Sudan, with its happy memories of official functions, balls and banquets spent in the company of the great and the good of Britain and Europe.

Curiously, the local newspaper did not see fit to publish an obituary to Kitty Wingate; it simply recorded her death, drawing attention to the Wingates' long years of marriage, adding that she had been awarded the DBE.[3] However, a few weeks later, the Governor of the Crown Colony of Aden published a memorial in *The Times* which informed readers that Lady Wingate's death had touched the hearts and minds of British people in the Colony; it was the closest that the press got to an official obituary, highlighting her family's place in the history of Aden for over a century:

> It was her father [Joseph Sparkinhall Rundle] who as Mate of the [HMS] *Volage* at the capture of Aden in 1839 raised the British flag ... In 1926 Lady Wingate and Sir Leslie Rundle [her brother] had presented the Red Ensign [planted by their father] to the Colony.[4]

Memorial services were held simultaneously at St Anne's Episcopal Church, Dunbar and St Margaret's Chapel, Westminster. At Dunbar the chief mourners were Wingate, son Ronald and Ronald's wife Mary. The funeral was attended by a large congregation, including many of the landed gentry in East Lothian, officials from the Dunbar Branch of the British Legion and Councillor A. J. Manderson representing the Town Council. Kitty Wingate's favourite hymn Psalm 121 'I to the hills will lift mine eyes' was sung. It was an appropriate choice; from Knockenhair, the Wingates had a clear and unrestricted view of gorse-covered Doon Hill and the Lammermuirs beyond. One can only speculate on how she might have spent summer evenings gazing at the gentle, rolling horizon when her husband was absent abroad. She would have seen them turn misty when it rained, then sharp and blue in early autumn, when the light seems to come from within Doon Hill.

Looking back on his long life during the few lonely years that were left to him, Wingate never forgot the numerous processions in open, horse-drawn carriages with flanking flunkeys and military escorts, the ceremonial state occasions and military parades, sumptuous banquets and spangled balls. At the end of his public life Wingate still bore emotional wounds that had never healed, the worst inflicted by A. J. Balfour and his associates in the Foreign Office. Many other colleagues failed or ignored him, not even troubling themselves to express appreciation for his invaluable work in the Sudan and Egypt. Few offered the consolation of friendship and sympathy in his fall from power. Wingate had often thought of writing his memoirs, which could have damned many for their cynical treatment of him; had he felt less oppressed, he might have turned his impressive and voluminous collection of private and public papers into the exciting narrative story that it cries out for; this author's attempt has merely skimmed the surface of the thousands of words he wrote and which are preserved in the University of Durham. Throughout his life Wingate disciplined himself to keep meticulous, dispassionate and detailed records of his activities while voyaging into the often choppy waters of public life in the service of king and country.

When Wingate fell from grace in 1919 one can imagine the comments of the great and good slumped in the overstuffed armchairs in places like White's Club in London:

Wingate? Rum chappie. Went native they say. Wanted to give independence to the Gyppos. Damned un-British thing to do, what? HMG wouldn't stand for it. Quite right too. Damned Gyppos holding a gun to our heads. Imagine that happening in India, God forbid. End of civilization, what? Serves the blighter right, getting the sack. Of course, what can you expect from a Scotchman, what? Explains it all. Damned Scotch. Always causing trouble. Damned lucky England took 'em over in 1707, what? Union of the Parliaments and all that. Best thing that ever happened to the Scotch.

Years later, Reginald Wingate would often be confused with his cousin Orde who waged guerrilla war against the Japanese in Burma. Again, one can imagine the comments about Orde in the Officers' Mess:

Damned unorthodox chappie. Fancied himself as a Lawrence of Judea. Strange cove, supporting the Jews. They say he converted. Didn't he have a relative who was kicked out of Egypt for disloyalty to the Crown after the first show? Rum lot, the Wingates.

All his life Wingate was a stickler for proper dress, sharing the trait with Edward VII and George V who insisted on the proper display of medals, forms of address, protocol and points of etiquette. Wingate took immense care of his own person; he waxed and pomaded his moustache, wore immaculate clothes (including the conventional white evening waistcoats so beloved of Victorians), antiquated spats over his shoes and a top hat to church almost until the day he died. He was noted for his well-manicured fingernails and his beautiful, almost feminine, hands. It was his custom to apply lavender water and use seven open razors numbered for every day of the week.

We have seen that Wingate never took the time to write his memoirs, nor did he even write another book after 1891. It is known that his London publisher, Edward Arnold, repeatedly invited him to produce his memoirs – he even signed a contract to that effect in 1939 – but pleaded the intervention of the Second World War as an excuse for his procrastination. Added to this rather lame excuse, he said he could not undertake such a task without the help of son Ronald who was of course in uniform and abroad in India. A brief flicker of enthusiasm for such a project resurfaced in 1945 but was extinguished a year later, when it was shelved yet again, this time on account of Wingate's declining health. One hazards a guess that Wingate felt too bitter about his treatment in 1919 to be dispassionate and detached – essential ingredients in historical writings – about his time in Egypt.

Wingate spent the remaining years of his life virtually alone, his only companions being a part-time housekeeper, nurse and a gardener. One can imagine him wandering through the rooms at Knockenhair, reminded of a past life by various artefacts and memorabilia – the Dervish weapons on the walls, the leopardskin stair carpet. It was said that Wingate had always intended to create a mausoleum in the grounds of Knockenhair for himself and his wife, which under Scots law is illegal. A more prosaic explanation is that the plot was used as a resting place for his deceased dogs.

Wingate made his last trip abroad in 1947 when he visited son Ronald in Brussels. He spent the winter of that year with daughter Victoria and her children in Kent. In frail and increasingly failing health, perhaps he was aware that he was saying a final goodbye to the last of his family. However, he managed a trip to London in November 1948, as is evinced by his manuscript note on a Christmas card illustrating the King's Troop, Royal Horse Artillery which he sent from Number Eleven, Woodville Gardens:

> This is the Troop that fired the salute of 41 guns today [15 November] from the Broad Walk, Hyde Park in celebration of the Royal Birth [of Prince Charles].

Poor health made it difficult for Wingate to observe his social obligations in Dunbar. Gradually, these tailed off after Lady Wingate's death. Even so, he was not forgotten. In September 1950 the Town Council sent a letter reminding him that he had been made a freeman of the Burgh fifty years earlier.[5] The Council also sent him congratulatory letters on the occasion of his birthday, particularly his ninetieth in June 1951.[6] Perhaps Wingate took the salute at the local war memorial on Armistice Sunday that year, the first and only time the author met him. It was probably one of his last public duties.

Due to health problems Wingate was obliged to vacate Knockenhair, as the mansion had become too expensive to heat and was unsuitable for domiciliary nursing care. According to the local newspaper, Wingate spent the last few years in the local Hotel Belle Vue from where he continued to receive visitors and kept up correspondence with his few surviving friends. While there he was attended by Nurse Helen Hutton, to whom he became greatly attached. He would draw his last breath while resident at the hotel in January 1953.

It is strange and perhaps not coincidental that, six days before his death, Wingate presented a Coptic-Christian censer to St Anne's Episcopal Church.[7] There was more than a little touch of feudal chivalry in this gesture – the dying knight bestowing a gift for prayers to be said for his soul. It was in keeping with Wingate's sense of tradition.

On Wednesday, 28 January 1953, General Sir Francis Reginald Wingate, the oldest and most decorated general in the British Army, finally breathed his last. The local newspaper published an obituary the following Friday,[8] which made mention of Winston Churchill, a man whom Wingate had always referred to as 'a young subaltern of mine' – probably a reference to Churchill's participation in the charge of the 21st Lancers at Omdurman in 1898. The same obituary also referred to the existence in Knockenhair of the *firwa*, or sheepskin rug, on which the Khalifa had knelt to await his death at the hands of Wingate's Sudanese battalions during the action at Um Dibaykarat on 23 November 1899. Ronald Evelyn Leslie Wingate inherited his father's honorific, becoming 2nd Baron Dunbar and Port Sudan, a title which became extinct at his death as he lacked a blood-line heir.

Telegrams and letters from all over the UK and the Middle East poured into Knockenhair; among the first were those from Queen Mary and Prime Minister Churchill. The Town Council minutes of 30 January 1953 recorded the following tribute:

> his interest and work in the Royal National Lifeboat Institution of which he was a member of the Executive Board ... Although he had not taken an active part in the administration of the Burgh affairs, Sir Reginald had at all times given encouragement to many local activities. He was a Deputy Lord Lieutenant of the county of Haddington, Freeman of the Burgh of Dunbar, Honorary Life Member of the Dunbar Lodge of Free-masons[9] and President of the local branch of the British Legion. Provost Manderson expressed the sentiments of the Town Council when he stated that the community would deeply mourn the loss of a very old and distinguished friend.[10]

In addition to these activities, Wingate had founded the local Horticultural Society, opened bazaars, fairs and swimming galas at which he often offici-ated as judge of competitions; the Wingates were also members of the East Lothian Antiquarian and Field Naturalists' Society (it still meets today).

In recognition of his long association with the British Army and rank at retirement from the Army Active List, the Army Council in London agreed that Wingate should be honoured with a military funeral and all the pomp and formality associated with such events.[11]

On 3 February 1953, a grey overcast day, the funeral arrangements began with a service at noon in St Anne's Episcopal Church. It was an impressive funeral, sombre and emotive, bringing a sense of occasion to the life of a small community. The overwhelming military presence was fitting; Wingate, the veteran soldier, had never forgotten his beginnings as a young lieutenant in the Royal Artillery at Woolwich, nor had he lost touch with his few remaining comrades-in-arms.

The service was conducted by the Episcopalian Bishop of Edinburgh, the Right Reverend K. C. H. Warner, and the local rector, the Reverend E. M. Ivans. The Bishop's address was simple and direct:

> We meet today to pay our respects to, and commend into the hands of Almighty God, one to whom was granted a long life in which he rendered signal service to his country. It is a rare thing that a man should give distinguished service under three monarchs [Victoria, Edward VII and George V] and live in retirement under three more [Edward VIII, George VI, and Elizabeth] ... Under his rule and administration [of the Sudan], sound economic planning replaced poverty and confusion. But this is not the time for laudatory speeches and flattering phrases, nor was he a man to approve of these, least of all for himself. For first and foremost, he was a Christian.[12]

The Bishop also related how, as a child one morning at breakfast, his father had read an account of the victory at Omdurman when it appeared in *The Daily Mail* of September 1898.

The many floral tributes included those from Sir Winston Churchill, the Army Council, the 7th Manchesters, the Egyptian Army Dinner Club, the Reginald Wingate (Freemasons) Lodge No 2954 EC, Khartoum and, touchingly, one from the trustees of the Gordon Memorial College, Khartoum, the Burgh Council and the Royal National Lifeboat Institution. Among the chief mourners were his son Sir Ronald Wingate and his wife, Lady Mary, Mrs Henry Dane (Victoria, Wingate's daughter) and her son Paul, Mrs Guy Street, Wingate's grand-daughter-in-law, and Colonel Walter Wingate Gray, a cousin. Mrs Helen Hutton, the nurse who had attended Wingate in his last years was also present, as was his gardener, William Baker. The dignitaries included Lieutenant General Sir Colin M. Barber, Commander in Chief, Scottish Command, representing the Army Council; C. G. Davies MC, Sudanese Agent in London, representing Sir Robert Howe, Governor General of the Sudan; Meccowi Akrat, Assistant Sudanese Agent, representing the Sudanese government in Khartoum and Ewan Campbell from the Sudanese Political Service. The Masonic Lodges of Egypt and the Sudan were also represented, as were the Town Council, the British Legion and various youth organizations in Dunbar. The Regimental party escorting the cortege was as follows:

	Officers	Other Ranks
Territorial Army	2	6
357th Medium Regiment	1	2
278th Field Regiment	1	2
414th Coast Regiment	1	2
587th Light Anti-Aircraft Regiment	1	2
Regular Army		
69th Heavy Anti-Aircraft Regiment (Redford Barracks, Midlothian) which provided the gun carriage	1	16

Other military representatives were drawn from 170 Provost Company, Corps of Royal Military Police; Trumpeters from the Boys' Regiment, Royal Artillery and the Pipes and Drums of 1st Argyll and Sutherland Highlanders, a regiment with which Wingate had connections.

Over 700 Dunbar schoolchildren were invited to line the route of the cortege along the High Street to pay their last respects to the Grand Old Man. It was a memorable occasion as the author, then aged ten, recalls; the hundreds who stood to attention as a mark of respect had hardly known the old man personally and few had little knowledge of his military and other public service achievements. Everyone in Dunbar knew him simply as 'The Sirdar' and that he was a great and generous man; perhaps a few discerning observers may have sensed that a page in British history had turned.

The cortege proceeded slowly from St Anne's along a hushed High Street, the Royal Artillery Guard/bearer party flanking the gun carriage bearing the coffin, marching at the slow step, the family members following behind. The coffin was draped with the Union Flag and bore Wingate's cocked hat, sword and a laurel wreath. The cortege passed the Town House and Town Chambers, the windows masked by drawn blinds, the Union Flag flying at half-mast from the roof. As the procession drew near the Parish Church, the Argylls played *The Flowers of the Forest*. If, all those years ago in 1908, Wingate had paid Dunbar a compliment by making it his home, some of the towns-people repaid the gesture on that February day.

Schoolchildren and townspeople were forbidden to attend the graveside ceremony. It was later made known that a short, dedicatory service had been held in a quiet corner of the cemetery where a lone piper played *Lochaber No More* as Wingate's remains were lowered into the grave. Two trumpeters from the Boys' Royal Artillery played *Last Post*, then *Reveille*.

After the funeral the *Haddingtonshire Courier* reporter for Dunbar paid his personal tribute to a man he admitted he had known only in the last few years of his life. He described Wingate as

The kindliest of men; the memory of his courtesy to all whatever their rank or creed, will be an inspiration to us who knew him. He loved a joke and was a raconteur ... 'The Captains and the Kings depart!' and we are left to wonder if we will ever look upon his like again.[13]

Fine words for a fine gentleman. Wingate was an honourable man, honest, kind and in many ways a prophet – and we know that a prophet is never honoured in his own country, especially by those in officialdom. The world has known few such men in modern times.

A memorial service was held in St Margaret's Chapel, Westminster at noon on 4 March, a fitting tribute to a loyal servant of the British Empire. His late wife Kitty had been commemorated there nearly seven years earlier. No doubt the service was attended by Sir Ronald and Lady Mary Wingate. Sir Ronald kept up an association with Dunbar for several years, albeit from a distance. Later that year, as recorded in the Council minutes, Sir Ronald presented an oil portrait to the Town Council by former soldier and prominent Maltese artist Edward Caruanan Dinghli (1877–1950). Painted in Malta in 1914, but contrary to the Town Council Minutes which describe the portrait as one of Reginald Wingate, it is in fact that of Sir Leslie Rundle, Wingate's brother-in-law and former Governor General of Malta from 1909 to 1915.[14] A few months later the Town Council received a letter dated 2 September from Wingate's executors intimating that he had left a legacy of £100 'to the poor of Dunbar'.[15] Other gifts followed, including Knockenhair House itself, presented to the people of Dunbar; the building was later converted into rented flats until these were finally sold privately.

In 1955, Sir Ronald published a history of his father's time in the Sudan, *Wingate of the Sudan*, which tells us very little of Wingate's private life because, as Ronald Wingate admitted in his second book, *Not in the Limelight*, he saw little of his father after attending boarding school and less during his career in the Indian Civil Service. Despite this, Ronald Wingate wrote loving words about his parents and his happy childhood in Cairo, Khartoum and Knockenhair.

By any military standards, Wingate was neither a military leader in the mould of his contemporaries – Kitchener, T. E. Lawrence, Orde Charles Wingate, nor was his career particularly heroic; he rarely had to resort to the use of rifle or bayonet, yet he achieved much in his army years and later in public administration. His genius lay in his mastery of languages, his perception of other men's minds, be they friend or enemy. His reputation as maker of the Anglo-Egyptian Sudan was built on a genuine concern for the people over whom he was appointed to rule; that and an ability to create a climate for social change based on sound economic principles. It could be argued that, during the campaign to free the Sudan, the success of his spy network and the steadfastness of General Sir Hector MacDonald gave Kitchener his victory at Omdurman. As Kitchener's spymaster, Wingate prepared the ground and MacDonald fought over and won it.

Wingate was devoted to the Sudan and its well-being and prosperity. His tolerance and trust of its people resulted in policies which did much to establish confidence in British (Christian) rule over a predominantly Muslim, Arab-oriented people. With the growth of Sudanese national consciousness, the country became independent with an elected representative parliament on 1 January 1956. Wingate would have been proud; in many ways the great moment was his legacy to a people he loved and respected.

Wingate was a man ahead of his time. Unlike many of his contemporaries he took the trouble to learn the language of the peoples of the Sudan and Egypt, respecting their customs, culture and religious beliefs. The author takes the view that Wingate was misunderstood, a scapegoat for what occurred in Egypt between 1917 and 1919. In seeking to understand Wingate, one is reminded of an anecdote about a learned QC who, having elaborately explained an admittedly confusing situation to a judge, was met with the response, 'I am none the wiser for your explanation', to which the barrister replied, 'No, My Lord, but you are now better informed.'

Statesman, civil servant, representative of Victoria, Edward VII and George V in the Sudan and Egypt, Wingate was energetic and tireless in his devotion to duty for Britain and these peoples. Even after his underhandedly blunt and undeserved dismissal, he worked on a comprehensive memorandum setting out his views on the future of Egypt. Perhaps his attention to duty was a powerful stimulant; a lesser man would have demitted office with bitterness, with a desire to get even, to blow the whistle, to accuse those who had unfairly wronged him. Wingate was a gentleman from his top hat to his spats, never vindictive, nearly always forgiving. He strove to do his best for his Egyptians and Sudanese who entertained hopes of achieving self-determination, hopes which the Foreign Office cynically dismissed as 'native aspirations'.

Wingate was supported by friends to whom he remained loyal and who reciprocated his friendship. Men like Lords Kitchener and Cromer, Rudolf von Slatin are examples of friendships which only ended with their deaths – Kitchener on 5 June 1916 in the sinking of HMS *Hampshire*; Cromer dying of ill-health on 29 January 1917 (uncannily almost thirty-six years to the day before Wingate's own death) and Slatin on 4 October 1931. There are enough letters written by these four men to fill several volumes. It is perhaps not a coincidence that during their careers all four were not only isolated geographically from the epicentre of power but also to a great extent remote in the political sense from the corridors of power in Whitehall. They never belonged to the cliques and *cabals* of their day.

Wingate was intelligent rather than intellectual, a realist rather than a romantic such as T. E. Lawrence. He felt the cold hand of history on his collar, knowing that his – and Britain's – time in Egypt would come to an end as it did in 1956, only three years after his death. The author hazards a guess that in his final years Wingate knew what would happen in Egypt although he could not have been able to predict with certainty that the Egyptian Army officer and politician Gamal Abd-El Nasser would become President in 1954, and would sign the Anglo-Egyptian agreement on the Suez Canal under which all British troops were to evacuate the Canal Zone by June 1956. Matters came to a head that year when Nasser nationalized the Suez Canal Company, precipitating an Anglo-French landing in the Canal Zone on 5 November 1956. The British and French claimed they were there in the role of peacekeepers to pre-empt a war between Egypt and Israel. It was a fiasco; the invaders failed to prevent the Egyptians from blocking the canal, there was an economic crisis as investors in the Canal Company bailed out and Prime Minister Anthony Eden was obliged to climb down.

It was not only the great and the good whose lives were touched by the extraordinary little Scotsman from Port Glasgow. The young officers who served under him in Khartoum and Cairo considered him an inspirational figure. They were loyal to him to such an extent that it must have ruffled the feathers of those in Whitehall, leading to an accusation that he was over familiar with his staff, a criticism levelled against those in government service who care about their staff. This trait is seen as weakness. Wingate's young men were not trained administrators, however; they were first and foremost soldiers but they placed their trust in him rather than in the politicians and mandarins of Whitehall. He inspired them by his example; some inevitably sacrificed their careers and promotion prospects in their devotion to him. In return, although he was unstinting in praise of them, he was acutely aware of the Machiavellian shifts and U-turns in the politics of his day. Wingate could smell the salt of a sea-change spreading over the British Empire. The Great War of 1914–18 proved that powerful empires pass away; the Ottoman Empire, the Russian Empire and the British Empire were all casualties in that hellish cauldron, that crucible which consumed the privilege and selfishness of the dynasties which had hitherto enjoyed unlimited power.

The Sudanese, Egyptians and Syrians with whom Wingate worked, loved, trusted and respected the man they dubbed 'The Father of the Ink'. If T. E. Lawrence was regarded in army and political circles as something of a visionary – a derogatory term in the eyes of Establishment – Wingate was, in his own quiet way, something of the same. He created and fostered the conditions under which young Sudanese men could become cadet officers and administrators. Wingate foresaw that Sudanese prosperity would make it less dependent on Egypt and thereby more self-sufficient in developing its own agriculture and building irrigation schemes to produce sufficient cotton as to ultimately transform the Sudanese economy from one in the red to one in the black.

Perhaps it is appropriate here to compare the rewards given to three of the men who to a greater or lesser degree administered the Sudan and Egypt. Kitchener received a Baronetcy and £30,000, followed by a Viscountcy and £50,000; he was finally elevated to the House of Lords after receiving an Earldom. Cromer got a Baronetcy, a Viscountcy, an Earldom and £50,000. Wingate received a Baronetcy and had to haggle to get a reduced Army pension of £1,300 a year in his capacity as a general.

These men were not without flaws; human beings are not perfect. They all shared one characteristic, however – they were dedicated to their profession and to Britain. Possibly, the positions of power they held made them intolerant sometimes. We cannot blame them for that. Their individual achievements, their loyalty to king and country and, ultimately, the people whom they served stand as testimony to their good faith. When they came to the Sudan, they entered a charnel-house, a chaotic, cruel, tyrannical part of the world. When Wingate, the last of them, left the Sudan, it had become a country enjoying peace and growing prosperity. His achievement is sadly now no more than a footnote in history. Wingate was a man with bottomless wells of humanity and energy, using his power not for personal gain but to improve the lives of the people over whom he was set to rule. He hid his humanitarianism under the cloak of Imperial duty; he believed that the Sudanese and the Egyptians would assume responsibility for themselves in due course, a freedom which would not be won without sacrifice, which throughout history has been the price men and women have to pay for achieving democracy.

Looking back, one asks again the obvious question – why did Wingate not seek out sympathetic ears among the backbenchers in the House of Commons in 1919 who might have saved him from the sack, or at least clamoured for his elevation to the peerage? 'Viscount Wingate of Khartoum' has a fine ring but it never became an entry in *Burke's Peerage*; perhaps Wingate was aware that sometimes even those who are in the right are better off keeping their counsel. Wingate and the shabby treatment he received from the Foreign Office and, by extension, the government of the day, is now a forgotten episode. He was but one of many casualties of his time. In many ways his end was accidental, a mere collision of the random and the inevitable in the politics of his day.

Fortunately Wingate's personal life was by and large happy. He was married to a vivacious woman: Kitty Rundle was a perfect match, supporting her husband in all he did. They loved one another without qualification but their lives were marred significantly by the deaths of two sons; their infant son Graham Andrew Leslie was born and sadly died in the same year of 1892, then in 1918 they lost Malcolm Roy in the Great War. Wingate's part of the family tree has bare branches; the family name has hardly survived, although Reginald and Kitty left descendants through their daughter Victoria, some of whose grandchildren live in the United Kingdom today.

There can be no absolute truth about a life lived, either in autobiography or biography. Who can know a person completely? No-one, not even the subject in question. Each generation distils its own view of an individual, coloured as that view will inevitably be by emotion, prejudice, ignorance and, of course, the politically correct *mores* of the time. Wingate lived in an era during which Britain coloured the map of the world pink, as many of this author's generation of schoolchildren were proud to learn. Since his death we have witnessed the geo-political consequences of that map although Wingate himself foresaw some of what would come to pass. We are presently witnessing a period of unrest in the Sudan, the even greater tragedy of the Israel-Palestine conflict, the rise of terrorism in many Middle East countries and the tragedies of conflict in Iraq and Afghanistan. What would the Sirdar, General Sir Reginald Wingate, make of it all?

The Wingate family lives on even if the military name barely does. Reginald and Kitty Wingate's immediate descendants survive through their daughter Victoria. This author is sure these descendants rightfully take great pride in their illustrious ancestor whose remains lie in Dunbar Churchyard beneath a simple cross of granite whose inscription honours him in the way he would have wished:

FRANCIS REGINALD

WINGATE

THE MAKER OF THE ANGLO-EGYPTIAN SUDAN

What better epitaph for a Scottish gentleman who loved the people of that remote country?

Notes

1. *HC*, 15 January 1946.
2. *The Sirdar*, Daly.
3. *HC*, 14 June 1946.
4. *Ibid.*, 5 July 1946.
5. *Dunbar Town Council Minutes*, 13 September 1950, SRO ref B 18/13/26.
6. *Ibid.*, 11 July 1951, SRO ref B 18/13/27.
7. *HC*, 23 January 1953.
8. *Ibid.*, 30 January 1953.
9. Wingate had also been Grand Master of Egypt and the Sudan and Grand Warden of England.
10. *Dunbar Town Council Minutes*, 30 January 1953, SRO ref B 18/13/29.
11. See papers on Wingate's funeral, SRO ref B 18/20/28.
12. *HC*, 6 February 1953.
13. *Ibid.*
14. *Dunbar Town Council Minutes*, 13 May and 10 June 1953, SRO ref B 18/13/29. These respectively read as follows:

    '... Provost Manderson stated that Sir Ronald Wingate had offered the Town Council a portrait of his father, the late General Sir Reginald Wingate and the Council unanimously agreed to accept the gift, with an expression of thanks to Sir Ronald, and to display the portrait suitably ...' (13 May 1953).

    '... The Council agreed that the portrait in oil should hang in a suitable place on the walls of the stairway leading to the Council Chambers ...' (10 June 1953).

    However, it may never have been put on public display as it is unframed and had been stored in the Town Council safe, where it languished for many years. The author recommended that the East Lothian Council Museums Service remove it to a place of safety as the painting, being by E. C. Dinghli, the renowned Maltese artist, may well be of great monetary value. Subsequently, investigation of the military decorations by the author has revealed that the subject is wearing the ribbon of the Queen's South Africa medal awarded to officers serving in the Boer War 1899–1902. As Wingate never served in this campaign, the portrait is without question that of Sir Leslie Rundle, who did; this view is also confirmed by close examination of contemporary photographs of Rundle.
15. *Dunbar Town Council Minutes*, 9 September 1953, SRO ref B 18/13/29.

Conclusion

So, was Francis Reginald Wingate an arch-imperialist? The answer seems to be yes and no.

Today the words 'Empire' and 'Imperialism' are seen as pejorative; modern, revisionist historians find it fashionable to write in derogatory terms about the British Empire, which, to a certain extent, is justified. No empire in world history has escaped censure, particularly those of Persia, Russia, India, China and Japan. The British Empire was the largest, ruling a quarter of the world's population and covering roughly the same proportion of land mass. Despite its excesses – racial prejudice, intolerance, exploitation, greed, arrogance and genocide – it nevertheless proved, in this author's opinion, the most civilized – and civilizing – empire of all in the course of the world's history.

Of course, empires are not won by gifts of bibles, convivial dinner parties and friendly handshakes; these are the business of the post-conquest administrators, after the guns have ceased firing. Empires are founded by ruthless individuals intent on power – soldiers and entrepreneurs who employ the sword and the bullet to achieve their aims. The British Empire was no different; it could not do without the gunboat. Speaking of the Empire in the House of Commons as early as 1766, Edmund Burke, the Member for Wendover, Buckinghamshire, had this to say, 'Without freedom [it] would not be a British Empire'. Taken out of context and at face value, Burke's statement is a contradiction in terms. Burke knew that empires are built through conquest, commerce, migration and settlement. Where the British Empire differed from its predecessors was the manner in which it enforced its rule. History has shown us that other empires were harsher in their treatment of their subject people. Even in modern times, the British people extol its virtues, viewing the past often through rose-tinted spectacles. Many thought – and still do – that the countries absorbed into the British Empire fared better than had they had been left to themselves. In many respects, this is true.

If the British Empire was won in battles fought by the English, it was the Scots and Irish who made a major contribution to sustaining it. F. R. Wingate was one such man. He believed in the Empire but also wished to improve the lot of the peoples over whom he was appointed to rule. Given Scotland's long struggle to preserve her independence from England, Scotsmen like Wingate were educated by their own country's experience to believe they should

275

demonstrate an enlightened approach to their administration of the nations occupied by Imperial Britain. This is perhaps graphically illustrated by comparing Wingate, a relatively small fish in the Middle East, to Lord George Curzon, Viceroy of India (1898–1905). Curzon was conservative from head to toe, expecting those over whom he was set to touch their forelocks and bow to their 'betters'. The same cannot be said of Wingate.

Did men like Curzon and Wingate perceive their primary duty as loyalty to king and country and serving British interests abroad? Of course they did. Curzon and his predecessors and successors who governed India, the jewel in the British crown, were determined to resist any attempts by the indigenous population to obtain independence. They did so because, while the Foreign Office once stated that it was the primary duty of the British Empire to prepare the nations they governed for independence, that independence was withheld – indefinitely – to suit British interests. Curzon in particular took the view that the idea of independence for India was unthinkable, with his 'I know better than you what is good for you because I am British' approach. Kitchener, the soldier, would have put it another way: 'We have got the Maxim gun which you have not.'

Wingate, a soldier first, then a statesman, was hardly unique. Of course he believed in the re-conquest of the Sudan by force but only because he believed passionately about the plight of the people tyrannized and enslaved by the Mahdists. However, he made the transition from serving soldier to civil administrator with surprising ease, which suggests he had found his true vocation, in 1899, when appointed Governor General of the Sudan, then High Commissioner of Egypt in 1917.

Wingate's administration of the Sudan was one of benign autocracy but he had a genuine concern for the welfare of the Sudanese people. His fluency in Arabic gave him a partiality towards them; a love of the Sudan remained fixed and constant throughout his life. From the outset, he abolished reactionary and even barbaric customs – for centuries, the Sudan economy was principally engaged in slave trading – and initiated reforms which improved the daily lives of the ordinary people. For example, he introduced a modern legal system – the Sudan previously had none – and embarked on an intensive education programme open to native men and women alike. He reformed the ineffective agricultural system, experimenting with new crops, irrigating hitherto unproductive desert areas, thus providing both food for the population and improving the export trade of a previously weak Sudanese economy. These were all cornerstones of British Imperial policy in countries which had failed to develop their potential either through ignorance or civil war.

It may be difficult for some today to acknowledge that, without a British Empire, the introduction of the framework of liberal capitalism would have taken much longer to achieve, if at all. The imposition of Imperial rule brought into existence the institutions of parliamentary democracy, which made the British Empire different, perhaps unique, among the empires of the world. Of course there were rebellions against British rule, uprisings fomented by nationalist elements seeking independence; these were put down with a force which was sometimes excessive and brutal. Wingate, knowing that the Empire did not have an unblemished record, did not relish such a prospect during his brief time as High Commissioner of Egypt. Egypt was second only to India in the hierarchy of nations ruled by the British, chiefly on account of the Suez Canal, in which Britain held the major share-holding since 1875.

When he arrived in Cairo to take up his new appointment in 1917, Wingate was acutely aware of not only the long-standing anti-British feelings in Egypt but also of the rise of the Egyptian Nationalist party seeking independence. He repeatedly sought clarification by the British government of the precise nature of the Protectorate agreement signed at the outbreak of the Great War, promising freedom to the Egyptians for their support against Germany and Turkey. His overtures to a resolute and insensitive Foreign Office about the need to recognize the growing power of the Nationalists fell on deaf ears. He warned the government that if it continued to ignore the Nationalists, there would be a violent backlash. Wingate's warnings were received first as irksome, second as weakness and third, as incompetence. These led to his downfall and dismissal.

So, was Wingate an arch-imperialist in the traditions of men like Curzon? The answer depends on the conditions obtaining in the countries over which he ruled. Had the Sudan been a rich, prosperous and sophisticated country, would Wingate have ruled it as he did? Also, had Egypt not been in close proximity to the Suez Canal, or if there had been no Canal at all, would Wingate have taken the same line with the British government? The answer to both questions is – probably not. Had the Sudan possessed vast oil reserves, the British government would certainly have treated matters differently; for one thing, there would have been stiff resistance to any moves for independence; for another, the country would have been occupied by a major British military force to protect the oil. As for Egypt, without Suez, the British government would have probably granted its independence in 1919.

The above picture is, however, purely this author's conjecture. Wingate the imperialist tempered his loyalty to king and country with a sincere and genuine compassion for the Sudanese people. As for Egypt, Curzon and his like deplored the arrogance of the nationalists, whereas Wingate detected a wind of change. Curzon was determined to resist any demands for self-government in Egypt because, were that to happen, it would send a direct and unequivocal signal to the nationalists in India.

Without doubt Wingate believed in the virtues of the British Empire but he knew it was only a matter of time before it would be dismantled, both as a result of its success and of the increasingly negative policies Britain followed at the beginning of the twentieth century, when there were distinct signs of imperial demise. Did Wingate mourn the passing of Empire when India was granted independence in 1947, the British withdrawing with almost unseemly haste, leaving behind a chaos that almost undid two centuries of orderly government? In all probability, Wingate was saddened by the spectacle, which answers the question posed at the outset. When General Sir Francis Reginald Wingate died in 1953, a part of the British Empire passed with him.

Appendix I

Declaration of Martial Law in Egypt

Extract from the *Journal Officiel du Gouvernement Egyptian* (Issue No. 146) dated 2 November 1914:

I, John Grenfell Maxwell, Lieutenant General Commanding His Britannic Majesty's Forces in Egypt, entrusted with the application of Martial Law, hereby give notice as follows:-

(1) The powers to be exercised under my authority by the Military Authorities are intended to supplement and not to supersede the Civil Administration, and all civil officials in the service of the Egyptian Government are hereby required to continue the punctual discharge of their respective duties.

(2) Private citizens will best serve the common end by abstaining from all action of a nature to disturb the public peace, to stir up disaffection, or to aid the enemies of His Britannic Majesty and His Allies, and by conforming promptly and cheerfully to all orders given under my authority for the maintenance of public peace and good order; and so long as they do so, they will be subject to no interference from the Military Authorities.

(3) All requisitions of services or of property which may be necessitated by military exigencies will be the subject of full compensation, to be assessed, in default of agreement, by an independent authority.

Cairo, November 2, 1914   (Signed) J. G. MAXWELL
Lieutenant General,
Commanding His Britannic Majesty's
Forces in Egypt

Appendix II

Turkish Propaganda Leaflet

Propaganda leaflet issued by the Turkish Government on 5 November 1914 marked 'secret' by the Intelligence Department, War Office, Cairo. The document is annotated thus:

> The attached are translations of Calls to the *Jehad* which have been issued in Turkey. A copy was obtained by this Department from Baghdad
>
> Translation
>
> To the Holy War. To the Holy War.
>
> A General call from the Society for uniting all the peoples of the Koran.
>
> > I take refuge in God from the cursed Satan.
> > In the name of God, the Merciful, the Compassionate.
> > Verily God hath bought the persons and substance of the Faithful and promised them Paradise in return: on the path of God shall they fight and slay, and be slain; this promise is given in the Law, in the Gospel, and in the Koran – and who more faithful to his engagement than God?
> > Rejoice, therefore, in the contract that ye have contracted; for this shall be the great bliss.
> > Peace be unto every Moslem believing in God and the Last Day, in the East and in the West, and the grace and blessings of God be on them.
> > My brethren in God, amongst other things which is not doubted by any sensible man and which has become quite clear and is taken for granted is the fact that the nations of Europe, the worshippers of the Cross, have determined from hundreds of years ago to fight Moslems, wipe out their religion and abolish their Sultanate from the face of the Earth. They make attacks on us nearly every day and take by violence and force a part of our countries and kingdom, without any reason. Their politicians and leaders like Gladstone, Hanotaux [French Minister of Foreign Affairs (1894–1898) and ardent supporter of the Franco-Russian Alliance] and Peter the Great have several times declared, and the actions of their Priests and Missionaries confirmed their declaration, that these infidels, who have ignored the Faith of God and His Apostles, intend surely to destroy the Kaaba [House of God in the centre of the Harem or courtyard of the Great Mosque at Mecca, which Muslims

believe was the first edifice erected for the worship of God] and the Tomb of the Prophet and to burn the Koran, wipe out Islam, convert Moslems to Christianity and baptize them by all possible means as they did centuries ago in Spain and days ago in the Balkan States.

In order to show the oppressions and atrocities of Europe and its savage dealings it is sufficient to recall to your memories their actions in Tripoli, Kharasan and Azerbijan [north west Persia], and in all the countries which they conquered in the Balkans.

Yesterday the principal beasts of the Balkan States: the Bulgarians, Servians [Serbians], Montenegrins and Greeks, the students of the European political professors, have attacked and killed your men with guns and rifles, and then turned to your women and children. They slew the children and violated the women in the most infamous manner. They also have burnt your Mosques, places of worship and the tombs of your grand-fathers.

Now Moslems, who are now in the last stage of glory and life, take up this invaluable opportunity in which God has caused His enemies to fight one another – Unite in the Union of Faith and gather together against these infidels and drive them out of your countries and homes. Fight them with the energy of those who care not for themselves and those who defend themselves, their Religion and Honour.

Help one another in this Holy War which is incumbent on you; even women and children should join in the War.

Also the Ulemas and Fikis should guard the grandeur of Islam and defend the Faith with money, soul and sound advice, God says in His Holy Book.

So make War on them: By your hands will God chastise them, and will put them to shame, will give you victory over them, will heal the bosoms of a people who believe and will take away the wrath of their hearts.

Take up the Holy War and sacrifice to it your souls and properties, whether you are light or burdened.

In the name of God, the Merciful, the Compassionate. Praise be to God who has favoured His creatures with the right Faith and taught all mankind and spirits, as is said in the Koran, that the right Faith is El Islam – and prayers and peace be on the guide of all creatures to the right path, the Holy Instructor and the Great Mediator our Lord and Prophet Mohammed El Mustafa, the Imam of the Apostles and the last of the Prophets, the Merciful, the Compassionate, and on all his noble family and reverend friends, the Imams of Moslems, the Lions of War in the Holy Places who hasten to comply with God's call.

We beg hereby to remind our Moslem brethren in the East and in the West of El Islam and its precepts, that the religious brotherhood is higher than the sexual brotherhood, and Moslems should in all circumstances be like a strong building, supporting one another. They should always be one in the Faith and work together for the honour of the word of God, obeying the order of God and united together against the enemies of God.

Their Faith instructs them that Moslems in the East should support Moslems in the West – It is not necessary to quote the verses of the Koran in this sense as these verses are known to all Ulemas of the Faith and to all the Faithful.

I address therefore the servants of God, the believers in the Koran, the Faithful who believe in God and the Great Prophet.

Is it becoming for men of energy, courage and honour, men of dignity and honour, to see the foreigners unite and come up together from all parts to conquer and occupy the countries of Moslems – to estrange them from their Faith, enjoy their women and daughters and possess their properties, and yet remain indolent, lazy, submissive, eating and drinking as if they were sheep – not caring for the deplorable state they are in and the state to which their brother Moslems in all parts of the world are subject, – miseries, calamities, murdering, burning, destruction, pillaging, etc, etc – the news of which taxes the heart.

You should, for such calamities to which your brother Moslems are subjected, be in mourning and remain so until you take revenge against their enemies and restore all that has been lost of their countries and the honour of their religion.

Wake up: therefore, O Brethren – May God guide you to the right path, wake up from the slumbers of humiliation and take support from God for the restoration of your honour – Unite together O Brethren, and if you do not feel pain from the calamities which befel [sic] your brother Moslems in the Balkan States, etc, which calamities affect even the stones, I will then with a broken heart call out "What a calamity, what a "Misery, what a Humiliation, what an Ending, let us lament 'El Islam'.

We are of God and to Him we shall return. There is no might nor power except in God.

Peace be unto you and the Mercy and Blessing of God.

(*Sudan Archive No. 133/4/45*, Durham University Library)

This was the document which Hussein, Emir of Mecca, refused to accept, using by way of excuse the fact that the Turks themselves were allied with non-Muslim Christian Germany. There was logic in his argument.

McMahon-Hussein Letter (excerpt)

In 1915–16 Sir Henry McMahon (1862–1949), British High Commissioner in Cairo, negotiated with Hussein Ibn Ali, the Sherif or Emir of Mecca. The British government promised to support his bid for the restoration of the Caliphate and leadership in the Arab world.

24 October 1915

I have received your letter of the 29th Shawal 1333 [the Islamic calendar date for 29 September 1915], with much pleasure and your expression of friendliness and sincerity have given me the greatest satisfaction.

I regret that you should have received from my last letter the impression that I regarded the question of limits and boundaries with coldness and hesitation, such was not the case, but it appeared to me that the time had not yet come when that question could be discussed in a conclusive manner.

I have realized, however, from your last letter that you regard this question as one of vital and urgent importance. I have, therefore, lost no time in informing the Government of Great Britain of the contents of your letter, and it is with great pleasure that I communicate to you on their behalf the following statement, which I am confident you will receive with satisfaction.

The two districts of Mersina and Alexandretta and portions of Syria lying to the west of the districts of Damascus, Homs, Hama and Aleppo *cannot be said to be purely Arab*, [author's italics] and should be excluded from the limits demanded.

With the above modification, and without prejudice to our existing treaties with Arab chiefs, we accept those limits.

As for those regions lying within those frontiers wherein Great Britain is free to act without detriment to the interests of her ally, France, I am empowered in the name of the Government of Great Britain to give the following assurances and make the following assurances and make the following reply to your letter.

(i) Subject to the above modifications, Great Britain is prepared to recognize and support the independence of the Arabs in all the regions within the limits demanded by the Sherif of Mecca [Hussein].

(ii) Great Britain will guarantee the Holy Places against all external aggression and will recognize their inviolability.

(iii) When the situation admits, Great Britain will give to the Arabs her advice and will assist them to establish what may appear to be the most suitable forms of government in those various territories.

(iv) On the other hand, it is understood that the Arabs have decided to seek the advice and guidance of Great Britain only, and that such European advisers and officials as may be required for the formation of a sound form of administration will be British.

(v) With regard to the vilayets [provinces of Turkey] of Baghdad and Basra, the Arabs will recognize that the established position and interests of Great Britain necessitate special administrative arrangements in order to secure these territories from foreign aggression, [ie Turkey] to promote the welfare of the local populations and to safeguard our mutual economic interests.

I am convinced that this declaration will assure you beyond all possible doubt of the sympathy of Great Britain towards the aspirations of her friends the Arabs and will result in a firm and lasting alliance, the immediate results of which will be the expulsion of the Turks from the Arab countries and the freeing of the Arab peoples from the Turkish yoke, which for so many years has pressed heavily upon them.

I have confined myself in this letter to the more vital and important questions, and if there are any other matters dealt with in your letters which I have omitted to mention, we may discuss them at some convenient date in the future.

It was with very great relief and satisfaction that I heard of the safe arrival of the Holy Carpet and the accompanying offerings which, thanks to the clearness of your directions and the excellence of your arrangements, were landed without trouble or mishap in spite of the dangers and difficulties occasioned by the present sad war. May God soon bring a lasting peace and freedom of all peoples.

I am sending this letter by the hand of your trusted and excellent messenger Sheik Mohammed ibn Arif ibn Uraifan, and he will inform you of the various matters of interest, but of less vital importance, which I have mentioned in this letter.

(Compliments)

(Signed) A. HENRY MCMAHON

(Source: *Great Britain: Parliamentary Papers*, 1939, Misc. No 3, Cmd. 5957)

The above McMahon-Hussein Agreement was accepted by the Palestinians as a promise by the British that, after the war, all land previously held by the Turks would be returned to the Arabs who occupied that land. The

Agreement would subsequently complicate Middle East history and politics, particularly after the signing of the Sykes-Picot Agreement. For his part, Hussein interpreted the correspondence as a clear indication that Palestine would be given to the Palestinians once the war was won. The British government would later dispute this interpretation; it was claimed that any land definitions were approximate and that Palestine was excluded from land to be returned to the Arab people. What is crucial to the above was the small phrase I have italicized; land that 'cannot be said to be purely Arab' was of course excluded from the McMahon Agreement as far as the British were concerned. Hussein, although not his son Prince Feisal, and many Arab people considered Palestine to be purely Arab. The British saw Palestine differently, since the Turks, while masters of Palestine, had allowed other religious groups, including the Jews, to reside in Jerusalem. The Balfour Declaration of 1917 complicated this further, offering a homeland for the Jews in Palestine. As mentioned in Chapter 8, Dr Chaim Weizmann had lobbied Prince Feisal at the Paris Peace Conference in 1919, seeking his agreement to Jewish settlement in Palestine. Feisal concurred as he considered the Palestinians only 'borderline Arabs'; he had no right to offer land to the Jews for it was not in his gift to do so. He was, of course, swayed by the charismatic Weizmann, as leader of the Zionist movement, and promised Jewish support for an independent Arab kingdom. In the protracted peace negotiations the Palestinian Question was conveniently ignored; the League of Nations subsequently granted the British a mandate to ensure law and order in Palestine, something which they found increasingly difficult to deliver. The trickle of Jewish settlers after 1919 became a flood when, in the 1930s, Nazi Germany commenced its persecution of the Jews. The rest is history. After the Second World War, when the extent of the Holocaust was known, the level of Jewish settlement in Palestine led to a declaration of war from the indigenous Arab population until, in 1948, the state of Israel was declared. The seemingly innocuous and small statement in Sir Henry McMahon's letter of October 1915 sowed seeds of dissension that neither he, nor anyone else, could have foreseen. Wingate was not party to the McMahon-Hussein correspondence in 1915 but knew of the Balfour Declaration and argued against it, warning the British government of the day that it would be unworkable.

Acknowledgement of Copyright Holders

Every effort has been made to obtain permission to use the photographs and graphics contained in this book. Most of the copyright holders are identified below by name. The majority of the illustrations belong to the University of Durham Library, Durham (Sudan Archive Department). I am grateful to the Library for allowing me to use these. The maps of the Battle of Omdurman are taken from *Omdurman* (Philip Zeigler). Attempts to trace the copyright holder of these have proved fruitless. However, should any information come to light subsequent to the publication of this book, the copyright holder should contact the publisher.

Illustrations

Front cover portrait of Wingate by courtesy of the National Portrait Gallery, London; back cover portrait of Wingate by courtesy of Mr Jamie Wilson.
1. Author's collection.
2. Courtesy of the Sudan Archive Department, Durham University Library.
3. *Ditto.*
4. *Ditto.*
5. Courtesy of the National Portrait Gallery, London.
6. *Ditto.*
7. *Ditto.*
8. Courtesy of the Sudan Archive Department, Durham University Library.
9. Author's collection.
10. *Ditto.*
11. Courtesy of the Sudan Archive Department, Durham University Library.
12. *Ditto.*
13. By kind permission of Dunbar Golf Club.
14. *Ditto.*
15. Author's collection.
16. *Ditto.*
17. *Ditto.*
18. Courtesy of the Sudan Archive Department, Durham University Library.
19. *Ditto.*
20. Courtesy of East Lothian Council Museum Service.

21. Author's collection.
22. Courtesy of the Sudan Archive Department, Durham University Library.
23. Courtesy of the National Portrait Gallery, London.
24. Courtesy of East Lothian Local History Centre.
25. Courtesy of the National Portrait Gallery, London.
26. *Ditto.*
27. Private collection.
28. Photograph Archive, Imperial War Museum, London [EA 21404].
29. Courtesy of the Sudan Archive Department, Durham University Library.
30. Author's collection.
31. *Ditto.*

List of Abbreviations

ADC	Aide-de-Camp
AJ	Arthur J. Balfour
Anzacs	Australians and New Zealanders (from Australian New Zealand Army Corps – ANZAC)
DU	Durham University Library
ELLHC	East Lothian Local History Centre
FO	Foreign Office
FRW	Francis Reginald Wingate
GOC	General Officer Commanding
HA	*Haddingtonshire Advertiser*
HC	*Haddingtonshire Courier* (now the *East Lothian Courier*)
HMG	His/Her Majesty's Government
HRH	His/Her Royal Highness
K of K	Horatio, Lord Kitchener of Khartoum
LG	David Lloyd George
RA	Royal Artillery
RAF	Royal Air Force
RELW	Ronald Evelyn Leslie Wingate
RN	Royal Navy
SAD	Sudan Archive Department
SDF	Sudan Defence Force
TA	Territorial Army
USAAF	United States Army Air Forces
WO	War Office
WP	Wingate Papers, Sudan Archive Department, Durham University Library
YMCA	Young Men's Christian Association

Bibliography

It would be nigh impossible to list all the memoirs, biographies, autobiographies, official papers, archives and histories which mention Sir Francis Reginald Wingate. However, among the many sources consulted in the course of writing this book, I list below the main sources. Foremost, of course, is Sir Ronald Wingate's *Wingate of the Sudan*, although Ronald admitted the book falls far short of being a biography of his father, and to a lesser extent, Ronald's autobiography *Not in the Limelight*.

In using several maps of the Sudan drawn from Philip Zeigler's invaluable book *Omdurman*, every effort has been made to trace the copyright holder but without success. The author and publisher apologize unreservedly for any breach of copyright; this was not intended. Any further information on these maps will be gratefully received should the identity of the copyright holder subsequently come to light.

Private Papers and Family Genealogy
Burke's Peerage and Baronetage (1937 edition).
Wingate Papers, Durham University.

Select Bibliography
Arthur, Sir George, *Life of Lord Kitchener* (3 vols, Macmillan, London, 1920).
Barrett, James W., *The War Work of the YMCA in Egypt* (H. K. Lewis & Co Ltd, London, 1919).
Brooke-Shephard, Gordon, *Between Two Flags: a Biography of Rudolf von Slatin* (Weidenfeld & Nicolson, London, 1973).
Bruce, Anthony, *The Last Crusade: the Palestine Campaign in the First World War* (John Murray, London, 2002).
Burleigh, Bennett, *Sirdar and Khalifa* (Chapman and Hall, London, 1898; reprint Nabu Press, 2010).
Carlyle, Gavin, *The Life and Work of the Reverend William Wingate* (A. Holness, London, 1901).
Carlyon, L. A., *Gallipoli* (Pan Macmillan, Australia, 2001).
Cecil, Hugh and Mirabel, *Imperial Marriage; an Edwardian War and Peace* (The History Press, London, 2005).
Churchill, Winston Spencer, *The River War* (Eyre and Spottiswoode, London, 1899).

Daly, M. W., *The Sirdar: Sir F. R. Wingate and the British Empire in the Middle East* (Memoirs of the American Philosophical Society, Philadelphia, USA, 1997).

Doolittle, Duncan D., *A Soldier's Hero: the Life of Sir Archibald Hunter* (Narragansett, Rhode Island, USA, 1991).

Harris, John V., *Dunbar Golf* (Kelso Graphics, Kelso, 2007).

Hill, Richard, *Slatin Pasha* (OUP, Oxford, 1965).

Holt, P. M. and Daly, M. W., *A History of the Sudan* (Harlow, 1961 and severally reprinted until 2000).

Howell, Georgina, *Daughter of the Desert: the Remarkable Life of Gertrude Bell* (Pan Macmillan, London 2006).

Kedourie, Elie, *The Chatham House version and other Middle Eastern studies* (Brandeis University Press, London 1970).

Kelly, Saul, *The Hunt for Zerzura* (John Murray, London, 2002).

Kenrick, Rosemary, *Sudan Tales* (Oleander Press, Cambridge, 1987).

Keown-Boyd, Henry, *A Good Dusting* (Secker and Warburg, London, 1986).

Keown-Boyd, Henry, *The Lion and the Sphinx; the rise and fall of the British in Egypt 1882–1956* (The Memoir Club, Spennymoor, Co. Durham, 2002).

King, John Wucher, *Historical dictionary of Egypt* (Scarecrow Press, New Jersey (1984).

Lawrence, T. E., *Seven Pillars of Wisdom* (Penguin Books Ltd, Middlesex, 1962).

Lloyd, Lord, *Egypt since Cromer* (Ams Press, London, 1933).

Long, C. W. R., *British Pro-Consuls in Egypt 1914–29; the challenge of nationalism* (Taylor and Francis, Oxford, 2007).

Magnus, Sir Phillip, *Kitchener: a Portrait of an Imperialist* (John Murray, London, 1958).

Marlowe, John, *Cromer in Egypt* (Praeger Publishing, New York, USA, 1970).

Nicolson, Harold: *Peacemaking, 1919* (Houghton and Mifflin & Co., London, 1933; reprinted Simon Publications, Bethesda MD, USA, 2001).

Ohrwalder, Father Joseph, *Ten Years Captivity in the Mahdi's Camp* (ed. F. R. Wingate; Sampson, Low, Marston and Co., London, 1892).

Pollock, John, *The Road to Omdurman* (Constable, London, 1998).

Royle, Trevor, *Orde Wingate Irregular Soldier* (Weidenfeld and Nicolson, London, 1995)

Royle, Trevor, *Orde Wingate: A Man of Genius, 1903–1944* (Frontline Books, Barnsley, 2010).

Slatin, Rudolf von, *Fire and Sword in the Soudan* (Arnold, London, 1896).

Steevens, G. W., *With Kitchener at Khartoum* (London, 1898; reprinted Darf, 1987 and Naval and Military Press, Uckfield, Sussex, 2009).

Sykes, Christopher, *Orde Wingate: the Official Biography* (World Publishing Co., London, 1959).

Warner, Phillip, *Dervish: The Rise and Fall of an African Empire* (Purnell Books Services Ltd, London, 1973).

Wilson, Jeremy, *Lawrence of Arabia: the Official Biography* (Heinemann, London, 1989).

Wingate, F. R., *Mahdiism and the Egyptian Sudan* (Macmillan, London, 1891, rep. Library of African Studies, general studies no. 44, London, 1968).

Wingate, Ronald, *Wingate of the Sudan* (John Murray, London, 1955).

Wingate, Ronald, *Not in the Limelight* (Hutchinson, London, 1959).

Winstone, H. V. F., *Illicit Adventure: the Story of Political and Military Intelligence in the Middle East from 1898 to 1926* (Jonathan Cape Ltd, London, 1982).

Ziegler, Philip, *Omdurman* (HarperCollins, London, 1973; reprinted Pen & Sword Books, Barnsley, 2006).

Index

Auda abu Tayi 169–70
Austria 100, 119, 247, 258

Bab el Habib 44
Bab-el-Mandeb 148
Baden-Powell, General Lord Robertson
    Stephenson Smyth 261
Baggara tribe 16, 18, 25, 30, 56–7
Baghdad 139–40, 280, 284
Bagnold, Colonel A. H. 23
Bagnold, Enid 23, 244
Bagnold, Major Ralph A. 244, 247
'Bagnold's Boys' (see Long Range Desert
    Group)
Baker, General Valentine 17
Baker, William 268
Baldwin, Stanley 232
Balfour, Arthur James 93, 95, 114, 173–5,
    179, 183–5, 194–5, 200–1, 203, 205,
    208–12, 214–15, 221–2, 225, 230, 237–8,
    248–9, 260, 264, 285
Balfour, Gerald 95
Balfour, Lady Frances 114, 230
Balliol College, Oxford 96
Barber, Lieutenant Colin M. 268
Baring, Sir Evelyn (see Cromer, Lord)
Baring, Thomas Cromer (Lord Northwood)
    24
Barrett, Sir James 214
Basra 133, 137, 284
Bayuda Desert 56–7
Beanley, serjeanty of, Northumberland 10
Beatrice, Princess 46
Bedouin tribe 152, 155, 175
Beersheba 170
Beijing 102
Belgian Congo 231
Belgian Congo Mining Company (see Board
    of Union Minière de Haute Katanga)
Bell, Gertrude 128–9, 134, 148, 173, 184, 205,
    249
Bell, Moberley 43
Benguela Railway Company 231, 259
Berber 52, 56–7, 59, 62, 83, 110, 113
Berbera, Port of 110
Bermann, Richard A. 244–5
Bigge, Sir Arthur J. 46, 88, 91, 258
Binyon, Laurence 224
Bir Abbas 156–7
Black Flag 65, 70–1, 74
Black Watch, The Royal Highland Regiment
    193
Black Week 87

Blair, General 13
Blitz, the London 232
Blue Nile 113, 230
Blunt, Wilfrid Scawen 75
Board du Minière du Haut Katanga 231–2, 258
Boer War, 1st (1880–81) 71
Boer War, 2nd (1899–1902) 72, 83, 85, 87, 91,
    98, 101, 108, 136, 225
Bombay (Mumbai) 12, 14
Bonar Law, Andrew 205, 216
Bonham Carter, Edgar 86, 102
Bowes-Lyon, Lady Elizabeth 231
Boxer Rebellion (1899–1901) 102–3
Boy Scouts' Association 261
Boyle, Captain William 148
Boys' Regiment, Royal Artillery 269
Bray, Captain 175
British (Non-Ferrous) Mining Corporation
    231
British Broadcasting Corporation (BBC) 232
British Cotton Growing Association 113–14
British High Command 168, 188
Broadwater Down, Tunbridge Wells 29, 90
Broadwood, Lieutenant General 66–7, 69
Bruce, Alexander Hugh (6th Lord Burleigh
    of Kennet) 225
Brussels 231, 266
Buckingham Palace 106, 207, 231, 254
Buddon Ness, Broughty Ferry 231
Burg el Arab 244
Burke, Edmund 275
Burke's Peerage 260, 273
Burleigh, Lord Balfour of 225
Byng, General 123

Cabinet (Cabinet Office) 20, 46, 50, 60, 86,
    132–3, 136, 168, 179, 190, 195, 198, 213,
    216
Cairo Intelligence Department 39, 173
Cairo Peace Conference 250
Cambysses, King of Persia 243
Camel Corps 67, 69, 81
Cameron Highlanders 66–7, 77
Campbell, Ewan 268
Canaan 183
Canada 207
Carchemish 129, 134, 156
Carey, Major William W. 185–6, 222
Carlyle, Thomas 47, 250
Carlyon, L. A. 137
Carnegie, Lord 233
Carrick, Dr 9
Carrick, Sarah 9
Caucasia 128

300

304